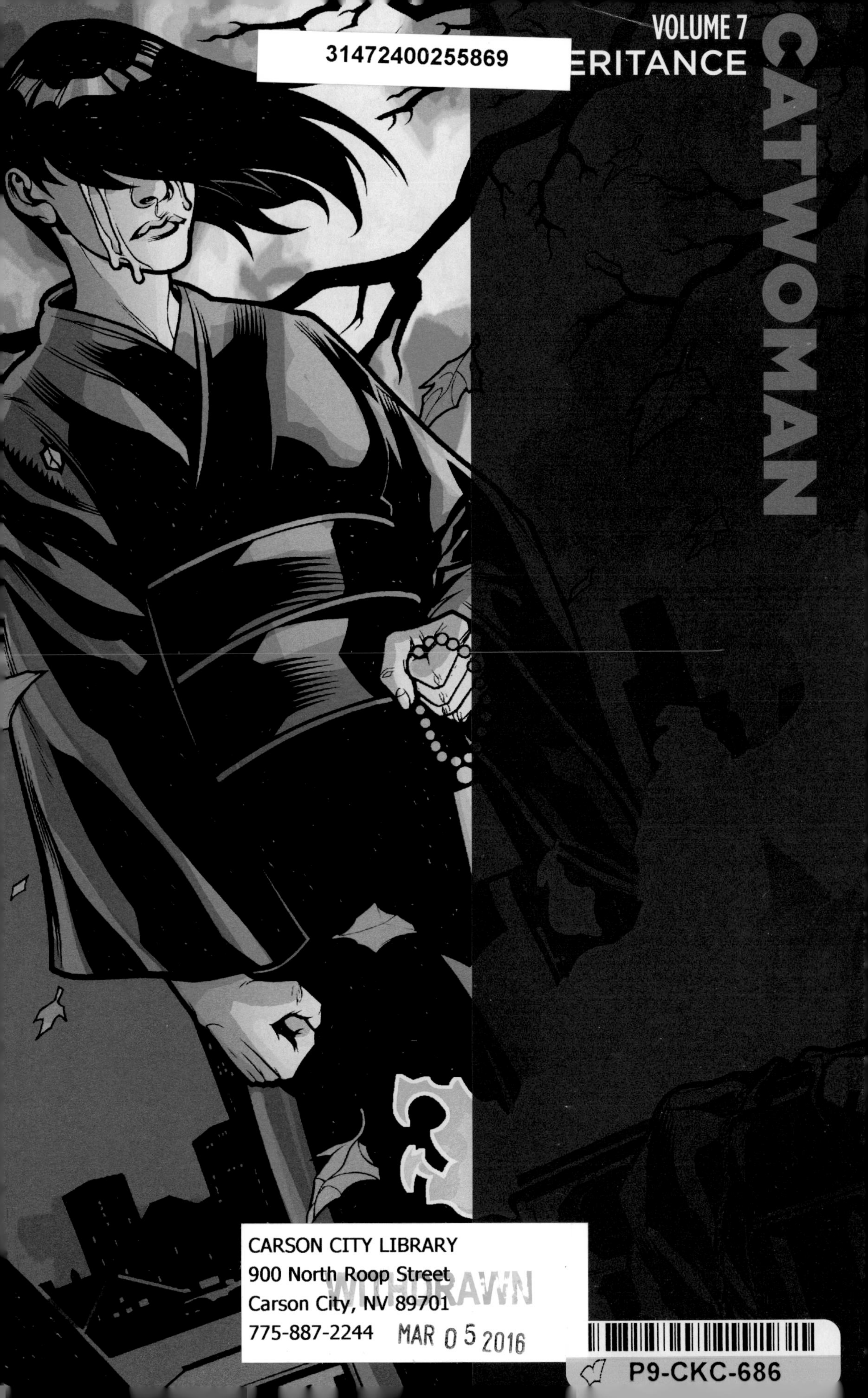
VOLUME 7
ERITANCE
CATWOMAN

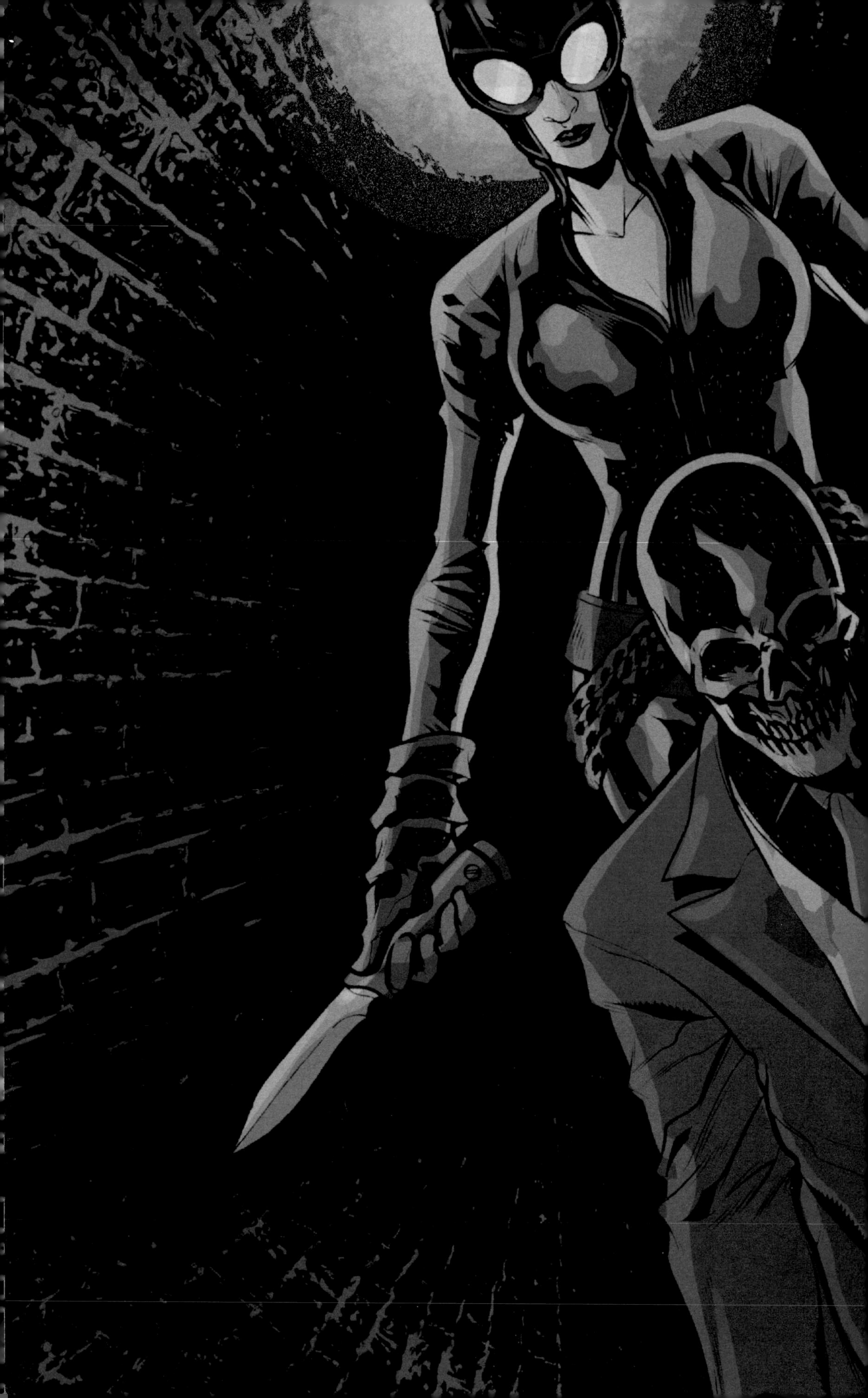

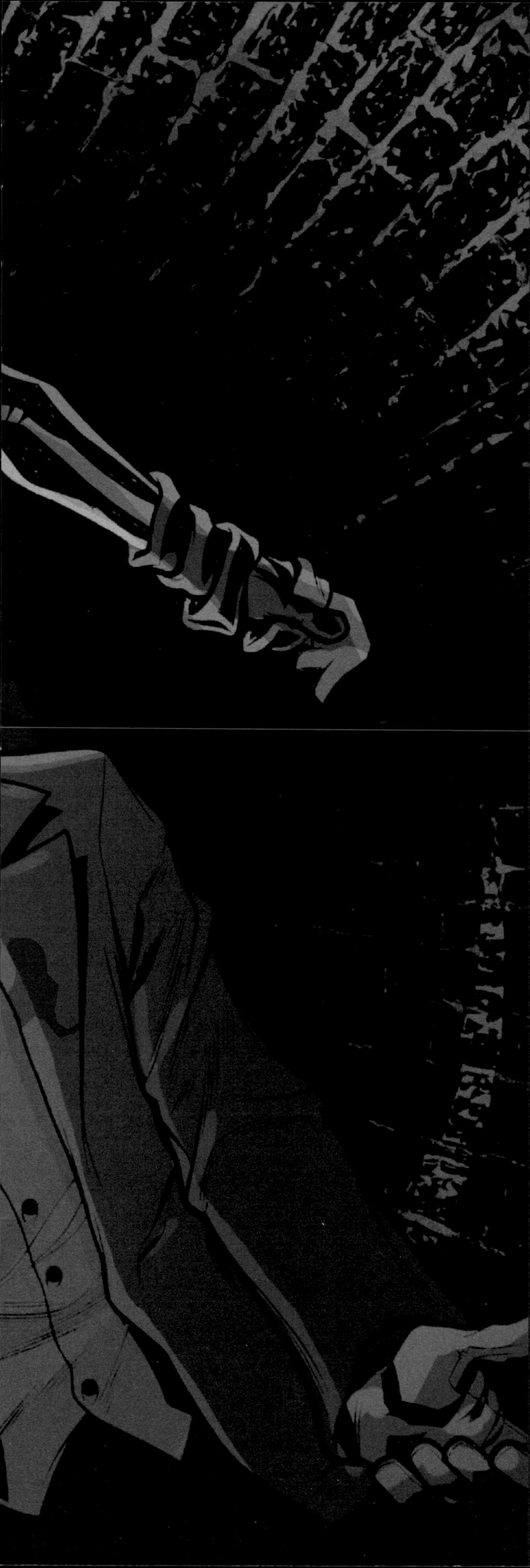

CATWOMAN

VOLUME 7
INHERITANCE

WRITER
GENEVIEVE VALENTINE

ARTISTS
DAVID MESSINA
GAETANO CARLUCCI

COLORIST
LEE LOUGHRIDGE

LETTERER
TRAVIS LANHAM

COLLECTION AND SERIES
COVER ARTIST
KEVIN WADA

BATMAN CREATED BY
BOB KANE WITH **BILL FINGER**

CATWOMAN VOLUME 7: INHERITANCE

Published by DC Comics. Compilation and all new material Copyright © 2016 DC Comics. All Rights Reserved. Originally published online as
CATWOMAN SNEAK PEEK and in single magazine form as CATWOMAN 41-46 Copyright © 2015 DC Comics. All Rights Reserved.
All characters, their distinctive likenesses and related elements featured in this publication are trademarks of DC Comics.
The stories, characters and incidents featured in this publication are entirely fictional. DC Comics does not read or accept
unsolicited ideas, stories or artwork.

DC Comics, 2900 West Alameda Ave., Burbank, CA 91505
Printed by RR Donnelley, Salem, VA, USA. 1/15/16. First Printing.
ISBN: 978-1-4012-6118-4

Names: Valentine, Genevieve, author. | Messina, illustrator.
Title: Catwoman. Volume 7, Inheritance / Genevieve Valentine, writer ; David
Messina, artist.
Other titles: Inheritance
Description: Burbank, CA : DC Comics, [2016]
Identifiers: LCCN 2015038019 | ISBN 9781401261184 (paperback)
Subjects: LCSH: Graphic novels. | Superhero comic books, strips, etc. |
BISAC: COMICS & GRAPHIC NOVELS / Superheroes.
Classification: LCC PN6728.C39 V36 2016 | DDC 741.5/973—dc23
LC record available at http://lccn.loc.gov/2015038019

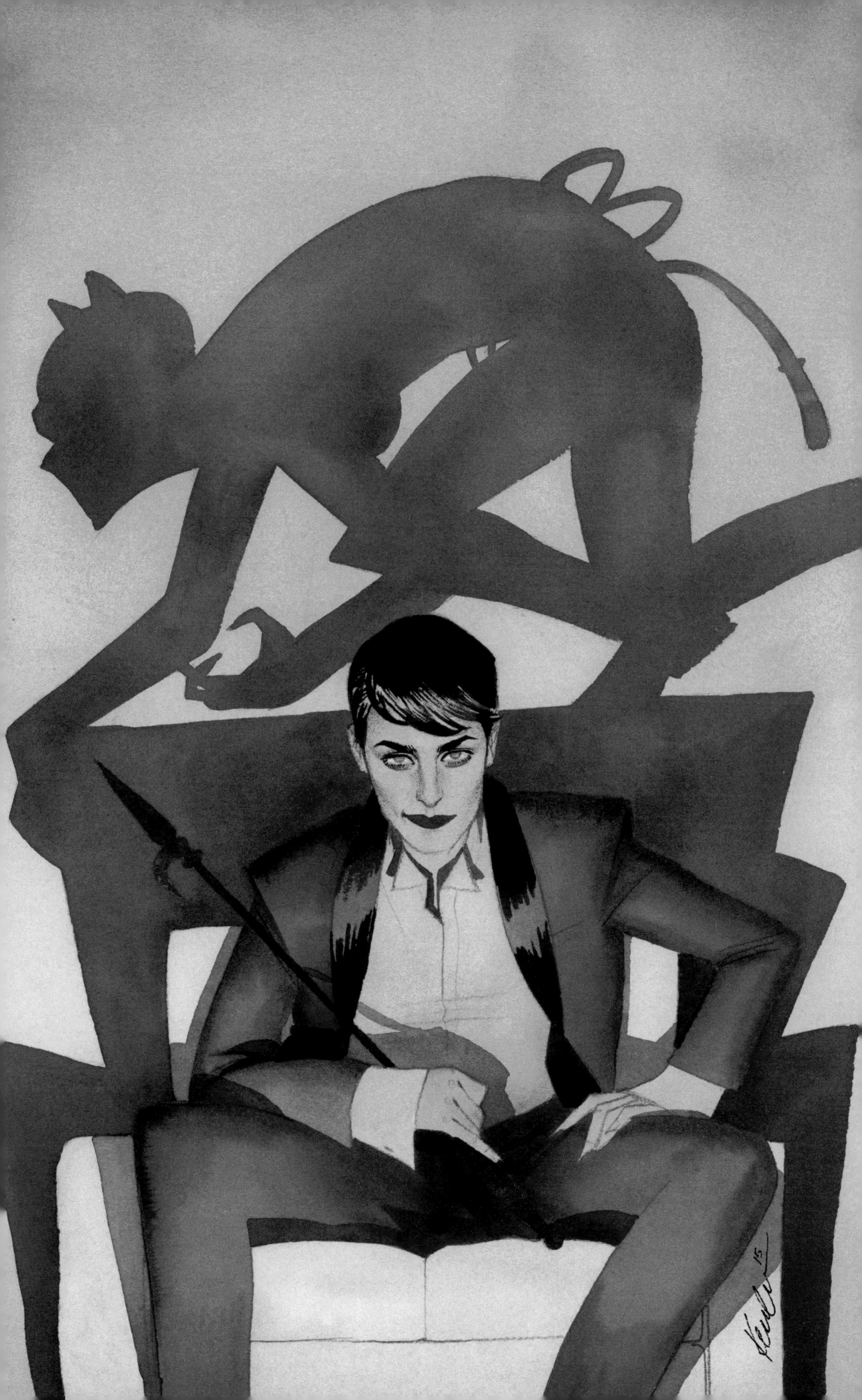

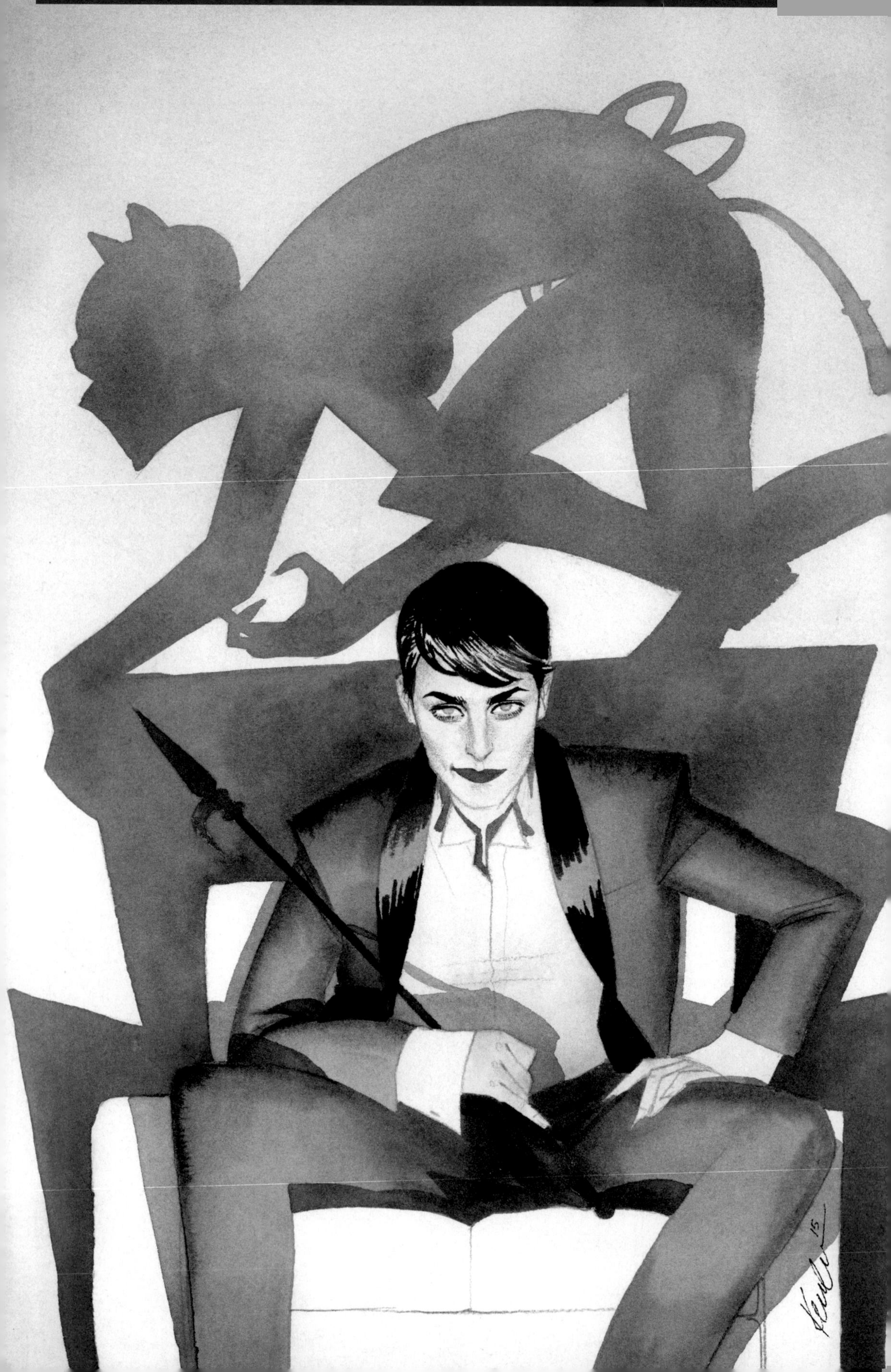

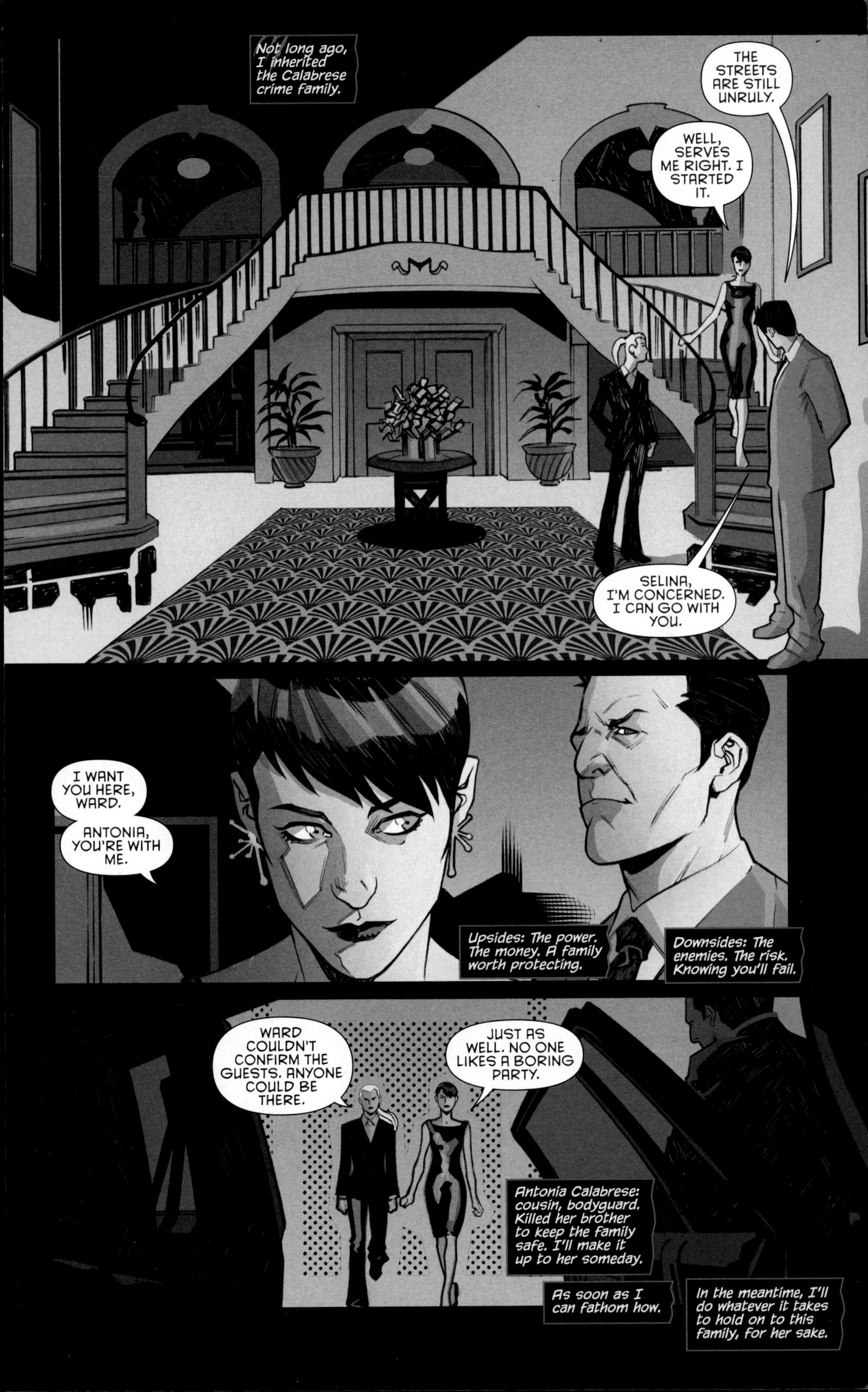
Not long ago, I inherited the Calabrese crime family.
THE STREETS ARE STILL UNRULY.
WELL, SERVES ME RIGHT. I STARTED IT.
SELINA, I'M CONCERNED. I CAN GO WITH YOU.
I WANT YOU HERE, WARD.
ANTONIA, YOU'RE WITH ME.
Upsides: The power. The money. A family worth protecting.
Downsides: The enemies. The risk. Knowing you'll fail.
WARD COULDN'T CONFIRM THE GUESTS. ANYONE COULD BE THERE.
JUST AS WELL. NO ONE LIKES A BORING PARTY.
Antonia Calabrese: cousin, bodyguard. Killed her brother to keep the family safe. I'll make it up to her someday.
As soon as I can fathom how.
In the meantime, I'll do whatever it takes to hold on to this family, for her sake.

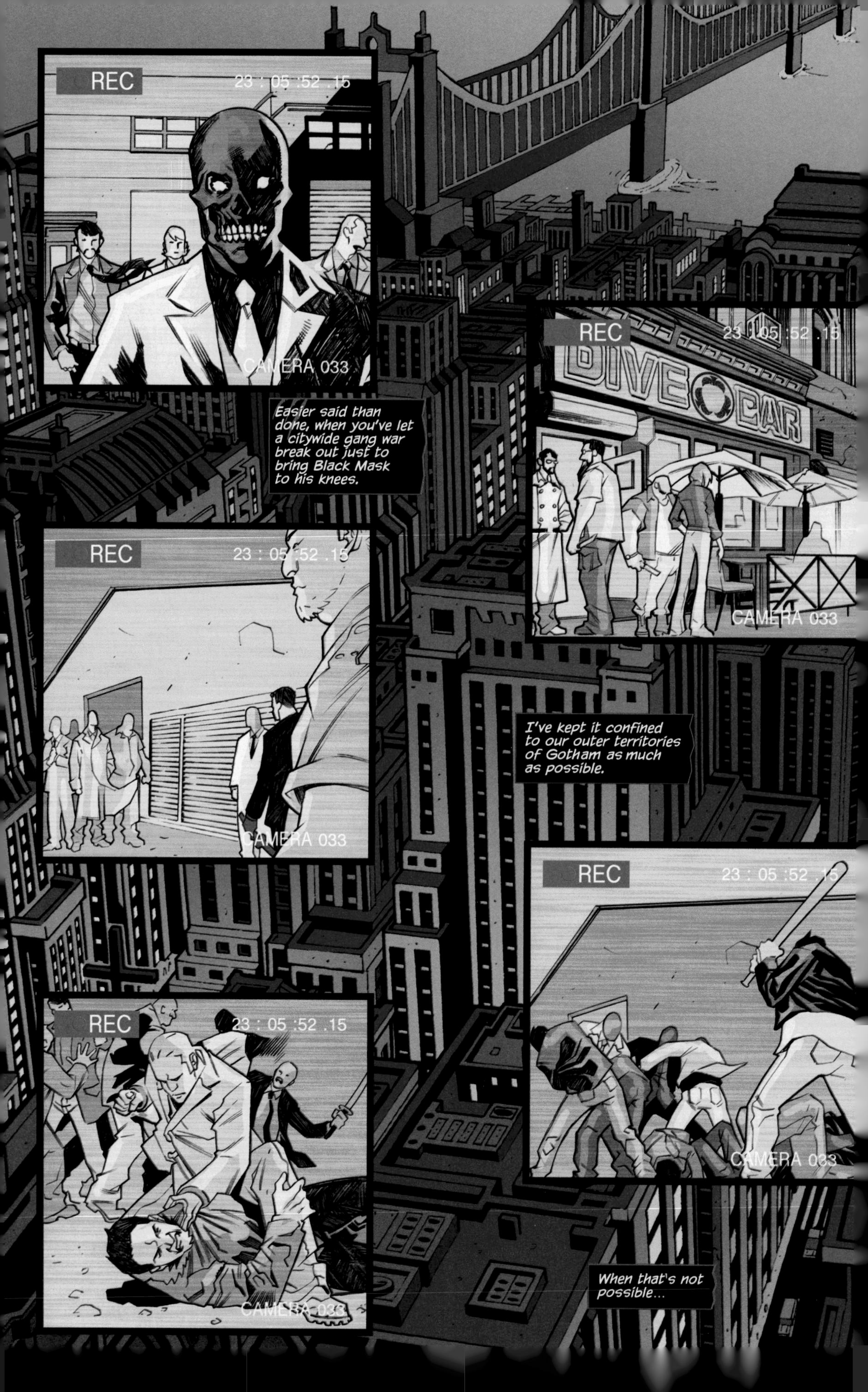
REC
23 : 05 :52 .15
CAMERA 033
Easier said than done, when you've let a citywide gang war break out just to bring Black Mask to his knees.
REC
23 : 05 :52 .15
DIVE BAR
CAMERA 033
REC
23 : 05 :52 .15
CAMERA 033
I've kept it confined to our outer territories of Gotham as much as possible.
REC
23 : 05 :52 .15
CAMERA 033
REC
23 : 05 :52 .15
CAMERA 033
When that's not possible...

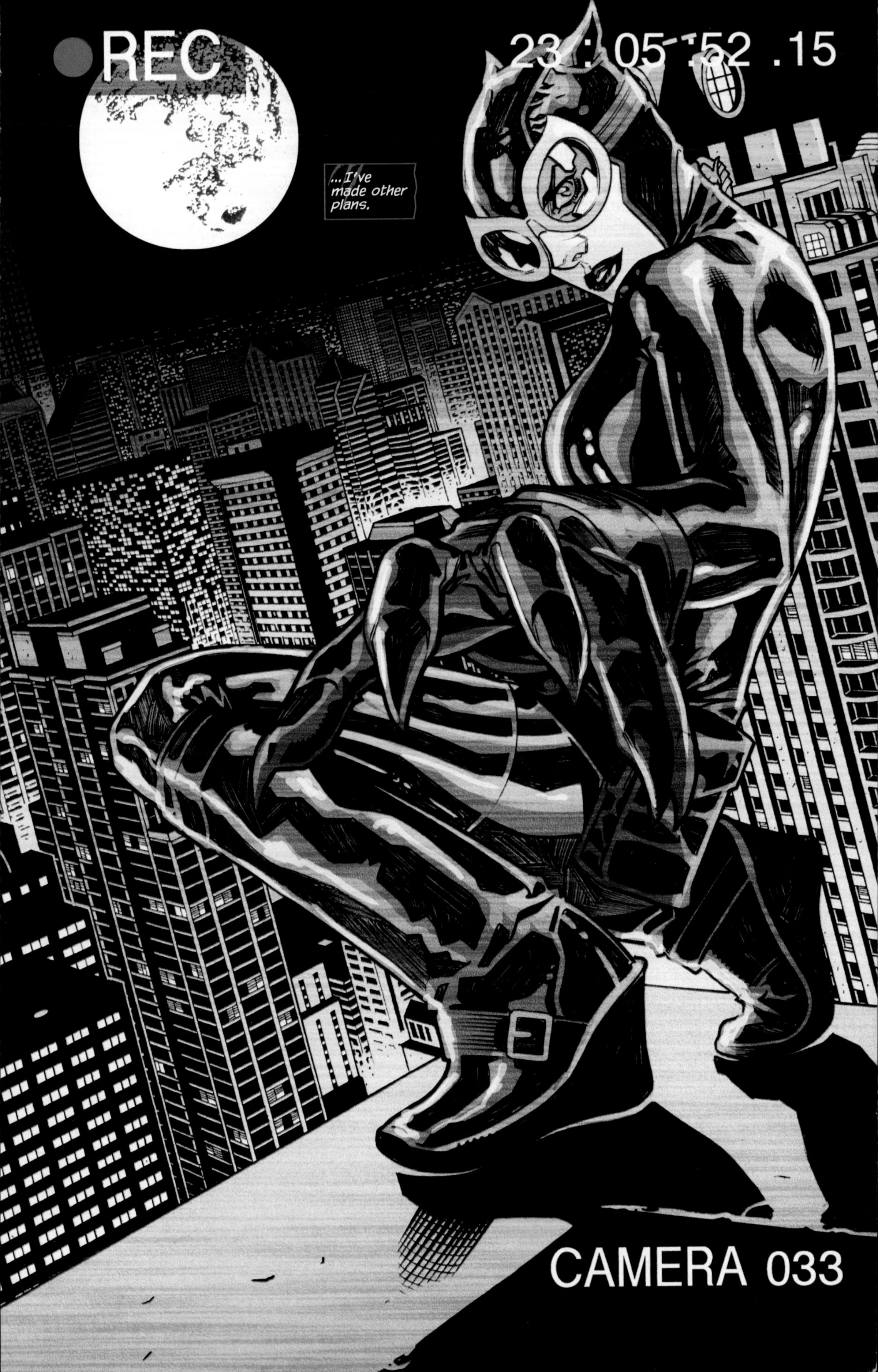
REC
23 : 05 :52 .15
...I've made other plans.
CAMERA 033

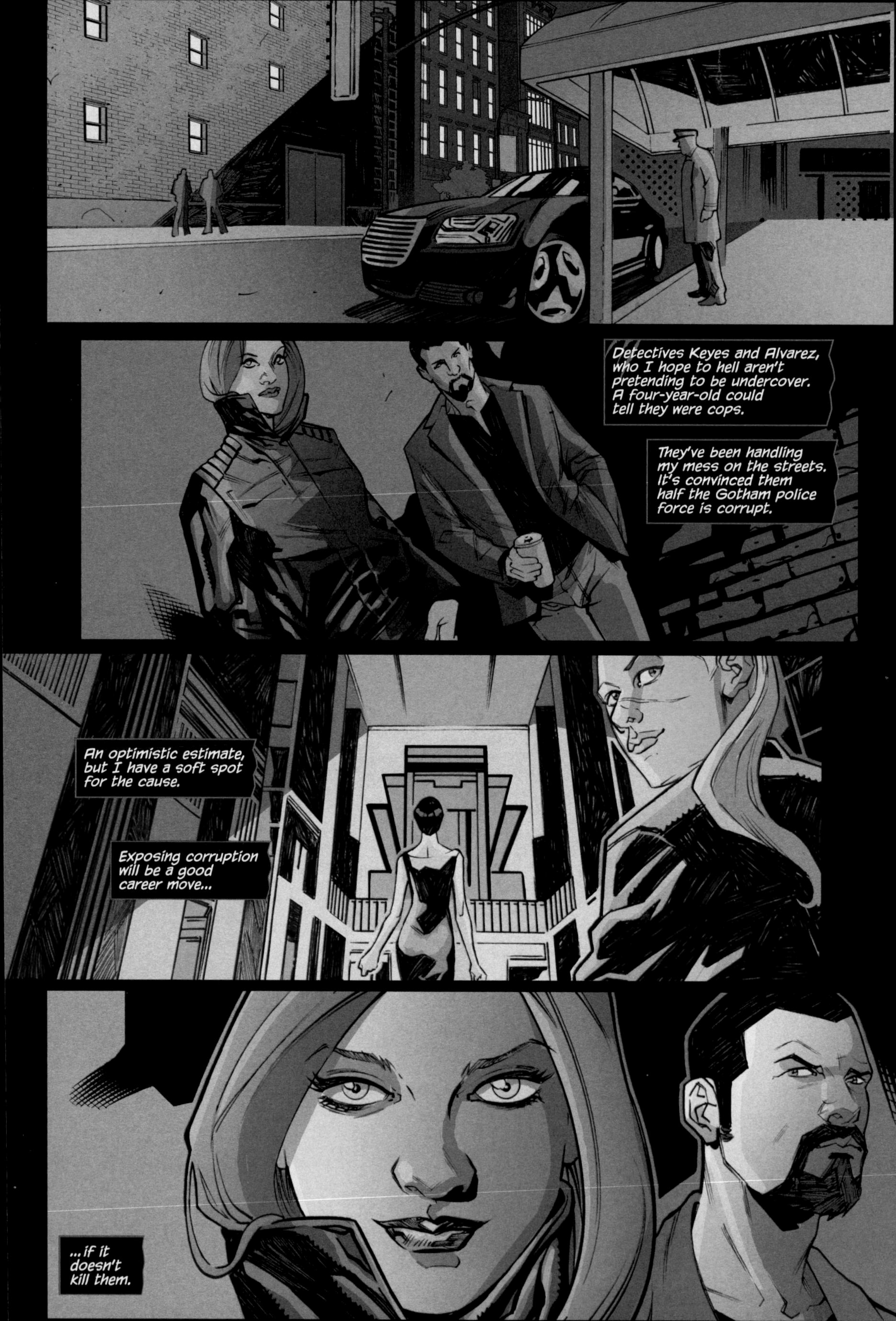
Detectives Keyes and Alvarez, who I hope to hell aren't pretending to be undercover. A four-year-old could tell they were cops.
They've been handling my mess on the streets. It's convinced them half the Gotham police force is corrupt.
An optimistic estimate, but I have a soft spot for the cause.
Exposing corruption will be a good career move...
...if it doesn't kill them.

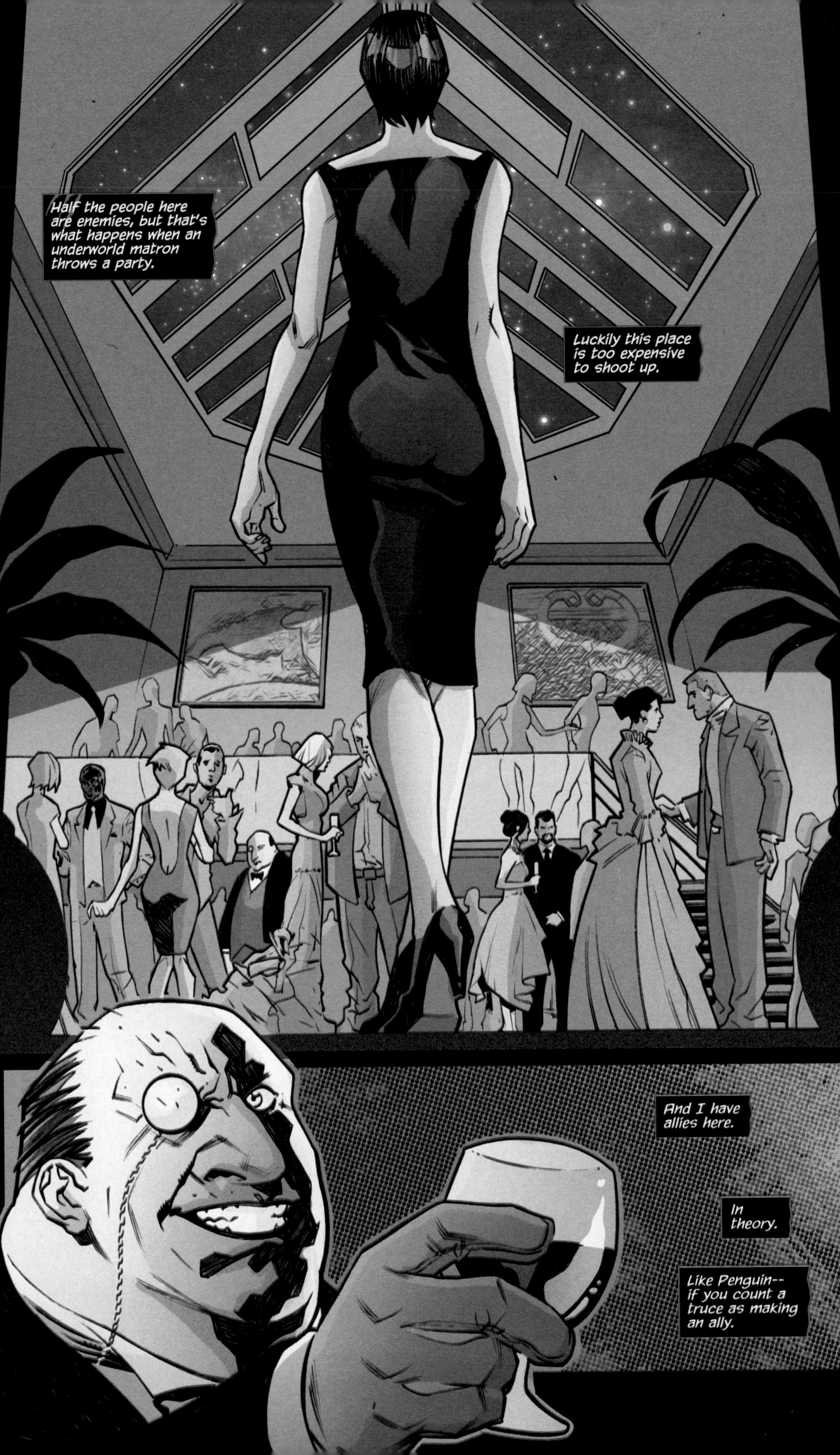
Half the people here are enemies, but that's what happens when an underworld matron throws a party.
Luckily this place is too expensive to shoot up.
And I have allies here.
In theory.
Like Penguin-- if you count a truce as making an ally.

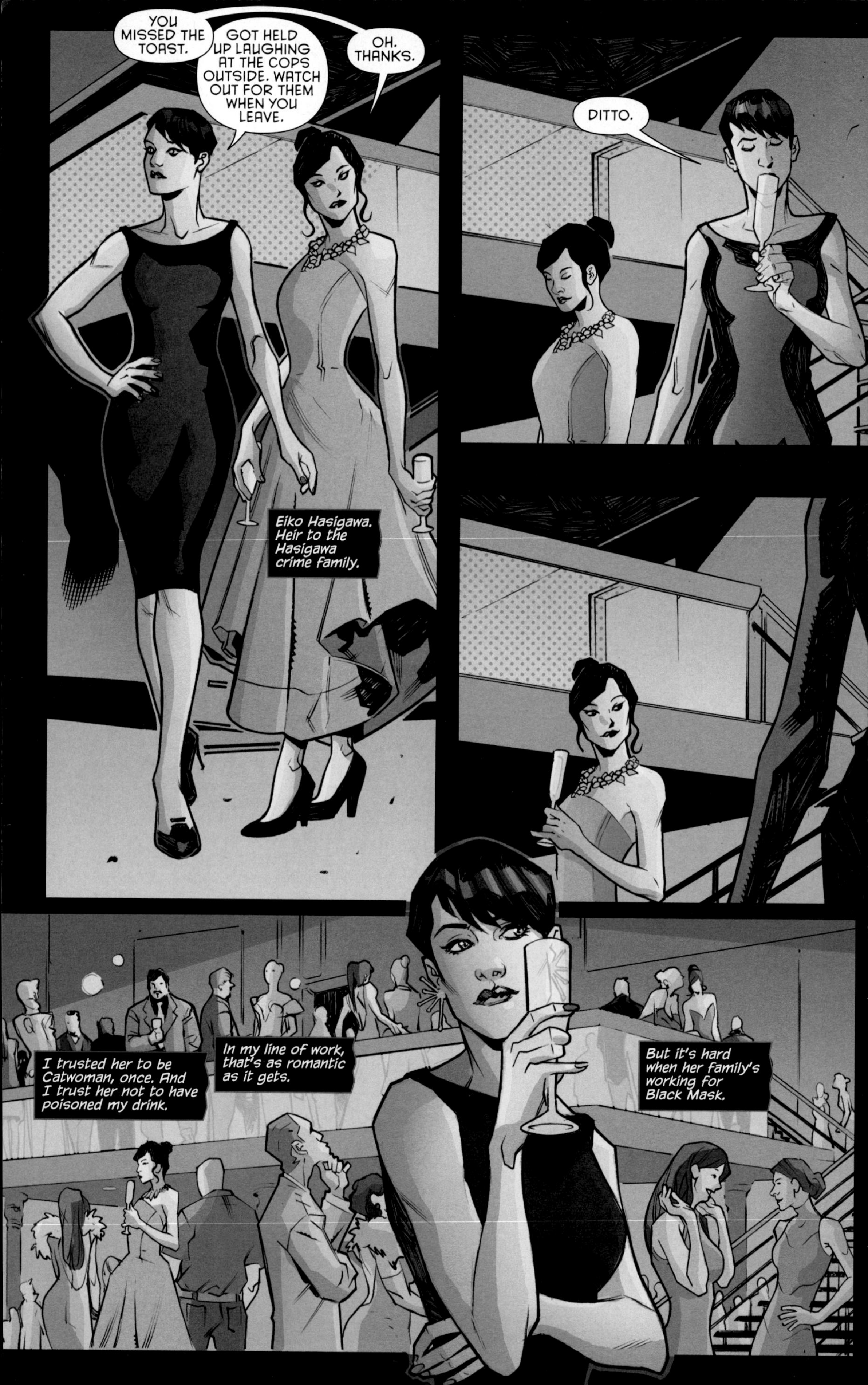
YOU MISSED THE TOAST.
GOT HELD UP LAUGHING AT THE COPS OUTSIDE. WATCH OUT FOR THEM WHEN YOU LEAVE.
OH. THANKS.
Eiko Hasigawa. Heir to the Hasigawa crime family.
DITTO.
I trusted her to be Catwoman, once. And I trust her not to have poisoned my drink.
In my line of work, that's as romantic as it gets.
But it's hard when her family's working for Black Mask.

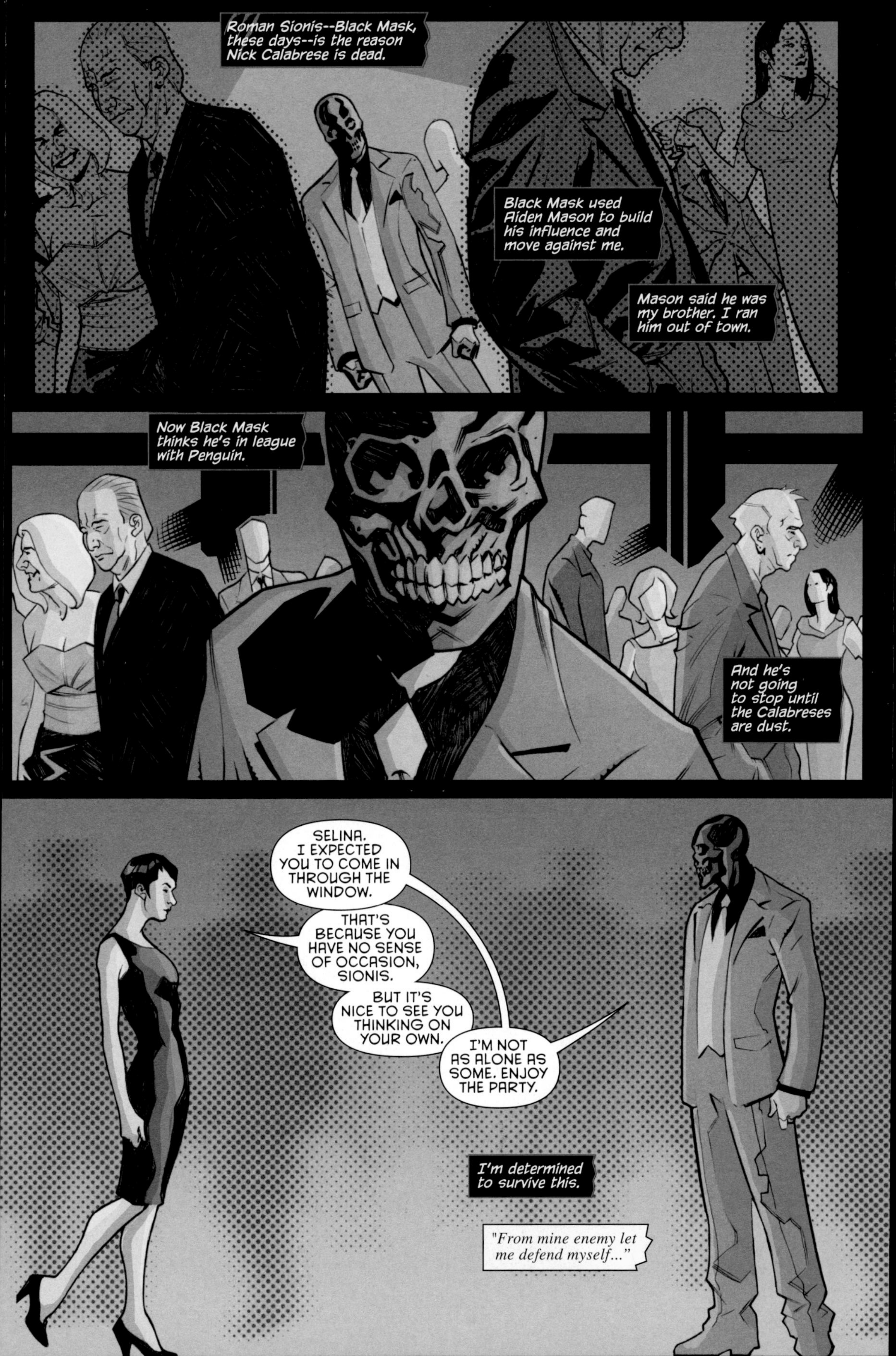

Roman Sionis--Black Mask, these days--is the reason Nick Calabrese is dead.
Black Mask used Aiden Mason to build his influence and move against me.
Mason said he was my brother. I ran him out of town.
Now Black Mask thinks he's in league with Penguin.
And he's not going to stop until the Calabreses are dust.
SELINA. I EXPECTED YOU TO COME IN THROUGH THE WINDOW.
THAT'S BECAUSE YOU HAVE NO SENSE OF OCCASION, SIONIS.
BUT IT'S NICE TO SEE YOU THINKING ON YOUR OWN.
I'M NOT AS ALONE AS SOME. ENJOY THE PARTY.
I'm determined to survive this.
"From mine enemy let me defend myself..."

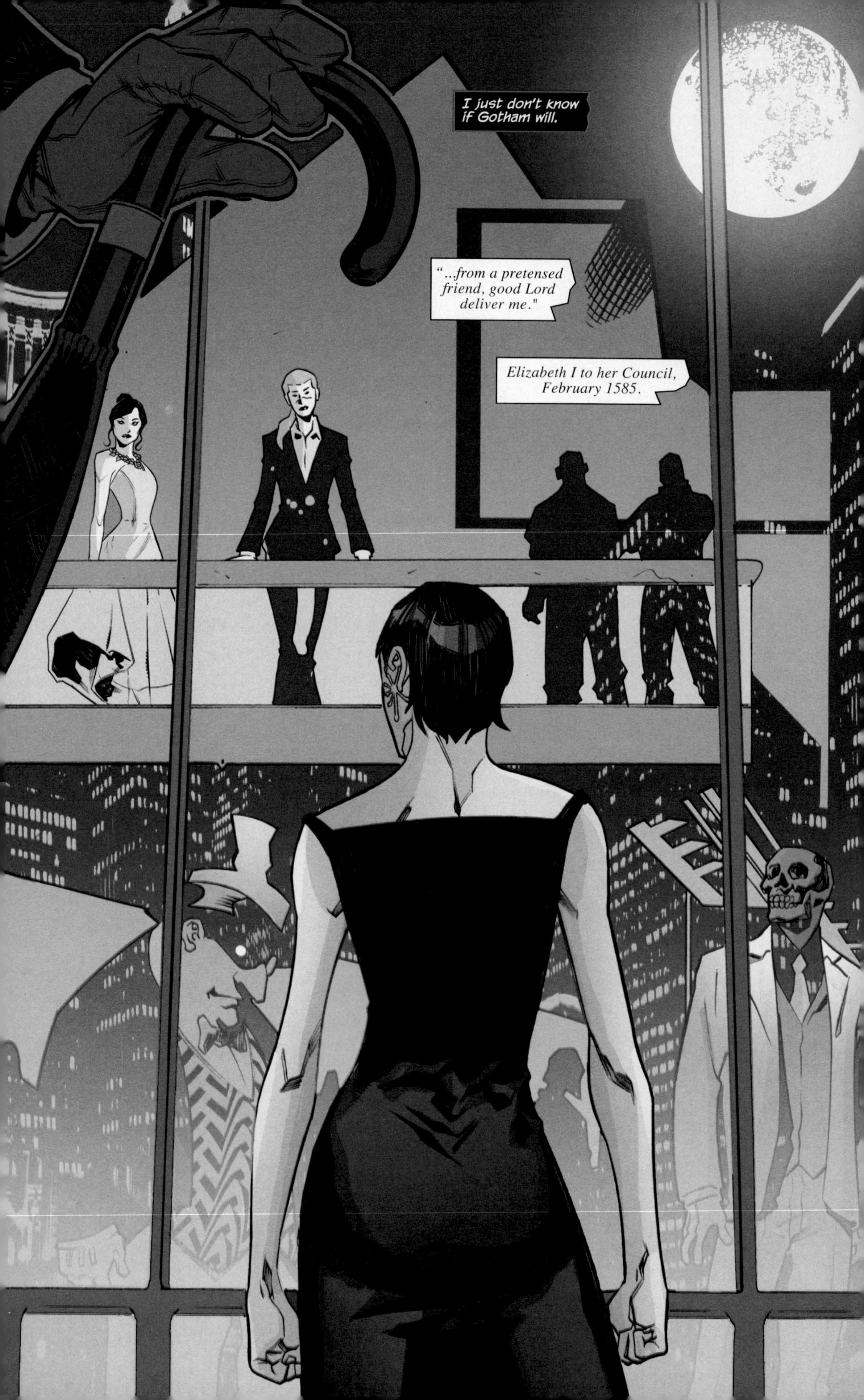
I just don't know if Gotham will.
"...from a pretensed friend, good Lord deliver me."
Elizabeth I to her Council, February 1585.

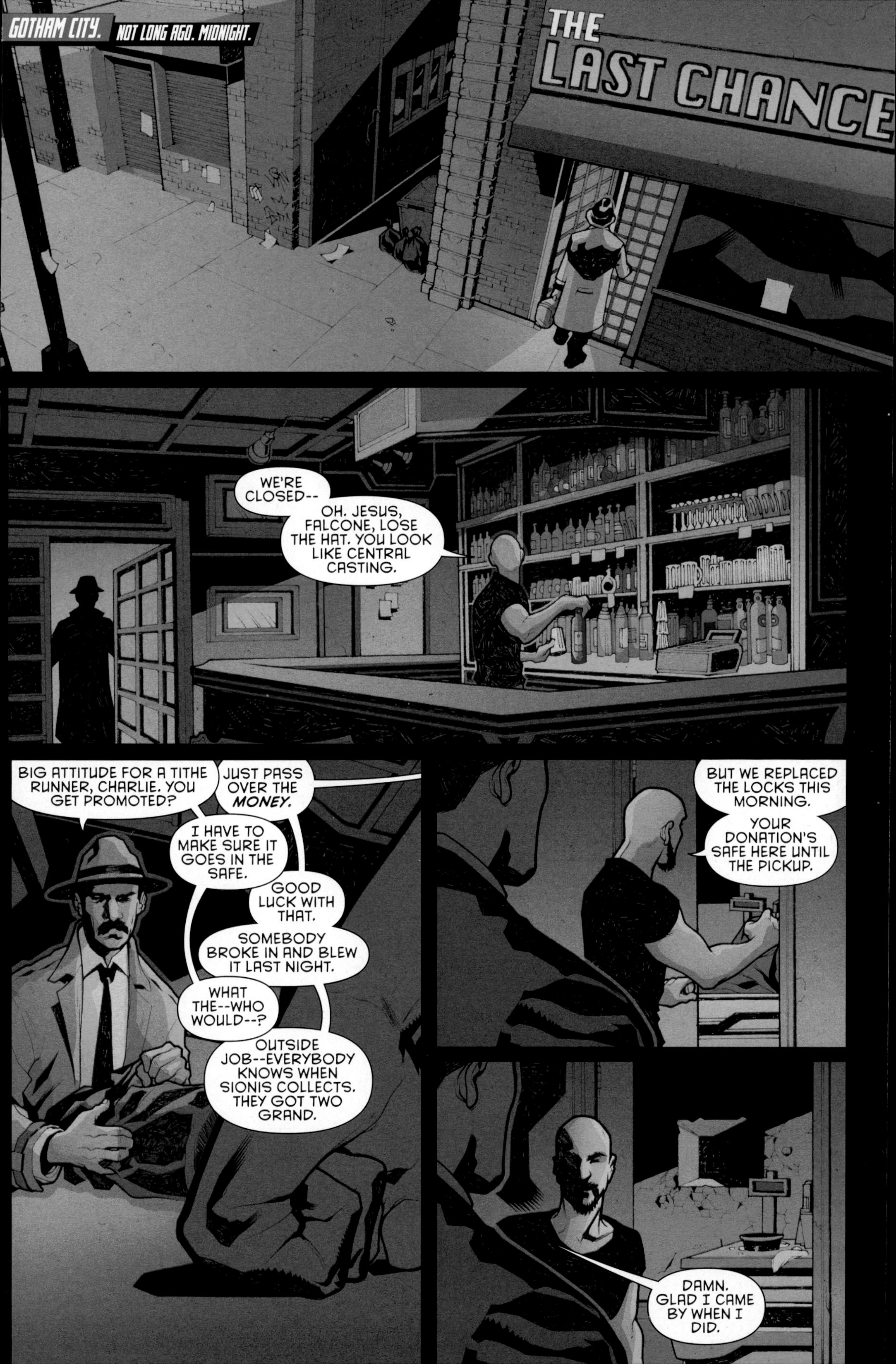
GOTHAM CITY.
NOT LONG AGO. MIDNIGHT.
THE LAST CHANCE
WE'RE CLOSED--
OH. JESUS, FALCONE, LOSE THE HAT. YOU LOOK LIKE CENTRAL CASTING.
BIG ATTITUDE FOR A TITHE RUNNER, CHARLIE. YOU GET PROMOTED?
JUST PASS OVER THE *MONEY.*
I HAVE TO MAKE SURE IT GOES IN THE SAFE.
GOOD LUCK WITH THAT.
SOMEBODY BROKE IN AND BLEW IT LAST NIGHT.
WHAT THE--WHO WOULD--?
OUTSIDE JOB--EVERYBODY KNOWS WHEN SIONIS COLLECTS. THEY GOT TWO GRAND.
BUT WE REPLACED THE LOCKS THIS MORNING.
YOUR DONATION'S SAFE HERE UNTIL THE PICKUP.
DAMN. GLAD I CAME BY WHEN I DID.

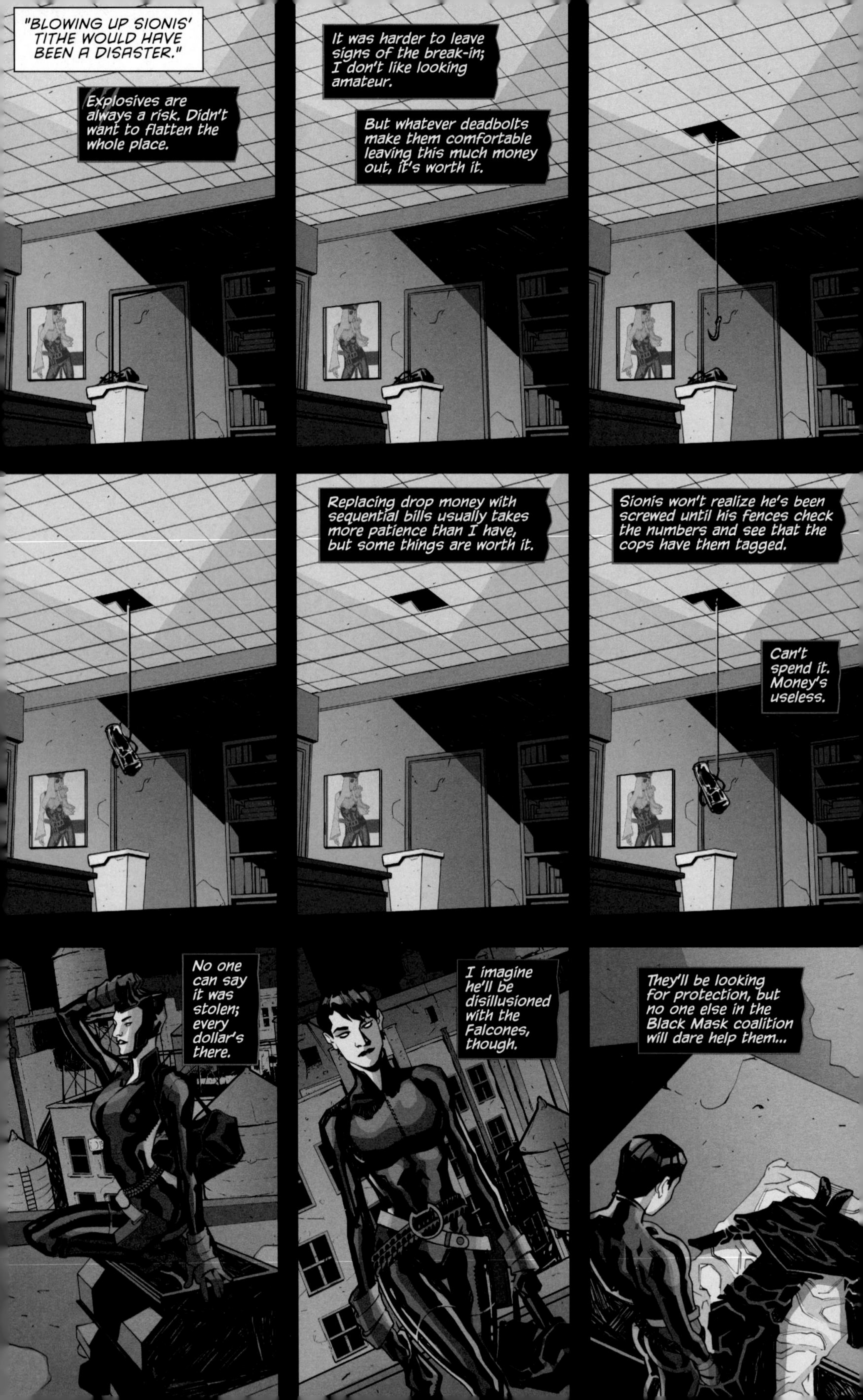
"BLOWING UP SIONIS' TITHE WOULD HAVE BEEN A DISASTER."
Explosives are always a risk. Didn't want to flatten the whole place.
It was harder to leave signs of the break-in; I don't like looking amateur.
But whatever deadbolts make them comfortable leaving this much money out, it's worth it.
Replacing drop money with sequential bills usually takes more patience than I have, but some things are worth it.
Sionis won't realize he's been screwed until his fences check the numbers and see that the cops have them tagged.
Can't spend it. Money's useless.
No one can say it was stolen; every dollar's there.
I imagine he'll be disillusioned with the Falcones, though.
They'll be looking for protection, but no one else in the Black Mask coalition will dare help them...

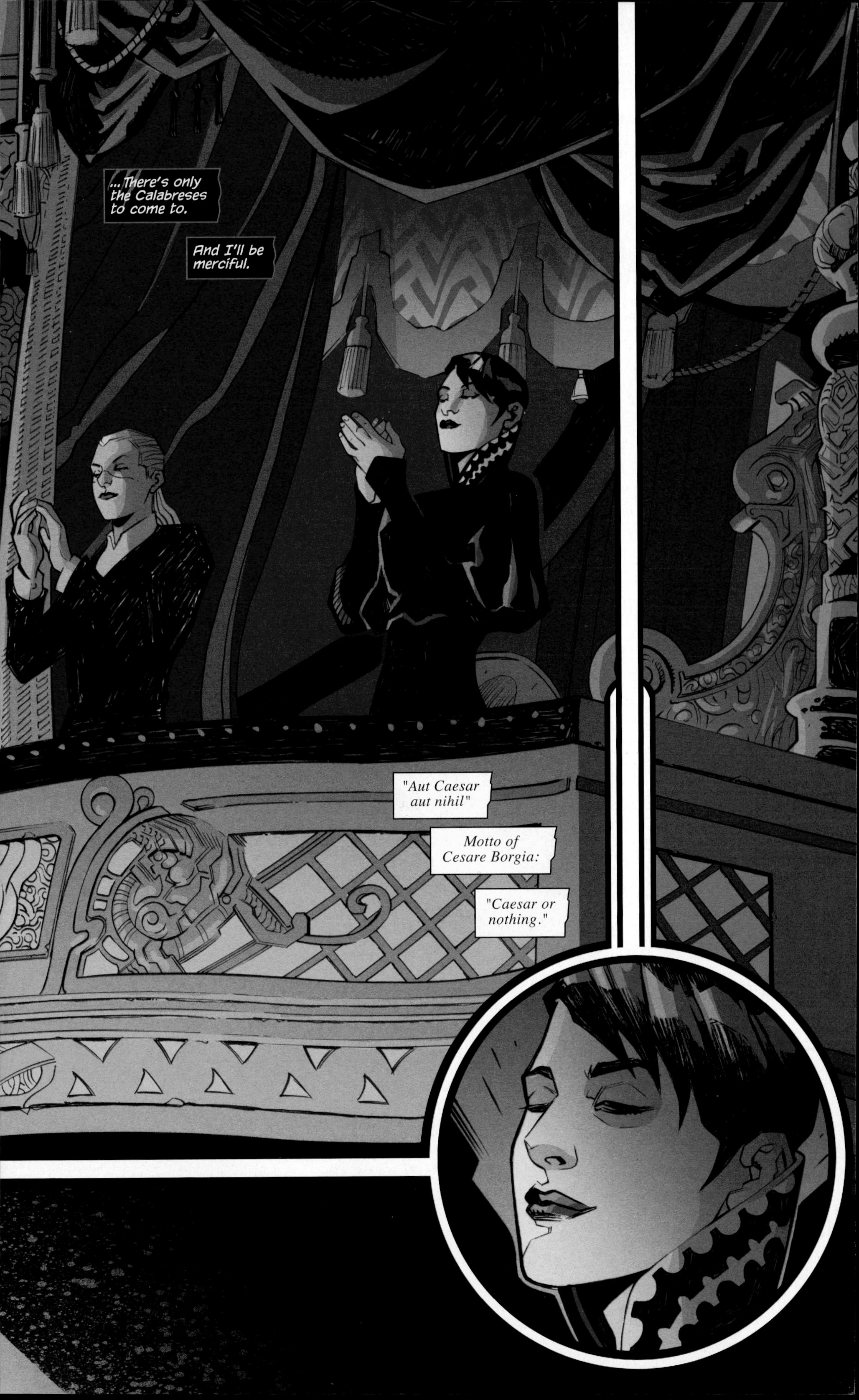
...There's only the Calabreses to come to.
And I'll be merciful.
"Aut Caesar aut nihil"
Motto of Cesare Borgia:
"Caesar or nothing."

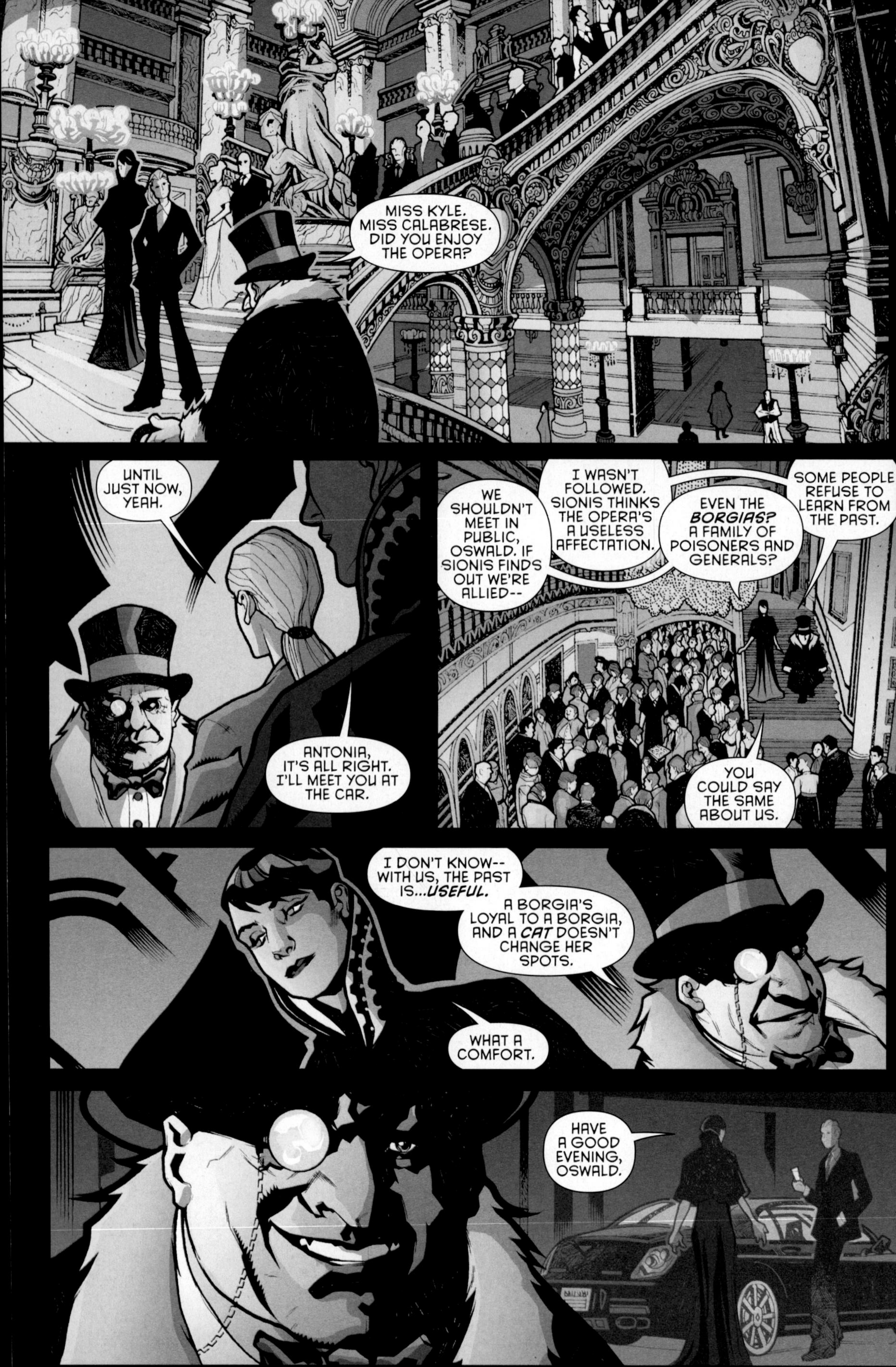
MISS KYLE. MISS CALABRESE. DID YOU ENJOY THE OPERA?
UNTIL JUST NOW, YEAH.
ANTONIA, IT'S ALL RIGHT. I'LL MEET YOU AT THE CAR.
WE SHOULDN'T MEET IN PUBLIC, OSWALD. IF SIONIS FINDS OUT WE'RE ALLIED--
I WASN'T FOLLOWED. SIONIS THINKS THE OPERA'S A USELESS AFFECTATION.
EVEN THE BORGIAS? A FAMILY OF POISONERS AND GENERALS?
SOME PEOPLE REFUSE TO LEARN FROM THE PAST.
YOU COULD SAY THE SAME ABOUT US.
I DON'T KNOW-- WITH US, THE PAST IS...USEFUL.
A BORGIA'S LOYAL TO A BORGIA, AND A CAT DOESN'T CHANGE HER SPOTS.
WHAT A COMFORT.
HAVE A GOOD EVENING, OSWALD.

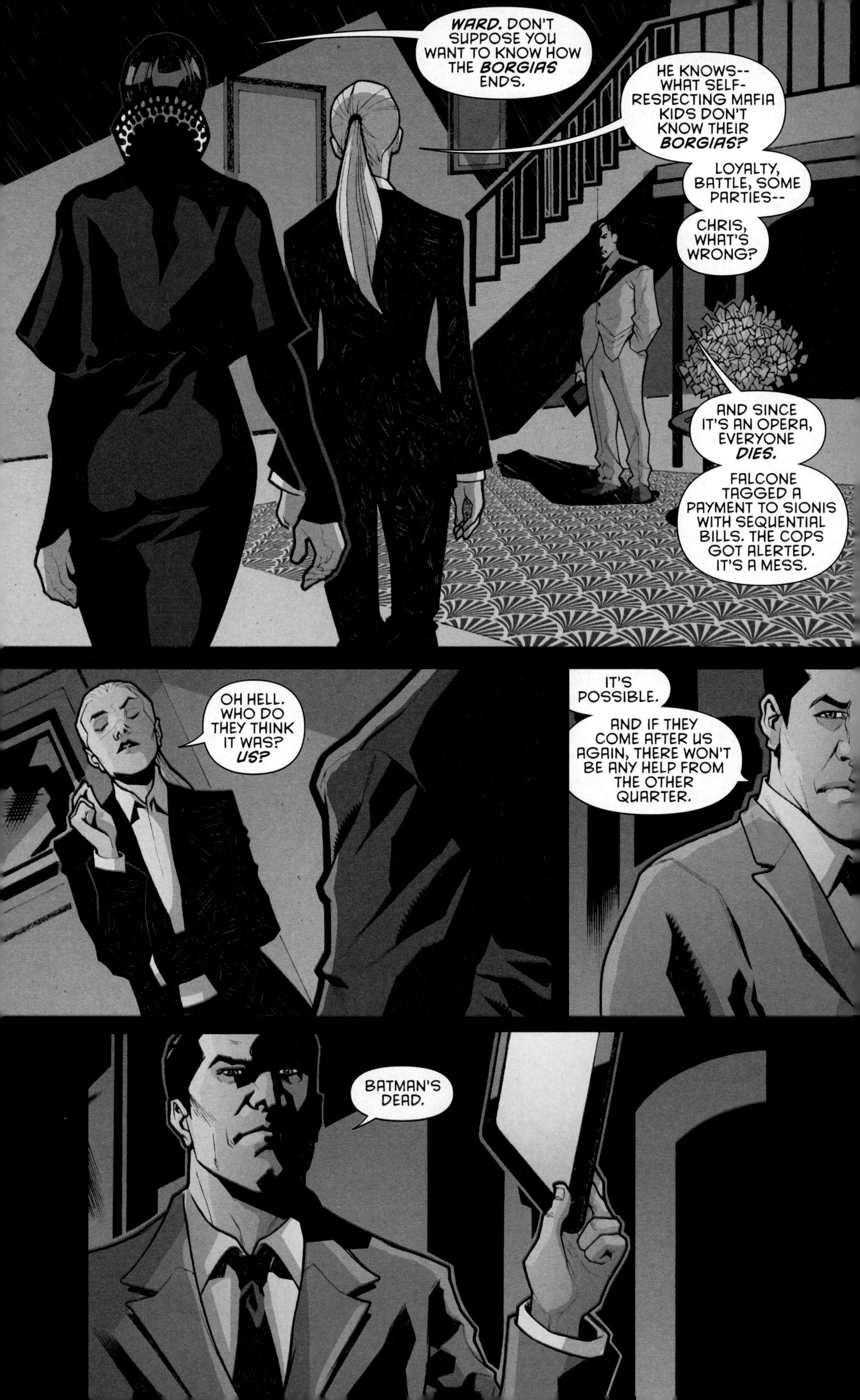
WARD. DON'T SUPPOSE YOU WANT TO KNOW HOW THE BORGIAS ENDS.
HE KNOWS-- WHAT SELF-RESPECTING MAFIA KIDS DON'T KNOW THEIR BORGIAS?
LOYALTY, BATTLE, SOME PARTIES--
CHRIS, WHAT'S WRONG?
AND SINCE IT'S AN OPERA, EVERYONE DIES.
FALCONE TAGGED A PAYMENT TO SIONIS WITH SEQUENTIAL BILLS. THE COPS GOT ALERTED. IT'S A MESS.
OH HELL. WHO DO THEY THINK IT WAS? US?
IT'S POSSIBLE.
AND IF THEY COME AFTER US AGAIN, THERE WON'T BE ANY HELP FROM THE OTHER QUARTER.
BATMAN'S DEAD.

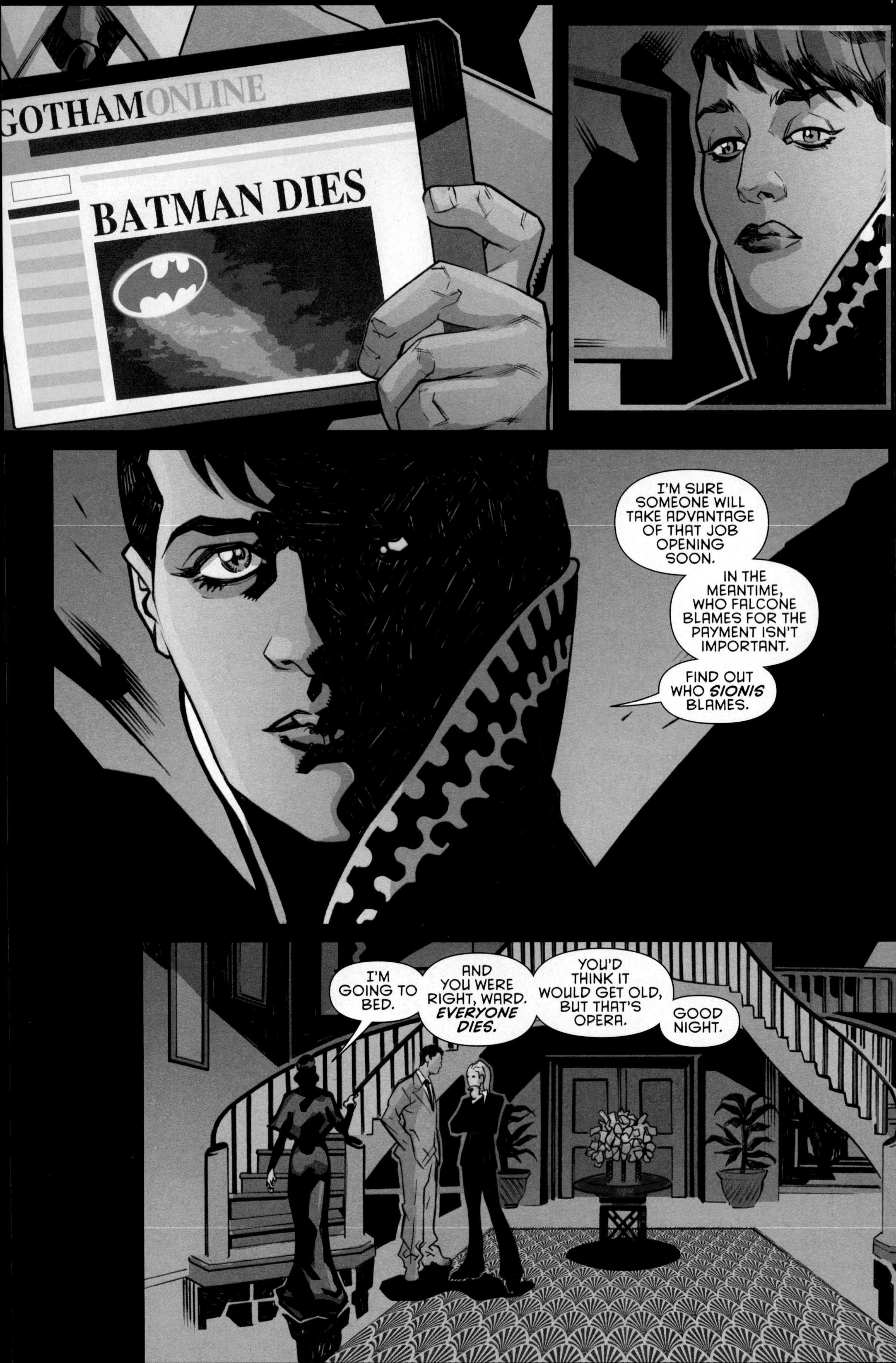
GOTHAM ONLINE
BATMAN DIES
I'M SURE SOMEONE WILL TAKE ADVANTAGE OF THAT JOB OPENING SOON.
IN THE MEANTIME, WHO FALCONE BLAMES FOR THE PAYMENT ISN'T IMPORTANT.
FIND OUT WHO *SIONIS* BLAMES.
I'M GOING TO BED.
AND YOU WERE RIGHT, WARD. *EVERYONE DIES.*
YOU'D THINK IT WOULD GET OLD, BUT THAT'S OPERA.
GOOD NIGHT.

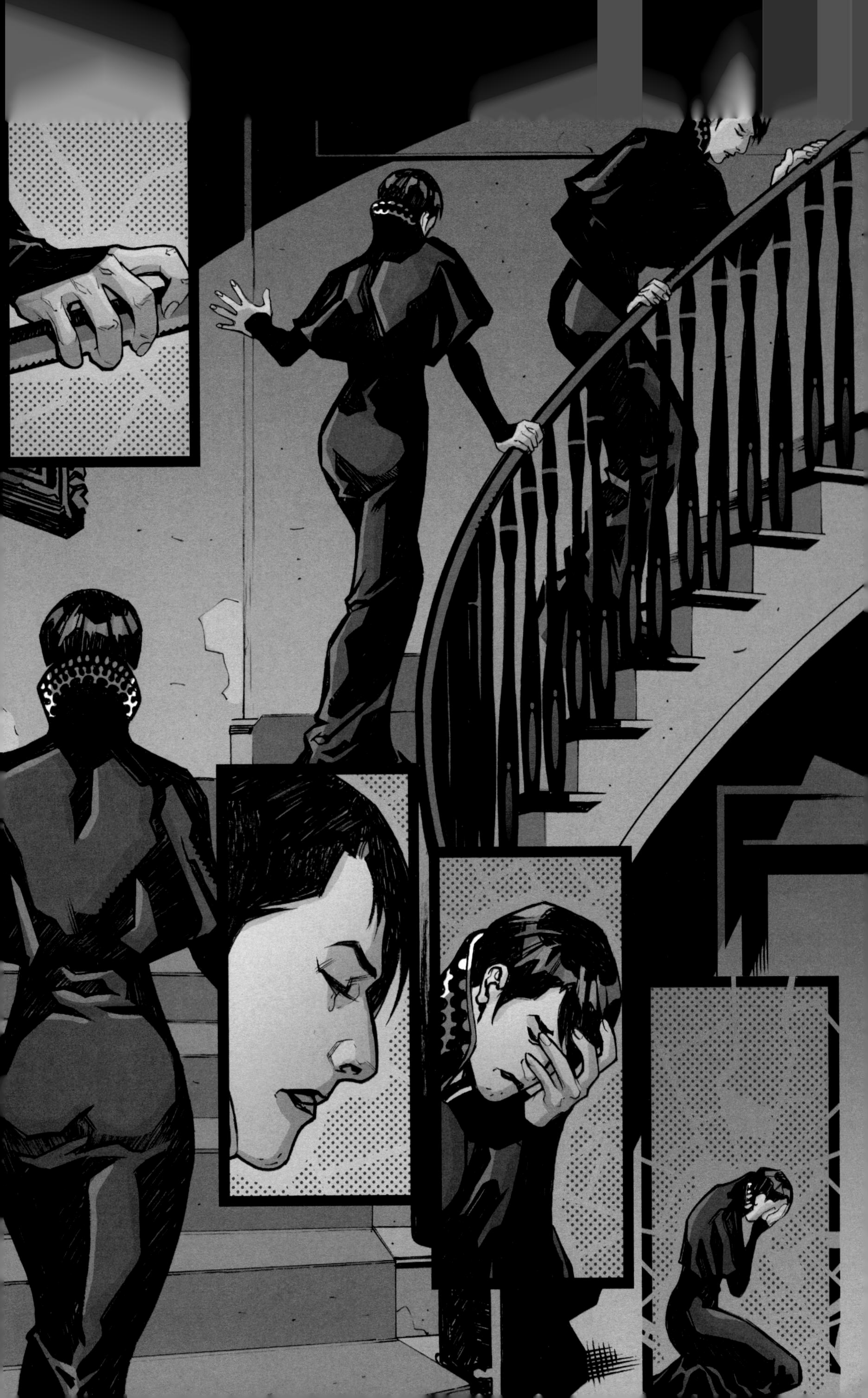

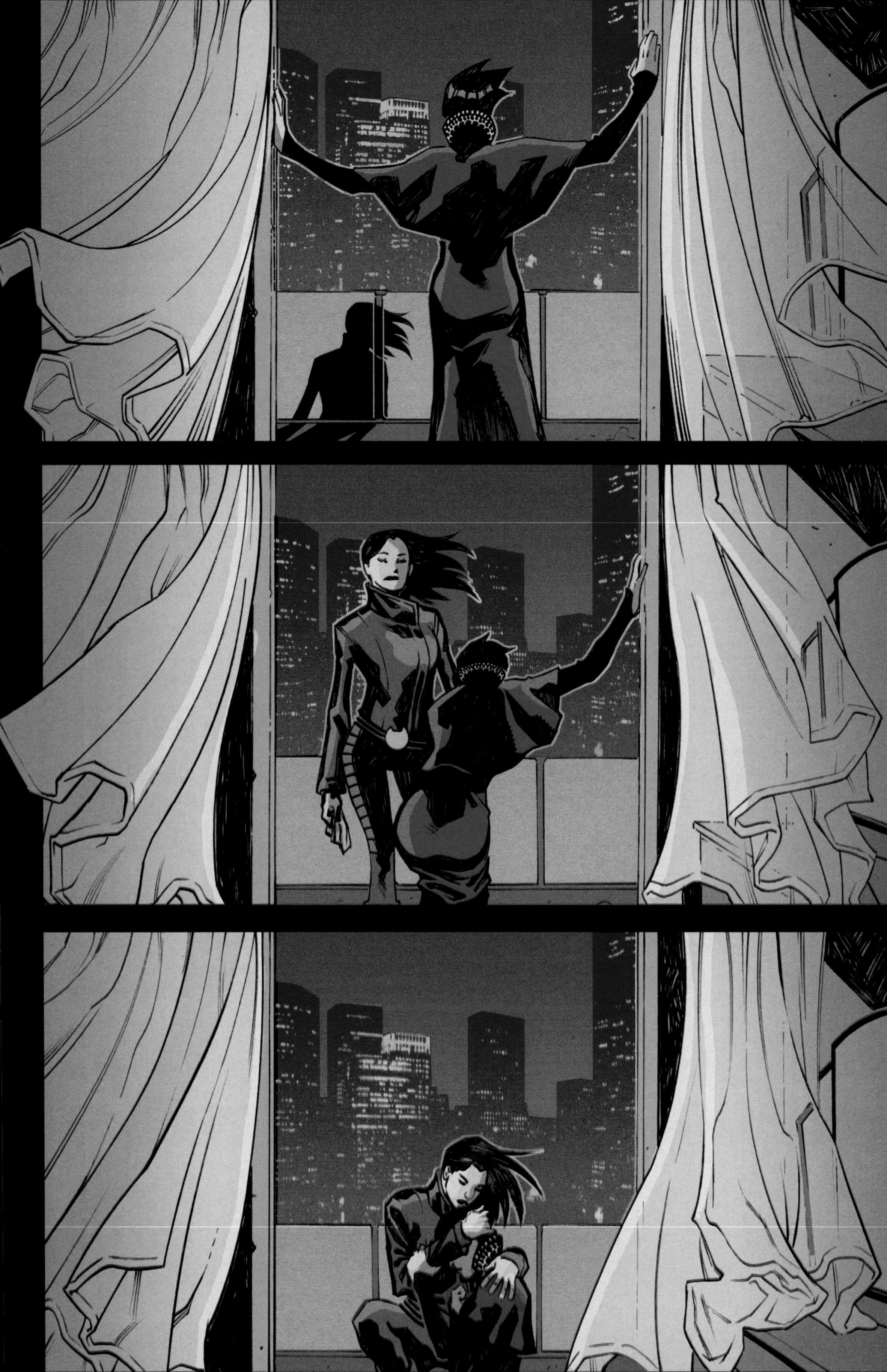

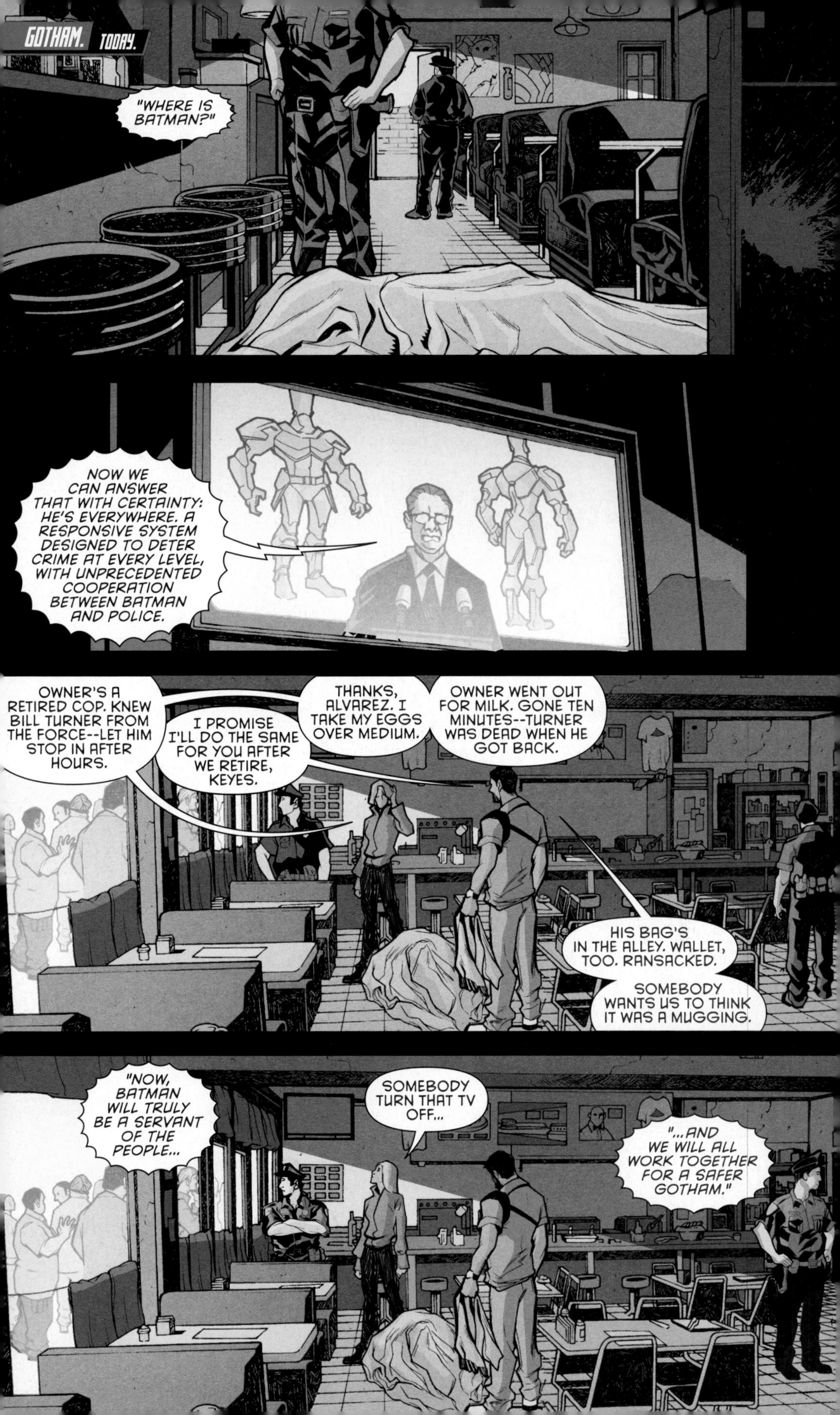
GOTHAM. TODAY.
"WHERE IS BATMAN?"
NOW WE CAN ANSWER THAT WITH CERTAINTY: HE'S EVERYWHERE. A RESPONSIVE SYSTEM DESIGNED TO DETER CRIME AT EVERY LEVEL, WITH UNPRECEDENTED COOPERATION BETWEEN BATMAN AND POLICE.
OWNER'S A RETIRED COP. KNEW BILL TURNER FROM THE FORCE--LET HIM STOP IN AFTER HOURS.
I PROMISE I'LL DO THE SAME FOR YOU AFTER WE RETIRE, KEYES.
THANKS, ALVAREZ. I TAKE MY EGGS OVER MEDIUM.
OWNER WENT OUT FOR MILK. GONE TEN MINUTES--TURNER WAS DEAD WHEN HE GOT BACK.
HIS BAG'S IN THE ALLEY. WALLET, TOO. RANSACKED.
SOMEBODY WANTS US TO THINK IT WAS A MUGGING.
"NOW, BATMAN WILL TRULY BE A SERVANT OF THE PEOPLE...
SOMEBODY TURN THAT TV OFF...
"...AND WE WILL ALL WORK TOGETHER FOR A SAFER GOTHAM."

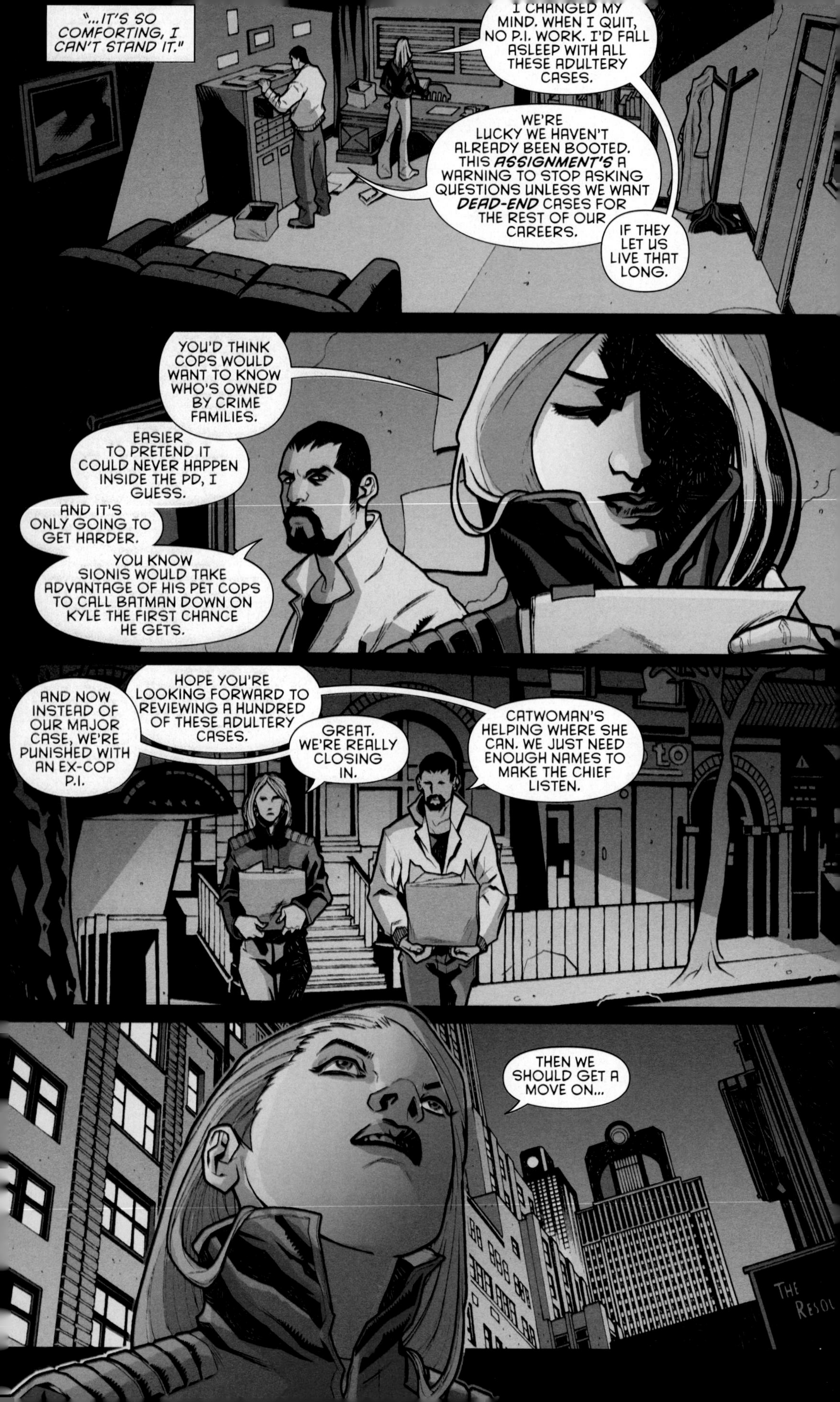
"...IT'S SO COMFORTING, I CAN'T STAND IT."
I CHANGED MY MIND. WHEN I QUIT, NO P.I. WORK. I'D FALL ASLEEP WITH ALL THESE ADULTERY CASES.
WE'RE LUCKY WE HAVEN'T ALREADY BEEN BOOTED. THIS ASSIGNMENT'S A WARNING TO STOP ASKING QUESTIONS UNLESS WE WANT DEAD-END CASES FOR THE REST OF OUR CAREERS.
IF THEY LET US LIVE THAT LONG.
YOU'D THINK COPS WOULD WANT TO KNOW WHO'S OWNED BY CRIME FAMILIES.
EASIER TO PRETEND IT COULD NEVER HAPPEN INSIDE THE PD, I GUESS.
AND IT'S ONLY GOING TO GET HARDER.
YOU KNOW SIONIS WOULD TAKE ADVANTAGE OF HIS PET COPS TO CALL BATMAN DOWN ON KYLE THE FIRST CHANCE HE GETS.
AND NOW INSTEAD OF OUR MAJOR CASE, WE'RE PUNISHED WITH AN EX-COP P.I.
HOPE YOU'RE LOOKING FORWARD TO REVIEWING A HUNDRED OF THESE ADULTERY CASES.
GREAT. WE'RE REALLY CLOSING IN.
CATWOMAN'S HELPING WHERE SHE CAN. WE JUST NEED ENOUGH NAMES TO MAKE THE CHIEF LISTEN.
THEN WE SHOULD GET A MOVE ON...

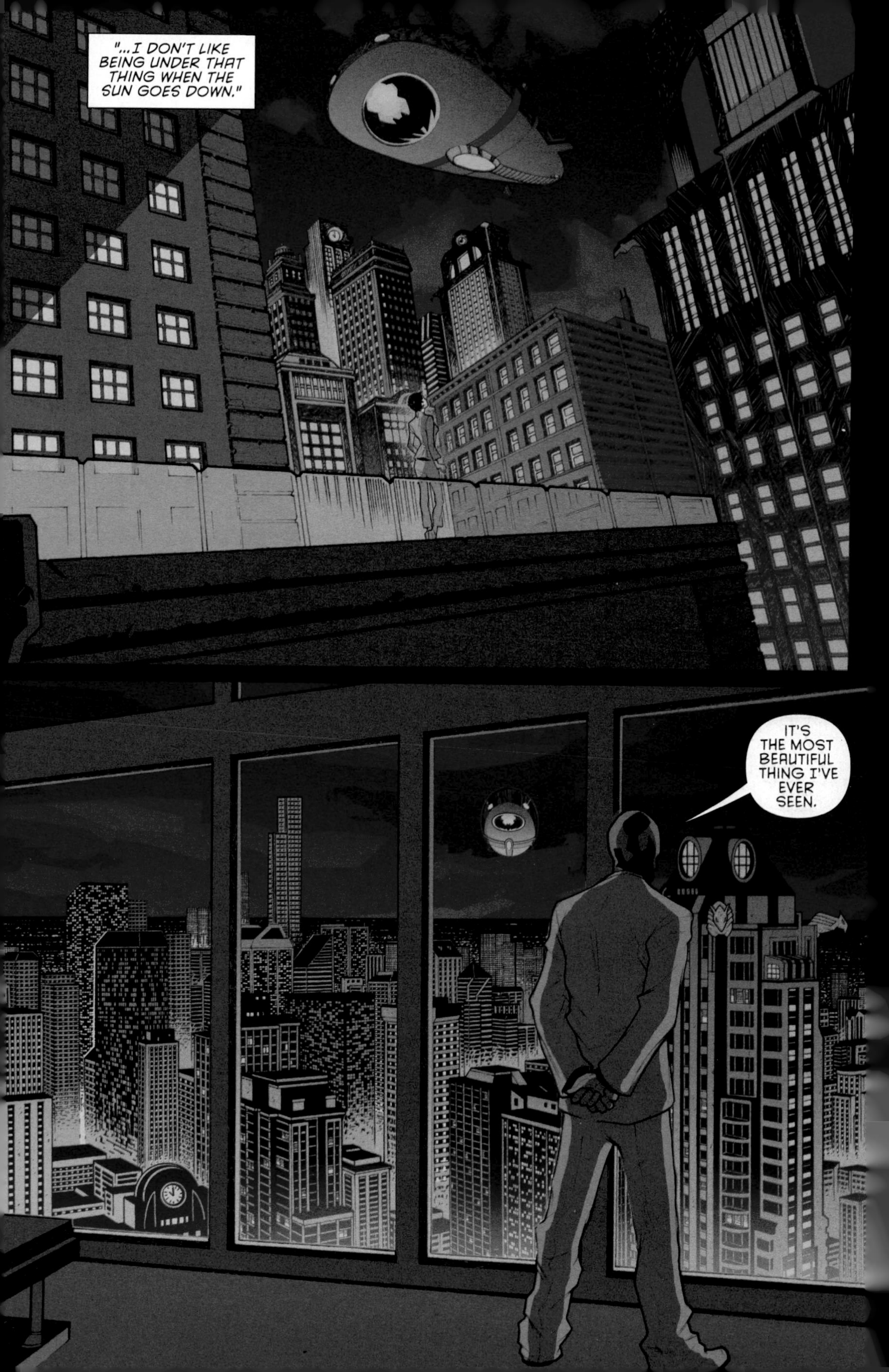
"...I DON'T LIKE BEING UNDER THAT THING WHEN THE SUN GOES DOWN."
IT'S THE MOST BEAUTIFUL THING I'VE EVER SEEN.

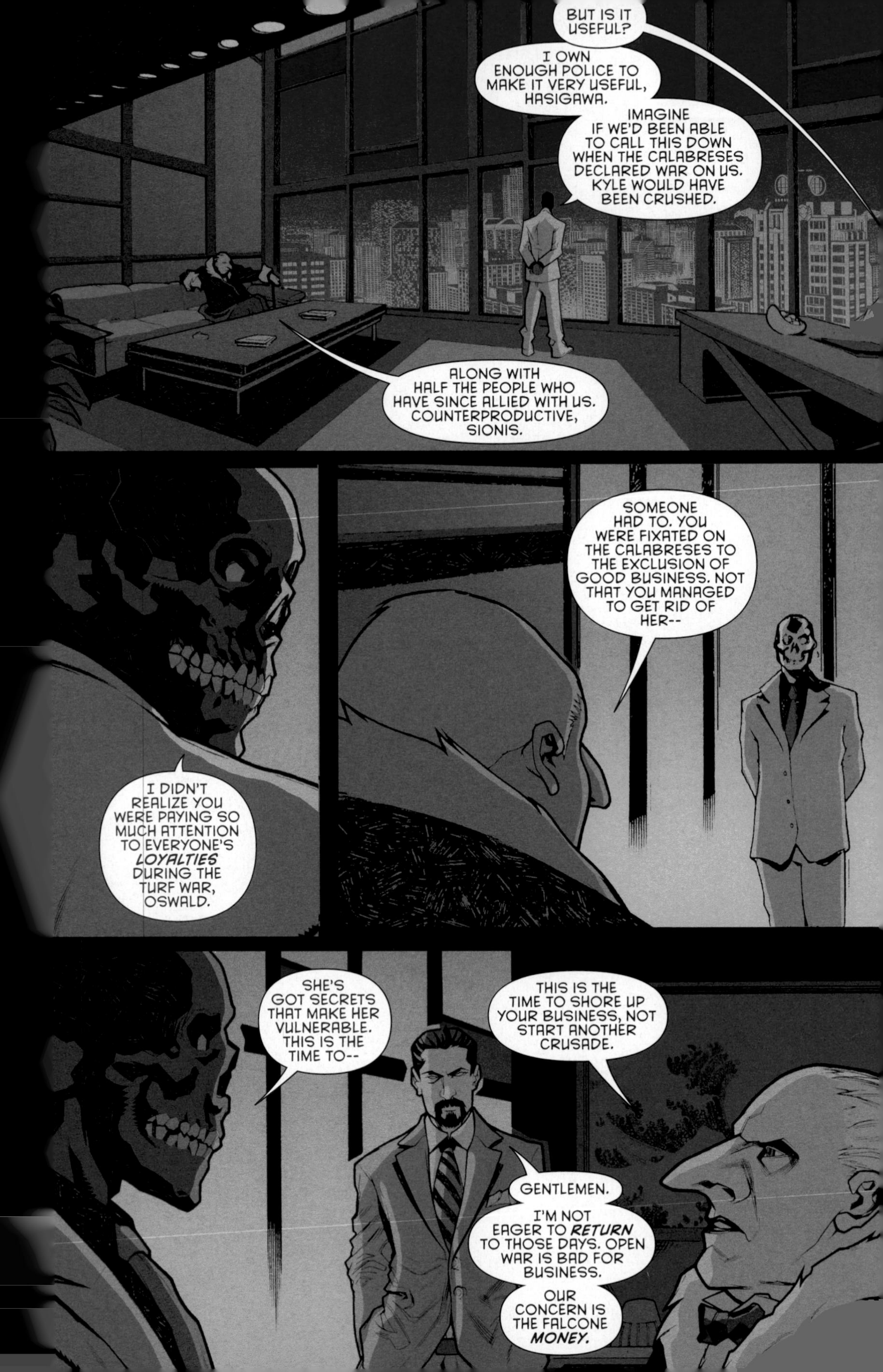
BUT IS IT USEFUL?
I OWN ENOUGH POLICE TO MAKE IT VERY USEFUL, HASIGAWA.
IMAGINE IF WE'D BEEN ABLE TO CALL THIS DOWN WHEN THE CALABRESES DECLARED WAR ON US. KYLE WOULD HAVE BEEN CRUSHED.
ALONG WITH HALF THE PEOPLE WHO HAVE SINCE ALLIED WITH US. COUNTERPRODUCTIVE, SIONIS.
SOMEONE HAD TO. YOU WERE FIXATED ON THE CALABRESES TO THE EXCLUSION OF GOOD BUSINESS. NOT THAT YOU MANAGED TO GET RID OF HER--
I DIDN'T REALIZE YOU WERE PAYING SO MUCH ATTENTION TO EVERYONE'S *LOYALTIES* DURING THE TURF WAR, OSWALD.
SHE'S GOT SECRETS THAT MAKE HER VULNERABLE. THIS IS THE TIME TO--
THIS IS THE TIME TO SHORE UP YOUR BUSINESS, NOT START ANOTHER CRUSADE.
GENTLEMEN.
I'M NOT EAGER TO ***RETURN*** TO THOSE DAYS. OPEN WAR IS BAD FOR BUSINESS.
OUR CONCERN IS THE FALCONE ***MONEY.***

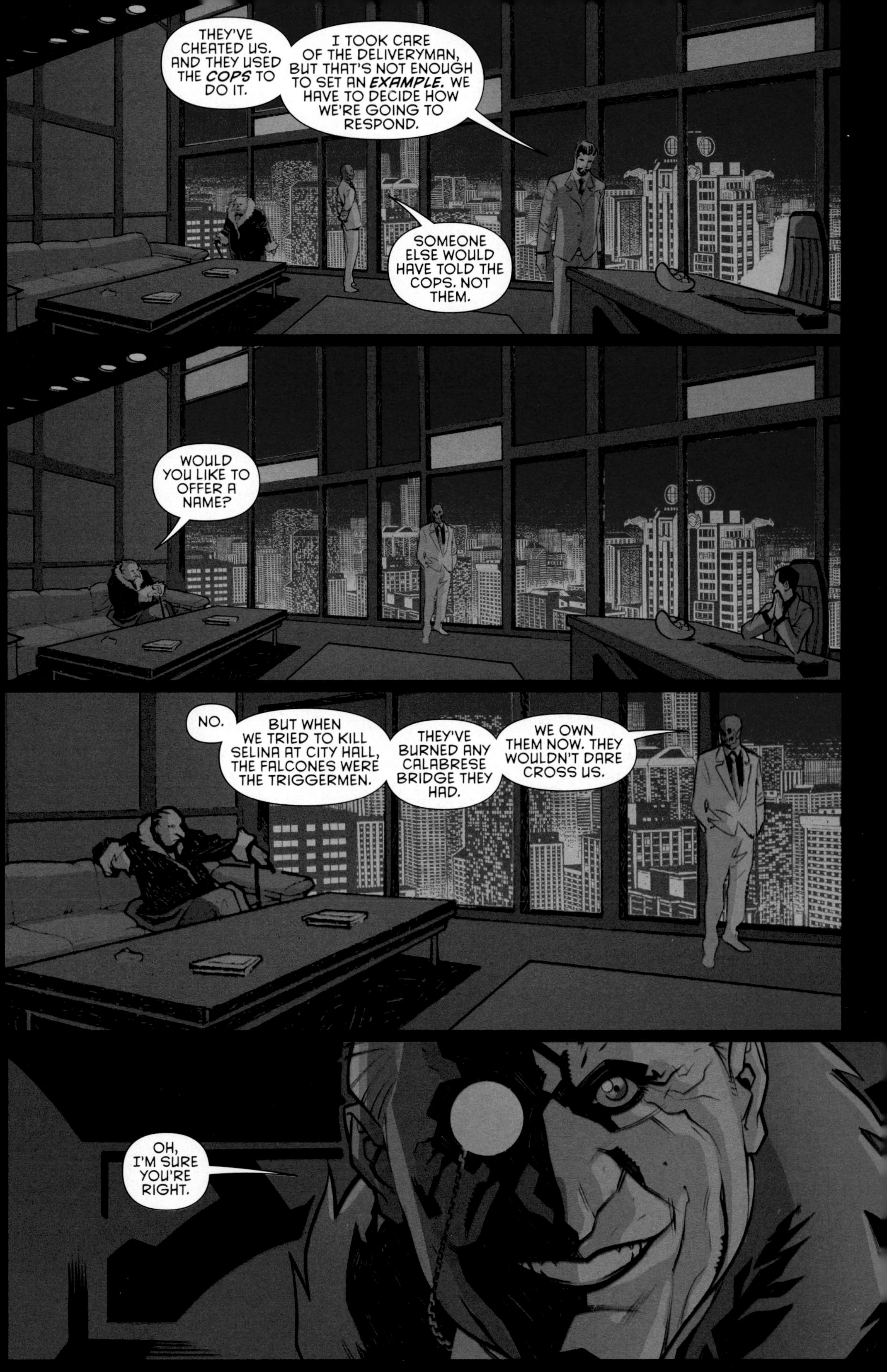
THEY'VE CHEATED US. AND THEY USED THE *COPS* TO DO IT.
I TOOK CARE OF THE DELIVERYMAN, BUT THAT'S NOT ENOUGH TO SET AN *EXAMPLE.* WE HAVE TO DECIDE HOW WE'RE GOING TO RESPOND.
SOMEONE ELSE WOULD HAVE TOLD THE COPS. NOT THEM.
WOULD YOU LIKE TO OFFER A NAME?
NO.
BUT WHEN WE TRIED TO KILL SELINA AT CITY HALL, THE FALCONES WERE THE TRIGGERMEN.
THEY'VE BURNED ANY CALABRESE BRIDGE THEY HAD.
WE OWN THEM NOW. THEY WOULDN'T DARE CROSS US.
OH, I'M SURE YOU'RE RIGHT.

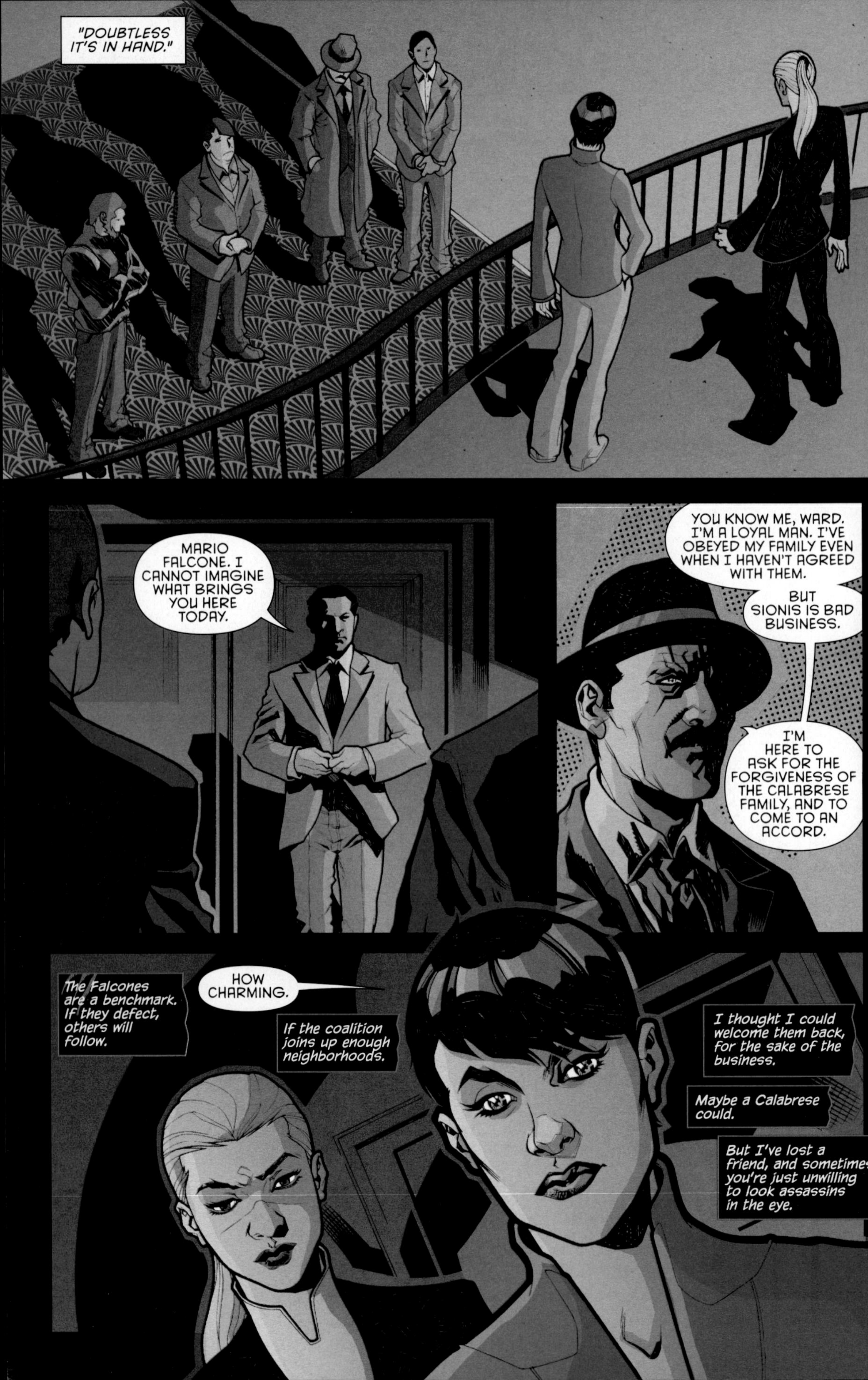
"DOUBTLESS IT'S IN HAND."
MARIO FALCONE. I CANNOT IMAGINE WHAT BRINGS YOU HERE TODAY.
YOU KNOW ME, WARD. I'M A LOYAL MAN. I'VE OBEYED MY FAMILY EVEN WHEN I HAVEN'T AGREED WITH THEM.
BUT SIONIS IS BAD BUSINESS.
I'M HERE TO ASK FOR THE FORGIVENESS OF THE CALABRESE FAMILY, AND TO COME TO AN ACCORD.
The Falcones are a benchmark. If they defect, others will follow.
HOW CHARMING.
If the coalition joins up enough neighborhoods.
I thought I could welcome them back, for the sake of the business.
Maybe a Calabrese could.
But I've lost a friend, and sometimes you're just unwilling to look assassins in the eye.

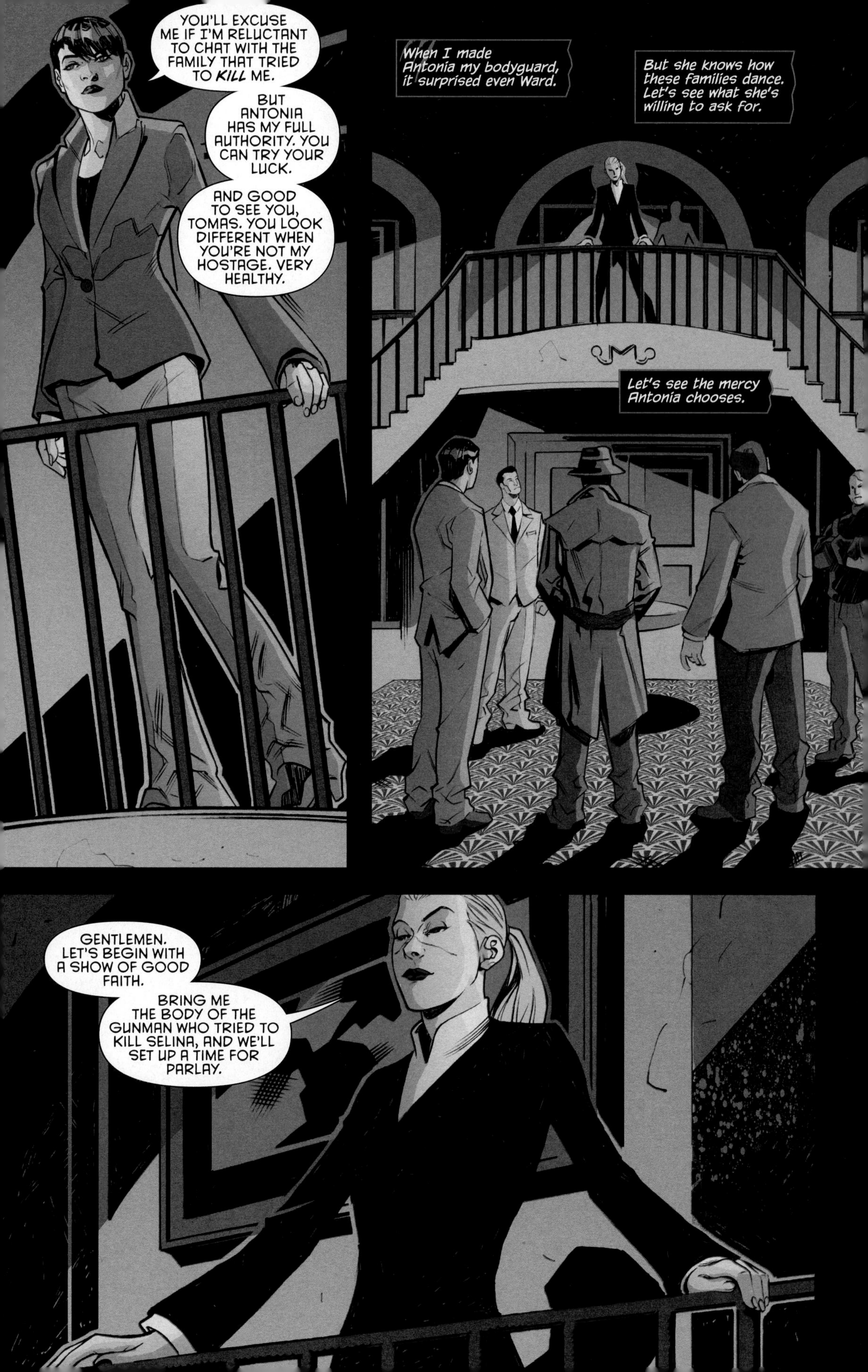
YOU'LL EXCUSE ME IF I'M RELUCTANT TO CHAT WITH THE FAMILY THAT TRIED TO KILL ME.
BUT ANTONIA HAS MY FULL AUTHORITY. YOU CAN TRY YOUR LUCK.
AND GOOD TO SEE YOU, TOMAS. YOU LOOK DIFFERENT WHEN YOU'RE NOT MY HOSTAGE. VERY HEALTHY.
When I made Antonia my bodyguard, it surprised even Ward.
But she knows how these families dance. Let's see what she's willing to ask for.
Let's see the mercy Antonia chooses.
GENTLEMEN. LET'S BEGIN WITH A SHOW OF GOOD FAITH.
BRING ME THE BODY OF THE GUNMAN WHO TRIED TO KILL SELINA, AND WE'LL SET UP A TIME FOR PARLAY.

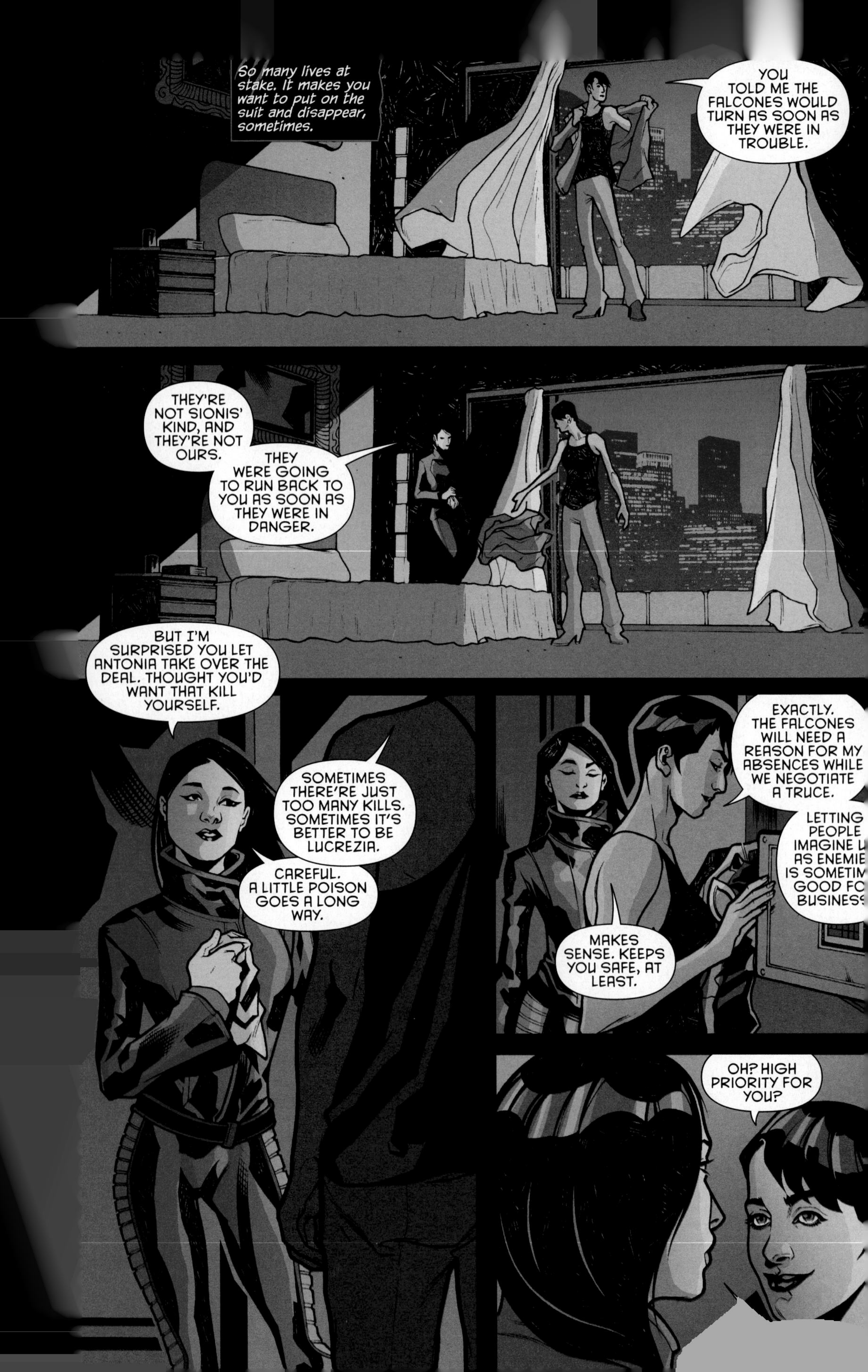
So many lives at stake. It makes you want to put on the suit and disappear, sometimes.
YOU TOLD ME THE FALCONES WOULD TURN AS SOON AS THEY WERE IN TROUBLE.
THEY'RE NOT SIONIS' KIND, AND THEY'RE NOT OURS.
THEY WERE GOING TO RUN BACK TO YOU AS SOON AS THEY WERE IN DANGER.
BUT I'M SURPRISED YOU LET ANTONIA TAKE OVER THE DEAL. THOUGHT YOU'D WANT THAT KILL YOURSELF.
SOMETIMES THERE'RE JUST TOO MANY KILLS. SOMETIMES IT'S BETTER TO BE LUCREZIA.
CAREFUL. A LITTLE POISON GOES A LONG WAY.
EXACTLY. THE FALCONES WILL NEED A REASON FOR MY ABSENCES WHILE WE NEGOTIATE A TRUCE.
MAKES SENSE. KEEPS YOU SAFE, AT LEAST.
OH? HIGH PRIORITY FOR YOU?

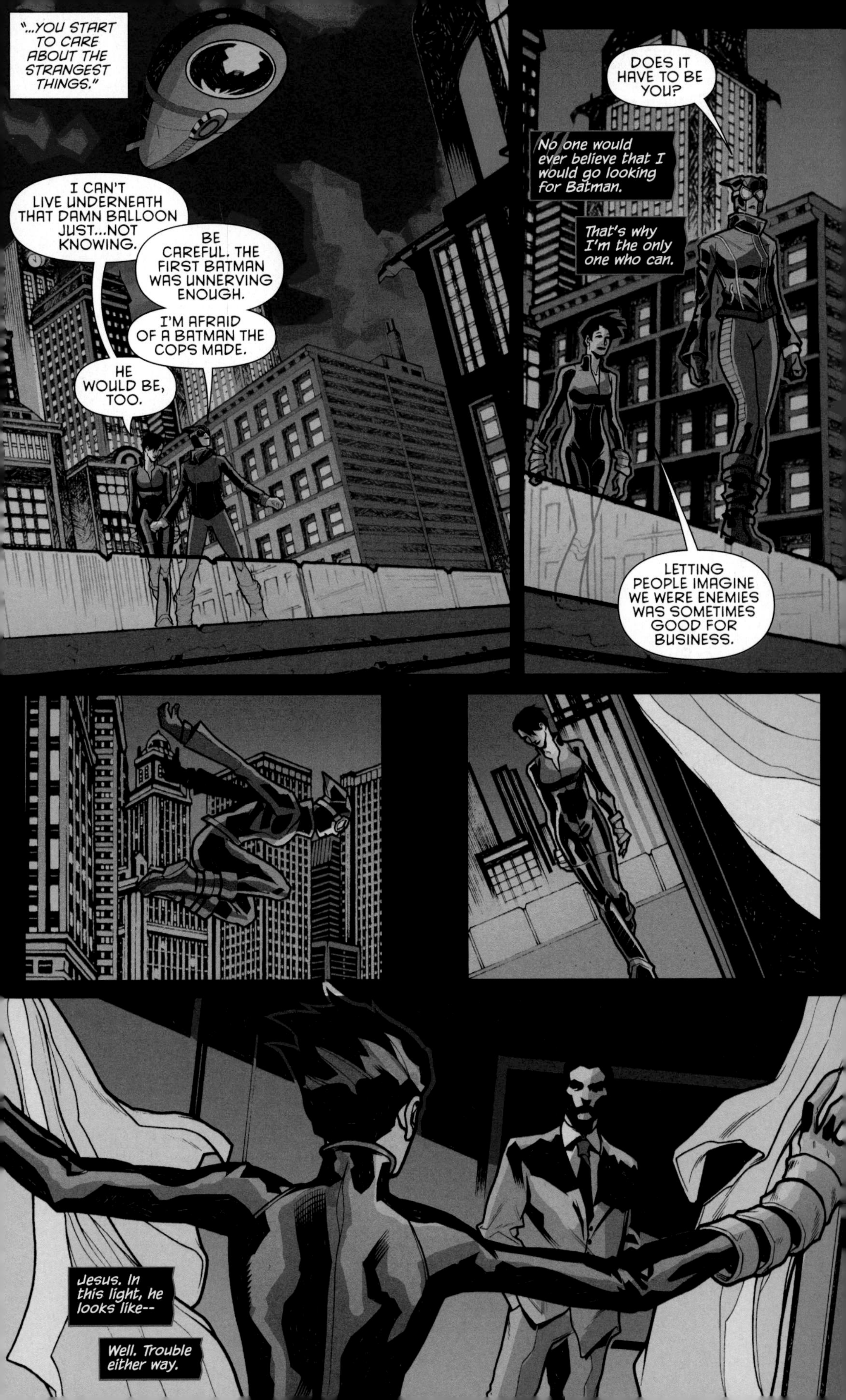
"...YOU START TO CARE ABOUT THE STRANGEST THINGS."
I CAN'T LIVE UNDERNEATH THAT DAMN BALLOON JUST...NOT KNOWING.
BE CAREFUL. THE FIRST BATMAN WAS UNNERVING ENOUGH.
I'M AFRAID OF A BATMAN THE COPS MADE.
HE WOULD BE, TOO.
DOES IT HAVE TO BE YOU?
No one would ever believe that I would go looking for Batman.
That's why I'm the only one who can.
LETTING PEOPLE IMAGINE WE WERE ENEMIES WAS SOMETIMES GOOD FOR BUSINESS.
Jesus. In this light, he looks like--
Well. Trouble either way.

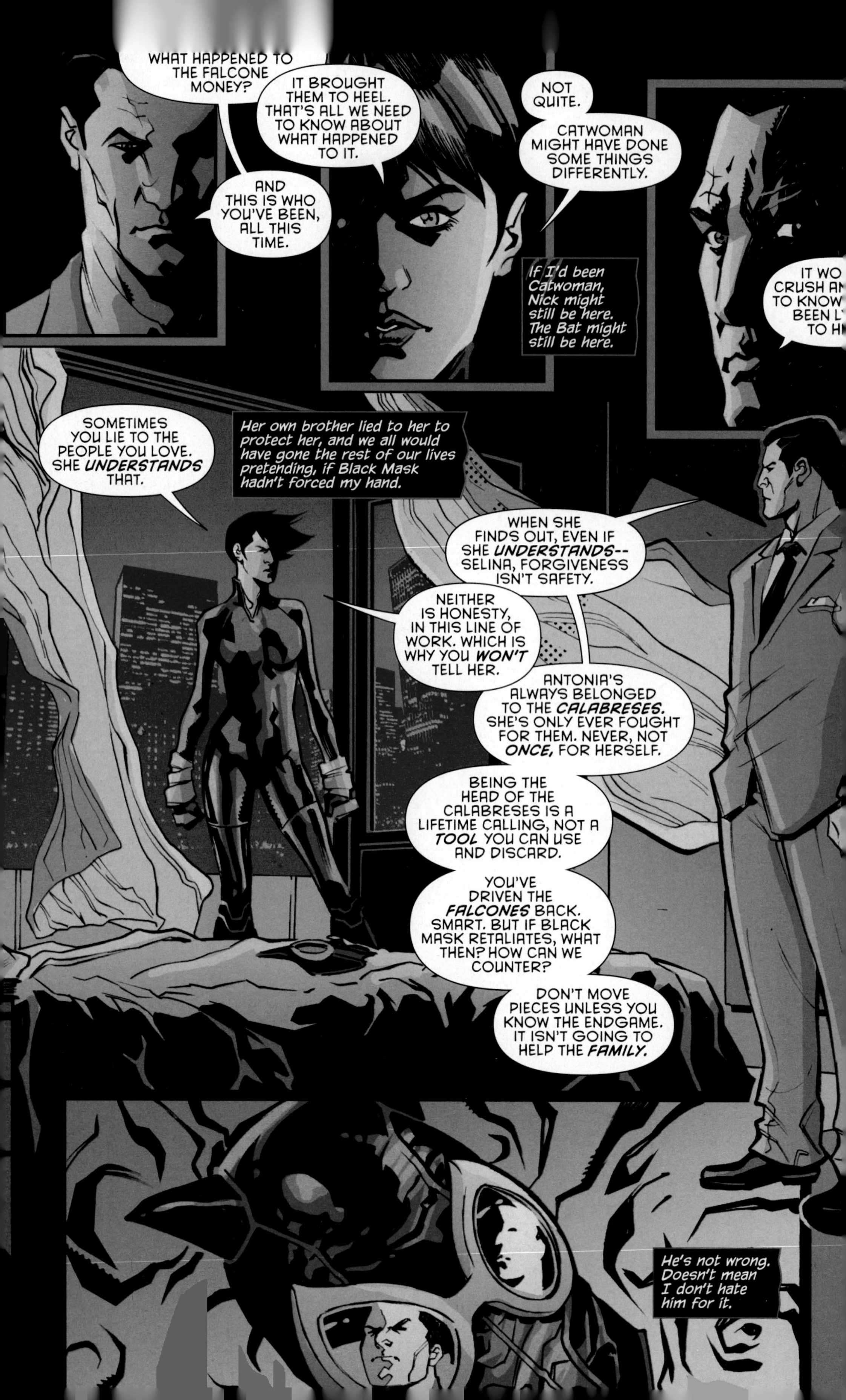

WHAT HAPPENED TO THE FALCONE MONEY?
IT BROUGHT THEM TO HEEL. THAT'S ALL WE NEED TO KNOW ABOUT WHAT HAPPENED TO IT.
AND THIS IS WHO YOU'VE BEEN, ALL THIS TIME.
NOT QUITE.
CATWOMAN MIGHT HAVE DONE SOME THINGS DIFFERENTLY.
If I'd been Catwoman, Nick might still be here. The Bat might still be here.
SOMETIMES YOU LIE TO THE PEOPLE YOU LOVE. SHE UNDERSTANDS THAT.
Her own brother lied to her to protect her, and we all would have gone the rest of our lives pretending, if Black Mask hadn't forced my hand.
WHEN SHE FINDS OUT, EVEN IF SHE UNDERSTANDS-- SELINA, FORGIVENESS ISN'T SAFETY.
NEITHER IS HONESTY, IN THIS LINE OF WORK. WHICH IS WHY YOU WON'T TELL HER.
ANTONIA'S ALWAYS BELONGED TO THE CALABRESES. SHE'S ONLY EVER FOUGHT FOR THEM. NEVER, NOT ONCE, FOR HERSELF.
BEING THE HEAD OF THE CALABRESES IS A LIFETIME CALLING, NOT A TOOL YOU CAN USE AND DISCARD.
YOU'VE DRIVEN THE FALCONES BACK. SMART. BUT IF BLACK MASK RETALIATES, WHAT THEN? HOW CAN WE COUNTER?
DON'T MOVE PIECES UNLESS YOU KNOW THE ENDGAME. IT ISN'T GOING TO HELP THE FAMILY.
He's not wrong. Doesn't mean I don't hate him for it.

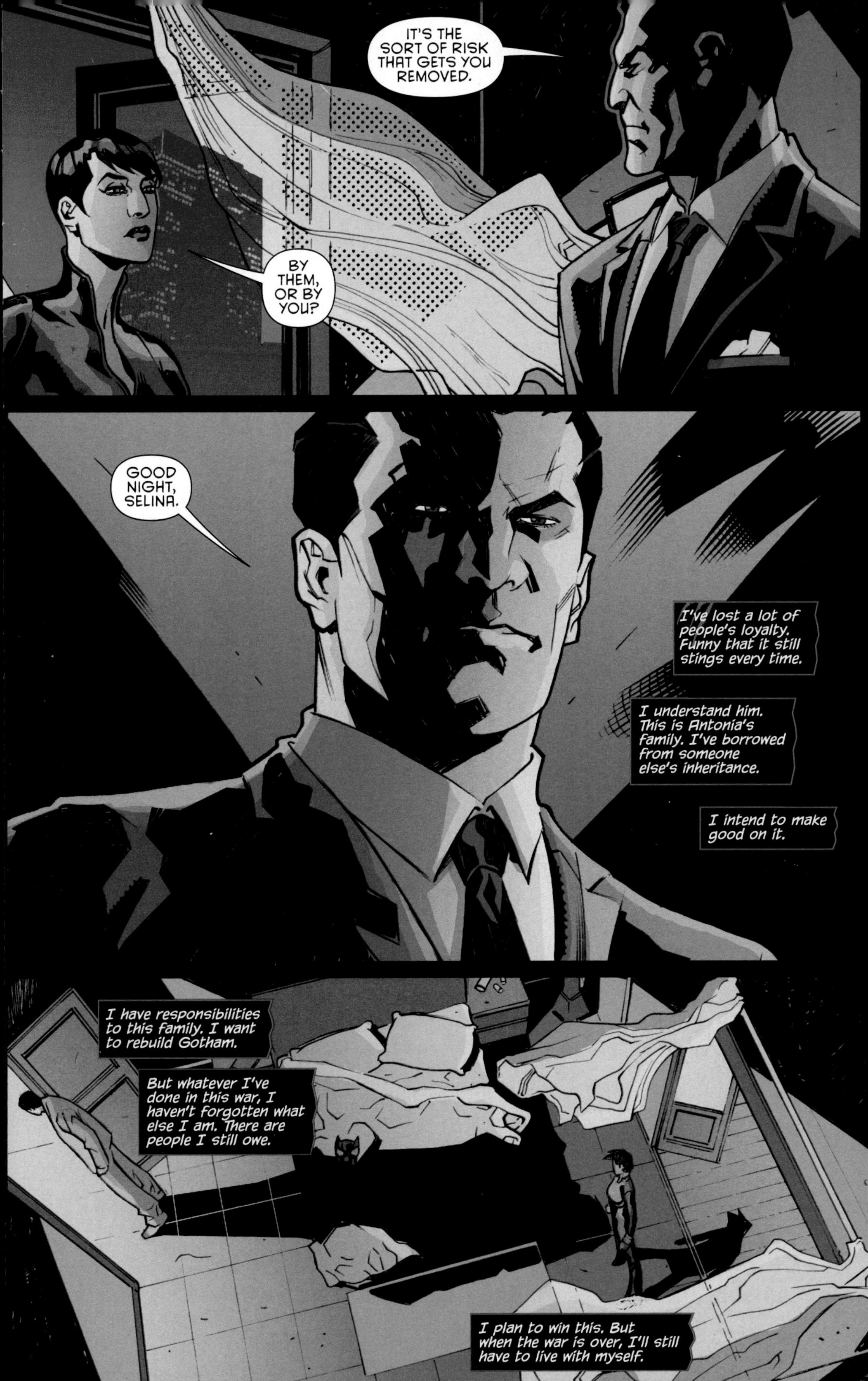
IT'S THE SORT OF RISK THAT GETS YOU REMOVED.
BY THEM, OR BY YOU?
GOOD NIGHT, SELINA.
I've lost a lot of people's loyalty. Funny that it still stings every time.
I understand him. This is Antonia's family. I've borrowed from someone else's inheritance.
I intend to make good on it.
I have responsibilities to this family. I want to rebuild Gotham.
But whatever I've done in this war, I haven't forgotten what else I am. There are people I still owe.
I plan to win this. But when the war is over, I'll still have to live with myself.

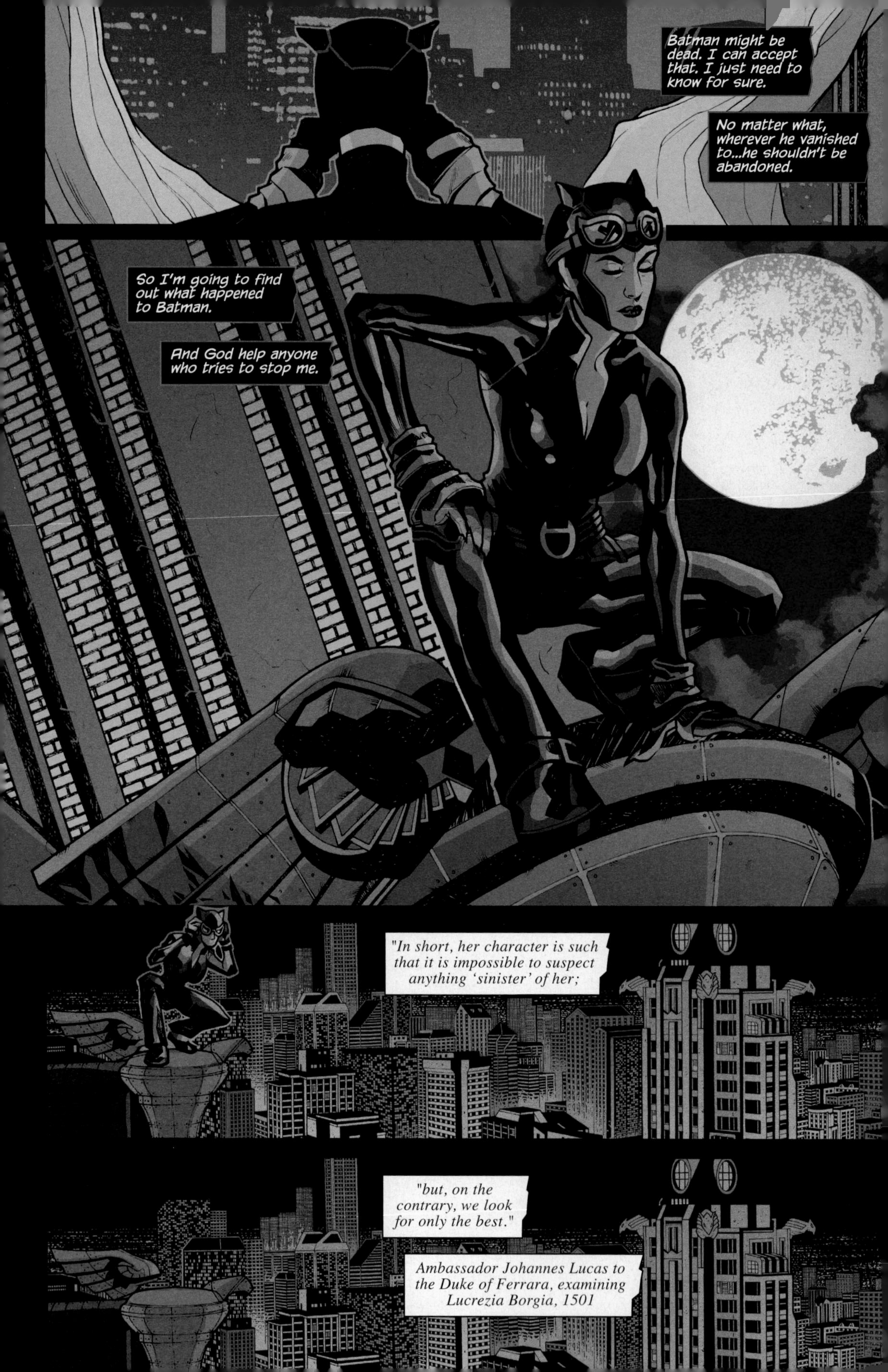
Batman might be dead. I can accept that. I just need to know for sure.
No matter what, wherever he vanished to...he shouldn't be abandoned.
So I'm going to find out what happened to Batman.
And God help anyone who tries to stop me.
"In short, her character is such that it is impossible to suspect anything 'sinister' of her;
"but, on the contrary, we look for only the best."
Ambassador Johannes Lucas to the Duke of Ferrara, examining Lucrezia Borgia, 1501

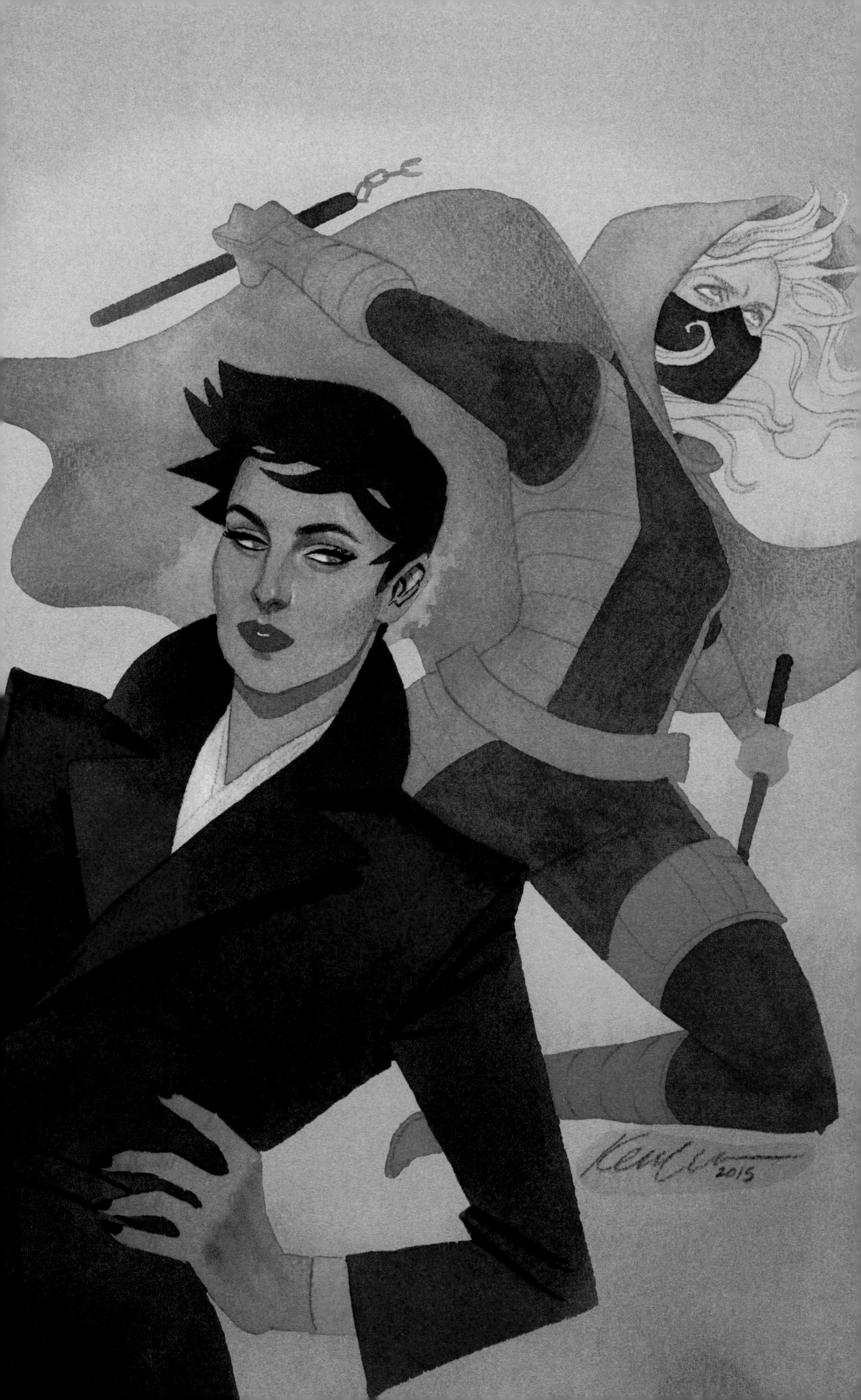
2015

writer DAVID HAHN artist LEE LOUGHRIDGE colorist TRAVIS LANHAM letterer cover art by KEVIN WADA

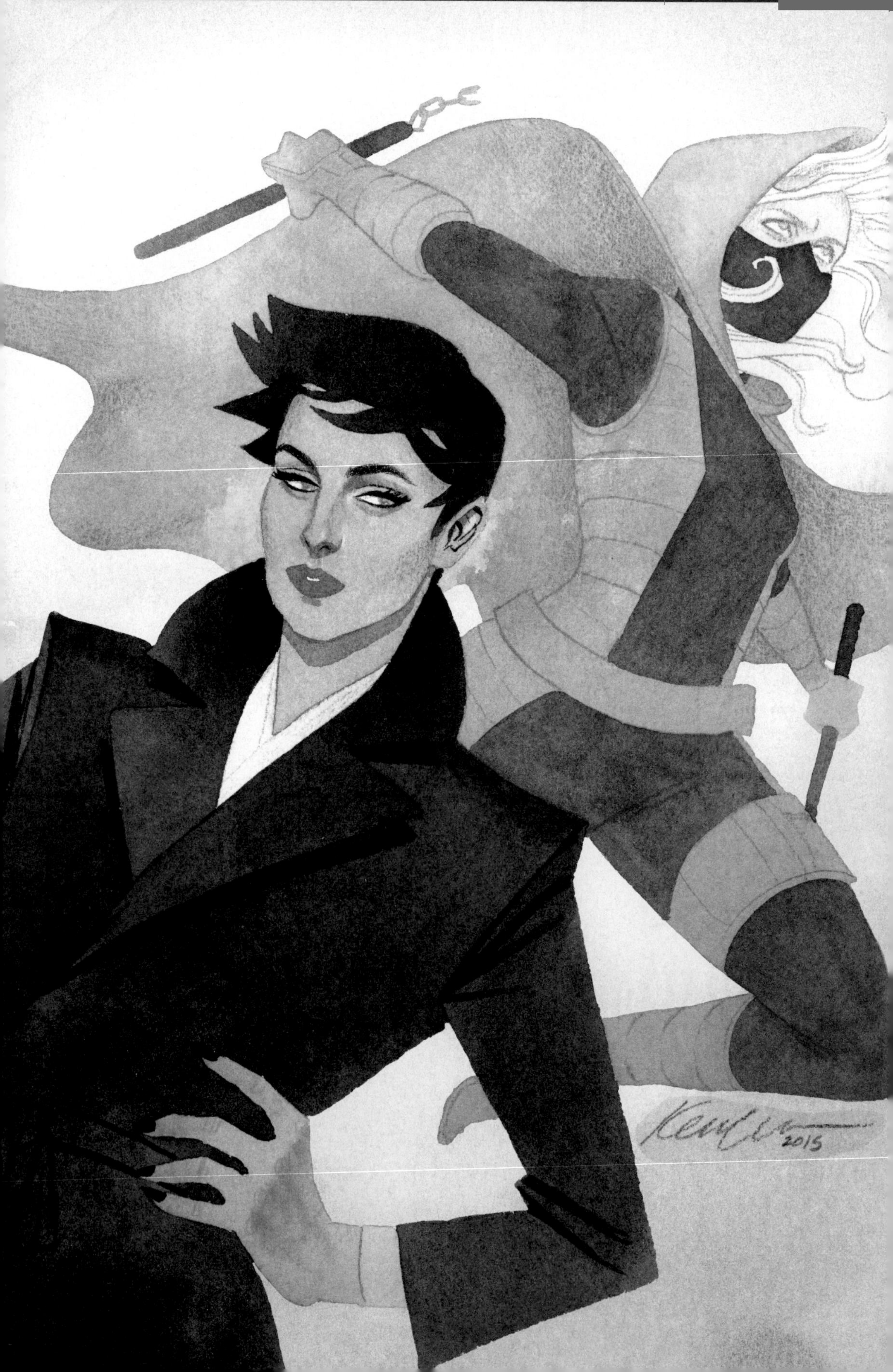

2015

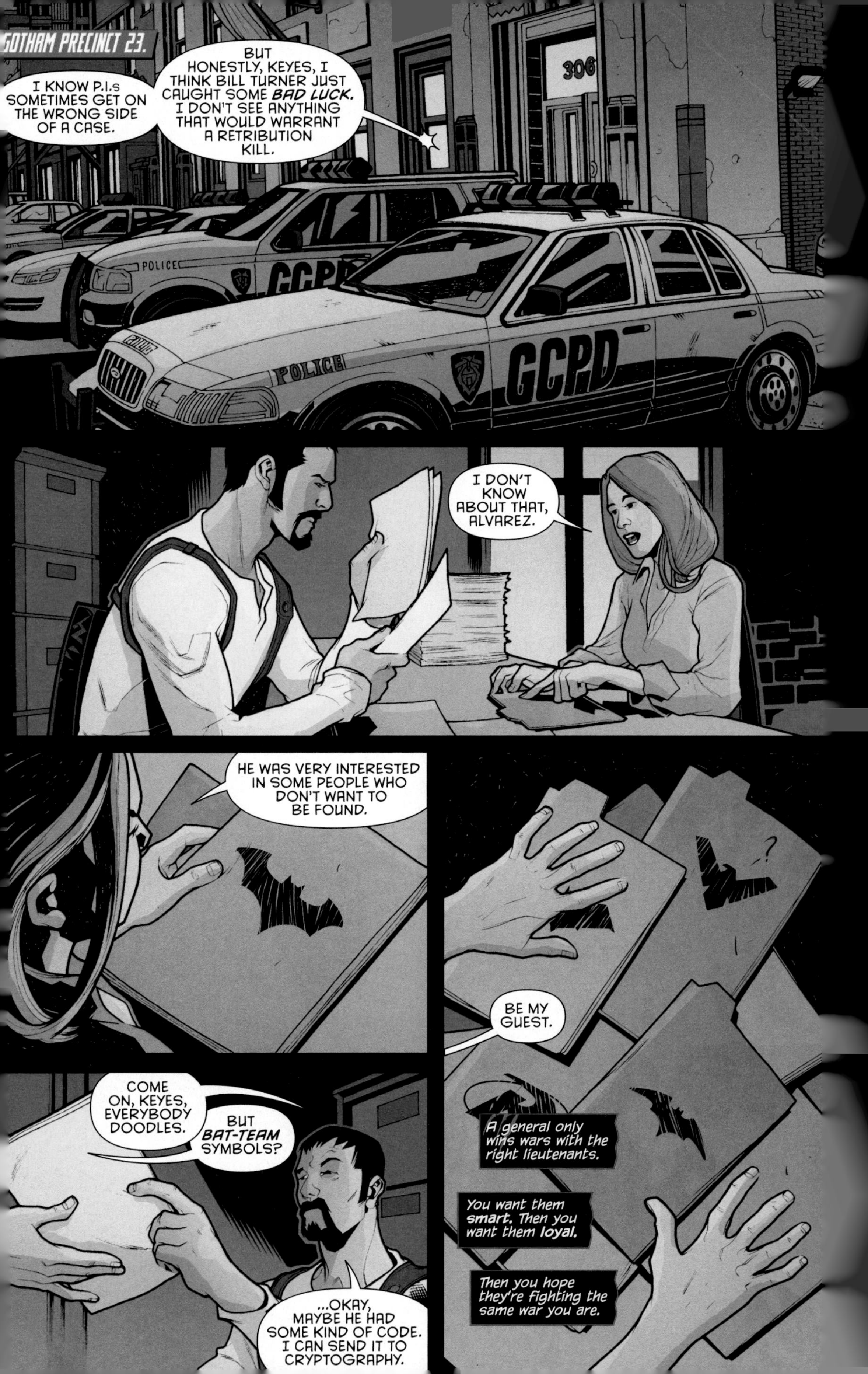
GOTHAM PRECINCT 23.
I KNOW P.I.s SOMETIMES GET ON THE WRONG SIDE OF A CASE.
BUT HONESTLY, KEYES, I THINK BILL TURNER JUST CAUGHT SOME BAD LUCK. I DON'T SEE ANYTHING THAT WOULD WARRANT A RETRIBUTION KILL.
306
POLICE
GCPD
POLICE
GCPD
I DON'T KNOW ABOUT THAT, ALVAREZ.
HE WAS VERY INTERESTED IN SOME PEOPLE WHO DON'T WANT TO BE FOUND.
BE MY GUEST.
COME ON, KEYES, EVERYBODY DOODLES.
BUT BAT-TEAM SYMBOLS?
...OKAY, MAYBE HE HAD SOME KIND OF CODE. I CAN SEND IT TO CRYPTOGRAPHY.
A general only wins wars with the right lieutenants.
You want them smart. Then you want them loyal.
Then you hope they're fighting the same war you are.

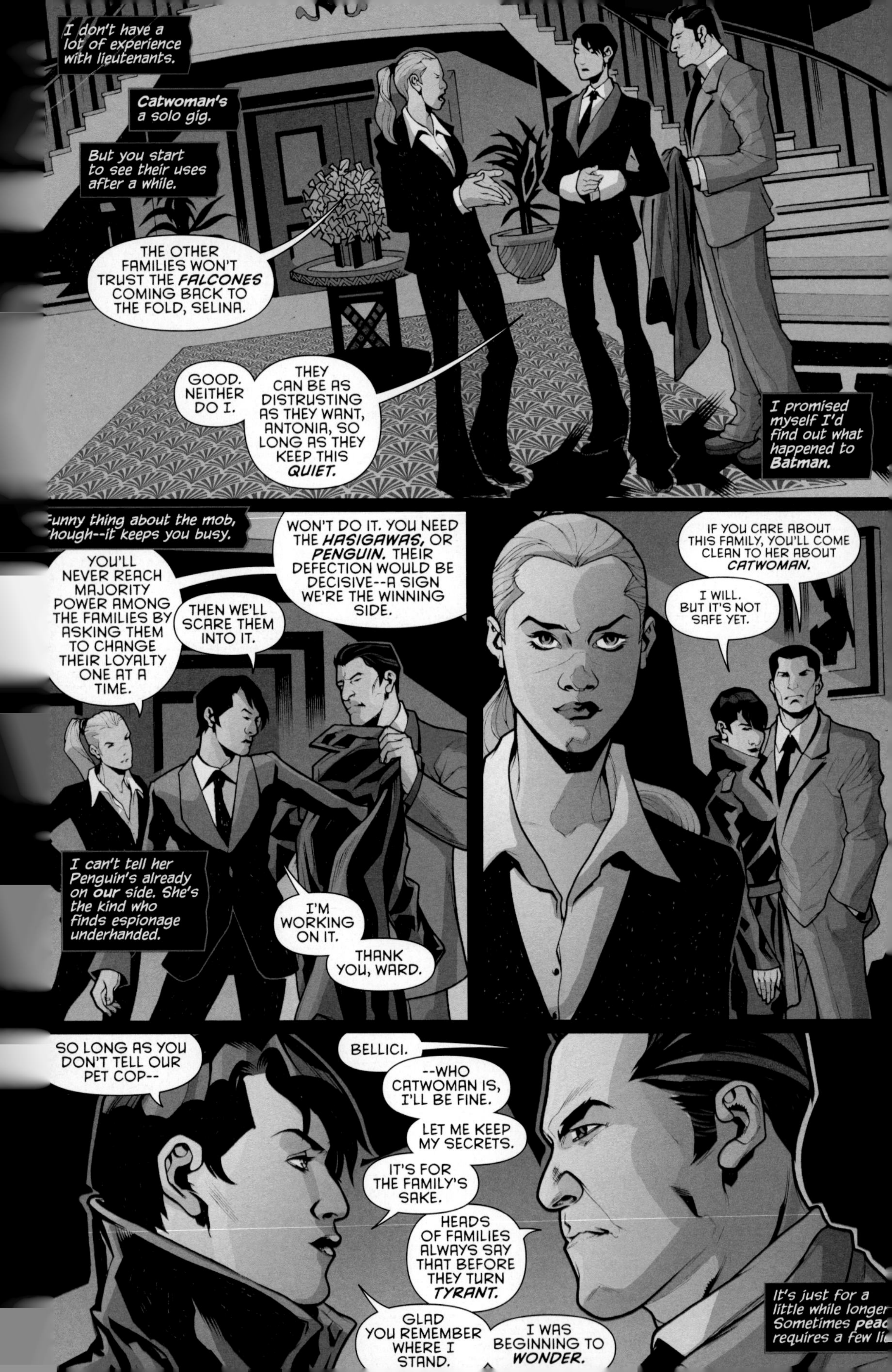
I don't have a lot of experience with lieutenants.
Catwoman's a solo gig.
But you start to see their uses after a while.
THE OTHER FAMILIES WON'T TRUST THE FALCONES COMING BACK TO THE FOLD, SELINA.
GOOD. NEITHER DO I.
THEY CAN BE AS DISTRUSTING AS THEY WANT, ANTONIA, SO LONG AS THEY KEEP THIS QUIET.
I promised myself I'd find out what happened to Batman.
unny thing about the mob, hough--it keeps you busy.
YOU'LL NEVER REACH MAJORITY POWER AMONG THE FAMILIES BY ASKING THEM TO CHANGE THEIR LOYALTY ONE AT A TIME.
THEN WE'LL SCARE THEM INTO IT.
WON'T DO IT. YOU NEED THE HASIGAWAS, OR PENGUIN. THEIR DEFECTION WOULD BE DECISIVE--A SIGN WE'RE THE WINNING SIDE.
I can't tell her Penguin's already on our side. She's the kind who finds espionage underhanded.
I'M WORKING ON IT.
THANK YOU, WARD.
IF YOU CARE ABOUT THIS FAMILY, YOU'LL COME CLEAN TO HER ABOUT CATWOMAN.
I WILL. BUT IT'S NOT SAFE YET.
SO LONG AS YOU DON'T TELL OUR PET COP--
BELLICI.
--WHO CATWOMAN IS, I'LL BE FINE.
LET ME KEEP MY SECRETS.
IT'S FOR THE FAMILY'S SAKE.
HEADS OF FAMILIES ALWAYS SAY THAT BEFORE THEY TURN TYRANT.
GLAD YOU REMEMBER WHERE I STAND.
I WAS BEGINNING TO WONDER.
It's just for a little while longer Sometimes peac requires a few li

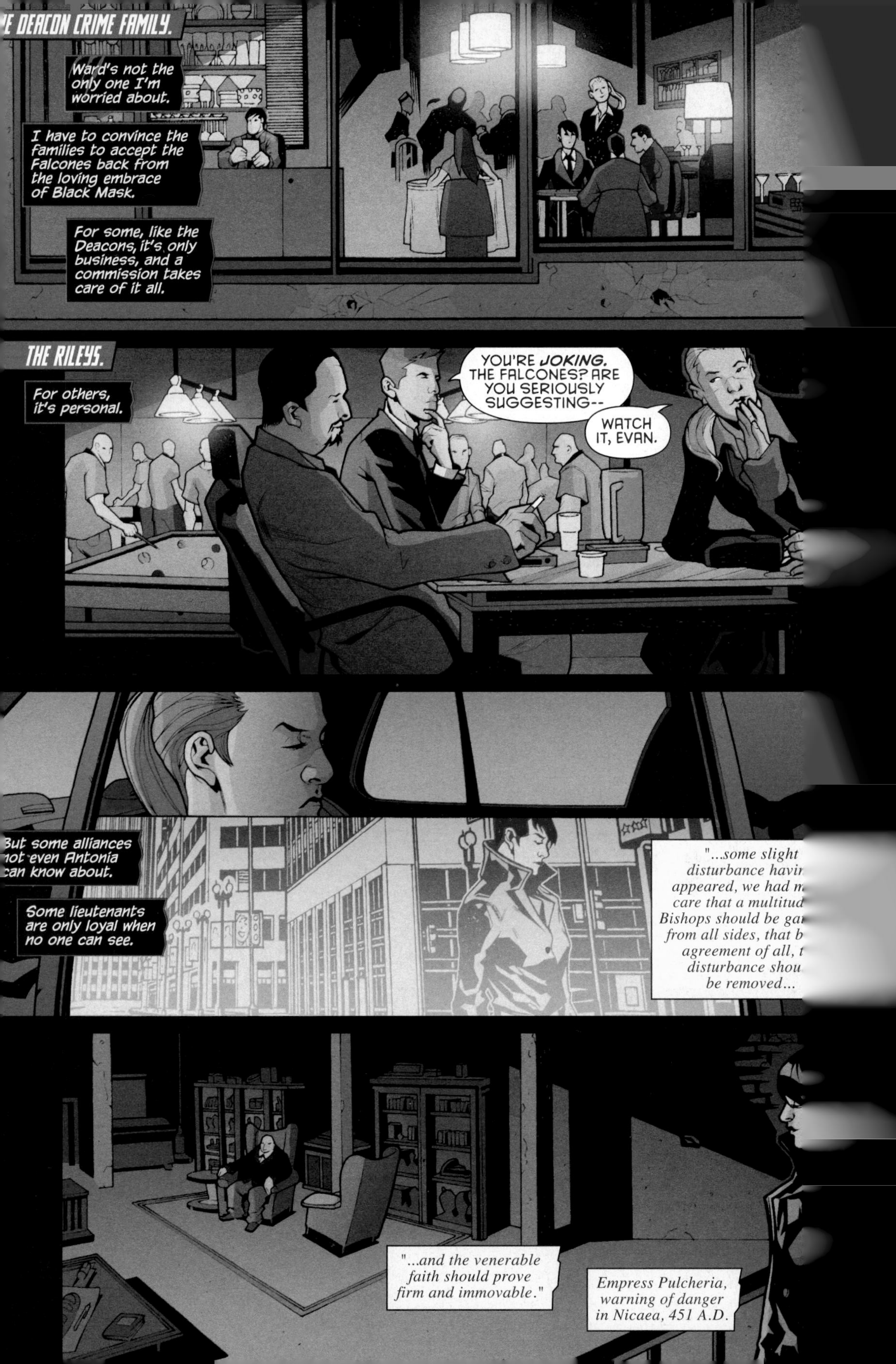
E DEACON CRIME FAMILY.
Ward's not the only one I'm worried about.
I have to convince the families to accept the Falcones back from the loving embrace of Black Mask.
For some, like the Deacons, it's only business, and a commission takes care of it all.
THE RILEYS.
For others, it's personal.
YOU'RE JOKING. THE FALCONES? ARE YOU SERIOUSLY SUGGESTING--
WATCH IT, EVAN.
But some alliances not even Antonia can know about.
Some lieutenants are only loyal when no one can see.
"...some slight disturbance havi appeared, we had m care that a multitud Bishops should be ga from all sides, that b agreement of all, t disturbance shou be removed...
"...and the venerable faith should prove firm and immovable."
Empress Pulcheria, warning of danger in Nicaea, 451 A.D.

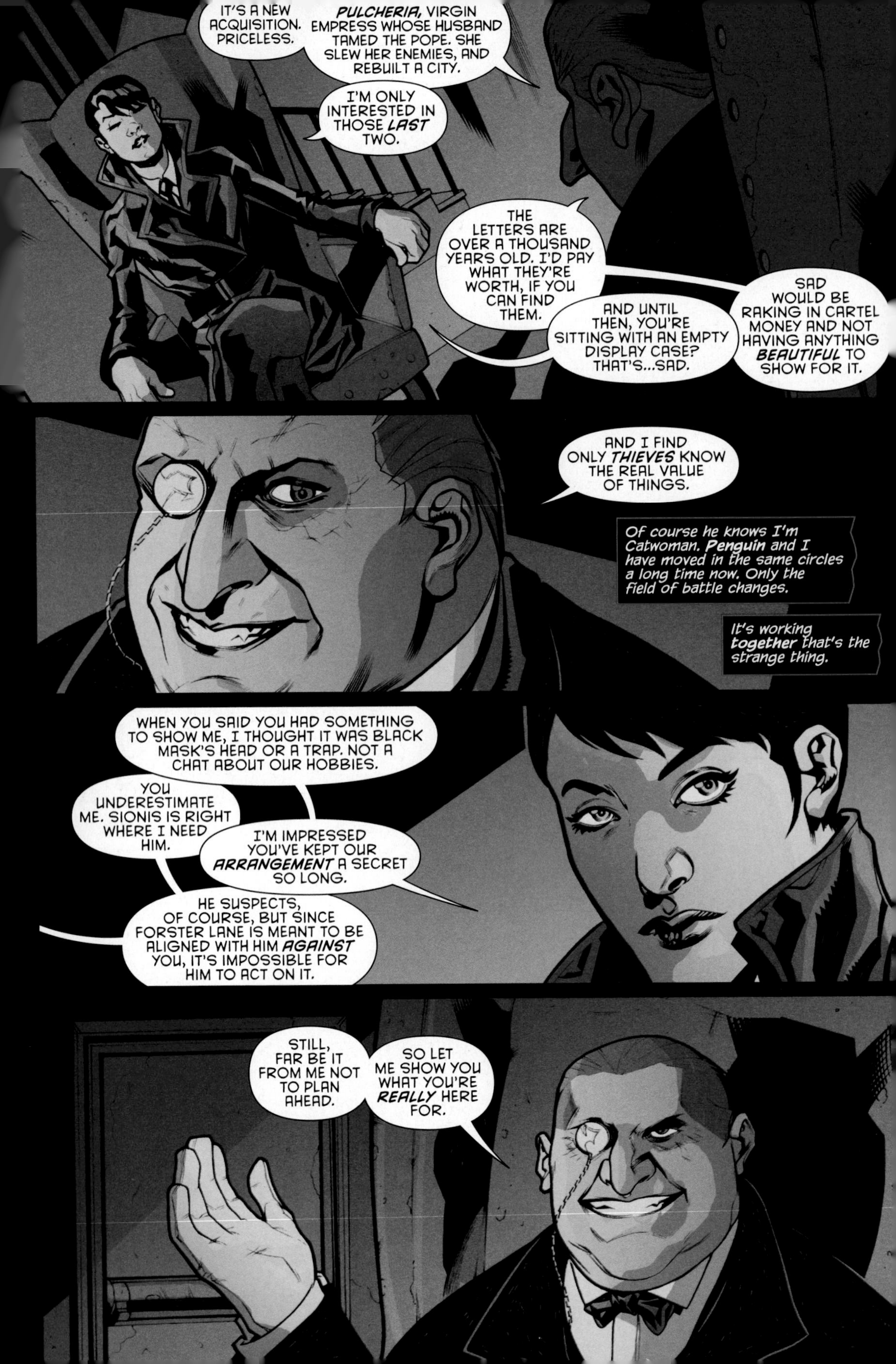
IT'S A NEW ACQUISITION. PRICELESS.
PULCHERIA, VIRGIN EMPRESS WHOSE HUSBAND TAMED THE POPE. SHE SLEW HER ENEMIES, AND REBUILT A CITY.
I'M ONLY INTERESTED IN THOSE LAST TWO.
THE LETTERS ARE OVER A THOUSAND YEARS OLD. I'D PAY WHAT THEY'RE WORTH, IF YOU CAN FIND THEM.
AND UNTIL THEN, YOU'RE SITTING WITH AN EMPTY DISPLAY CASE? THAT'S...SAD.
SAD WOULD BE RAKING IN CARTEL MONEY AND NOT HAVING ANYTHING BEAUTIFUL TO SHOW FOR IT.
AND I FIND ONLY THIEVES KNOW THE REAL VALUE OF THINGS.
Of course he knows I'm Catwoman. Penguin and I have moved in the same circles a long time now. Only the field of battle changes.
It's working together that's the strange thing.
WHEN YOU SAID YOU HAD SOMETHING TO SHOW ME, I THOUGHT IT WAS BLACK MASK'S HEAD OR A TRAP. NOT A CHAT ABOUT OUR HOBBIES.
YOU UNDERESTIMATE ME. SIONIS IS RIGHT WHERE I NEED HIM.
I'M IMPRESSED YOU'VE KEPT OUR ARRANGEMENT A SECRET SO LONG.
HE SUSPECTS, OF COURSE, BUT SINCE FORSTER LANE IS MEANT TO BE ALIGNED WITH HIM AGAINST YOU, IT'S IMPOSSIBLE FOR HIM TO ACT ON IT.
STILL, FAR BE IT FROM ME NOT TO PLAN AHEAD.
SO LET ME SHOW YOU WHAT YOU'RE REALLY HERE FOR.

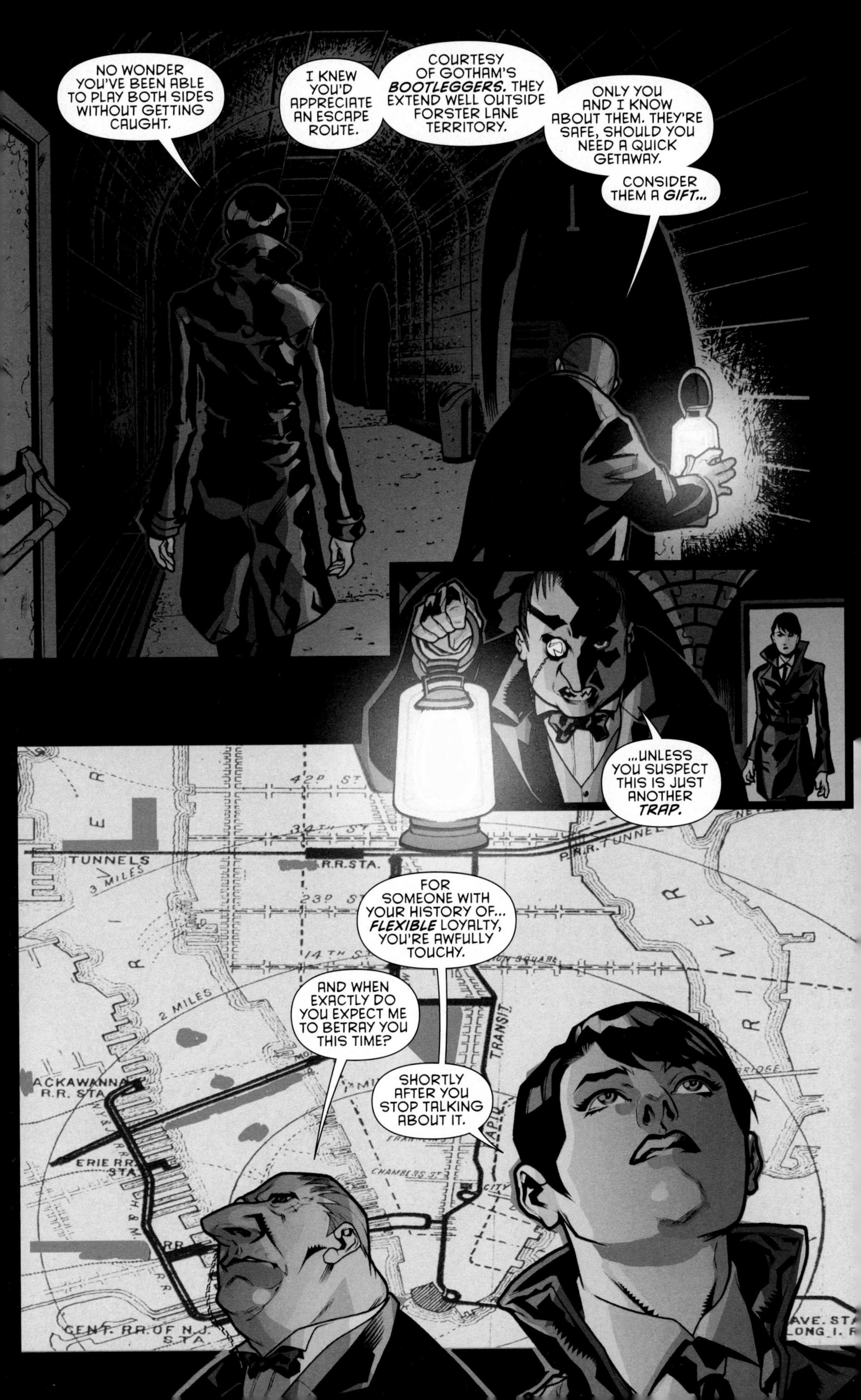
NO WONDER YOU'VE BEEN ABLE TO PLAY BOTH SIDES WITHOUT GETTING CAUGHT.
I KNEW YOU'D APPRECIATE AN ESCAPE ROUTE.
COURTESY OF GOTHAM'S **BOOTLEGGERS.** THEY EXTEND WELL OUTSIDE FORSTER LANE TERRITORY.
ONLY YOU AND I KNOW ABOUT THEM. THEY'RE SAFE, SHOULD YOU NEED A QUICK GETAWAY.
CONSIDER THEM A ***GIFT...***
...UNLESS YOU SUSPECT THIS IS JUST ANOTHER ***TRAP.***
FOR SOMEONE WITH YOUR HISTORY OF... ***FLEXIBLE*** LOYALTY, YOU'RE AWFULLY TOUCHY.
AND WHEN EXACTLY DO YOU EXPECT ME TO BETRAY YOU THIS TIME?
SHORTLY AFTER YOU STOP TALKING ABOUT IT.
TUNNELS
3 MILES
R.R.STA.
P.R.R. TUNNEL
2 MILES
TRANSIT
R.R. STA
ERIE RR STA
CHAMBERS ST
CENT. RR. OF N.J. STA
AVE. STA

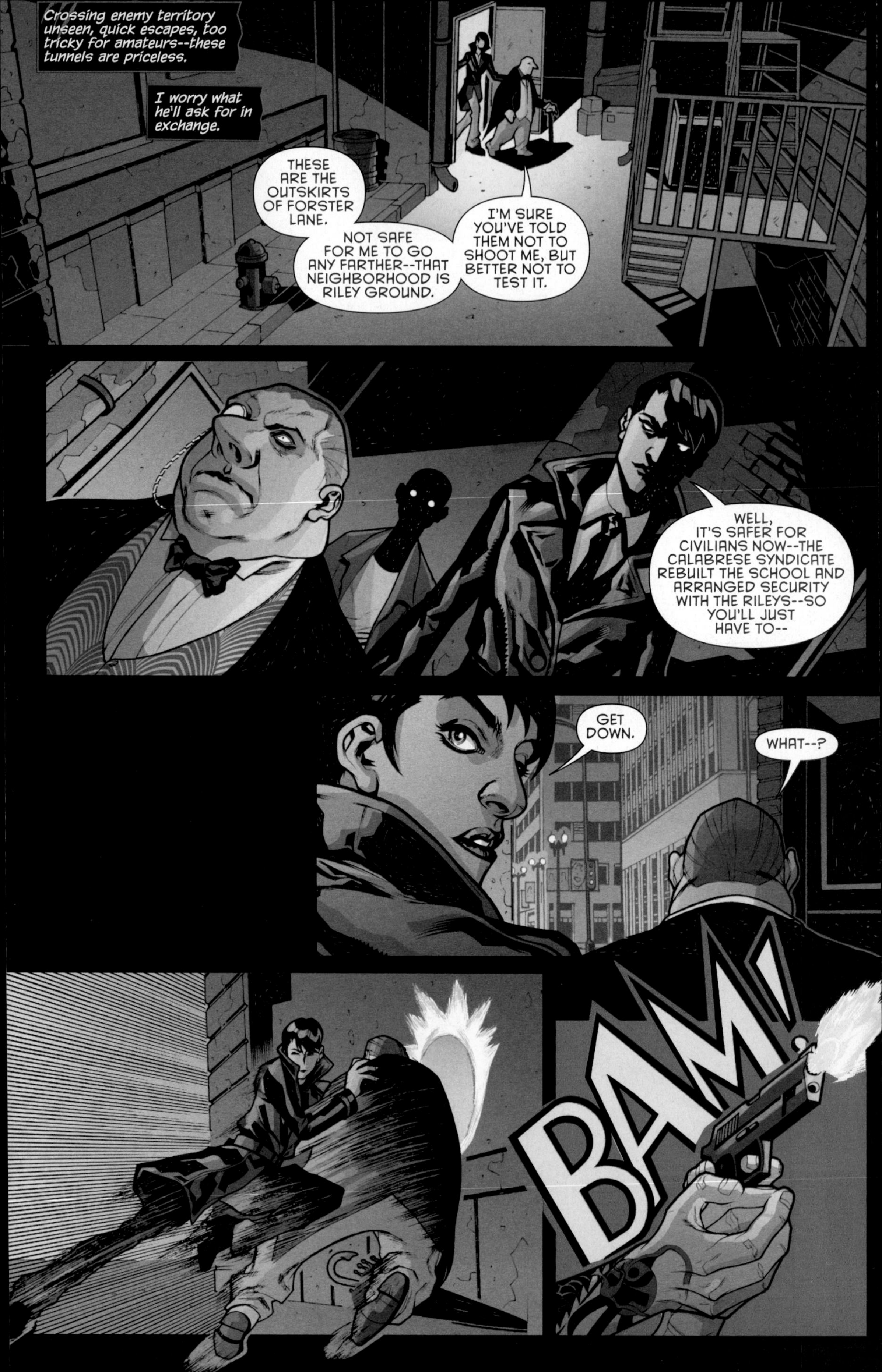
Crossing enemy territory unseen, quick escapes, too tricky for amateurs--these tunnels are priceless.
I worry what he'll ask for in exchange.
THESE ARE THE OUTSKIRTS OF FORSTER LANE.
NOT SAFE FOR ME TO GO ANY FARTHER--THAT NEIGHBORHOOD IS RILEY GROUND.
I'M SURE YOU'VE TOLD THEM NOT TO SHOOT ME, BUT BETTER NOT TO TEST IT.
WELL, IT'S SAFER FOR CIVILIANS NOW--THE CALABRESE SYNDICATE REBUILT THE SCHOOL AND ARRANGED SECURITY WITH THE RILEYS--SO YOU'LL JUST HAVE TO--
GET DOWN.
WHAT--?
BAM!

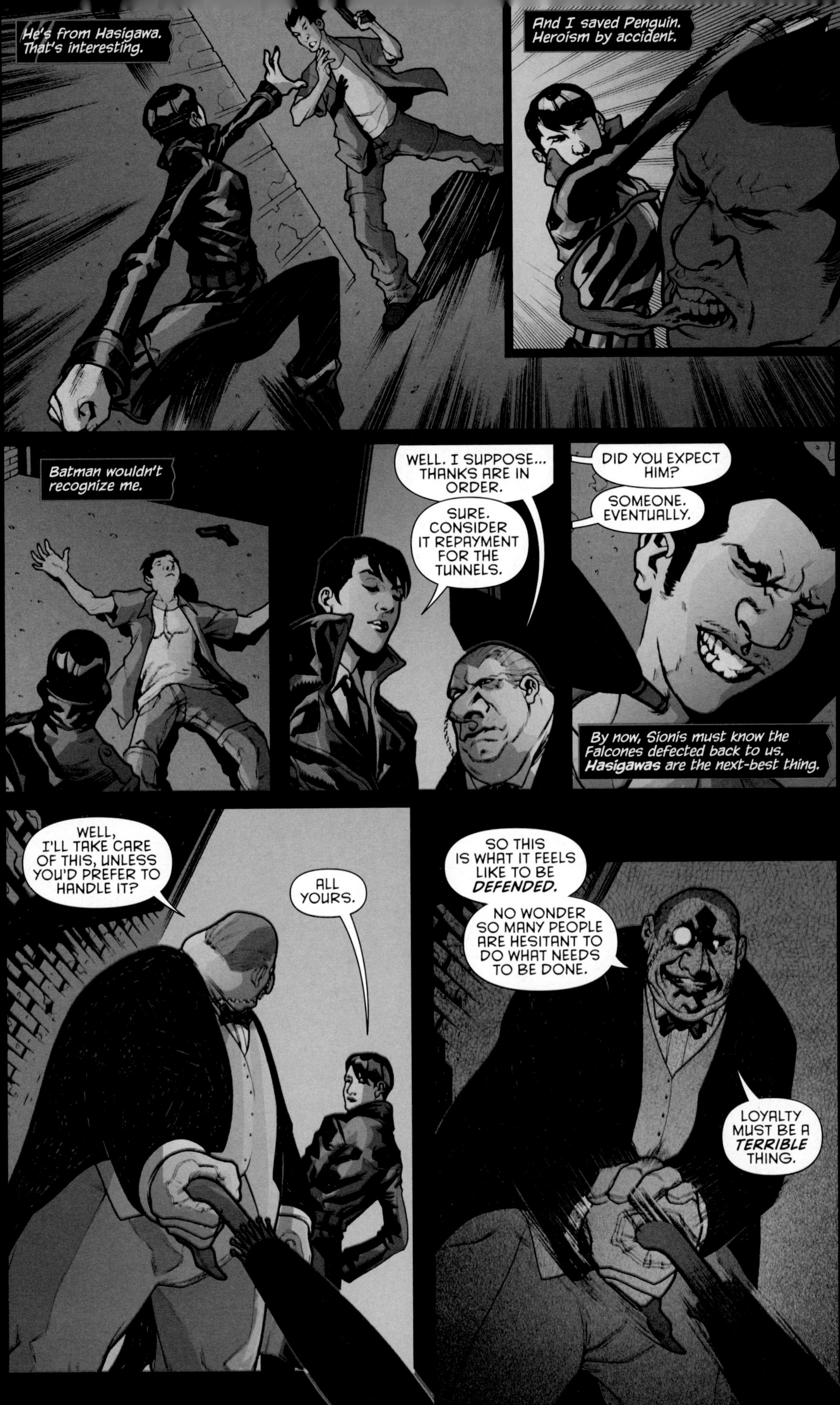
He's from Hasigawa. That's interesting.
And I saved Penguin. Heroism by accident.
Batman wouldn't recognize me.
WELL. I SUPPOSE... THANKS ARE IN ORDER.
SURE. CONSIDER IT REPAYMENT FOR THE TUNNELS.
DID YOU EXPECT HIM?
SOMEONE. EVENTUALLY.
By now, Sionis must know the Falcones defected back to us. **Hasigawas** are the next-best thing.
WELL, I'LL TAKE CARE OF THIS, UNLESS YOU'D PREFER TO HANDLE IT?
ALL YOURS.
SO THIS IS WHAT IT FEELS LIKE TO BE ***DEFENDED.***
NO WONDER SO MANY PEOPLE ARE HESITANT TO DO WHAT NEEDS TO BE DONE.
LOYALTY MUST BE A ***TERRIBLE*** THING.

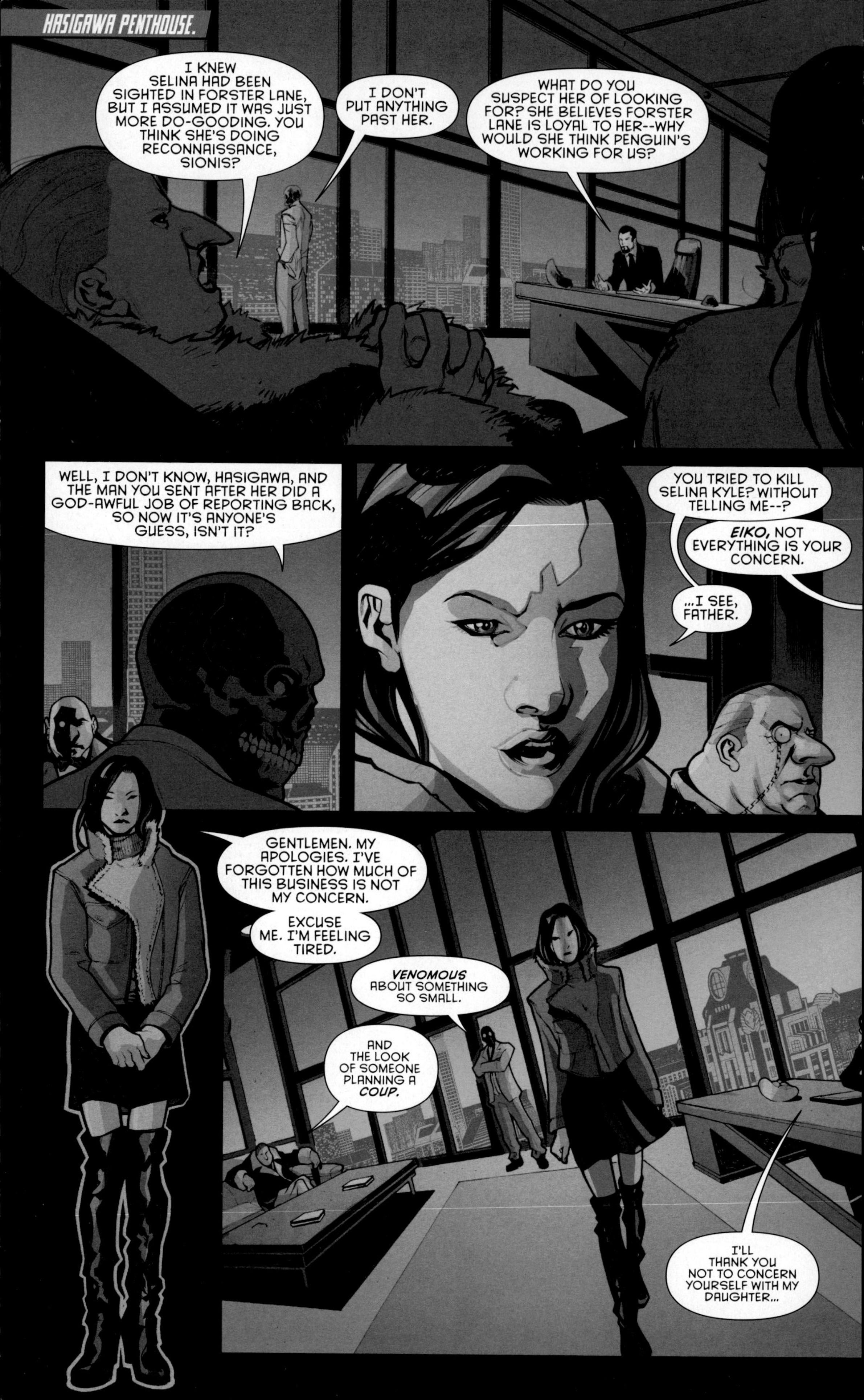
HASIGAWA PENTHOUSE.
I KNEW SELINA HAD BEEN SIGHTED IN FORSTER LANE, BUT I ASSUMED IT WAS JUST MORE DO-GOODING. YOU THINK SHE'S DOING RECONNAISSANCE, SIONIS?
I DON'T PUT ANYTHING PAST HER.
WHAT DO YOU SUSPECT HER OF LOOKING FOR? SHE BELIEVES FORSTER LANE IS LOYAL TO HER--WHY WOULD SHE THINK PENGUIN'S WORKING FOR US?
WELL, I DON'T KNOW, HASIGAWA, AND THE MAN YOU SENT AFTER HER DID A GOD-AWFUL JOB OF REPORTING BACK, SO NOW IT'S ANYONE'S GUESS, ISN'T IT?
YOU TRIED TO KILL SELINA KYLE? WITHOUT TELLING ME--?
EIKO, NOT EVERYTHING IS YOUR CONCERN.
...I SEE, FATHER.
GENTLEMEN. MY APOLOGIES. I'VE FORGOTTEN HOW MUCH OF THIS BUSINESS IS NOT MY CONCERN.
EXCUSE ME. I'M FEELING TIRED.
VENOMOUS ABOUT SOMETHING SO SMALL.
AND THE LOOK OF SOMEONE PLANNING A COUP.
I'LL THANK YOU NOT TO CONCERN YOURSELF WITH MY DAUGHTER...

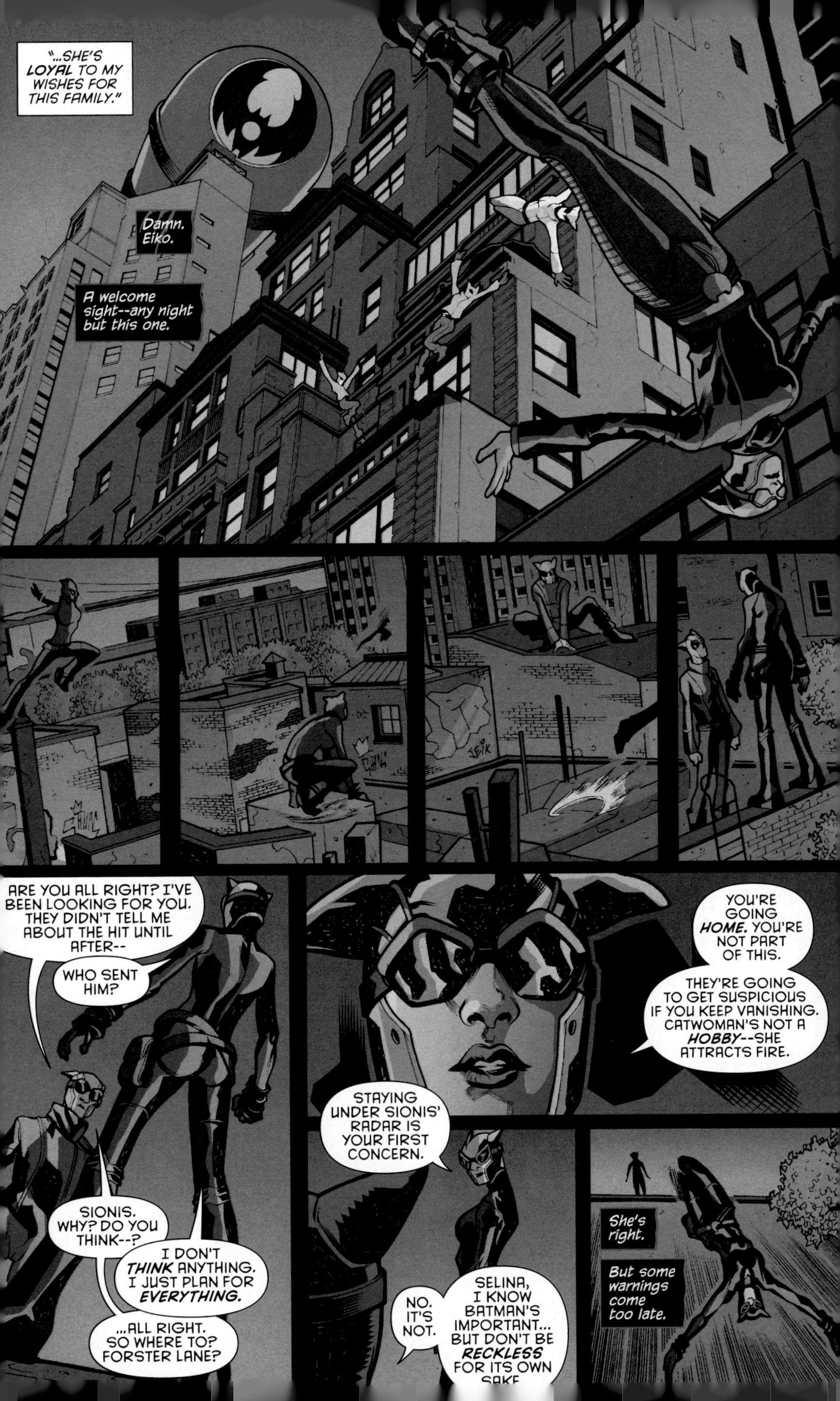
"...SHE'S LOYAL TO MY WISHES FOR THIS FAMILY."
Damn, Eiko.
A welcome sight--any night but this one.
ARE YOU ALL RIGHT? I'VE BEEN LOOKING FOR YOU. THEY DIDN'T TELL ME ABOUT THE HIT UNTIL AFTER--
WHO SENT HIM?
SIONIS. WHY? DO YOU THINK--?
I DON'T THINK ANYTHING. I JUST PLAN FOR EVERYTHING.
...ALL RIGHT. SO WHERE TO? FORSTER LANE?
YOU'RE GOING HOME. YOU'RE NOT PART OF THIS.
THEY'RE GOING TO GET SUSPICIOUS IF YOU KEEP VANISHING. CATWOMAN'S NOT A HOBBY--SHE ATTRACTS FIRE.
STAYING UNDER SIONIS' RADAR IS YOUR FIRST CONCERN.
NO. IT'S NOT.
SELINA, I KNOW BATMAN'S IMPORTANT... BUT DON'T BE RECKLESS FOR ITS OWN SAKE.
She's right.
But some warnings come too late.

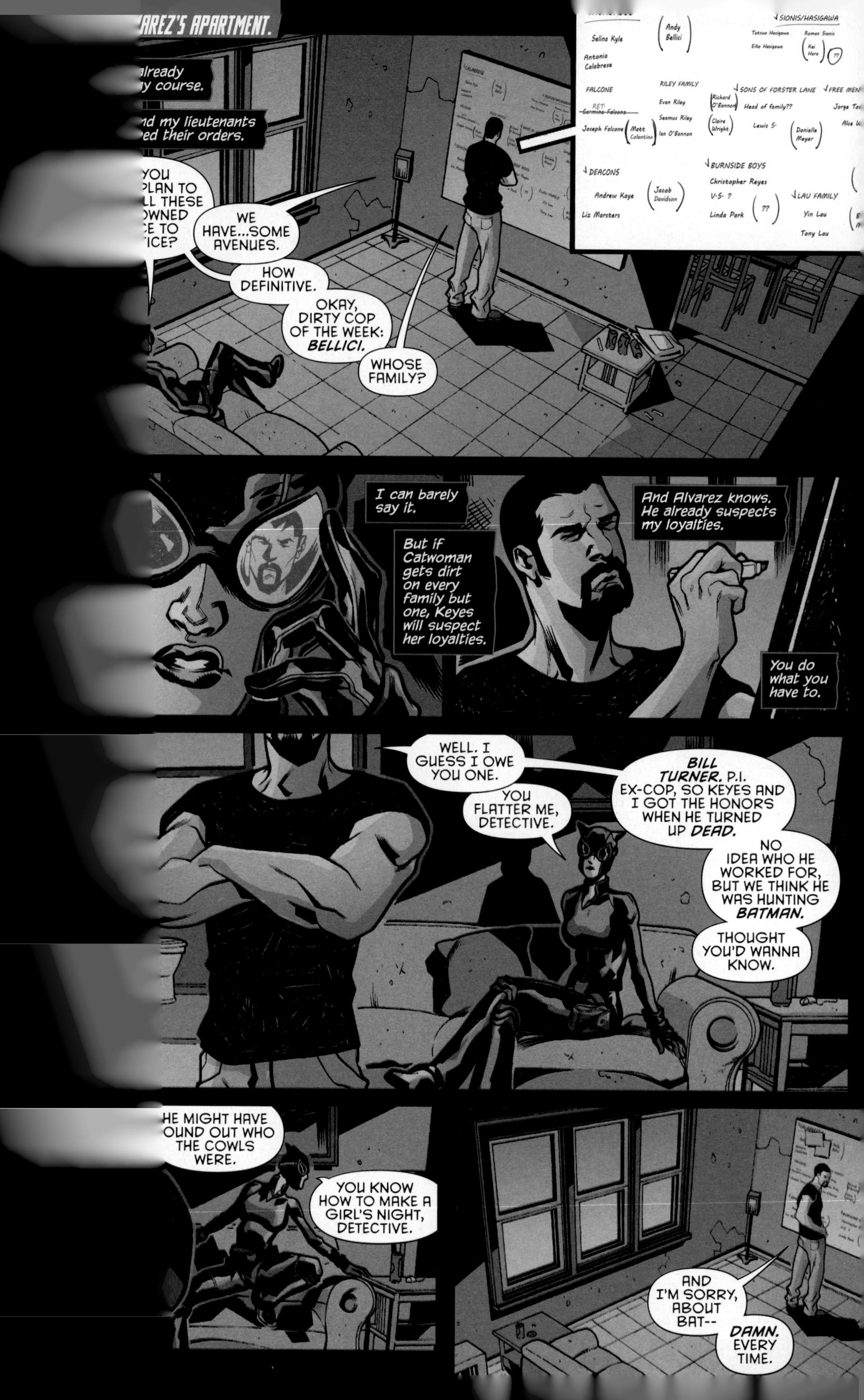

VAREZ'S APARTMENT.
already
y course.
nd my lieutenants
ed their orders.
YOU PLAN TO LL THESE OWNED CE TO ICE?
WE HAVE...SOME AVENUES.
HOW DEFINITIVE.
OKAY, DIRTY COP OF THE WEEK: BELLICI.
WHOSE FAMILY?
Selina Kyle
Andy Bellici
Antonio Calabrese
SIONIS/HASIGAWA
Tatsuo Hasigawa
Roman Sionis
Eiko Hasigawa
Kei Hara
??
FALCONE
RET. Carmine Falcone
Joseph Falcone
Matt Colantino
RILEY FAMILY
Evan Riley
Seamus Riley
Ian O'Bannon
Richard O'Bannon
Head of family??
Claire Wright
SONS OF FORSTER LANE
Lewis S.
Danielle Meyer
FREE MEN
Jorge To
Alce W
DEACONS
Andrew Kaye
Jacob Davidson
Liz Marsters
BURNSIDE BOYS
Christopher Reyes
V.S. ?
Linda Park
??
LAU FAMILY
Yin Lau
Tony Lau
I can barely say it.
But if Catwoman gets dirt on every family but one, Keyes will suspect her loyalties.
And Alvarez knows. He already suspects my loyalties.
You do what you have to.
WELL. I GUESS I OWE YOU ONE.
YOU FLATTER ME, DETECTIVE.
BILL TURNER. P.I. EX-COP, SO KEYES AND I GOT THE HONORS WHEN HE TURNED UP DEAD.
NO IDEA WHO HE WORKED FOR, BUT WE THINK HE WAS HUNTING BATMAN.
THOUGHT YOU'D WANNA KNOW.
HE MIGHT HAVE OUND OUT WHO THE COWLS WERE.
YOU KNOW HOW TO MAKE A GIRL'S NIGHT, DETECTIVE.
AND I'M SORRY, ABOUT BAT--
DAMN. EVERY TIME.

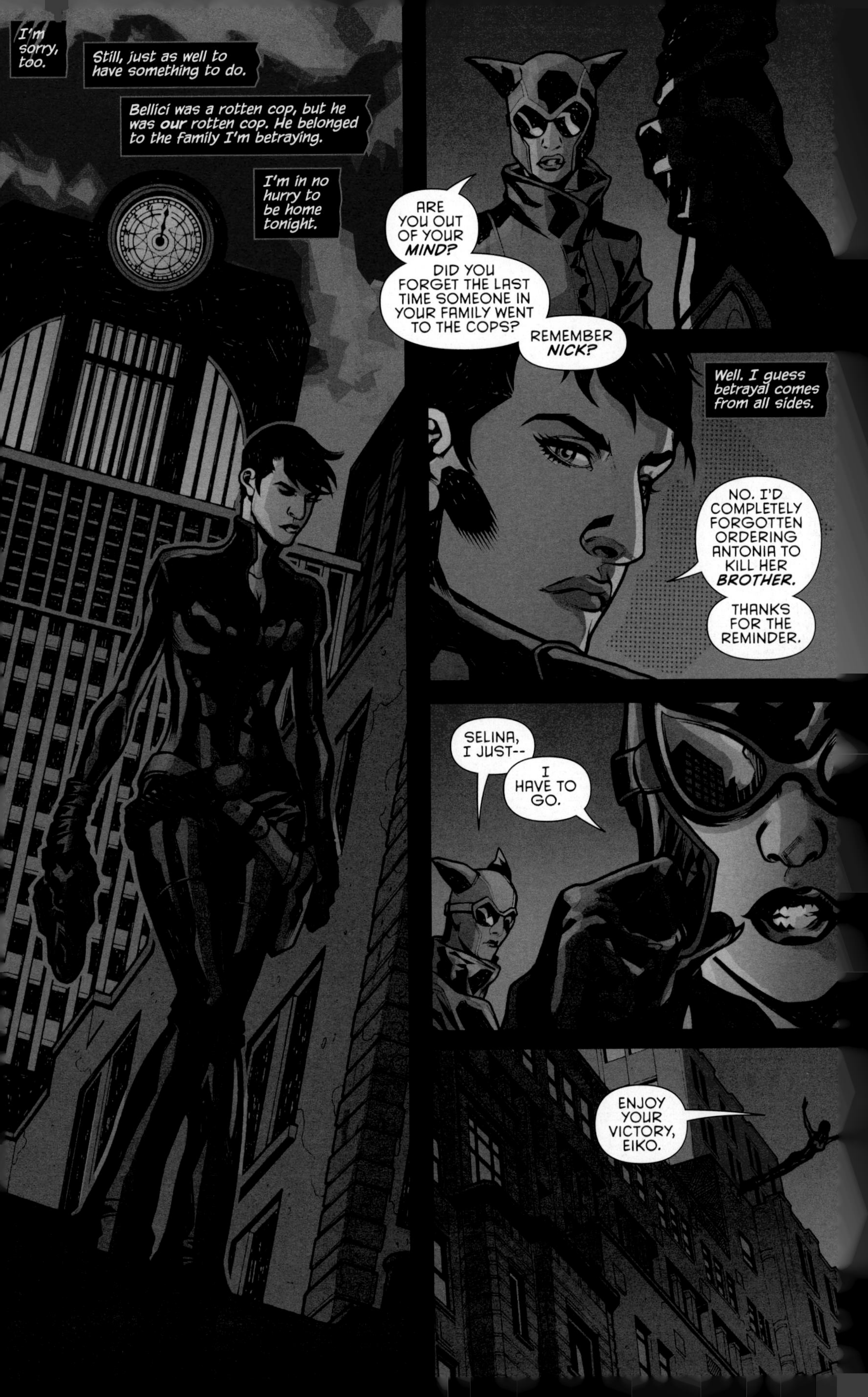

I'm sorry, too.
Still, just as well to have something to do.
Bellici was a rotten cop, but he was our rotten cop. He belonged to the family I'm betraying.
I'm in no hurry to be home tonight.
ARE YOU OUT OF YOUR MIND?
DID YOU FORGET THE LAST TIME SOMEONE IN YOUR FAMILY WENT TO THE COPS?
REMEMBER NICK?
Well. I guess betrayal comes from all sides.
NO. I'D COMPLETELY FORGOTTEN ORDERING ANTONIA TO KILL HER BROTHER.
THANKS FOR THE REMINDER.
SELINA, I JUST--
I HAVE TO GO.
ENJOY YOUR VICTORY, EIKO.

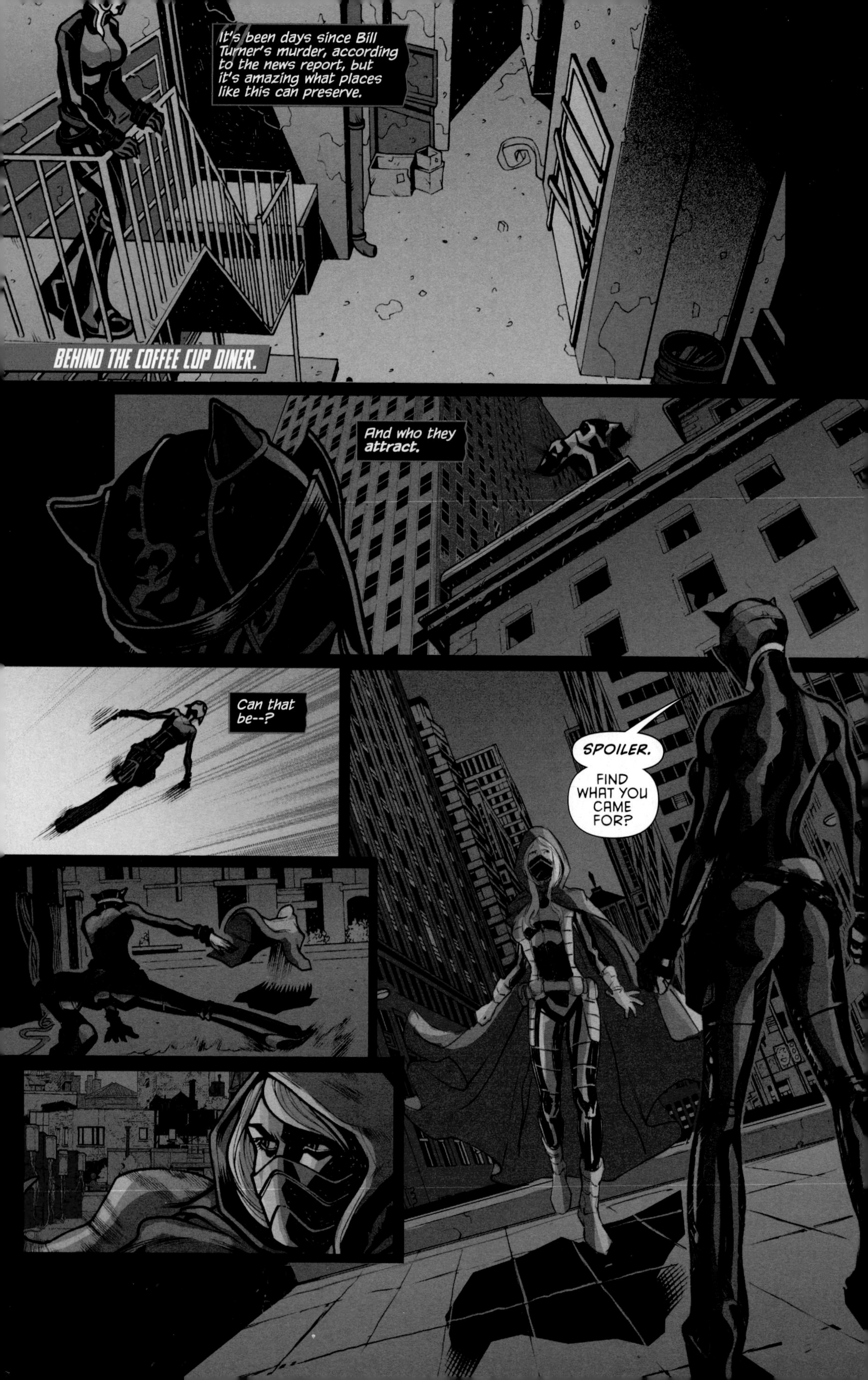
It's been days since Bill Turner's murder, according to the news report, but it's amazing what places like this can preserve.
BEHIND THE COFFEE CUP DINER.
And who they attract.
Can that be--?
SPOILER.
FIND WHAT YOU CAME FOR?

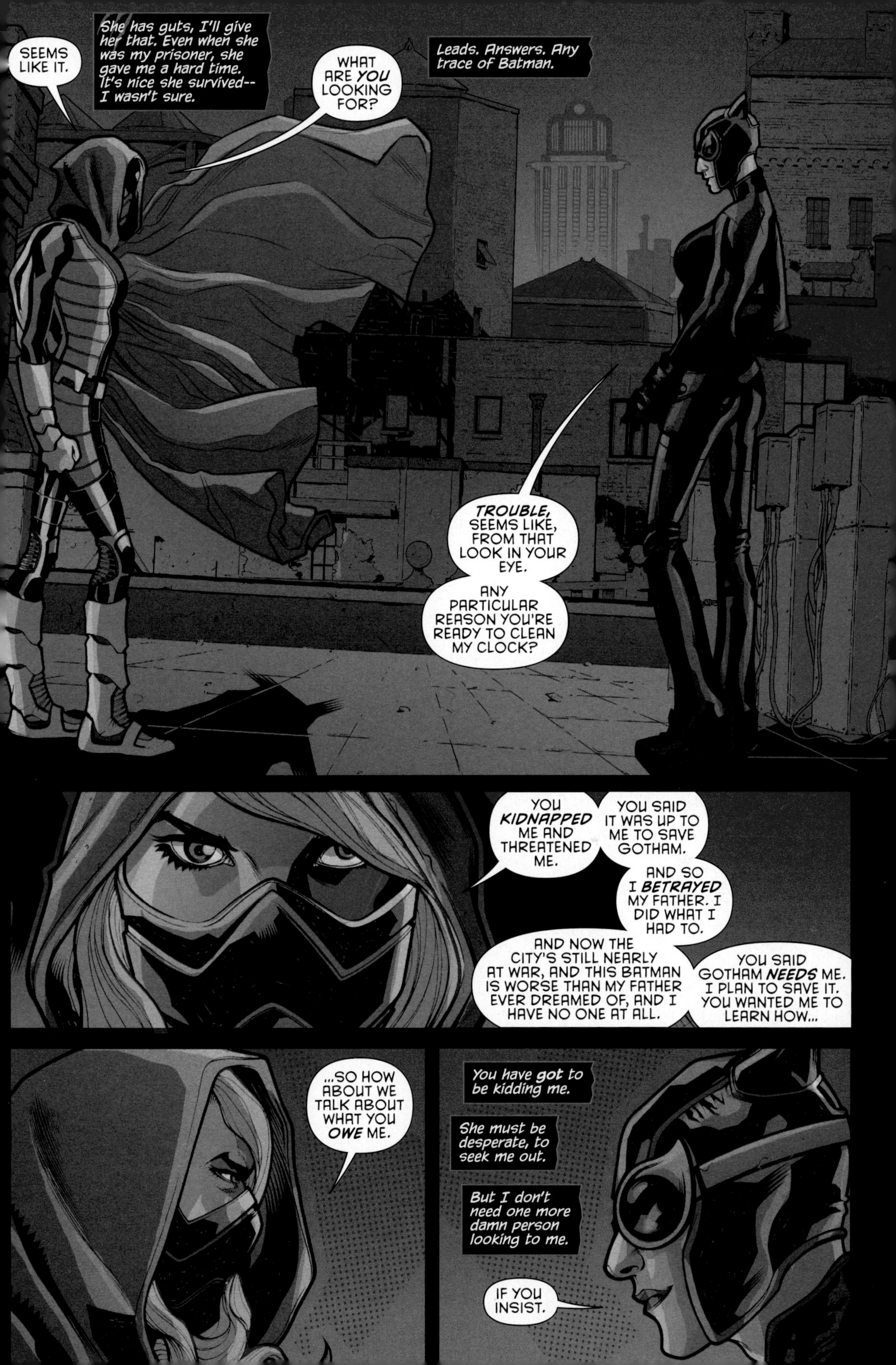

SEEMS LIKE IT.
She has guts, I'll give her that. Even when she was my prisoner, she gave me a hard time. It's nice she survived-- I wasn't sure.
WHAT ARE YOU LOOKING FOR?
Leads. Answers. Any trace of Batman.
TROUBLE, SEEMS LIKE, FROM THAT LOOK IN YOUR EYE.
ANY PARTICULAR REASON YOU'RE READY TO CLEAN MY CLOCK?
YOU KIDNAPPED ME AND THREATENED ME.
YOU SAID IT WAS UP TO ME TO SAVE GOTHAM.
AND SO I BETRAYED MY FATHER. I DID WHAT I HAD TO.
AND NOW THE CITY'S STILL NEARLY AT WAR, AND THIS BATMAN IS WORSE THAN MY FATHER EVER DREAMED OF, AND I HAVE NO ONE AT ALL.
YOU SAID GOTHAM NEEDS ME. I PLAN TO SAVE IT. YOU WANTED ME TO LEARN HOW...
...SO HOW ABOUT WE TALK ABOUT WHAT YOU OWE ME.
You have got to be kidding me.
She must be desperate, to seek me out.
But I don't need one more damn person looking to me.
IF YOU INSIST.

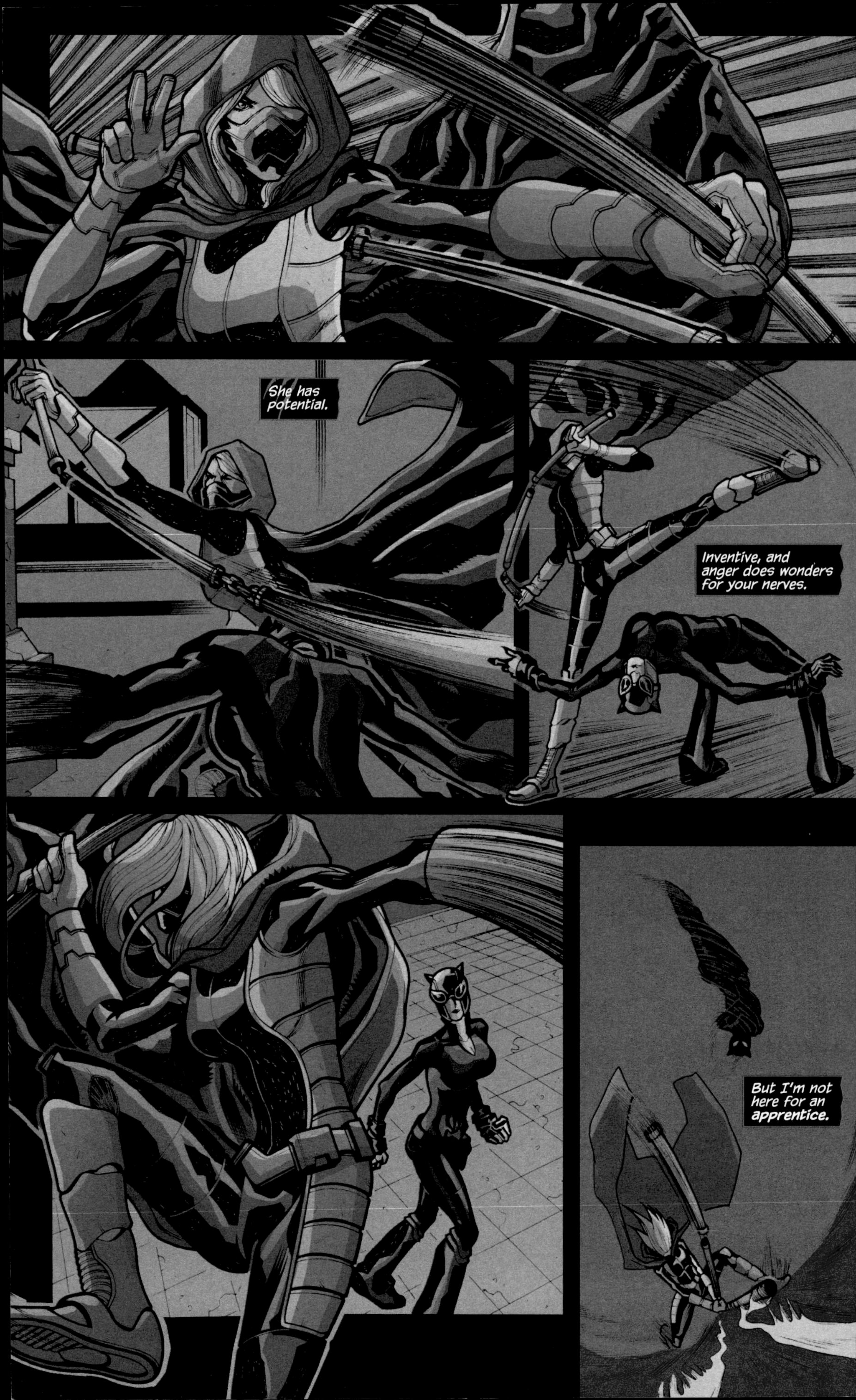
She has potential.
Inventive, and anger does wonders for your nerves.
But I'm not here for an **apprentice.**

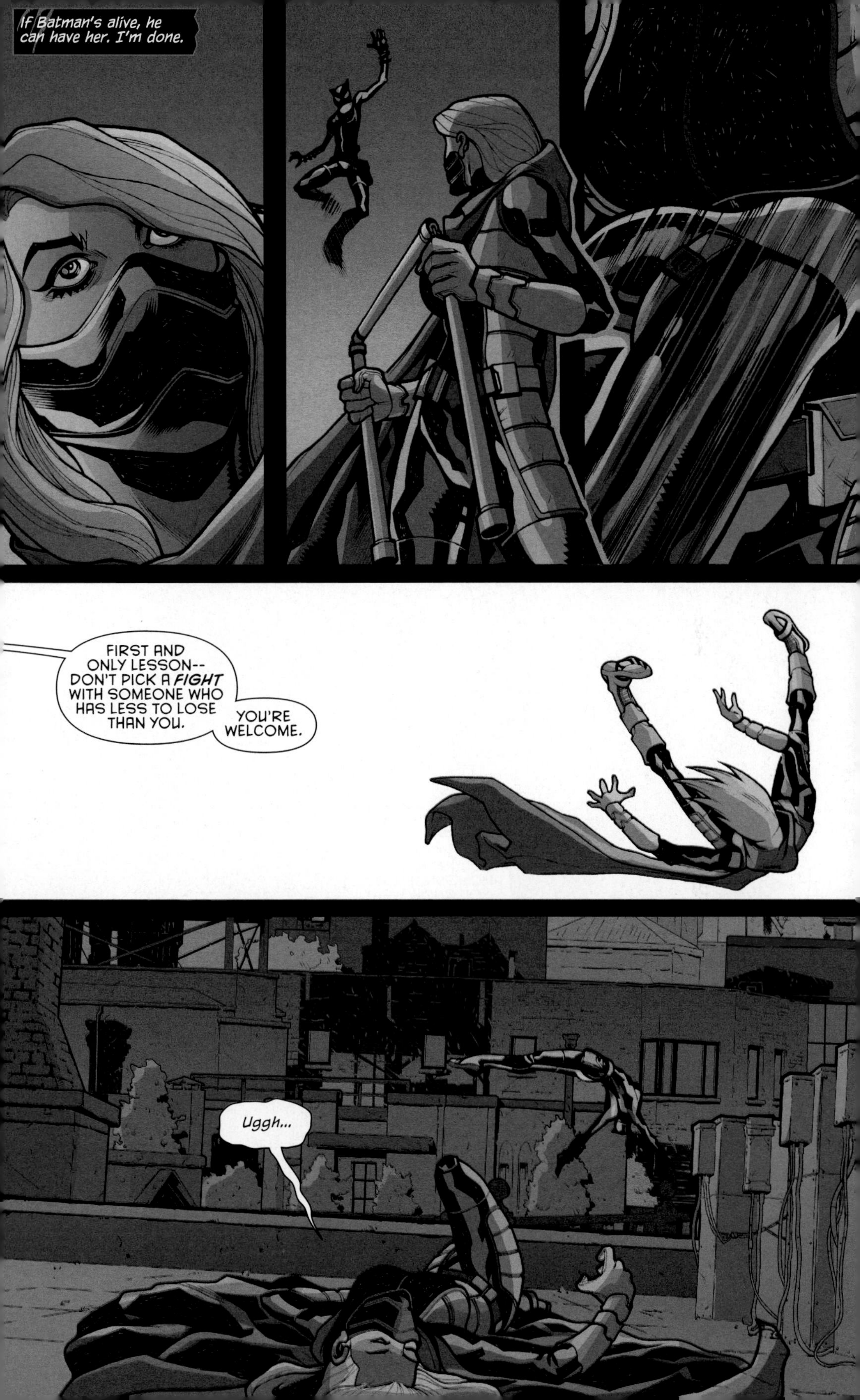

If Batman's alive, he can have her. I'm done.
FIRST AND ONLY LESSON-- DON'T PICK A *FIGHT* WITH SOMEONE WHO HAS LESS TO LOSE THAN YOU.
YOU'RE WELCOME.
Uggh...

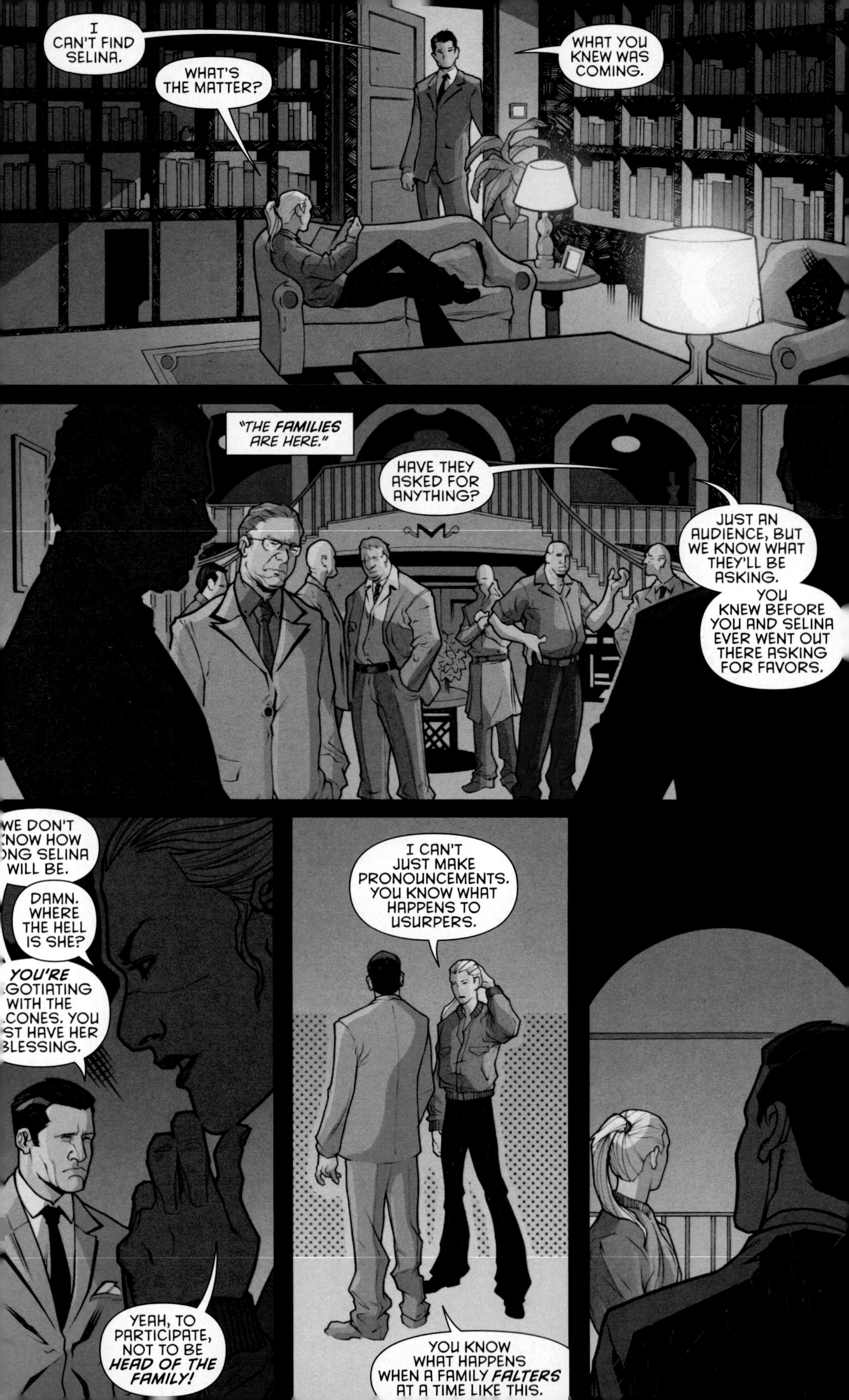

I CAN'T FIND SELINA.
WHAT'S THE MATTER?
WHAT YOU KNEW WAS COMING.
"THE FAMILIES ARE HERE."
HAVE THEY ASKED FOR ANYTHING?
JUST AN AUDIENCE, BUT WE KNOW WHAT THEY'LL BE ASKING.
YOU KNEW BEFORE YOU AND SELINA EVER WENT OUT THERE ASKING FOR FAVORS.
WE DON'T KNOW HOW ONG SELINA WILL BE.
DAMN. WHERE THE HELL IS SHE?
YOU'RE EGOTIATING WITH THE CONES. YOU ST HAVE HER BLESSING.
YEAH, TO PARTICIPATE, NOT TO BE HEAD OF THE FAMILY!
I CAN'T JUST MAKE PRONOUNCEMENTS. YOU KNOW WHAT HAPPENS TO USURPERS.
YOU KNOW WHAT HAPPENS WHEN A FAMILY FALTERS AT A TIME LIKE THIS.

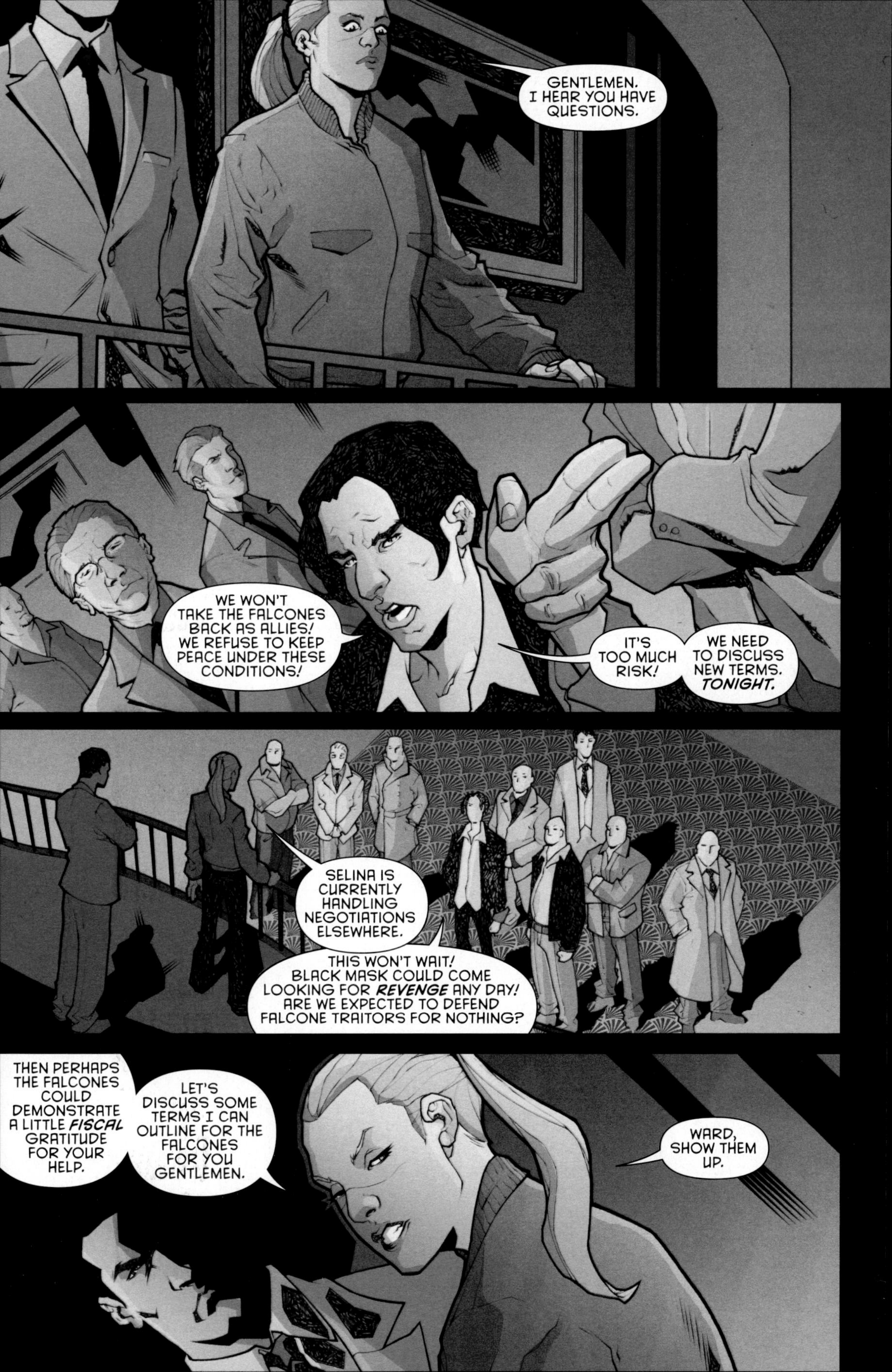
GENTLEMEN. I HEAR YOU HAVE QUESTIONS.
WE WON'T TAKE THE FALCONES BACK AS ALLIES! WE REFUSE TO KEEP PEACE UNDER THESE CONDITIONS!
IT'S TOO MUCH RISK!
WE NEED TO DISCUSS NEW TERMS. *TONIGHT.*
SELINA IS CURRENTLY HANDLING NEGOTIATIONS ELSEWHERE.
THIS WON'T WAIT! BLACK MASK COULD COME LOOKING FOR *REVENGE* ANY DAY! ARE WE EXPECTED TO DEFEND FALCONE TRAITORS FOR NOTHING?
THEN PERHAPS THE FALCONES COULD DEMONSTRATE A LITTLE *FISCAL* GRATITUDE FOR YOUR HELP.
LET'S DISCUSS SOME TERMS I CAN OUTLINE FOR THE FALCONES FOR YOU GENTLEMEN.
WARD, SHOW THEM UP.

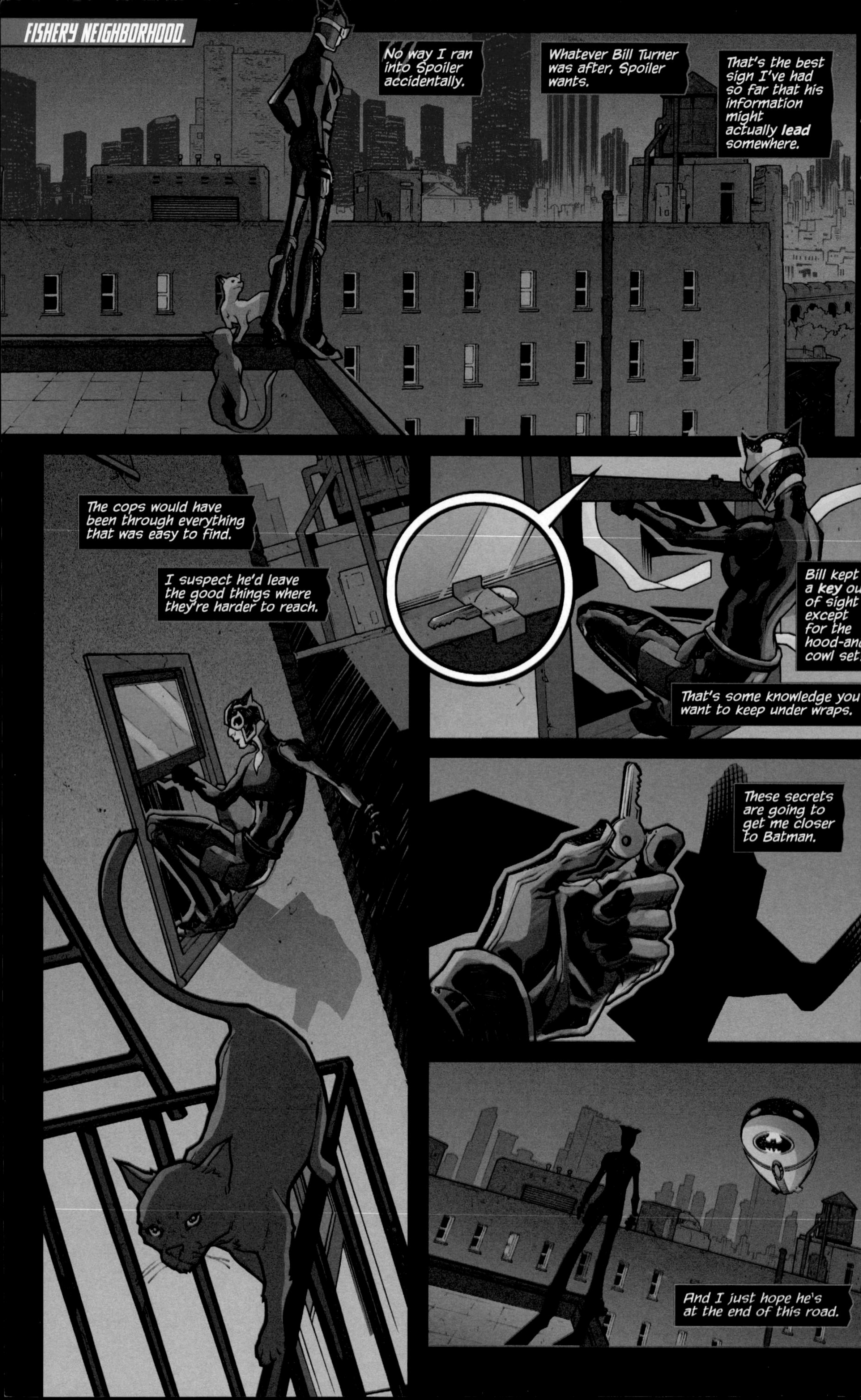
FISHERY NEIGHBORHOOD.
No way I ran into Spoiler accidentally.
Whatever Bill Turner was after, Spoiler wants.
That's the best sign I've had so far that his information might actually lead somewhere.
The cops would have been through everything that was easy to find.
I suspect he'd leave the good things where they're harder to reach.
Bill kept a key ou of sight except for the hood-and cowl set.
That's some knowledge you want to keep under wraps.
These secrets are going to get me closer to Batman.
And I just hope he's at the end of this road.

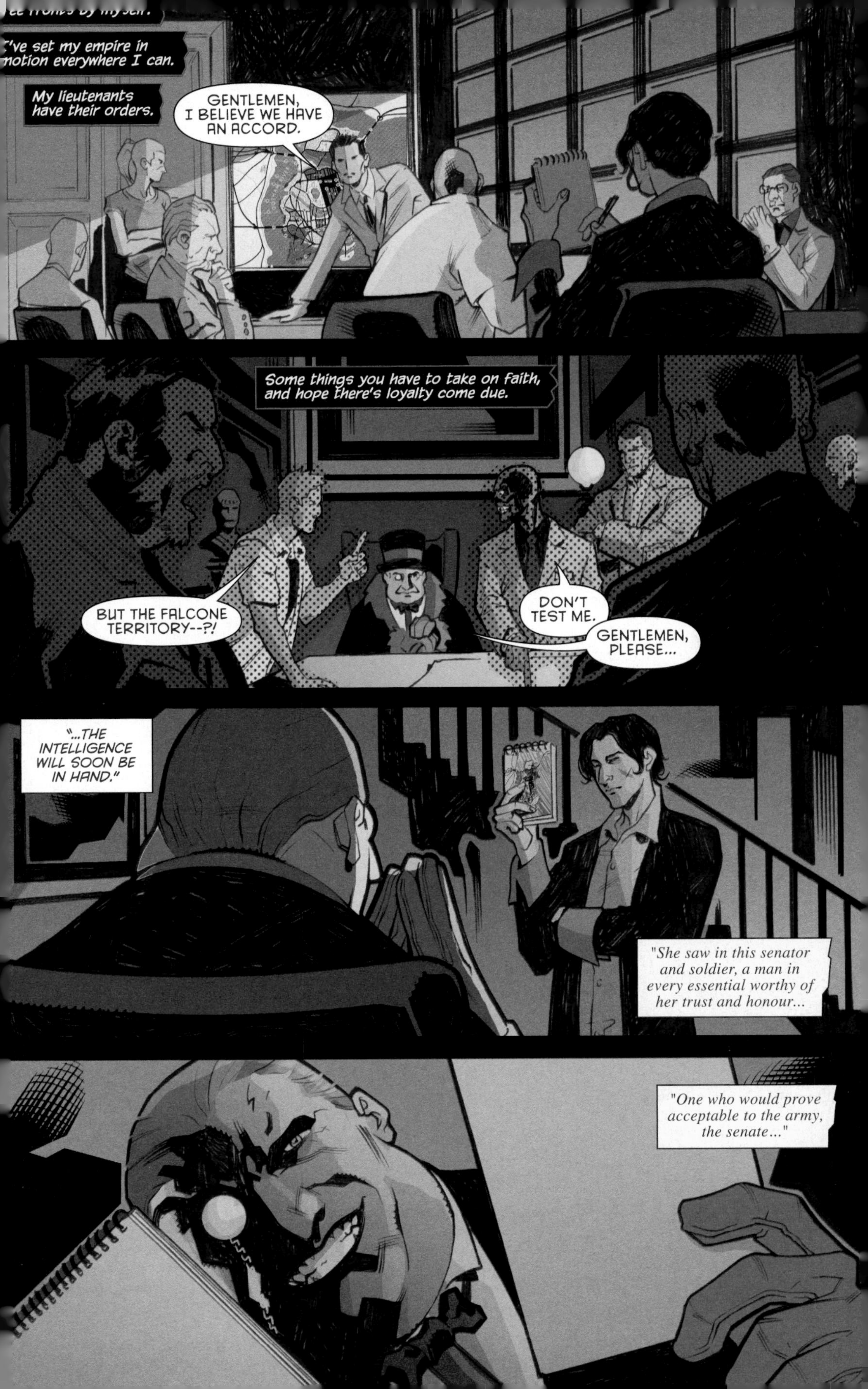
I've set my empire in motion everywhere I can.
My lieutenants have their orders.
GENTLEMEN, I BELIEVE WE HAVE AN ACCORD.
Some things you have to take on faith, and hope there's loyalty come due.
BUT THE FALCONE TERRITORY--?!
DON'T TEST ME.
GENTLEMEN, PLEASE...
"...THE INTELLIGENCE WILL SOON BE IN HAND."
"She saw in this senator and soldier, a man in every essential worthy of her trust and honour...
"One who would prove acceptable to the army, the senate..."

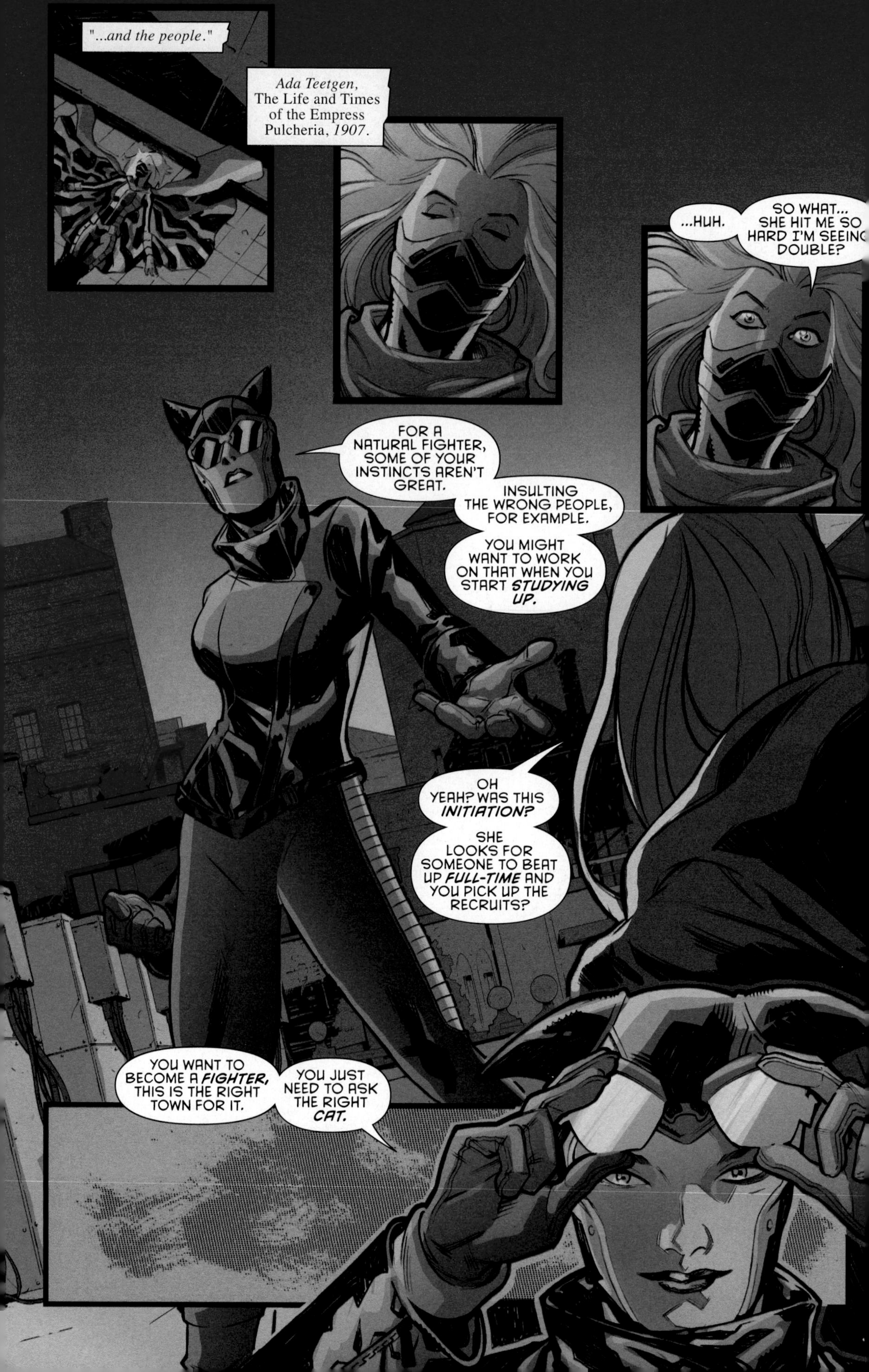
"...and the people."
Ada Teetgen, The Life and Times of the Empress Pulcheria, *1907*.
...HUH.
SO WHAT... SHE HIT ME SO HARD I'M SEEING DOUBLE?
FOR A NATURAL FIGHTER, SOME OF YOUR INSTINCTS AREN'T GREAT.
INSULTING THE WRONG PEOPLE, FOR EXAMPLE.
YOU MIGHT WANT TO WORK ON THAT WHEN YOU START *STUDYING UP.*
OH YEAH? WAS THIS *INITIATION?*
SHE LOOKS FOR SOMEONE TO BEAT UP *FULL-TIME* AND YOU PICK UP THE RECRUITS?
YOU WANT TO BECOME A *FIGHTER,* THIS IS THE RIGHT TOWN FOR IT.
YOU JUST NEED TO ASK THE RIGHT *CAT.*

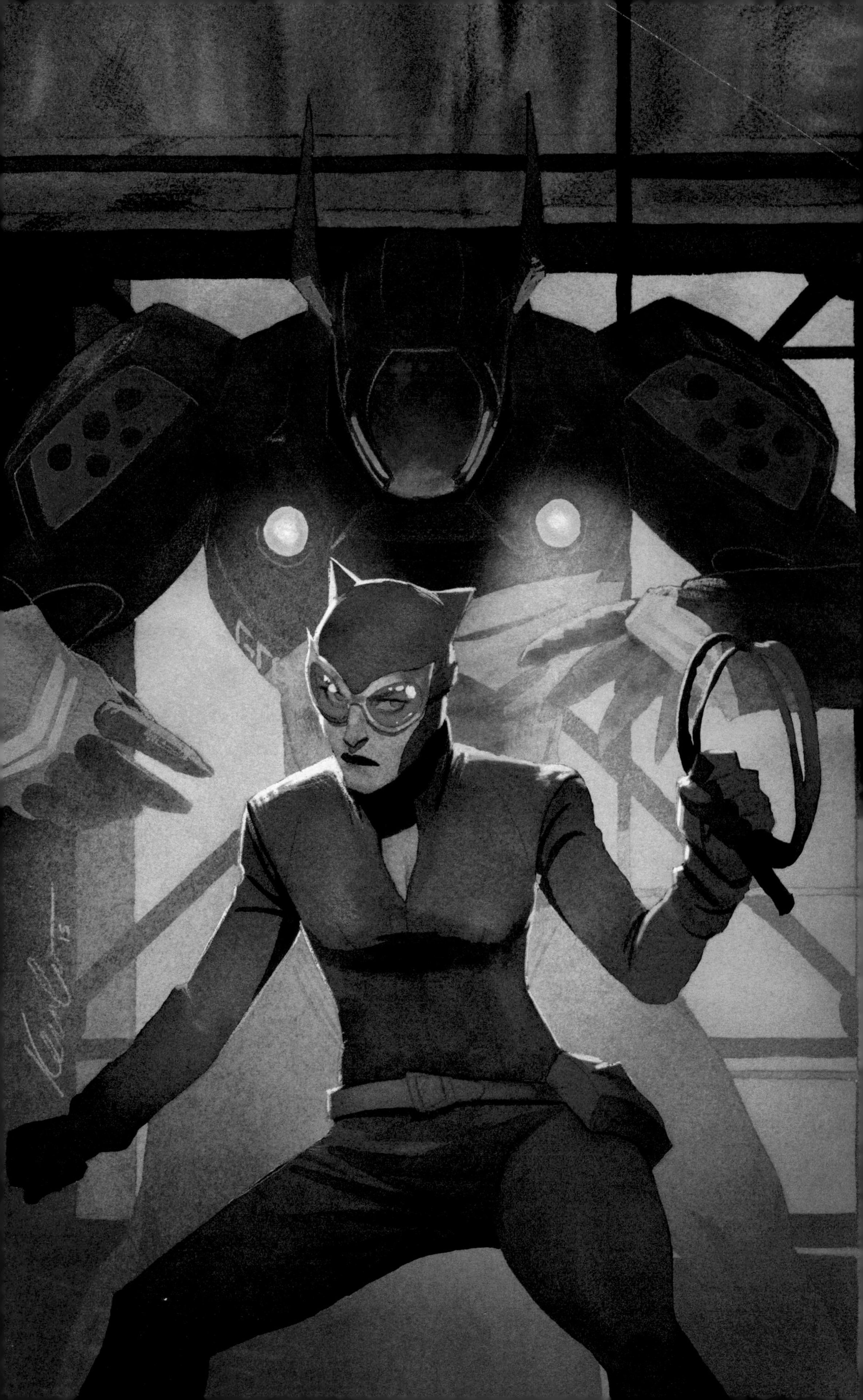

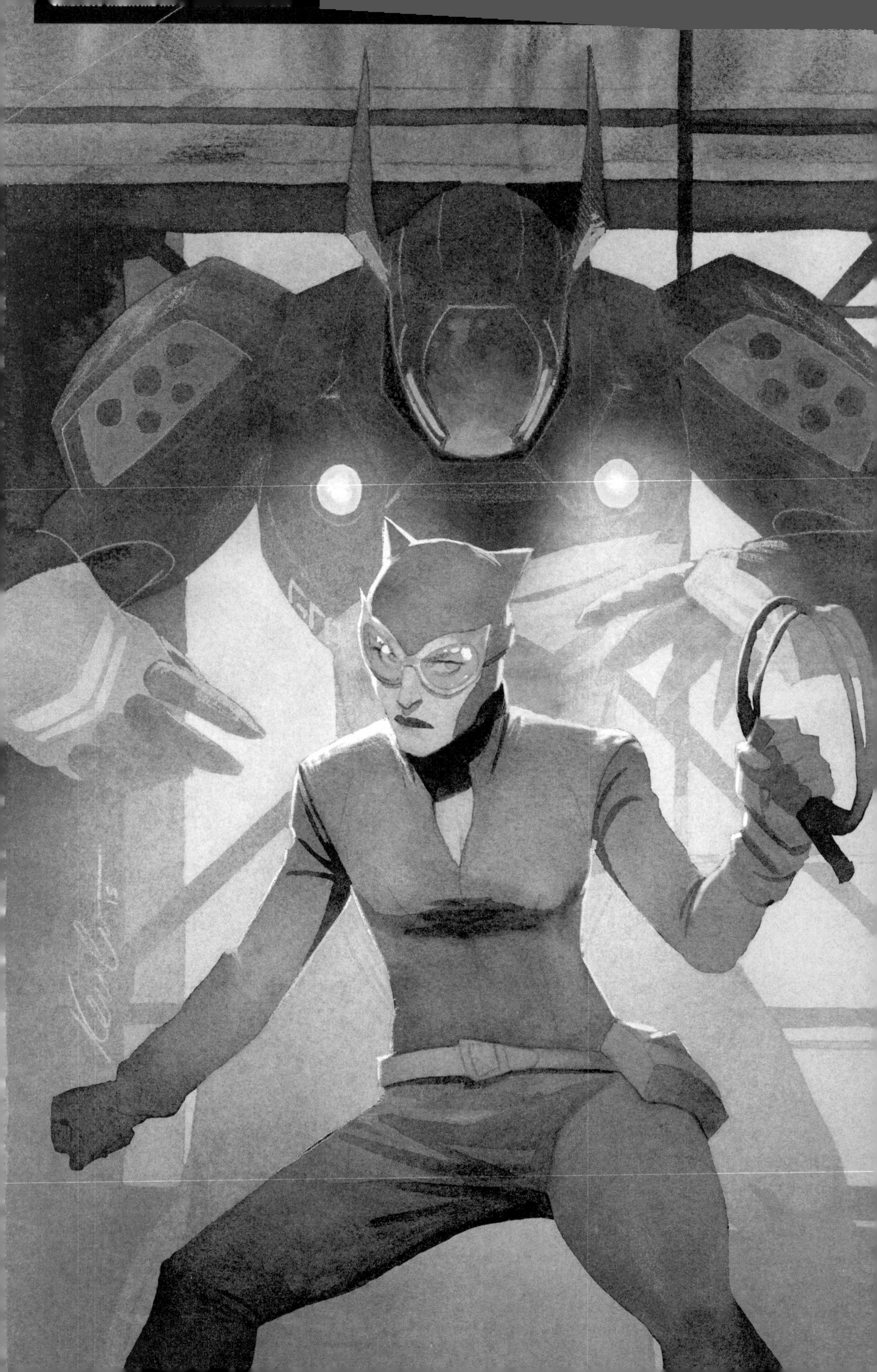

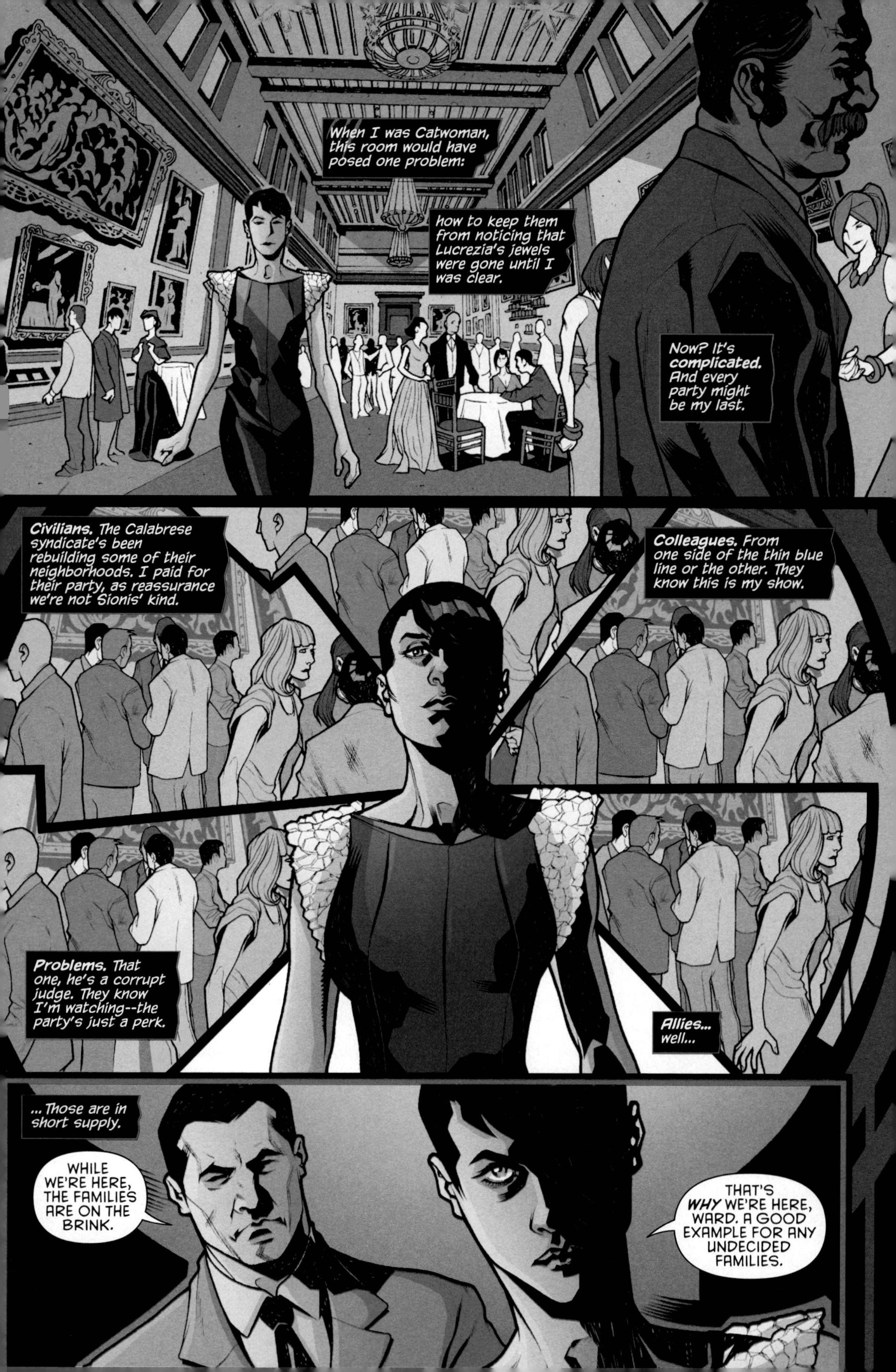

When I was Catwoman, this room would have posed one problem:
how to keep them from noticing that Lucrezia's jewels were gone until I was clear.
Now? It's complicated. And every party might be my last.
Civilians. The Calabrese syndicate's been rebuilding some of their neighborhoods. I paid for their party, as reassurance we're not Sionis' kind.
Colleagues. From one side of the thin blue line or the other. They know this is my show.
Problems. That one, he's a corrupt judge. They know I'm watching--the party's just a perk.
Allies... well...
...Those are in short supply.
WHILE WE'RE HERE, THE FAMILIES ARE ON THE BRINK.
THAT'S WHY WE'RE HERE, WARD. A GOOD EXAMPLE FOR ANY UNDECIDED FAMILIES.

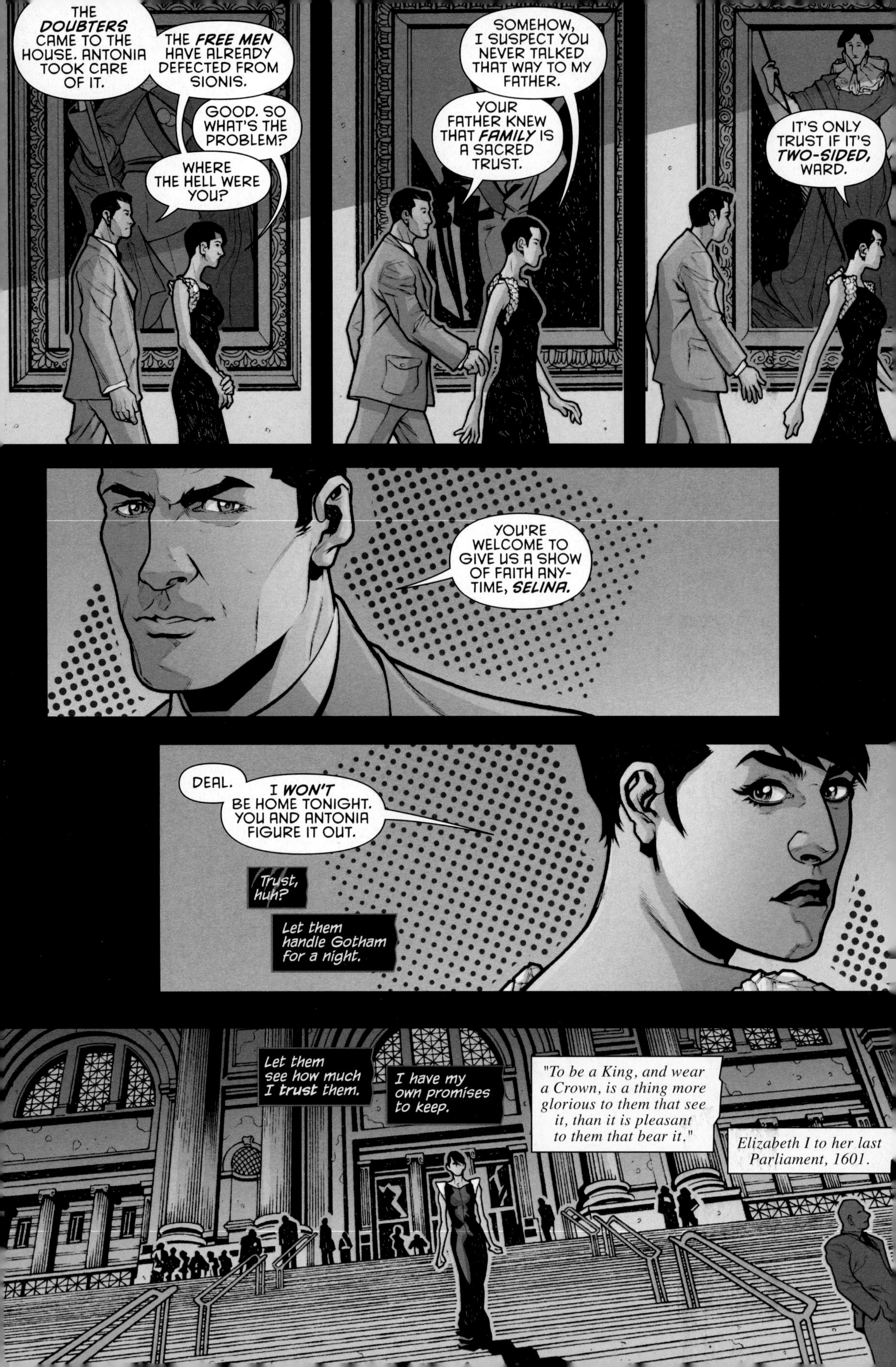
THE DOUBTERS CAME TO THE HOUSE. ANTONIA TOOK CARE OF IT.
THE FREE MEN HAVE ALREADY DEFECTED FROM SIONIS.
GOOD. SO WHAT'S THE PROBLEM?
WHERE THE HELL WERE YOU?
SOMEHOW, I SUSPECT YOU NEVER TALKED THAT WAY TO MY FATHER.
YOUR FATHER KNEW THAT FAMILY IS A SACRED TRUST.
IT'S ONLY TRUST IF IT'S TWO-SIDED, WARD.
YOU'RE WELCOME TO GIVE US A SHOW OF FAITH ANY-TIME, SELINA.
DEAL.
I WON'T BE HOME TONIGHT. YOU AND ANTONIA FIGURE IT OUT.
Trust, huh?
Let them handle Gotham for a night.
Let them see how much I trust them.
I have my own promises to keep.
"To be a King, and wear a Crown, is a thing more glorious to them that see it, than it is pleasant to them that bear it."
Elizabeth I to her last Parliament, 1601.

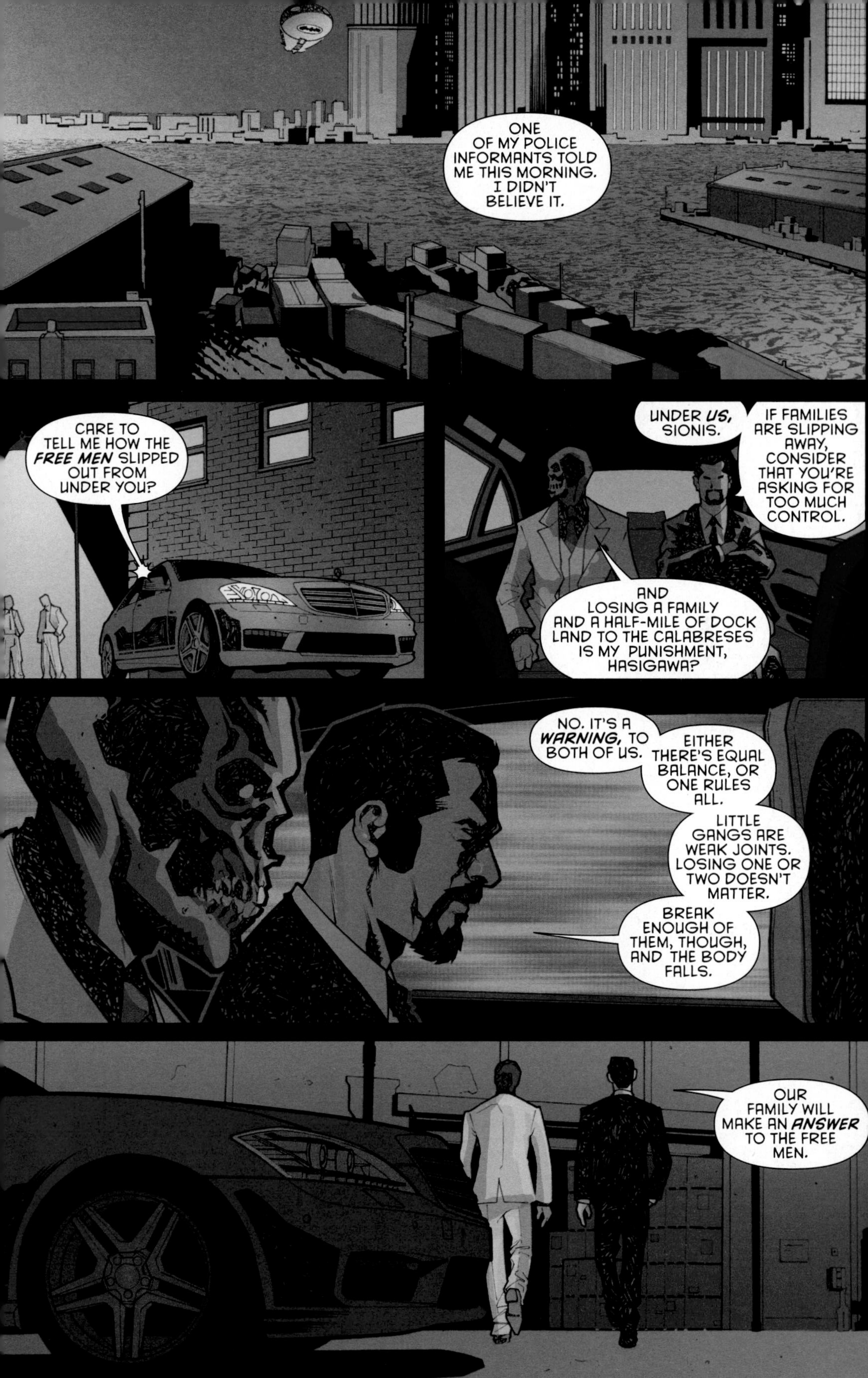
ONE OF MY POLICE INFORMANTS TOLD ME THIS MORNING. I DIDN'T BELIEVE IT.
CARE TO TELL ME HOW THE FREE MEN SLIPPED OUT FROM UNDER YOU?
UNDER US, SIONIS.
IF FAMILIES ARE SLIPPING AWAY, CONSIDER THAT YOU'RE ASKING FOR TOO MUCH CONTROL.
AND LOSING A FAMILY AND A HALF-MILE OF DOCK LAND TO THE CALABRESES IS MY PUNISHMENT, HASIGAWA?
NO. IT'S A WARNING, TO BOTH OF US.
EITHER THERE'S EQUAL BALANCE, OR ONE RULES ALL.
LITTLE GANGS ARE WEAK JOINTS. LOSING ONE OR TWO DOESN'T MATTER.
BREAK ENOUGH OF THEM, THOUGH, AND THE BODY FALLS.
OUR FAMILY WILL MAKE AN ANSWER TO THE FREE MEN.

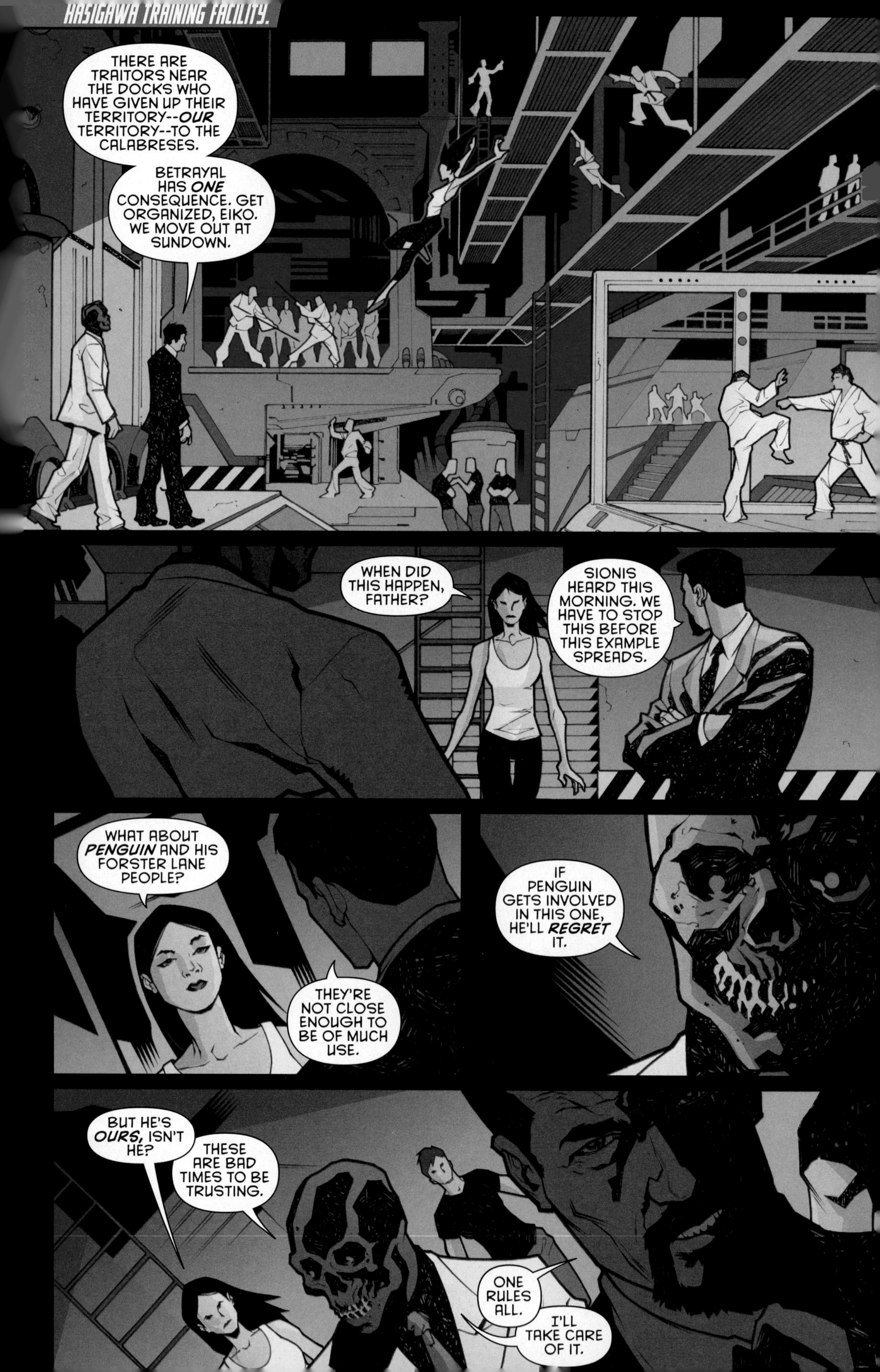
HASIGAWA TRAINING FACILITY.
THERE ARE TRAITORS NEAR THE DOCKS WHO HAVE GIVEN UP THEIR TERRITORY--OUR TERRITORY--TO THE CALABRESES.
BETRAYAL HAS ONE CONSEQUENCE. GET ORGANIZED, EIKO. WE MOVE OUT AT SUNDOWN.
WHEN DID THIS HAPPEN, FATHER?
SIONIS HEARD THIS MORNING. WE HAVE TO STOP THIS BEFORE THIS EXAMPLE SPREADS.
WHAT ABOUT PENGUIN AND HIS FORSTER LANE PEOPLE?
THEY'RE NOT CLOSE ENOUGH TO BE OF MUCH USE.
IF PENGUIN GETS INVOLVED IN THIS ONE, HE'LL REGRET IT.
BUT HE'S OURS, ISN'T HE?
THESE ARE BAD TIMES TO BE TRUSTING.
ONE RULES ALL.
I'LL TAKE CARE OF IT.

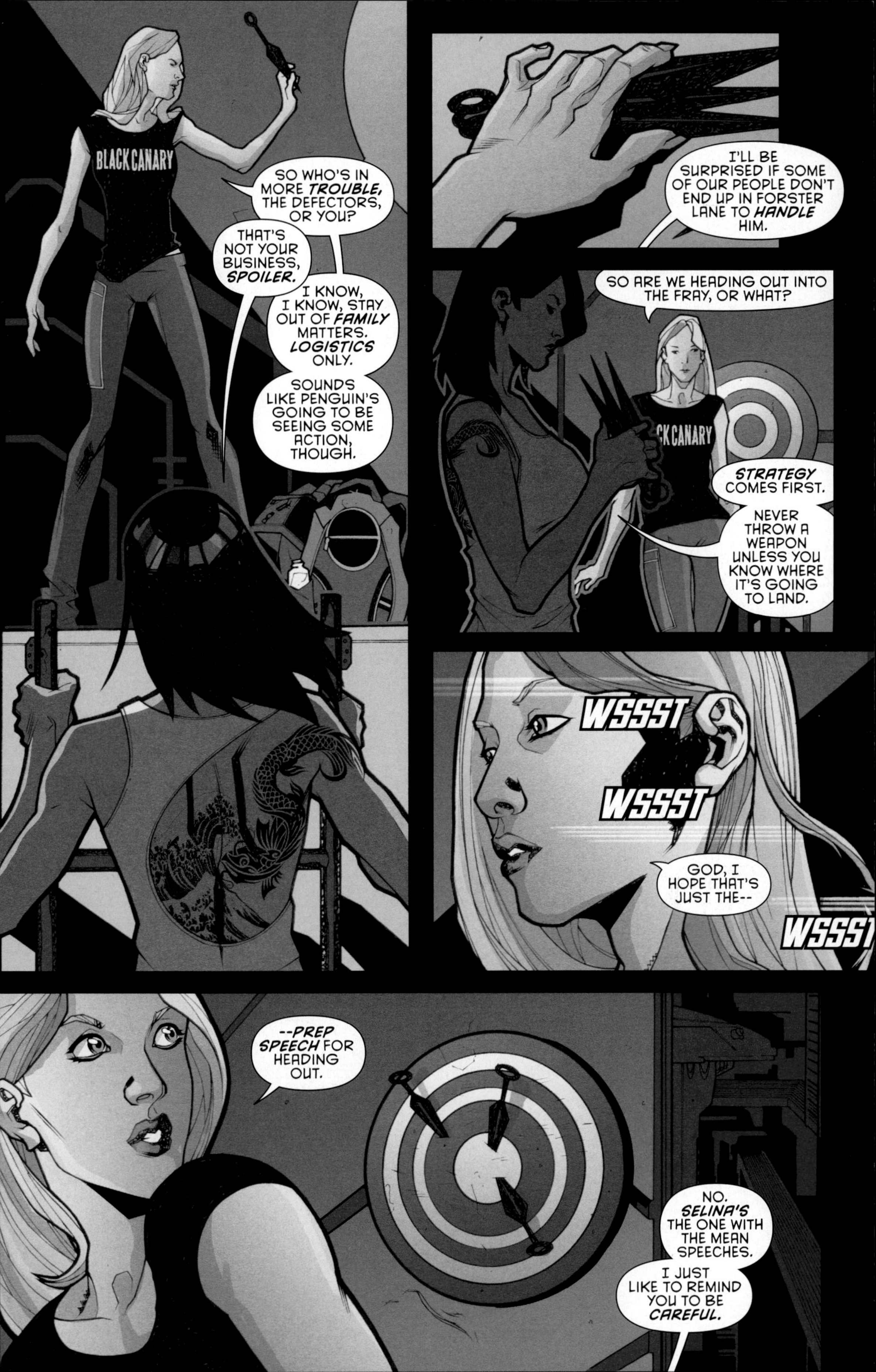
BLACK CANARY
SO WHO'S IN MORE TROUBLE, THE DEFECTORS, OR YOU?
THAT'S NOT YOUR BUSINESS, SPOILER.
I KNOW, I KNOW, STAY OUT OF FAMILY MATTERS. LOGISTICS ONLY.
SOUNDS LIKE PENGUIN'S GOING TO BE SEEING SOME ACTION, THOUGH.
I'LL BE SURPRISED IF SOME OF OUR PEOPLE DON'T END UP IN FORSTER LANE TO HANDLE HIM.
SO ARE WE HEADING OUT INTO THE FRAY, OR WHAT?
CK CANARY
STRATEGY COMES FIRST.
NEVER THROW A WEAPON UNLESS YOU KNOW WHERE IT'S GOING TO LAND.
WSSST
WSSST
GOD, I HOPE THAT'S JUST THE--
WSSST
--PREP SPEECH FOR HEADING OUT.
NO. SELINA'S THE ONE WITH THE MEAN SPEECHES.
I JUST LIKE TO REMIND YOU TO BE CAREFUL.

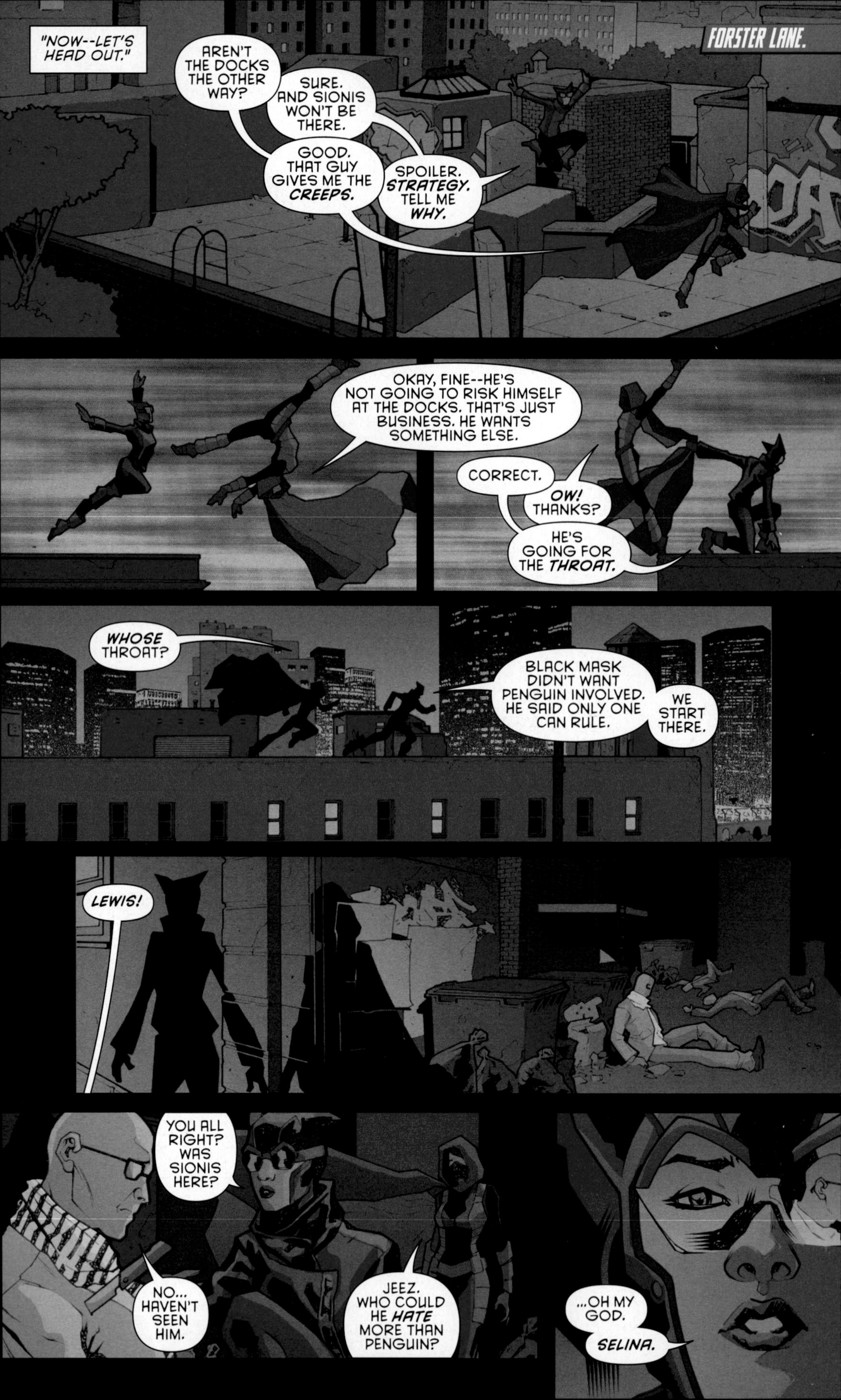
"NOW--LET'S HEAD OUT."
FORSTER LANE.
AREN'T THE DOCKS THE OTHER WAY?
SURE. AND SIONIS WON'T BE THERE.
GOOD. THAT GUY GIVES ME THE CREEPS.
SPOILER. STRATEGY. TELL ME WHY.
OKAY, FINE--HE'S NOT GOING TO RISK HIMSELF AT THE DOCKS. THAT'S JUST BUSINESS. HE WANTS SOMETHING ELSE.
CORRECT.
OW! THANKS?
HE'S GOING FOR THE THROAT.
WHOSE THROAT?
BLACK MASK DIDN'T WANT PENGUIN INVOLVED. HE SAID ONLY ONE CAN RULE.
WE START THERE.
LEWIS!
YOU ALL RIGHT? WAS SIONIS HERE?
NO... HAVEN'T SEEN HIM.
JEEZ. WHO COULD HE HATE MORE THAN PENGUIN?
...OH MY GOD.
SELINA.

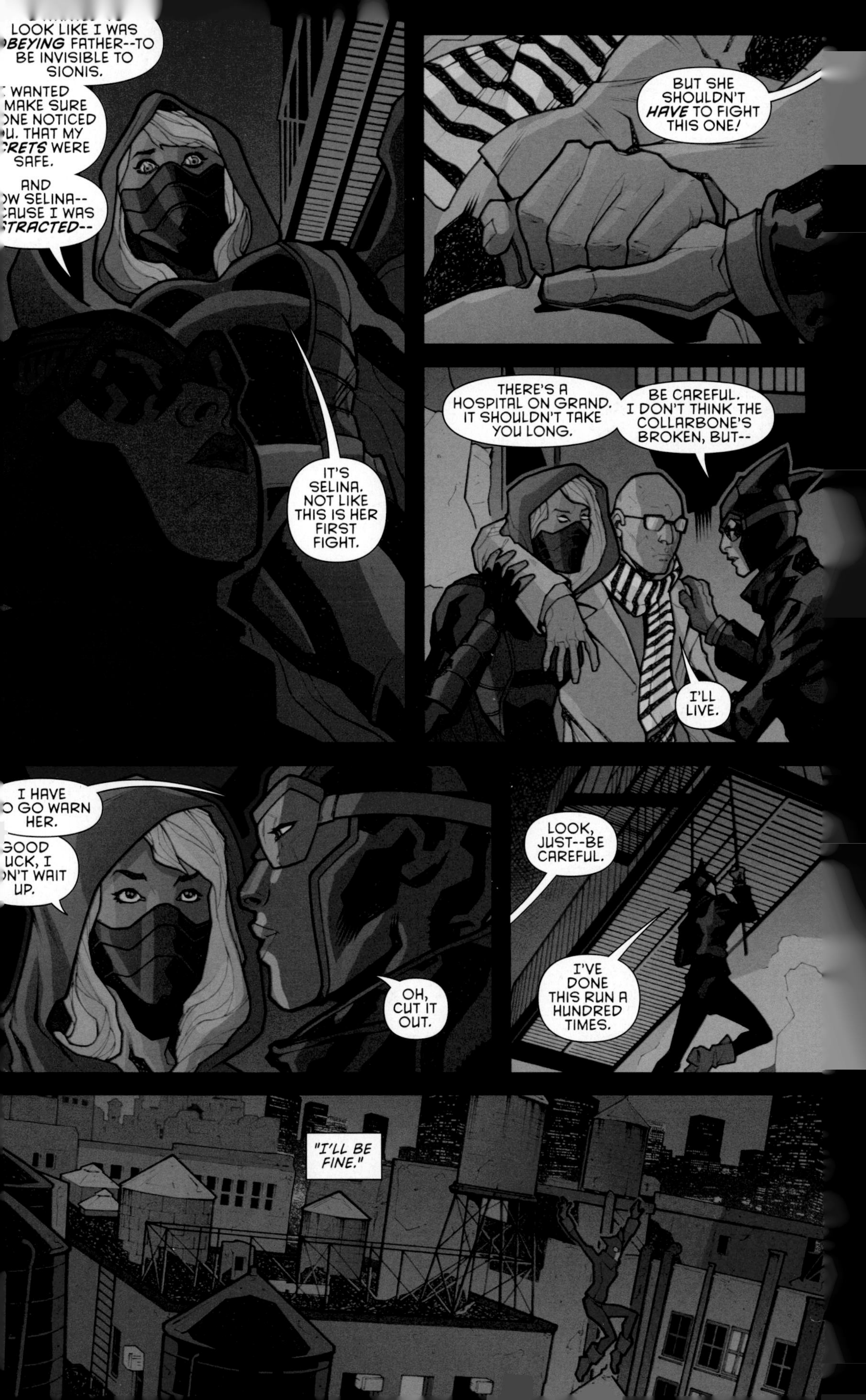

LOOK LIKE I WAS BEYING FATHER--TO BE INVISIBLE TO SIONIS.
WANTED MAKE SURE ONE NOTICED U. THAT MY CRETS WERE SAFE.
AND W SELINA-- CAUSE I WAS STRACTED--
IT'S SELINA. NOT LIKE THIS IS HER FIRST FIGHT.
BUT SHE SHOULDN'T HAVE TO FIGHT THIS ONE!
THERE'S A HOSPITAL ON GRAND. IT SHOULDN'T TAKE YOU LONG.
BE CAREFUL. I DON'T THINK THE COLLARBONE'S BROKEN, BUT--
I'LL LIVE.
I HAVE O GO WARN HER.
GOOD UCK, I N'T WAIT UP.
OH, CUT IT OUT.
LOOK, JUST--BE CAREFUL.
I'VE DONE THIS RUN A HUNDRED TIMES.
"I'LL BE FINE."

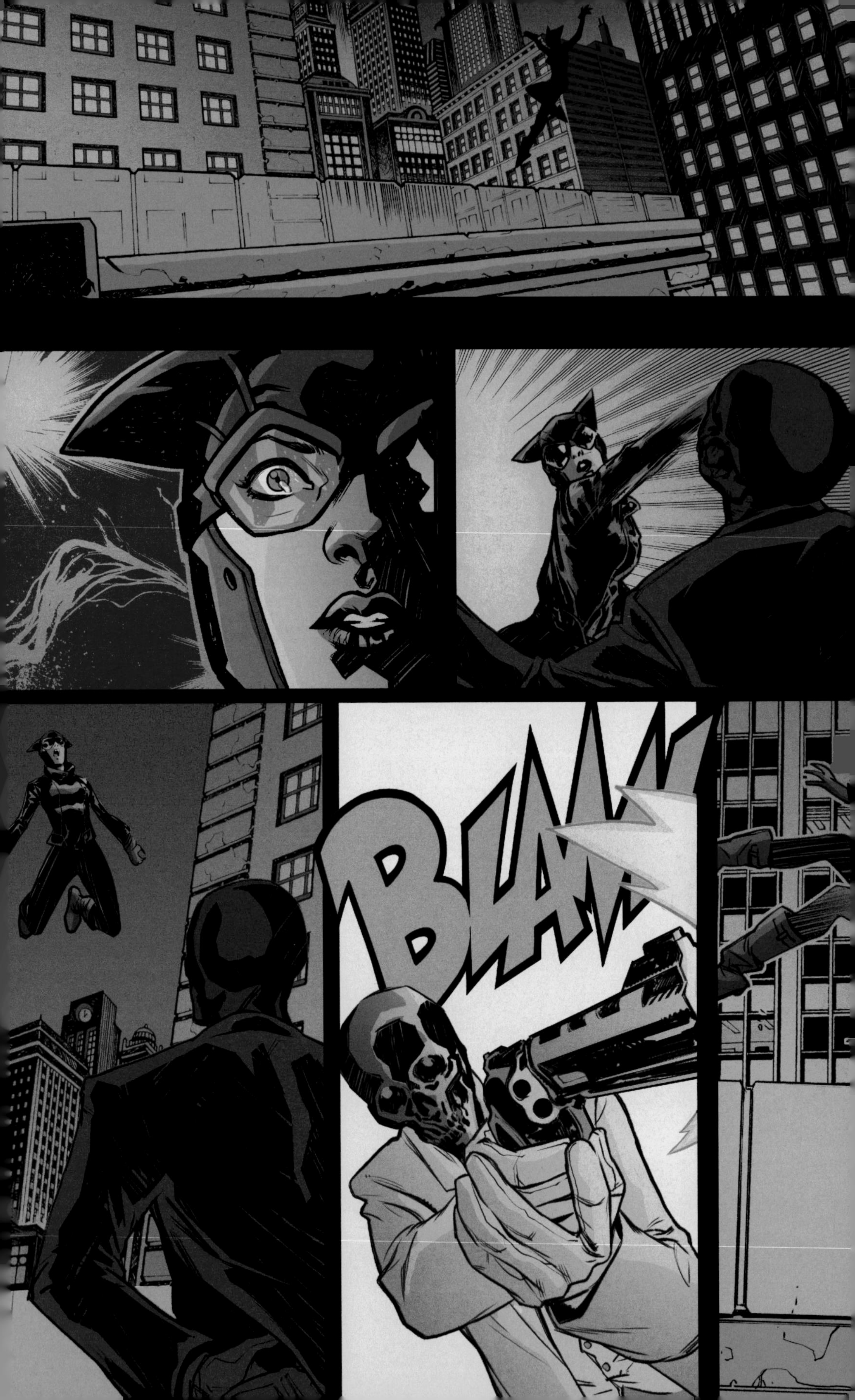
BLAM

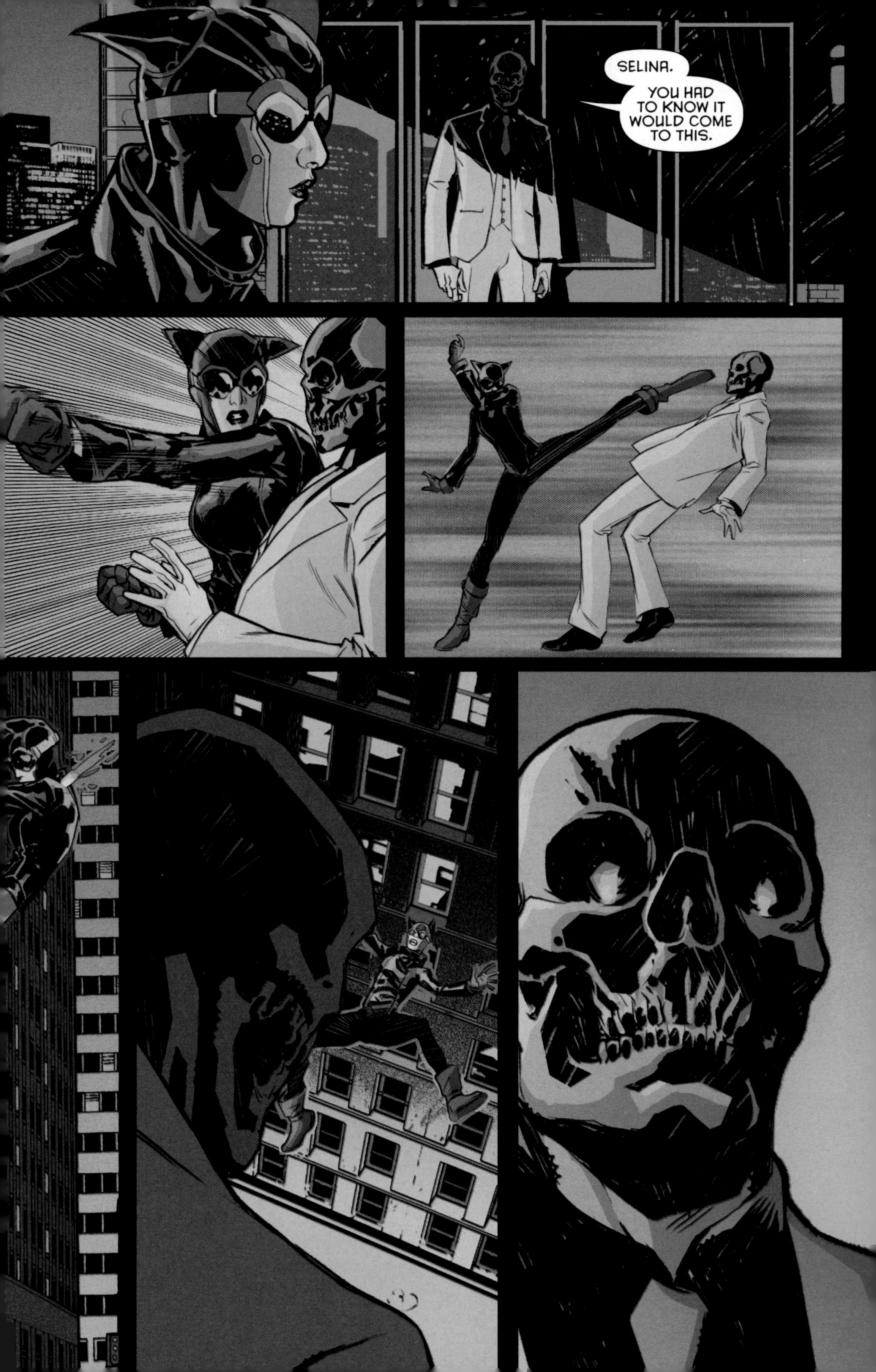
SELINA.
YOU HAD TO KNOW IT WOULD COME TO THIS.

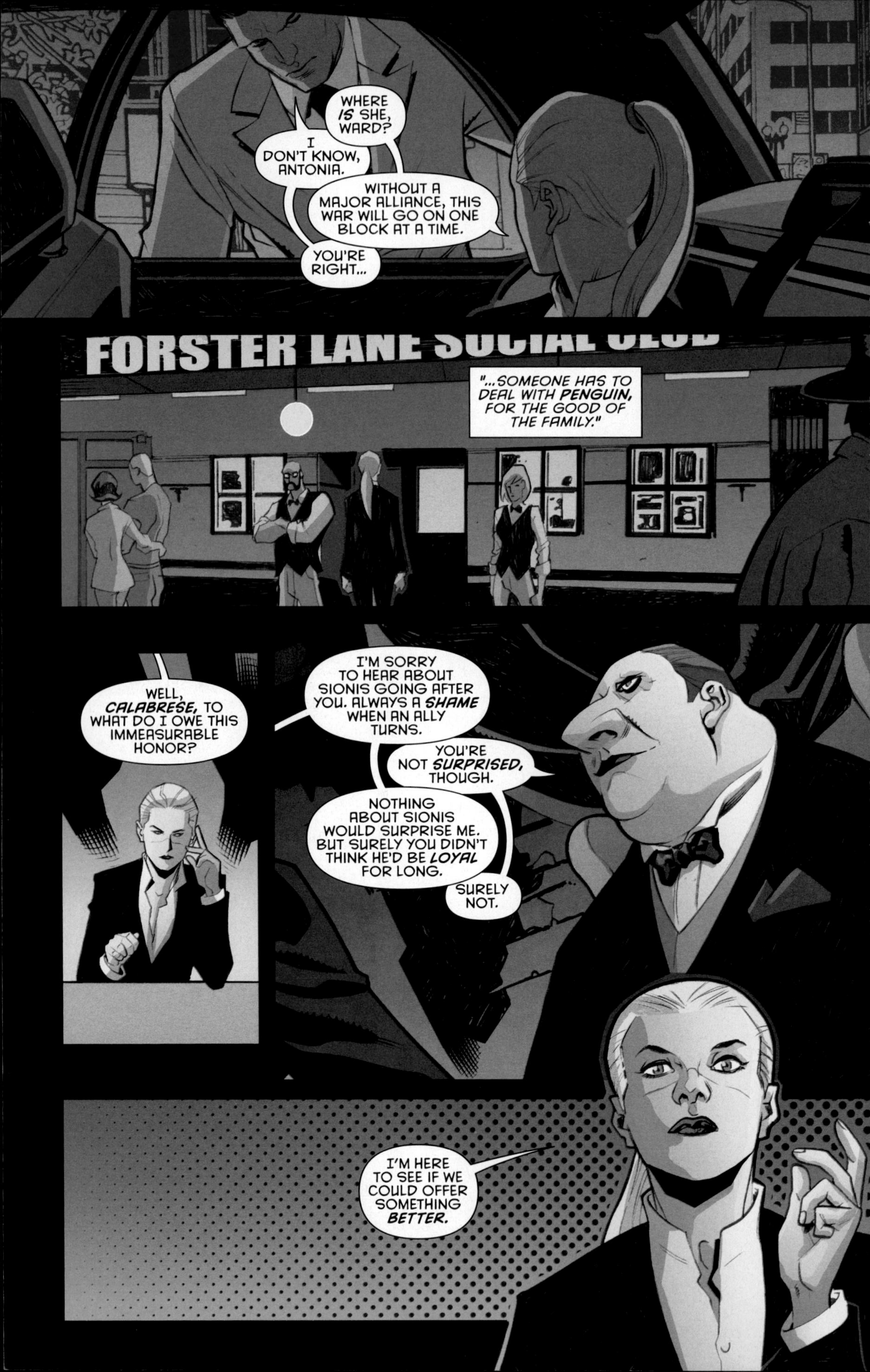
WHERE *IS* SHE, WARD?
I DON'T KNOW, ANTONIA.
WITHOUT A MAJOR ALLIANCE, THIS WAR WILL GO ON ONE BLOCK AT A TIME.
YOU'RE RIGHT...
FORSTER LANE SOCIAL CLUB
"...SOMEONE HAS TO DEAL WITH **PENGUIN**, FOR THE GOOD OF THE FAMILY."
WELL, ***CALABRESE,*** TO WHAT DO I OWE THIS IMMEASURABLE HONOR?
I'M SORRY TO HEAR ABOUT SIONIS GOING AFTER YOU. ALWAYS A ***SHAME*** WHEN AN ALLY TURNS.
YOU'RE NOT ***SURPRISED,*** THOUGH.
NOTHING ABOUT SIONIS WOULD SURPRISE ME. BUT SURELY YOU DIDN'T THINK HE'D BE ***LOYAL*** FOR LONG.
SURELY NOT.
I'M HERE TO SEE IF WE COULD OFFER SOMETHING ***BETTER.***

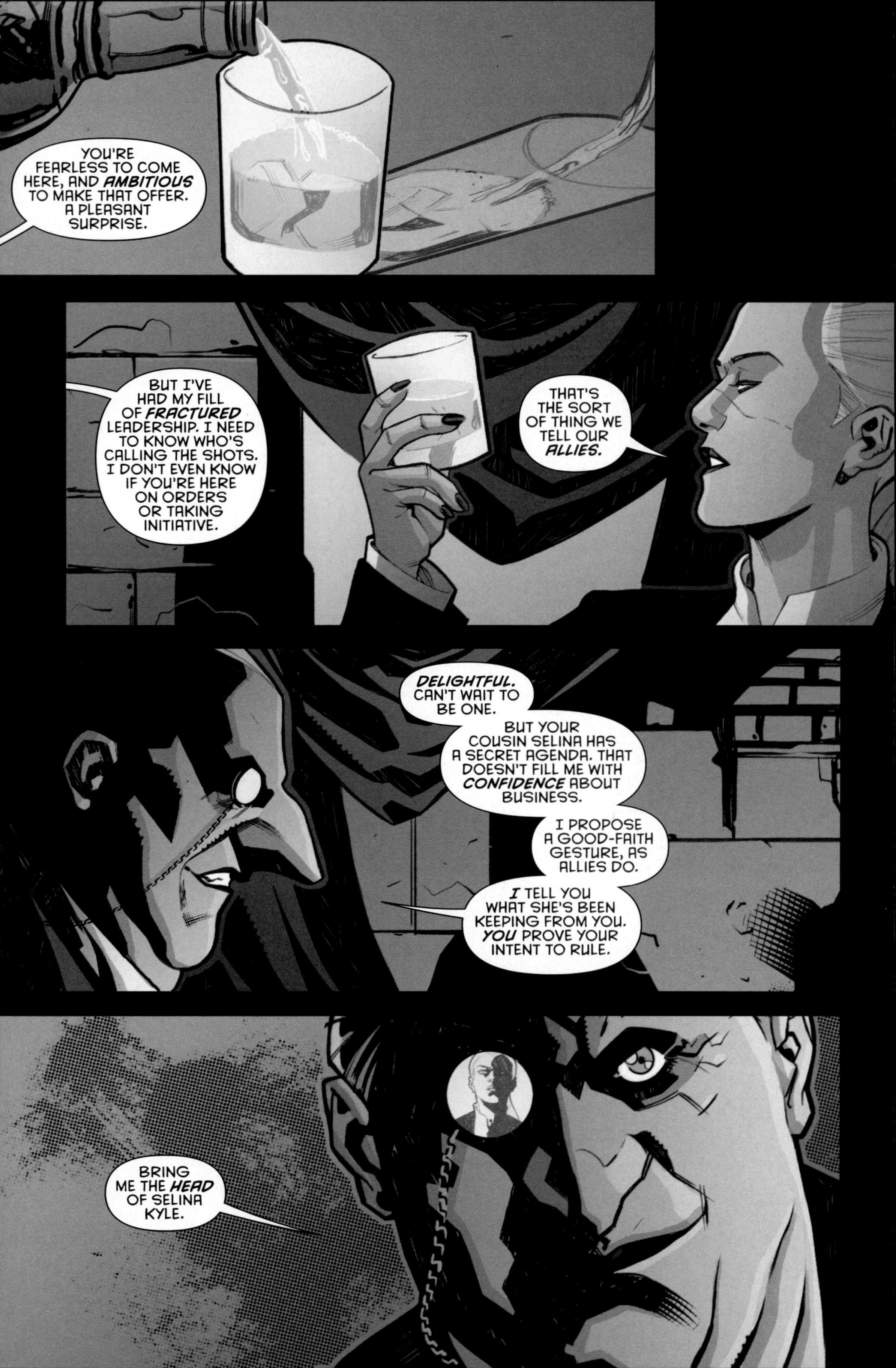

YOU'RE FEARLESS TO COME HERE, AND AMBITIOUS TO MAKE THAT OFFER. A PLEASANT SURPRISE.
BUT I'VE HAD MY FILL OF FRACTURED LEADERSHIP. I NEED TO KNOW WHO'S CALLING THE SHOTS. I DON'T EVEN KNOW IF YOU'RE HERE ON ORDERS OR TAKING INITIATIVE.
THAT'S THE SORT OF THING WE TELL OUR ALLIES.
DELIGHTFUL. CAN'T WAIT TO BE ONE.
BUT YOUR COUSIN SELINA HAS A SECRET AGENDA. THAT DOESN'T FILL ME WITH CONFIDENCE ABOUT BUSINESS.
I PROPOSE A GOOD-FAITH GESTURE, AS ALLIES DO.
I TELL YOU WHAT SHE'S BEEN KEEPING FROM YOU. YOU PROVE YOUR INTENT TO RULE.
BRING ME THE HEAD OF SELINA KYLE.

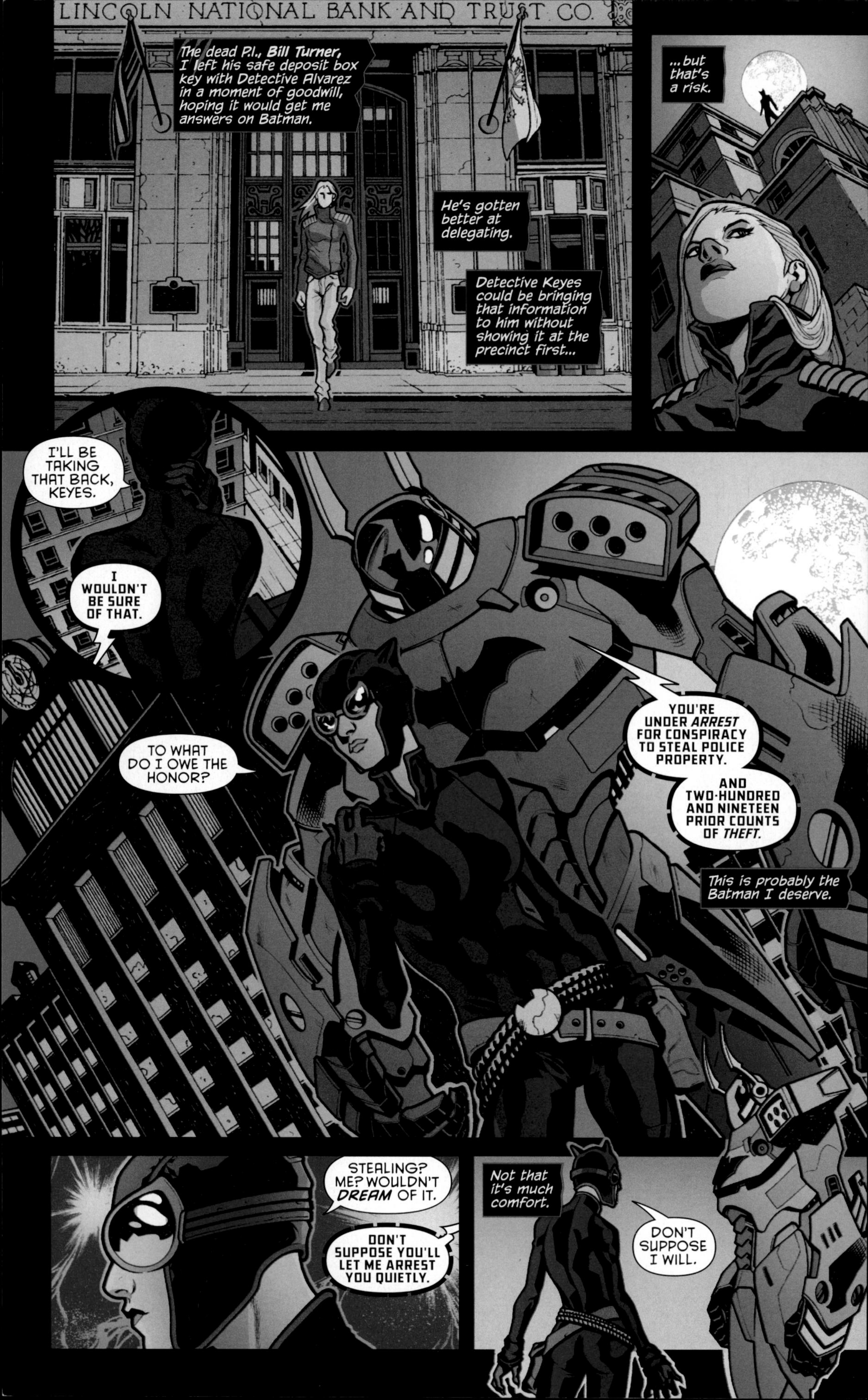
LINCOLN NATIONAL BANK AND TRUST CO.
The dead P.I., Bill Turner, I left his safe deposit box key with Detective Alvarez in a moment of goodwill, hoping it would get me answers on Batman.
He's gotten better at delegating.
Detective Keyes could be bringing that information to him without showing it at the precinct first...
...but that's a risk.
I'LL BE TAKING THAT BACK, KEYES.
I WOULDN'T BE SURE OF THAT.
TO WHAT DO I OWE THE HONOR?
YOU'RE UNDER ARREST FOR CONSPIRACY TO STEAL POLICE PROPERTY.
AND TWO-HUNDRED AND NINETEEN PRIOR COUNTS OF THEFT.
This is probably the Batman I deserve.
STEALING? ME? WOULDN'T DREAM OF IT.
DON'T SUPPOSE YOU'LL LET ME ARREST YOU QUIETLY.
Not that it's much comfort.
DON'T SUPPOSE I WILL.

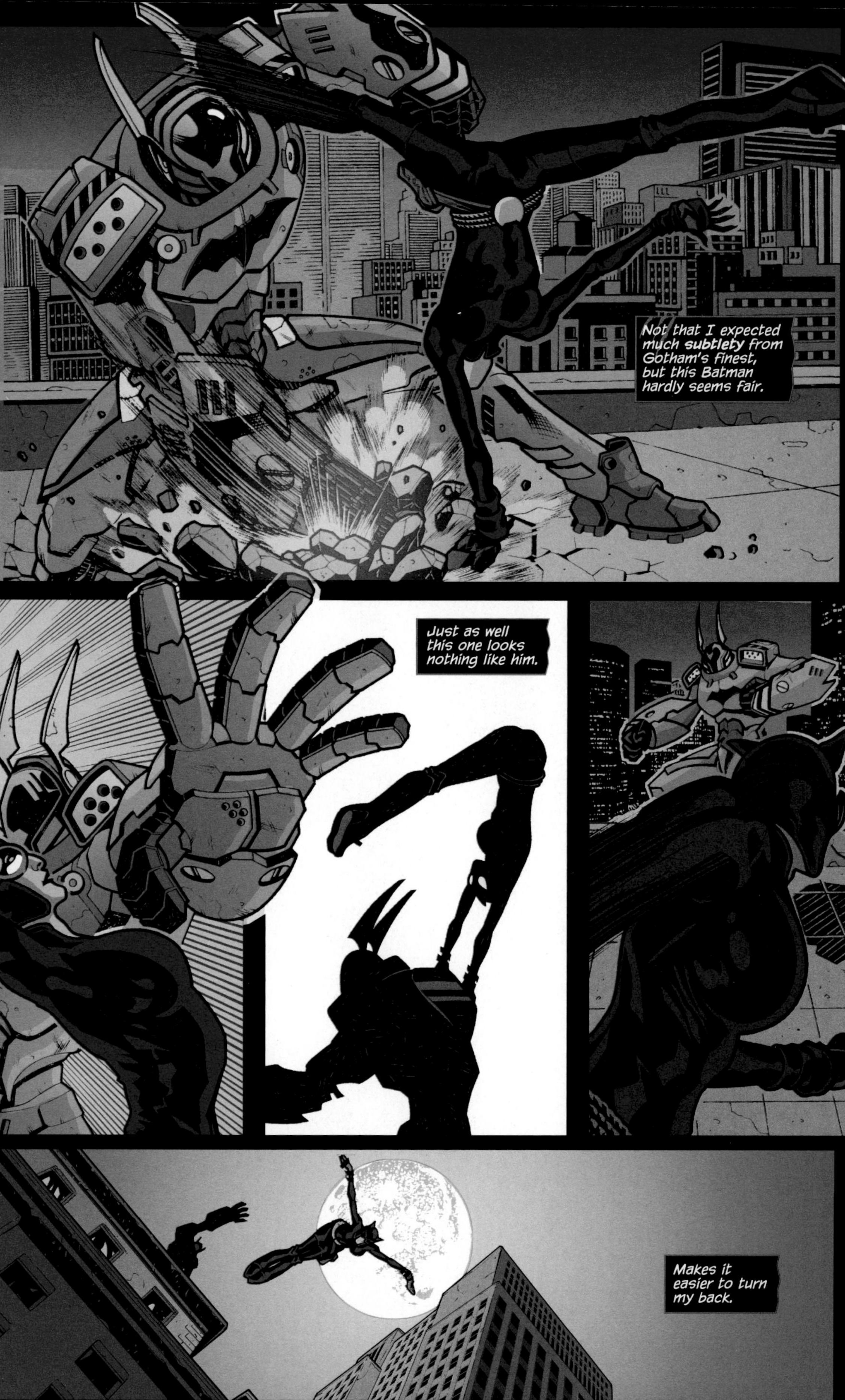
Not that I expected much subtlety from Gotham's finest, but this Batman hardly seems fair.
Just as well this one looks nothing like him.
Makes it easier to turn my back.

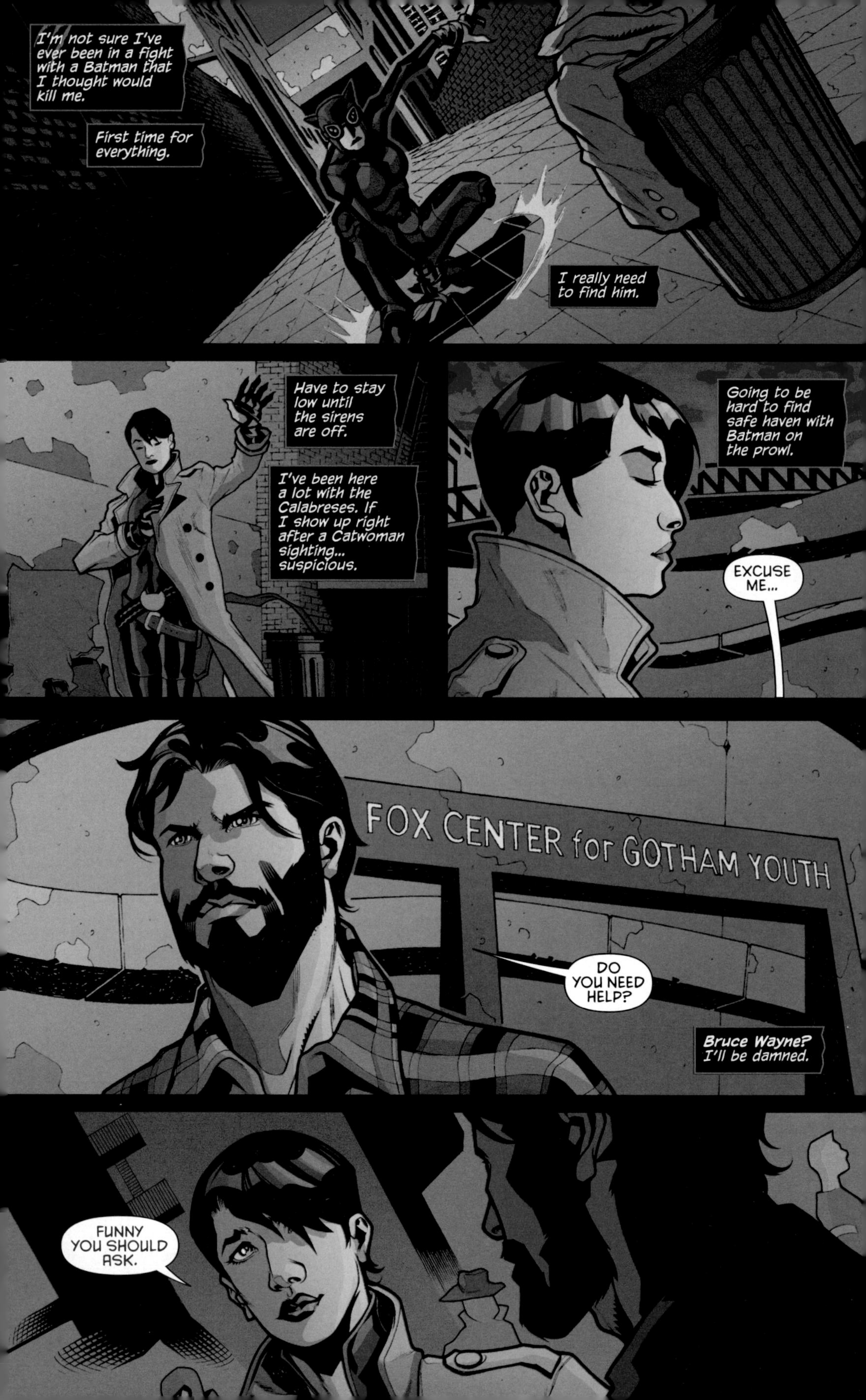
I'm not sure I've ever been in a fight with a Batman that I thought would kill me.
First time for everything.
I really need to find him.
Have to stay low until the sirens are off.
I've been here a lot with the Calabreses. If I show up right after a Catwoman sighting... suspicious.
Going to be hard to find safe haven with Batman on the prowl.
EXCUSE ME...
FOX CENTER for GOTHAM YOUTH
DO YOU NEED HELP?
Bruce Wayne? I'll be damned.
FUNNY YOU SHOULD ASK.

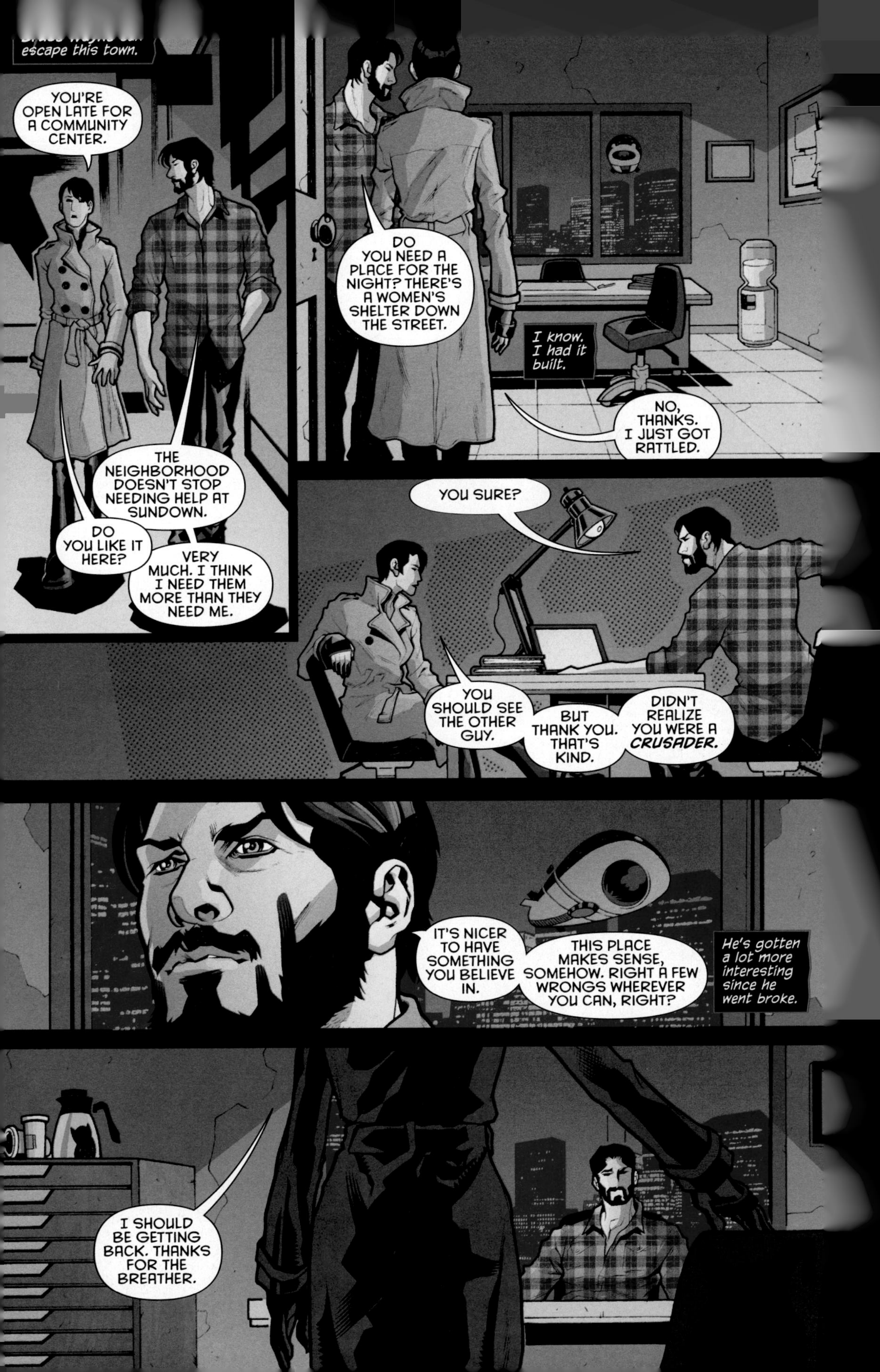
escape this town.
YOU'RE OPEN LATE FOR A COMMUNITY CENTER.
THE NEIGHBORHOOD DOESN'T STOP NEEDING HELP AT SUNDOWN.
DO YOU LIKE IT HERE?
VERY MUCH. I THINK I NEED THEM MORE THAN THEY NEED ME.
DO YOU NEED A PLACE FOR THE NIGHT? THERE'S A WOMEN'S SHELTER DOWN THE STREET.
I know. I had it built.
NO, THANKS. I JUST GOT RATTLED.
YOU SURE?
YOU SHOULD SEE THE OTHER GUY.
BUT THANK YOU. THAT'S KIND.
DIDN'T REALIZE YOU WERE A CRUSADER.
IT'S NICER TO HAVE SOMETHING YOU BELIEVE IN.
THIS PLACE MAKES SENSE, SOMEHOW. RIGHT A FEW WRONGS WHEREVER YOU CAN, RIGHT?
He's gotten a lot more interesting since he went broke.
I SHOULD BE GETTING BACK. THANKS FOR THE BREATHER.

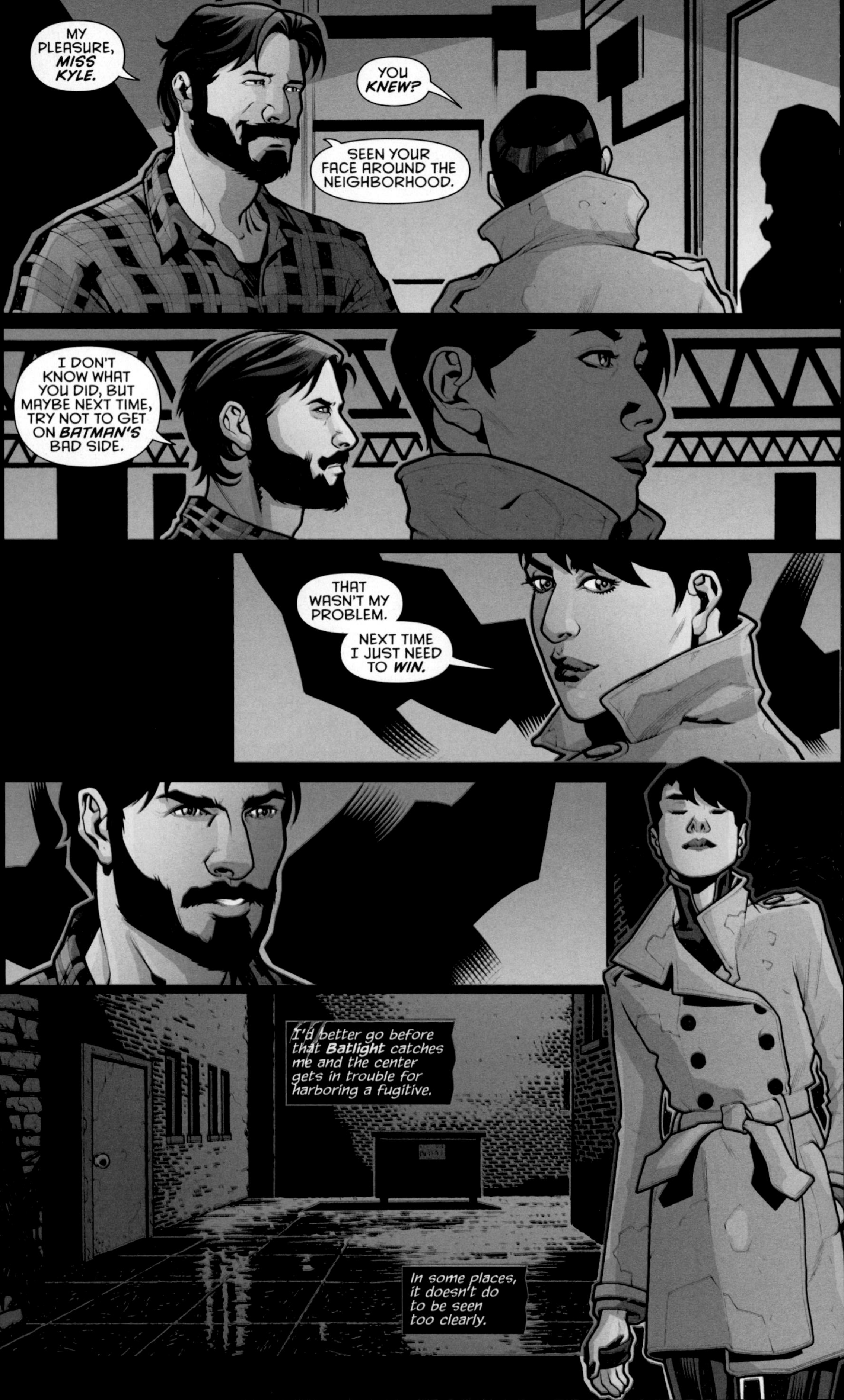
MY PLEASURE, MISS KYLE.
YOU KNEW?
SEEN YOUR FACE AROUND THE NEIGHBORHOOD.
I DON'T KNOW WHAT YOU DID, BUT MAYBE NEXT TIME, TRY NOT TO GET ON BATMAN'S BAD SIDE.
THAT WASN'T MY PROBLEM.
NEXT TIME I JUST NEED TO WIN.
I'd better go before that Batlight catches me and the center gets in trouble for harboring a fugitive.
In some places, it doesn't do to be seen too clearly.

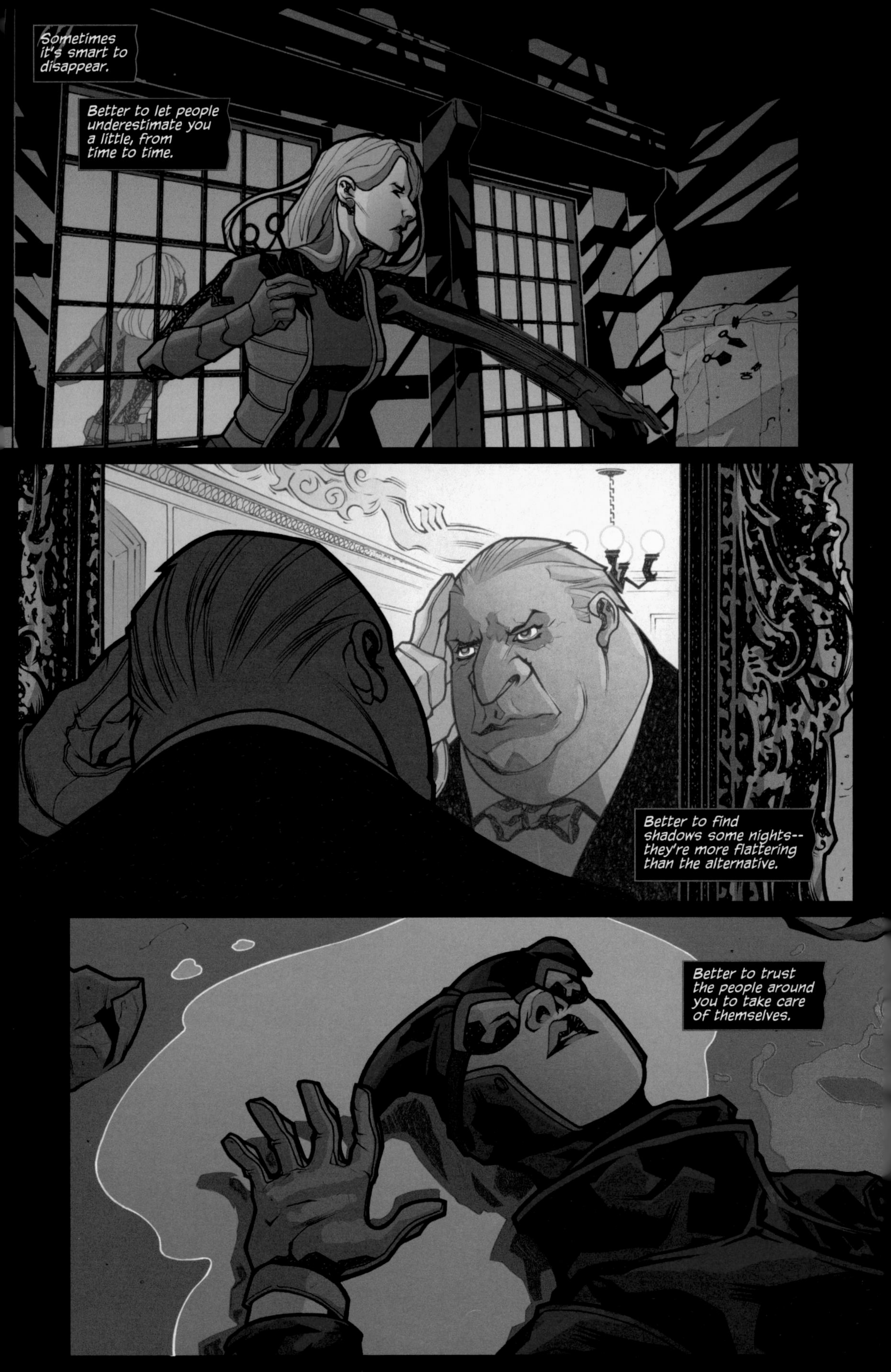
Sometimes it's smart to disappear.
Better to let people underestimate you a little, from time to time.
Better to find shadows some nights--they're more flattering than the alternative.
Better to trust the people around you to take care of themselves.

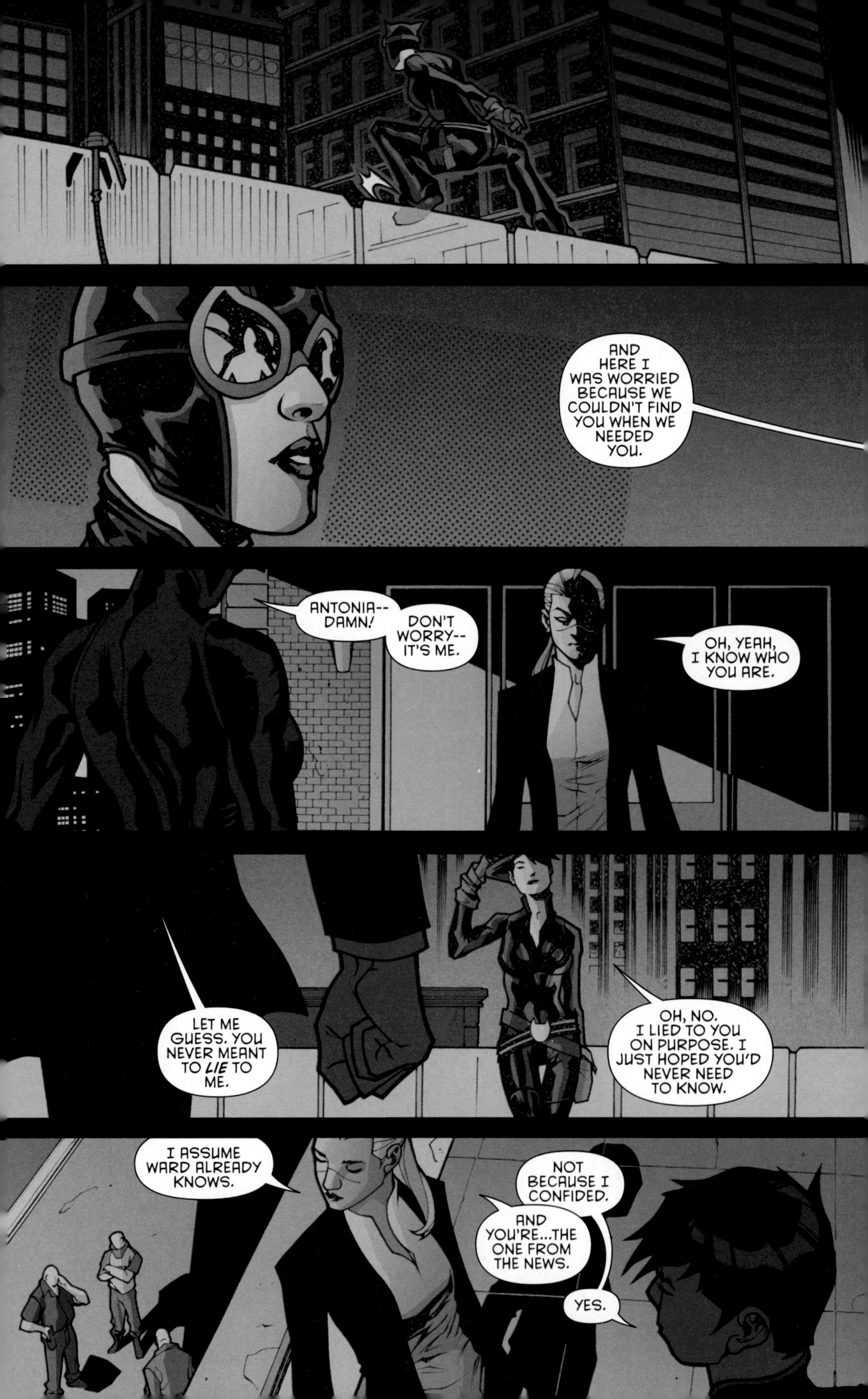
AND HERE I WAS WORRIED BECAUSE WE COULDN'T FIND YOU WHEN WE NEEDED YOU.
ANTONIA-- DAMN!
DON'T WORRY-- IT'S ME.
OH, YEAH, I KNOW WHO YOU ARE.
LET ME GUESS. YOU NEVER MEANT TO *LIE* TO ME.
OH, NO. I LIED TO YOU ON PURPOSE. I JUST HOPED YOU'D NEVER NEED TO KNOW.
I ASSUME WARD ALREADY KNOWS.
NOT BECAUSE I CONFIDED.
AND YOU'RE...THE ONE FROM THE NEWS.
YES.

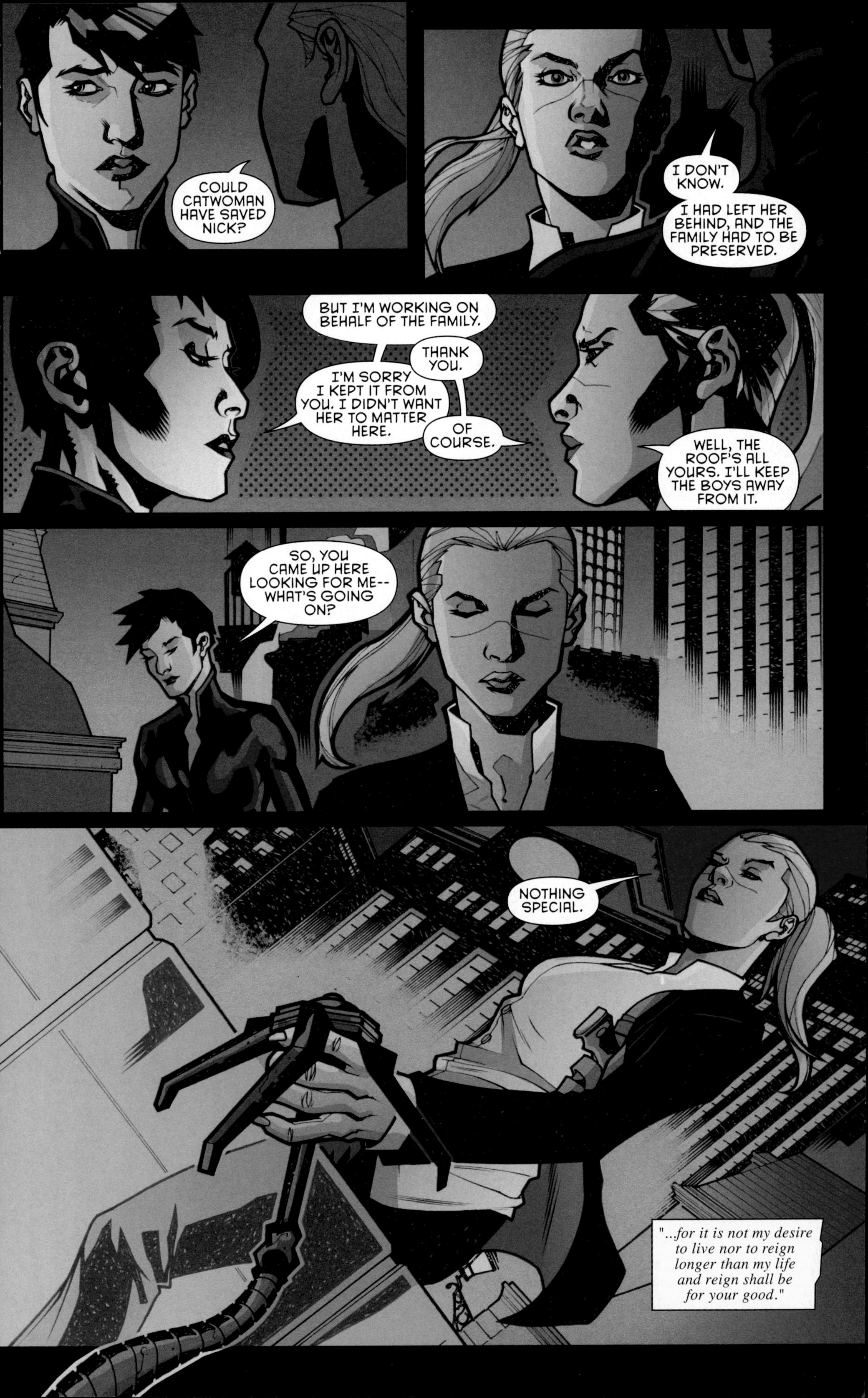

COULD CATWOMAN HAVE SAVED NICK?
I DON'T KNOW.
I HAD LEFT HER BEHIND, AND THE FAMILY HAD TO BE PRESERVED.
BUT I'M WORKING ON BEHALF OF THE FAMILY.
I'M SORRY I KEPT IT FROM YOU. I DIDN'T WANT HER TO MATTER HERE.
THANK YOU.
OF COURSE.
WELL, THE ROOF'S ALL YOURS. I'LL KEEP THE BOYS AWAY FROM IT.
SO, YOU CAME UP HERE LOOKING FOR ME--WHAT'S GOING ON?
NOTHING SPECIAL.
"...for it is not my desire to live nor to reign longer than my life and reign shall be for your good."

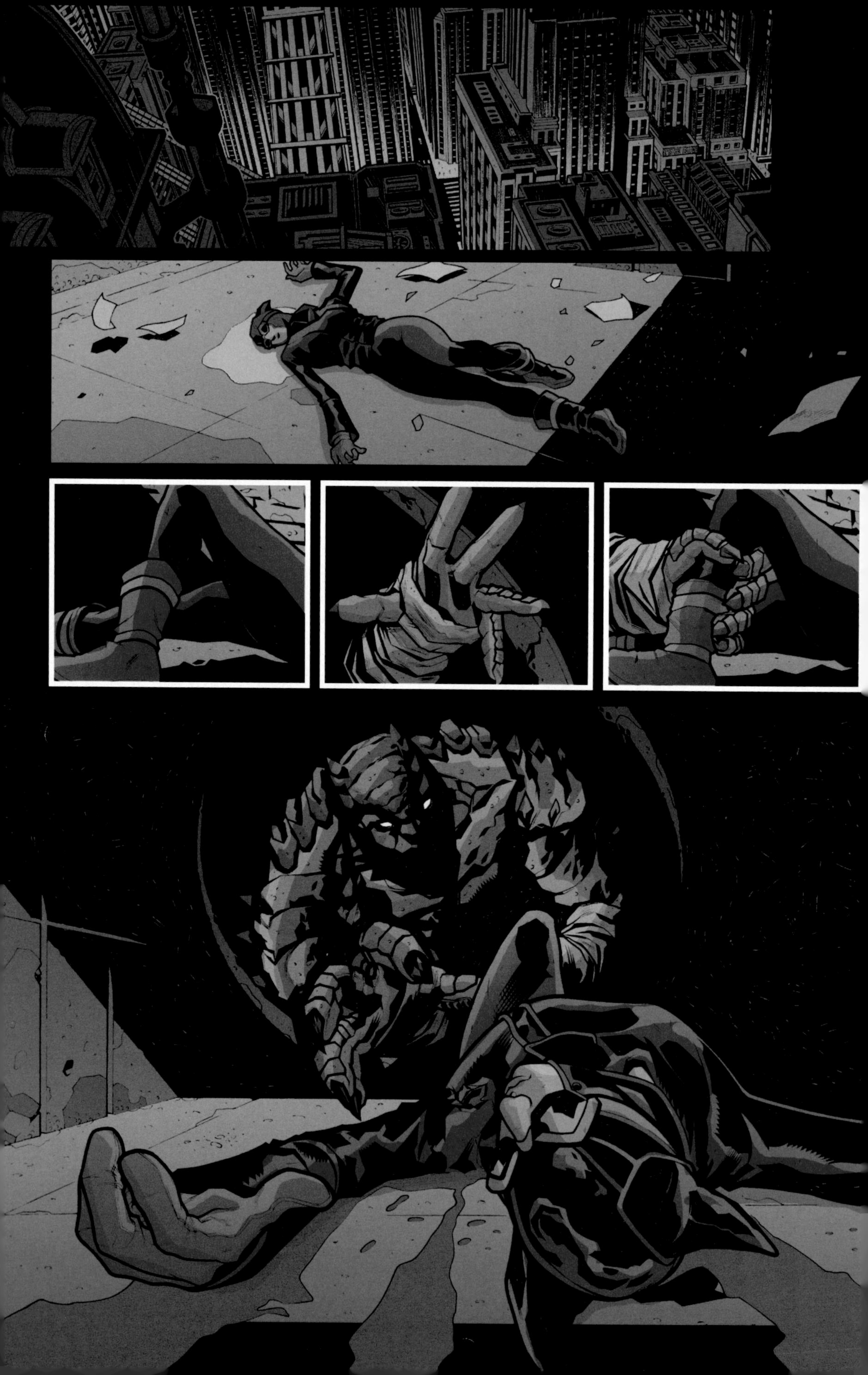

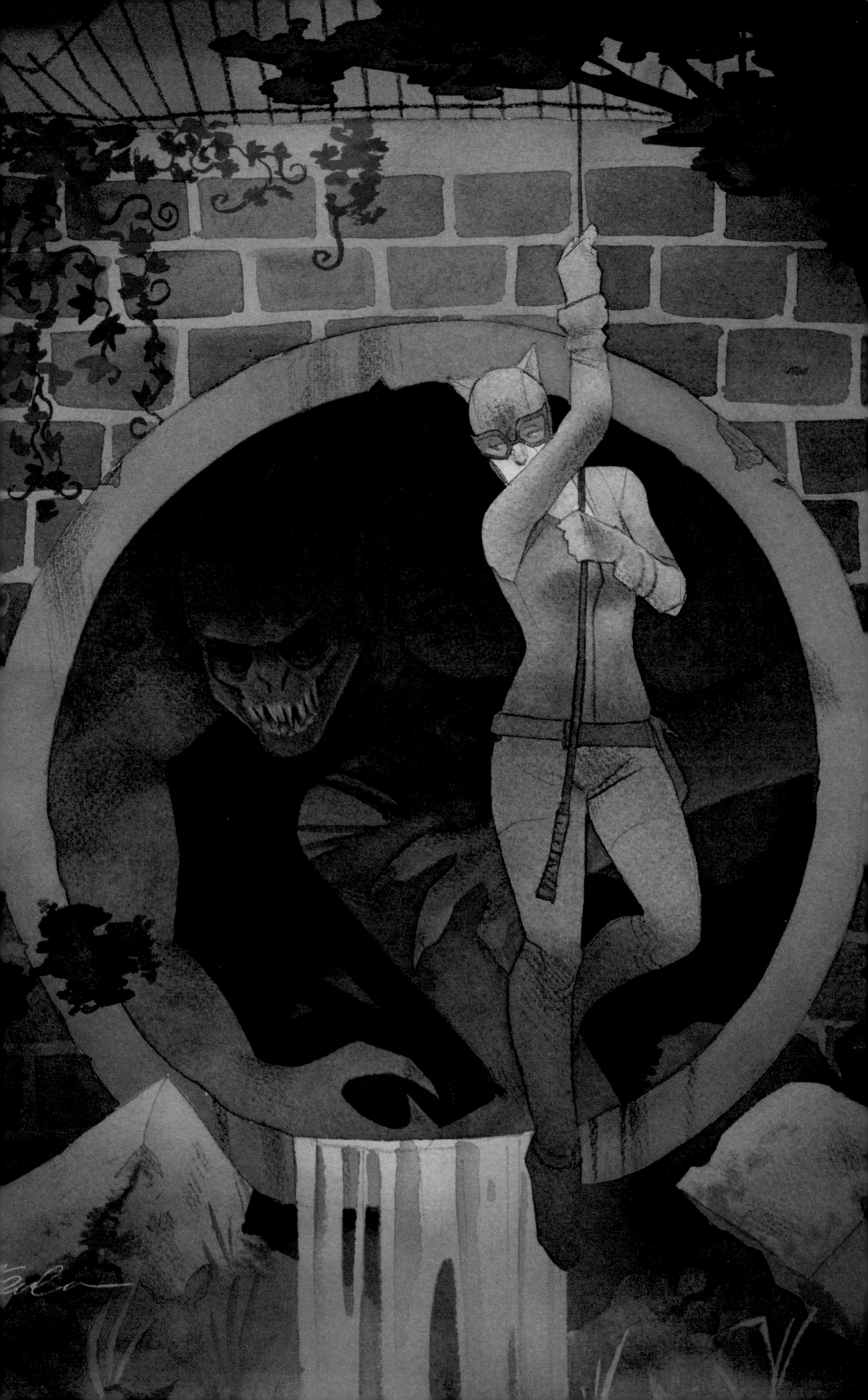

FIRE

GENEVIEVE VALENTINE writer **DAVID MESSINA** penciller **GAETANO CARLUCCI** inker **LEE LOUGHRIDGE** colorist **TRAVIS LANHAM** letterer cover art by **KEVIN WADA**

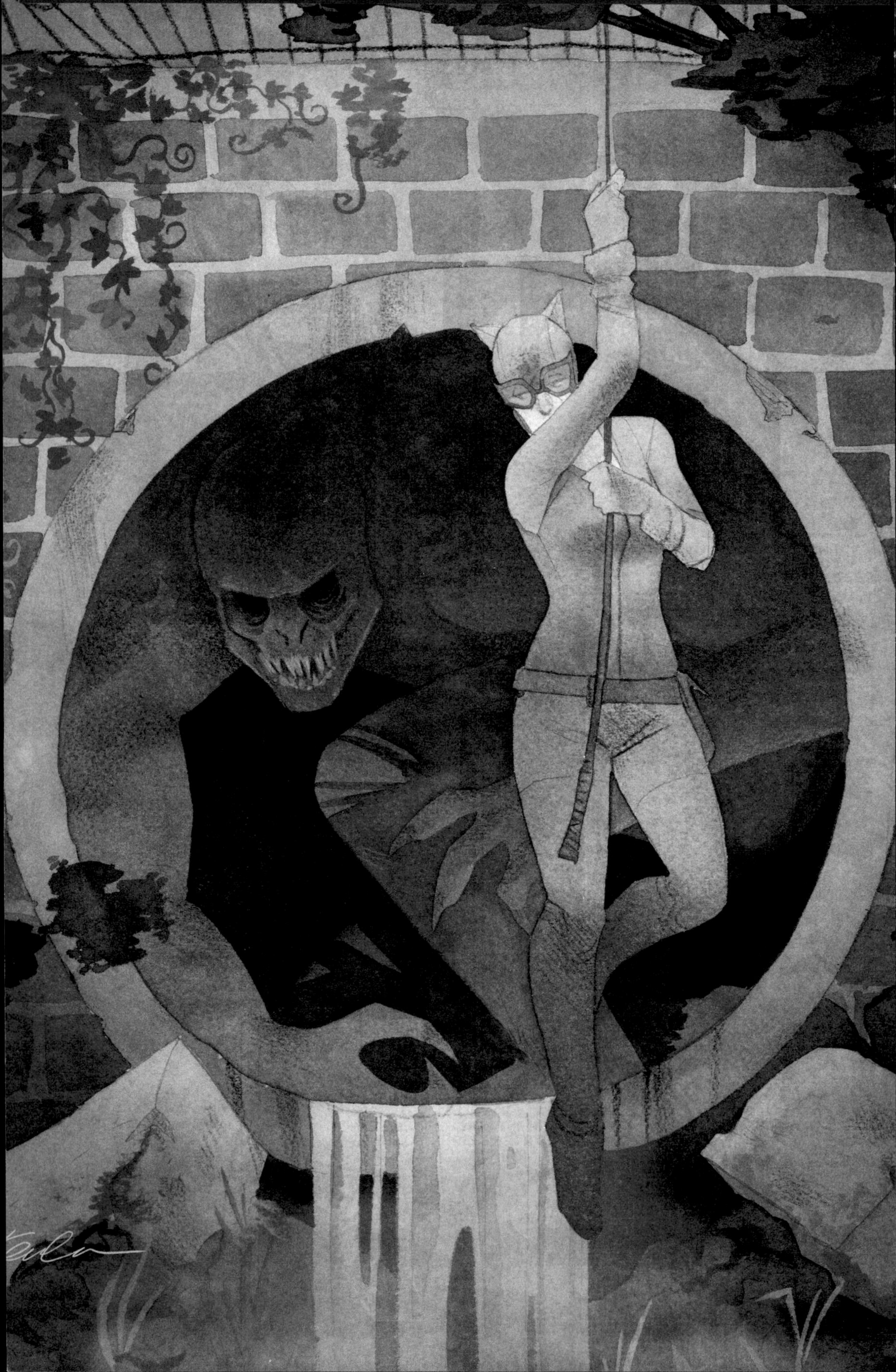

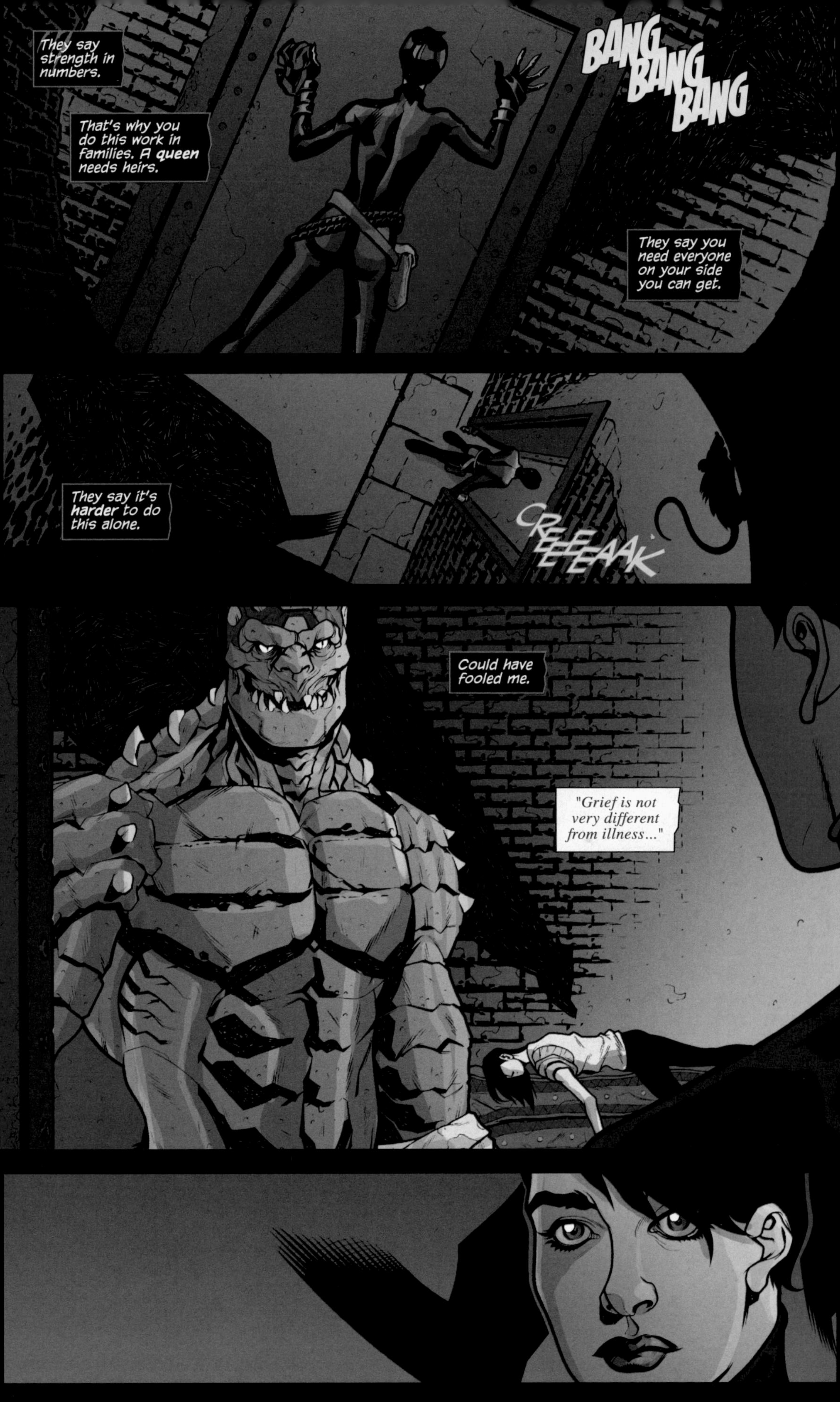
They say strength in numbers.
BANG BANG BANG
That's why you do this work in families. A **queen** needs heirs.
They say you need everyone on your side you can get.
They say it's **harder** to do this alone.
CREEEEAAK
Could have fooled me.
"Grief is not very different from illness..."

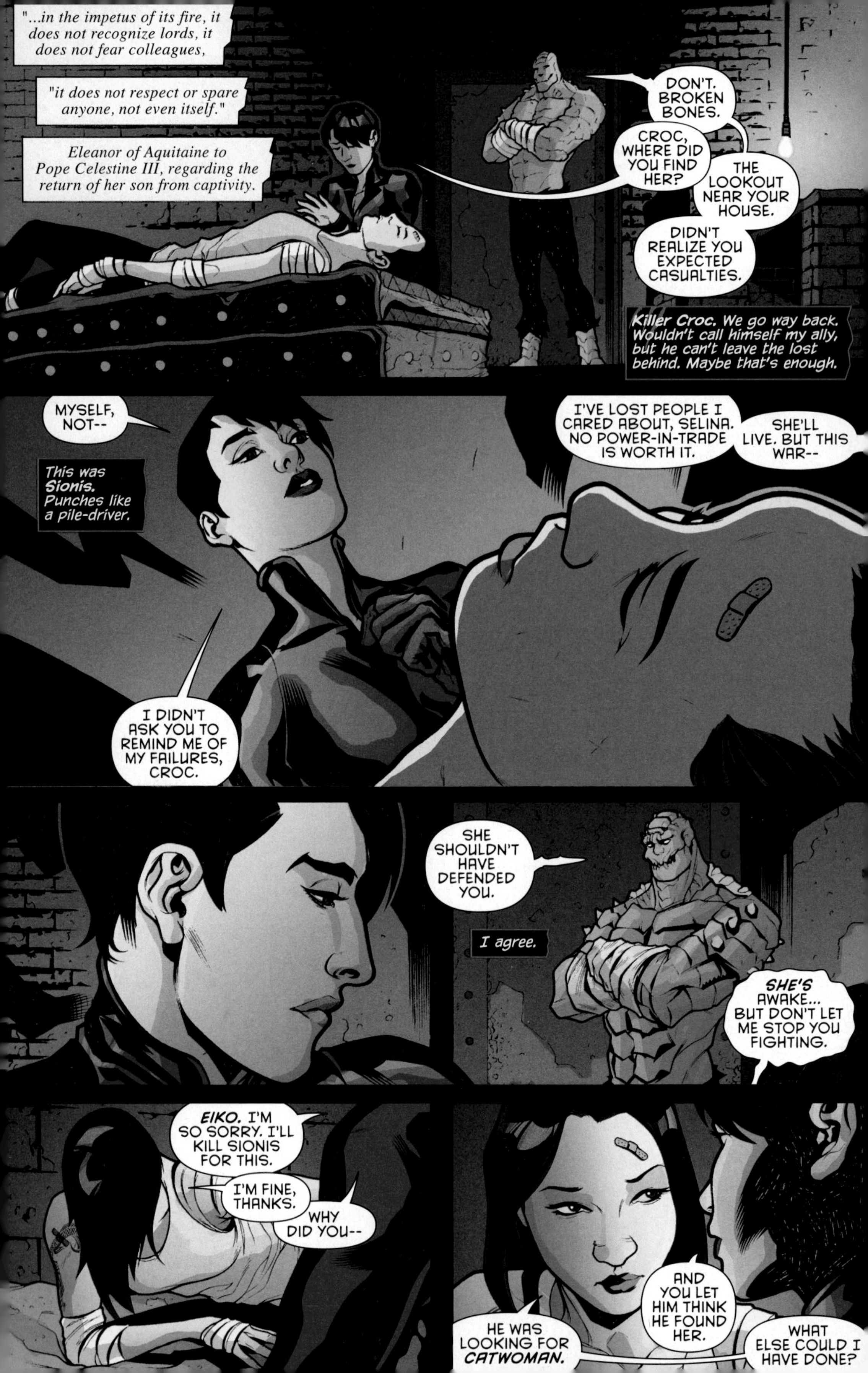
"...in the impetus of its fire, it does not recognize lords, it does not fear colleagues,
"it does not respect or spare anyone, not even itself."
Eleanor of Aquitaine to Pope Celestine III, regarding the return of her son from captivity.
DON'T. BROKEN BONES.
CROC, WHERE DID YOU FIND HER?
THE LOOKOUT NEAR YOUR HOUSE.
DIDN'T REALIZE YOU EXPECTED CASUALTIES.
Killer Croc. We go way back. Wouldn't call himself my ally, but he can't leave the lost behind. Maybe that's enough.
MYSELF, NOT--
This was Sionis. Punches like a pile-driver.
I'VE LOST PEOPLE I CARED ABOUT, SELINA. NO POWER-IN-TRADE IS WORTH IT.
SHE'LL LIVE. BUT THIS WAR--
I DIDN'T ASK YOU TO REMIND ME OF MY FAILURES, CROC.
SHE SHOULDN'T HAVE DEFENDED YOU.
I agree.
SHE'S AWAKE... BUT DON'T LET ME STOP YOU FIGHTING.
EIKO. I'M SO SORRY. I'LL KILL SIONIS FOR THIS.
I'M FINE, THANKS.
WHY DID YOU--
HE WAS LOOKING FOR CATWOMAN.
AND YOU LET HIM THINK HE FOUND HER.
WHAT ELSE COULD I HAVE DONE?

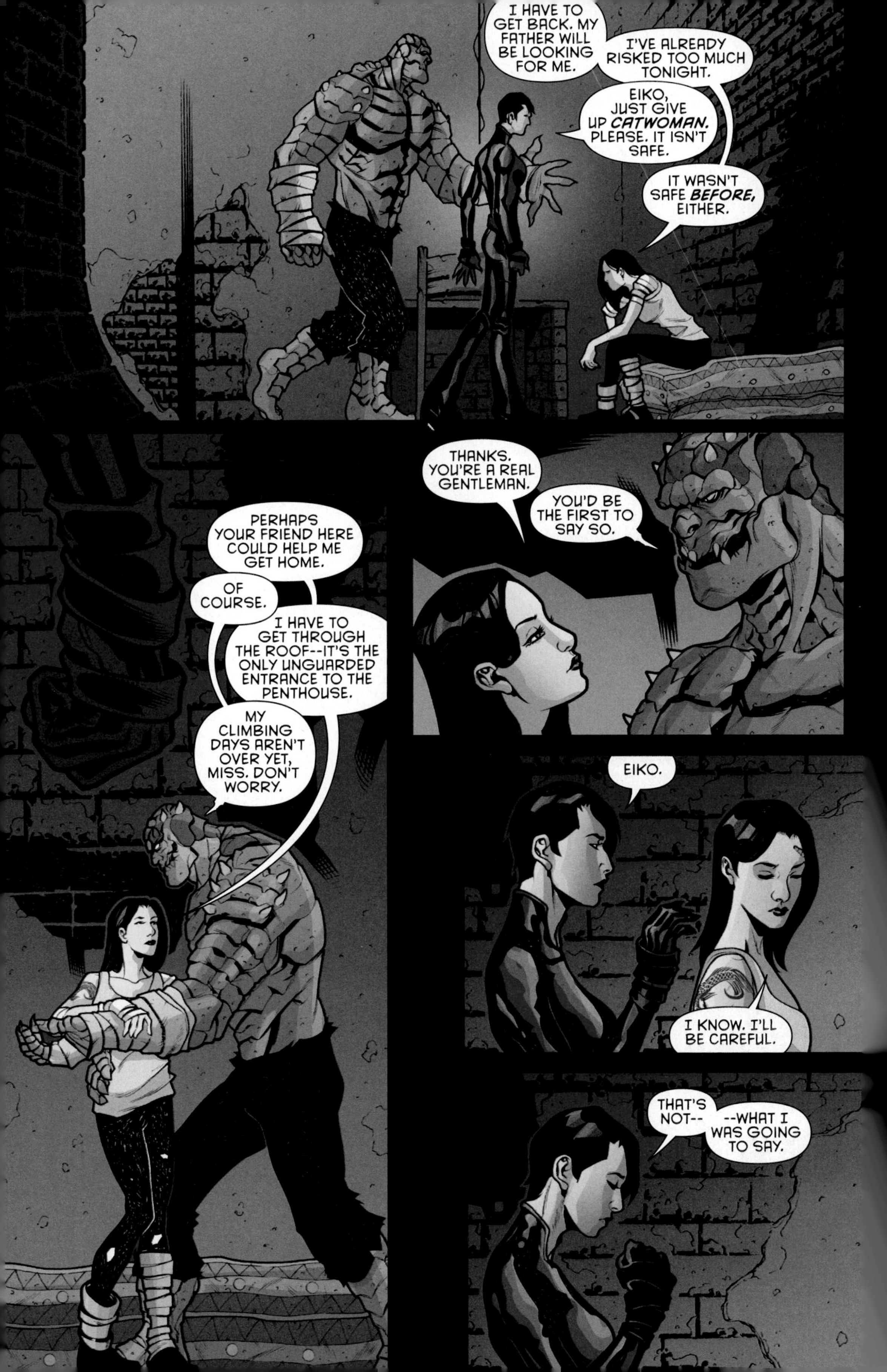
I HAVE TO GET BACK. MY FATHER WILL BE LOOKING FOR ME.
I'VE ALREADY RISKED TOO MUCH TONIGHT.
EIKO, JUST GIVE UP CATWOMAN. PLEASE. IT ISN'T SAFE.
IT WASN'T SAFE BEFORE, EITHER.
PERHAPS YOUR FRIEND HERE COULD HELP ME GET HOME.
OF COURSE.
I HAVE TO GET THROUGH THE ROOF--IT'S THE ONLY UNGUARDED ENTRANCE TO THE PENTHOUSE.
MY CLIMBING DAYS AREN'T OVER YET, MISS. DON'T WORRY.
THANKS. YOU'RE A REAL GENTLEMAN.
YOU'D BE THE FIRST TO SAY SO.
EIKO.
I KNOW. I'LL BE CAREFUL.
THAT'S NOT--
--WHAT I WAS GOING TO SAY.

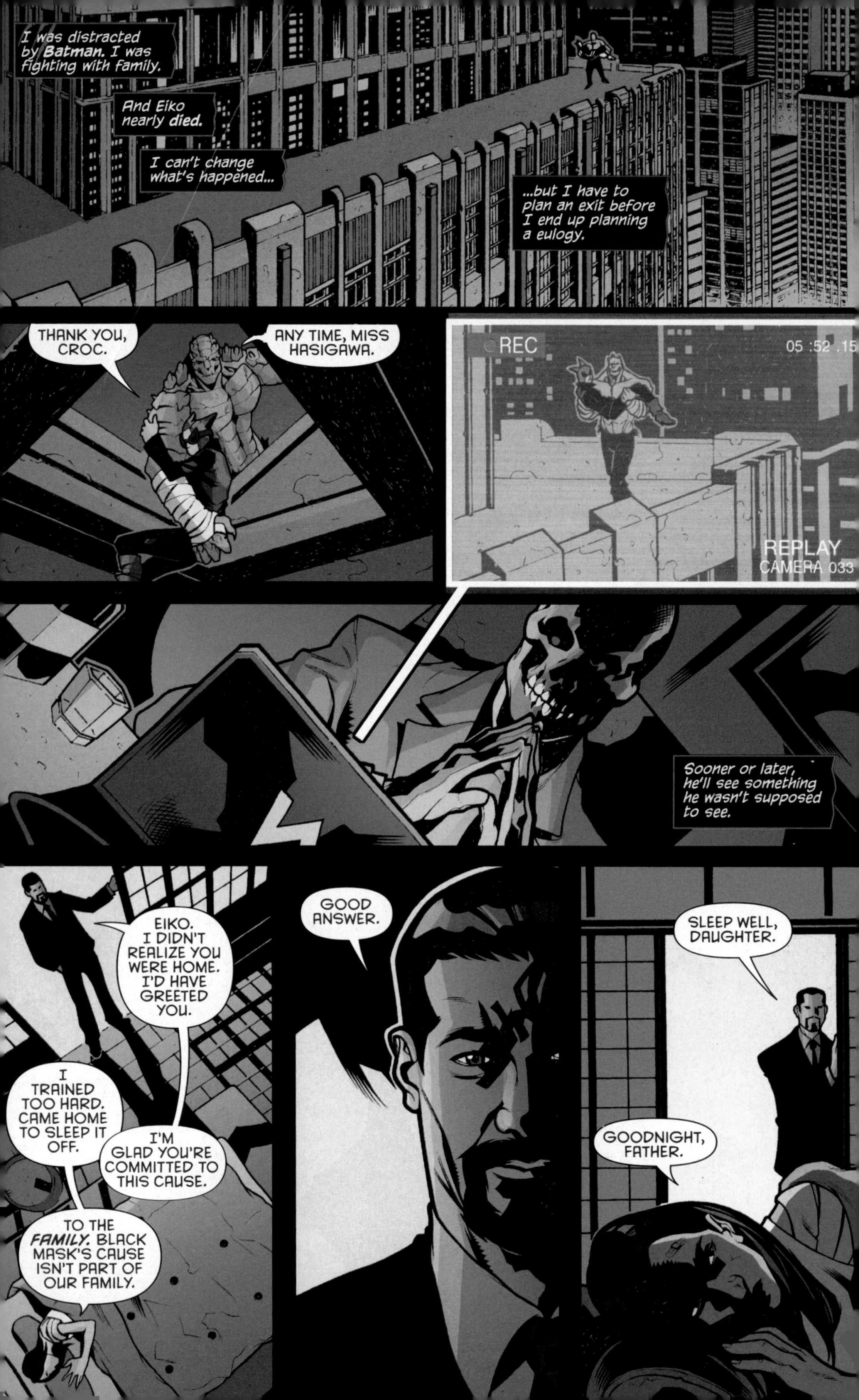
I was distracted by **Batman**. I was fighting with family.
And Eiko nearly **died**.
I can't change what's happened...
...but I have to plan an exit before I end up planning a eulogy.
THANK YOU, CROC.
ANY TIME, MISS HASIGAWA.
REC
05 :52 .15
REPLAY
CAMERA 033
Sooner or later, he'll see something he wasn't supposed to see.
EIKO. I DIDN'T REALIZE YOU WERE HOME. I'D HAVE GREETED YOU.
I TRAINED TOO HARD. CAME HOME TO SLEEP IT OFF.
I'M GLAD YOU'RE COMMITTED TO THIS CAUSE.
TO THE *FAMILY.* BLACK MASK'S CAUSE ISN'T PART OF OUR FAMILY.
GOOD ANSWER.
SLEEP WELL, DAUGHTER.
GOODNIGHT, FATHER.

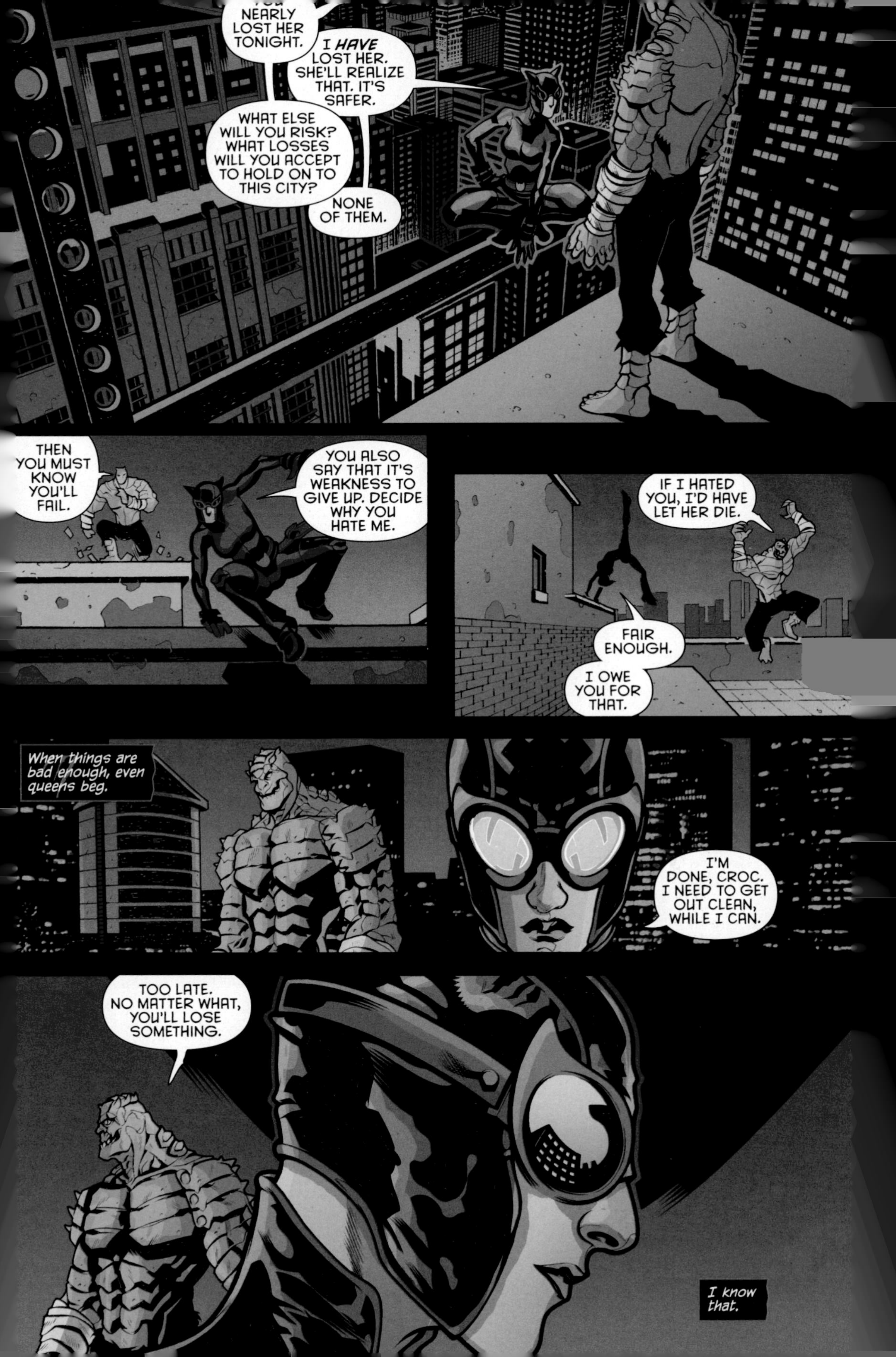
NEARLY LOST HER TONIGHT.
I ***HAVE*** LOST HER. SHE'LL REALIZE THAT. IT'S SAFER.
WHAT ELSE WILL YOU RISK? WHAT LOSSES WILL YOU ACCEPT TO HOLD ON TO THIS CITY?
NONE OF THEM.
THEN YOU MUST KNOW YOU'LL FAIL.
YOU ALSO SAY THAT IT'S WEAKNESS TO GIVE UP. DECIDE WHY YOU HATE ME.
IF I HATED YOU, I'D HAVE LET HER DIE.
FAIR ENOUGH.
I OWE YOU FOR THAT.
When things are bad enough, even queens beg.
I'M DONE, CROC. I NEED TO GET OUT CLEAN, WHILE I CAN.
TOO LATE. NO MATTER WHAT, YOU'LL LOSE SOMETHING.
I know that.

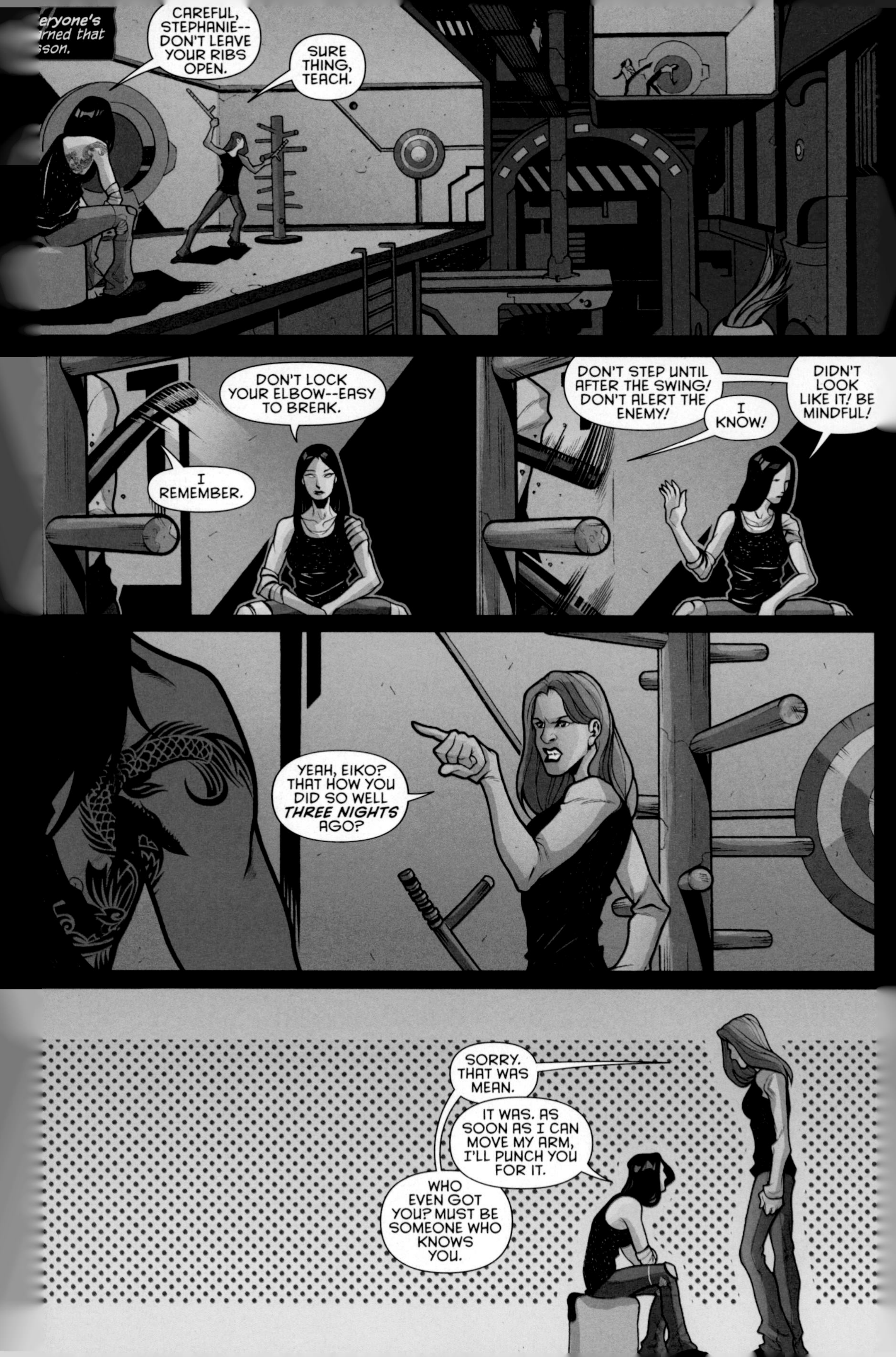

...eryone's
...rned that
...sson.
CAREFUL, STEPHANIE-- DON'T LEAVE YOUR RIBS OPEN.
SURE THING, TEACH.
DON'T LOCK YOUR ELBOW--EASY TO BREAK.
I REMEMBER.
DON'T STEP UNTIL AFTER THE SWING! DON'T ALERT THE ENEMY!
I KNOW!
DIDN'T LOOK LIKE IT! BE MINDFUL!
YEAH, EIKO? THAT HOW YOU DID SO WELL *THREE NIGHTS* AGO?
SORRY. THAT WAS MEAN.
IT WAS. AS SOON AS I CAN MOVE MY ARM, I'LL PUNCH YOU FOR IT.
WHO EVEN GOT YOU? MUST BE SOMEONE WHO KNOWS YOU.

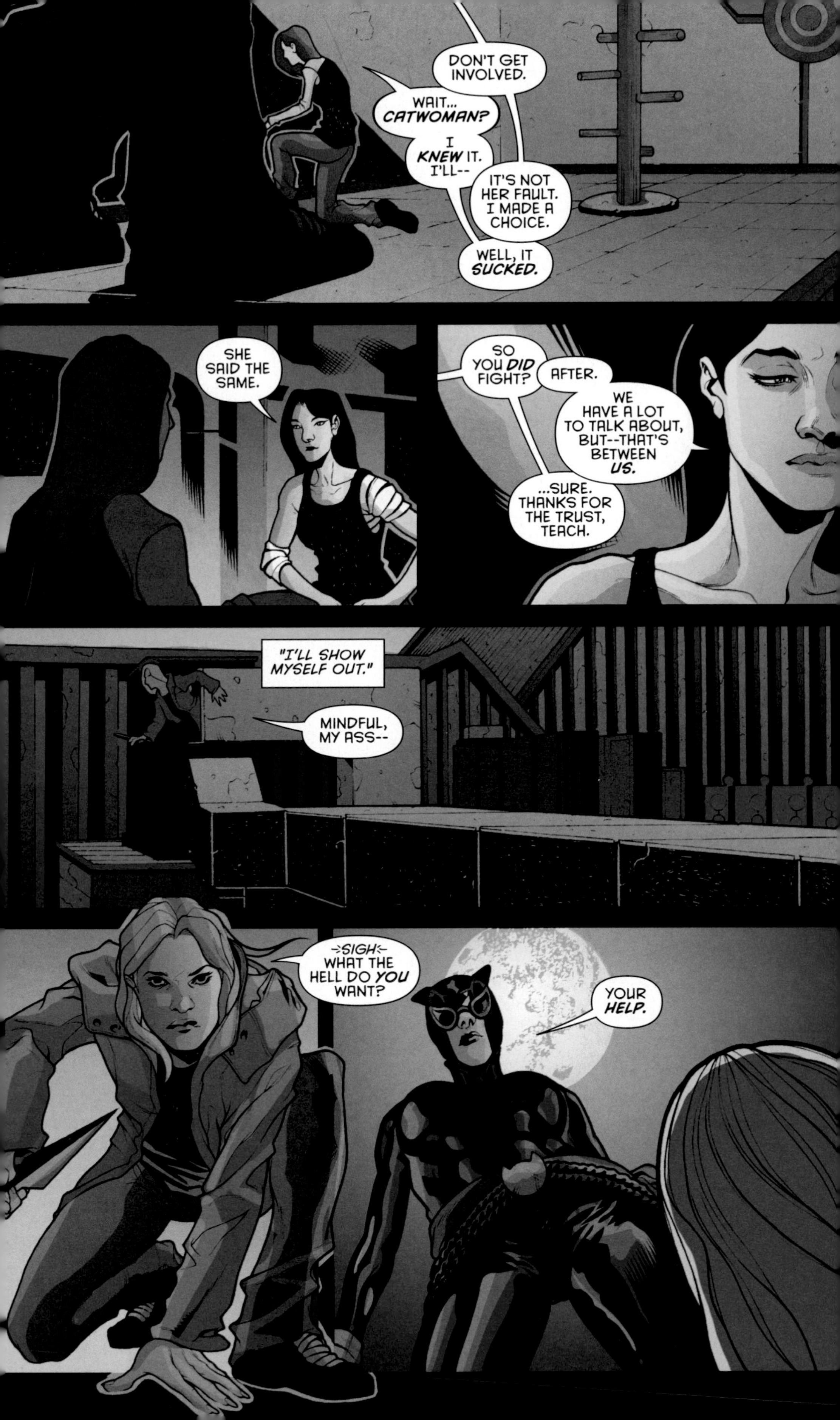
DON'T GET INVOLVED.
WAIT... CATWOMAN?
I KNEW IT. I'LL--
IT'S NOT HER FAULT. I MADE A CHOICE.
WELL, IT SUCKED.
SHE SAID THE SAME.
SO YOU DID FIGHT?
AFTER.
WE HAVE A LOT TO TALK ABOUT, BUT--THAT'S BETWEEN US.
...SURE. THANKS FOR THE TRUST, TEACH.
"I'LL SHOW MYSELF OUT."
MINDFUL, MY ASS--
SIGH
WHAT THE HELL DO YOU WANT?
YOUR HELP.

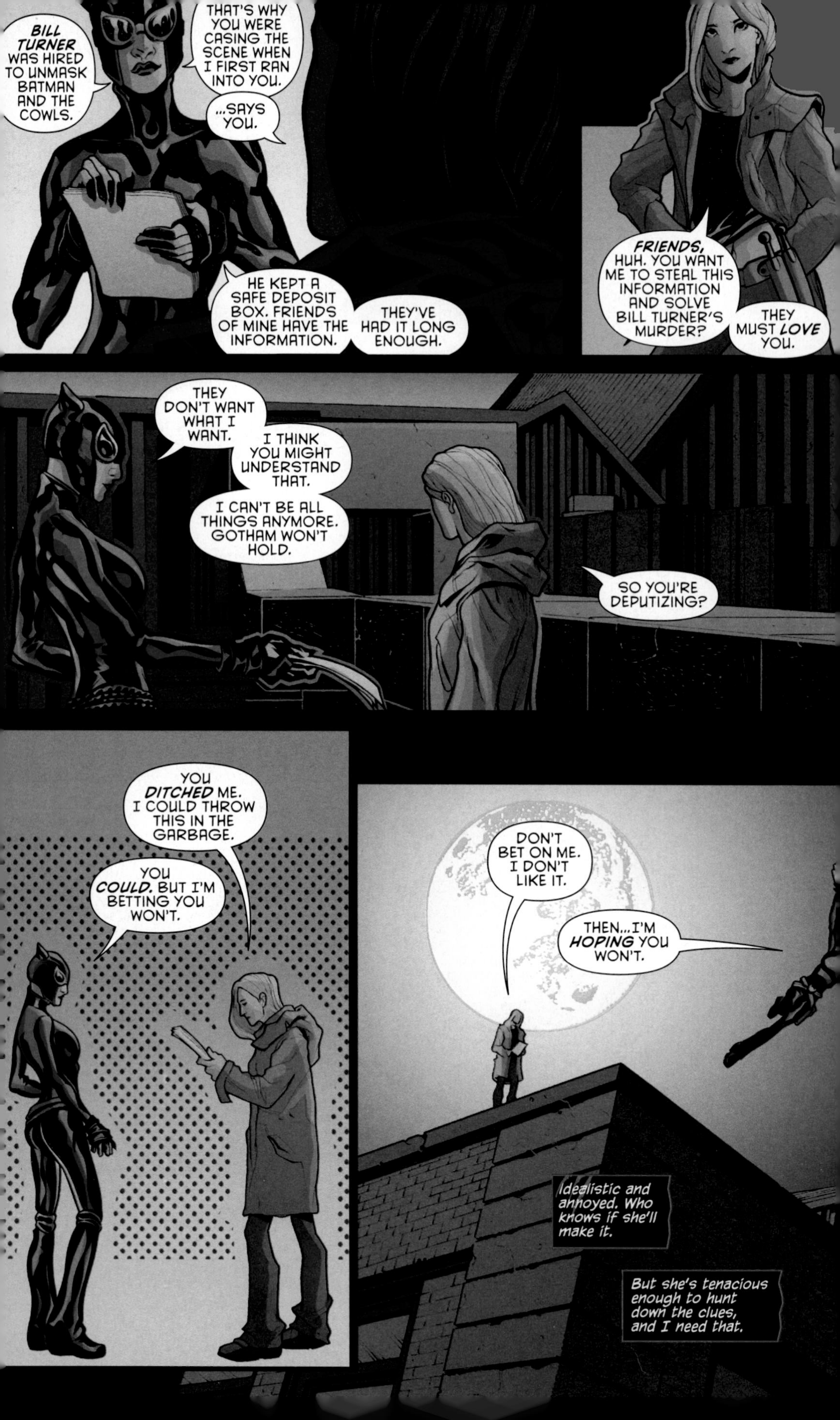

BILL TURNER WAS HIRED TO UNMASK BATMAN AND THE COWLS.
THAT'S WHY YOU WERE CASING THE SCENE WHEN I FIRST RAN INTO YOU.
...SAYS YOU.
HE KEPT A SAFE DEPOSIT BOX. FRIENDS OF MINE HAVE THE INFORMATION.
THEY'VE HAD IT LONG ENOUGH.
FRIENDS, HUH. YOU WANT ME TO STEAL THIS INFORMATION AND SOLVE BILL TURNER'S MURDER?
THEY MUST LOVE YOU.
THEY DON'T WANT WHAT I WANT.
I THINK YOU MIGHT UNDERSTAND THAT.
I CAN'T BE ALL THINGS ANYMORE. GOTHAM WON'T HOLD.
SO YOU'RE DEPUTIZING?
YOU DITCHED ME. I COULD THROW THIS IN THE GARBAGE.
YOU COULD. BUT I'M BETTING YOU WON'T.
DON'T BET ON ME. I DON'T LIKE IT.
THEN...I'M HOPING YOU WON'T.
Idealistic and annoyed. Who knows if she'll make it.
But she's tenacious enough to hunt down the clues, and I need that.

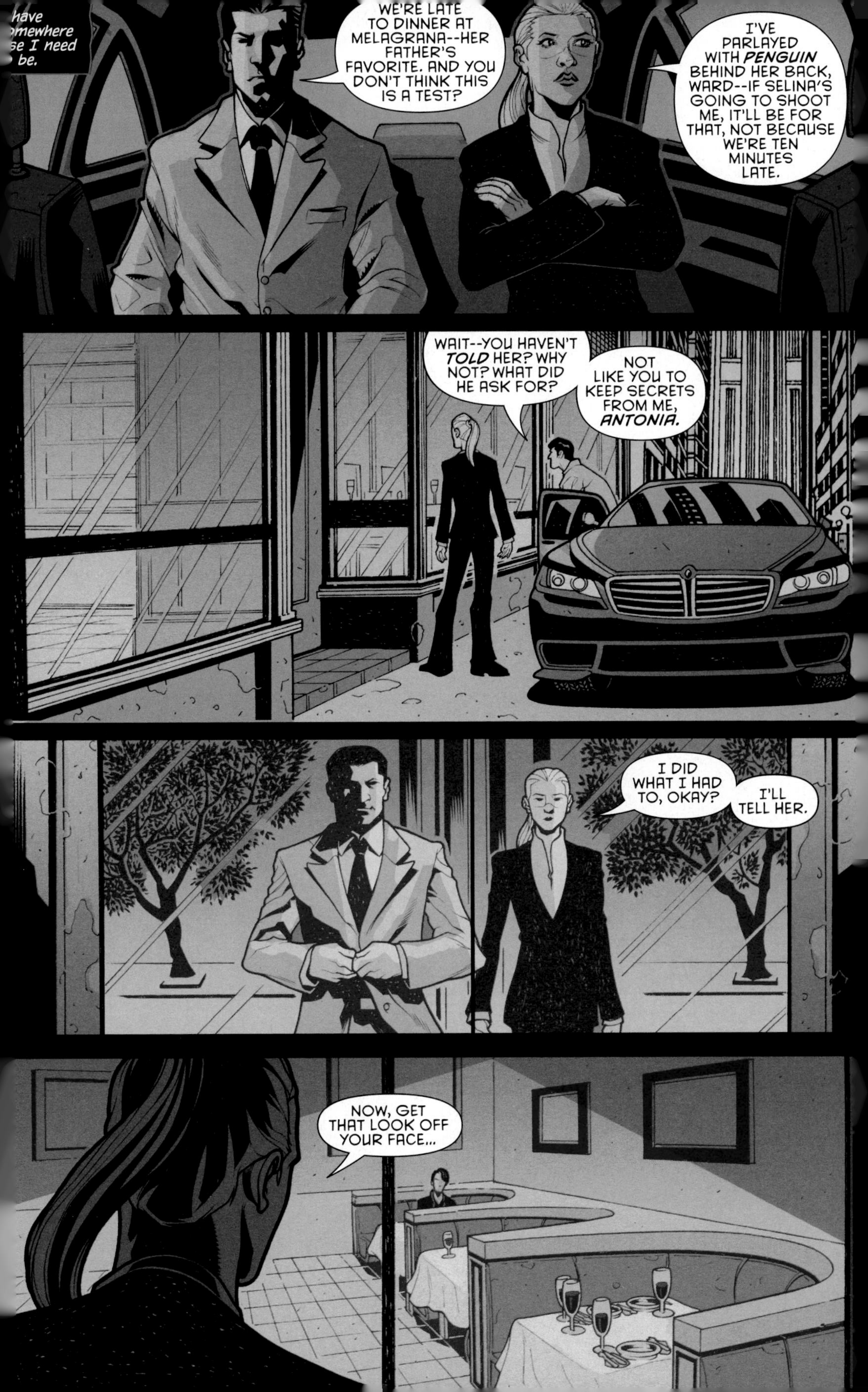

have
I need
be.
WE'RE LATE TO DINNER AT MELAGRANA--HER FATHER'S FAVORITE. AND YOU DON'T THINK THIS IS A TEST?
I'VE PARLAYED WITH *PENGUIN* BEHIND HER BACK, WARD--IF SELINA'S GOING TO SHOOT ME, IT'LL BE FOR THAT, NOT BECAUSE WE'RE TEN MINUTES LATE.
WAIT--YOU HAVEN'T *TOLD* HER? WHY NOT? WHAT DID HE ASK FOR?
NOT LIKE YOU TO KEEP SECRETS FROM ME, *ANTONIA.*
I DID WHAT I HAD TO, OKAY?
I'LL TELL HER.
NOW, GET THAT LOOK OFF YOUR FACE...

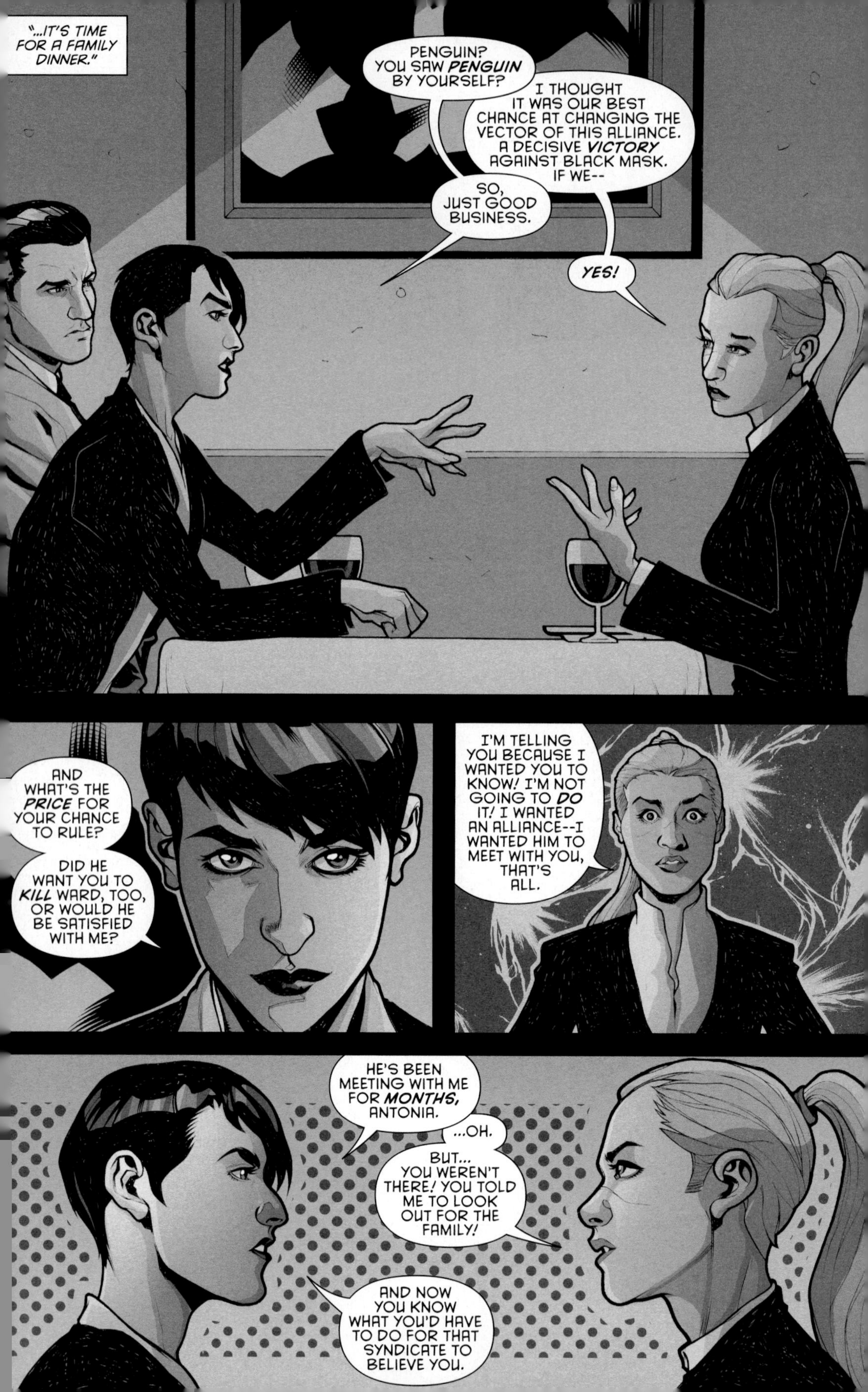
"...IT'S TIME FOR A FAMILY DINNER."
PENGUIN? YOU SAW PENGUIN BY YOURSELF?
I THOUGHT IT WAS OUR BEST CHANCE AT CHANGING THE VECTOR OF THIS ALLIANCE. A DECISIVE VICTORY AGAINST BLACK MASK. IF WE--
SO, JUST GOOD BUSINESS.
YES!
AND WHAT'S THE PRICE FOR YOUR CHANCE TO RULE?
DID HE WANT YOU TO KILL WARD, TOO, OR WOULD HE BE SATISFIED WITH ME?
I'M TELLING YOU BECAUSE I WANTED YOU TO KNOW! I'M NOT GOING TO DO IT! I WANTED AN ALLIANCE--I WANTED HIM TO MEET WITH YOU, THAT'S ALL.
HE'S BEEN MEETING WITH ME FOR MONTHS, ANTONIA.
...OH.
BUT... YOU WEREN'T THERE! YOU TOLD ME TO LOOK OUT FOR THE FAMILY!
AND NOW YOU KNOW WHAT YOU'D HAVE TO DO FOR THAT SYNDICATE TO BELIEVE YOU.

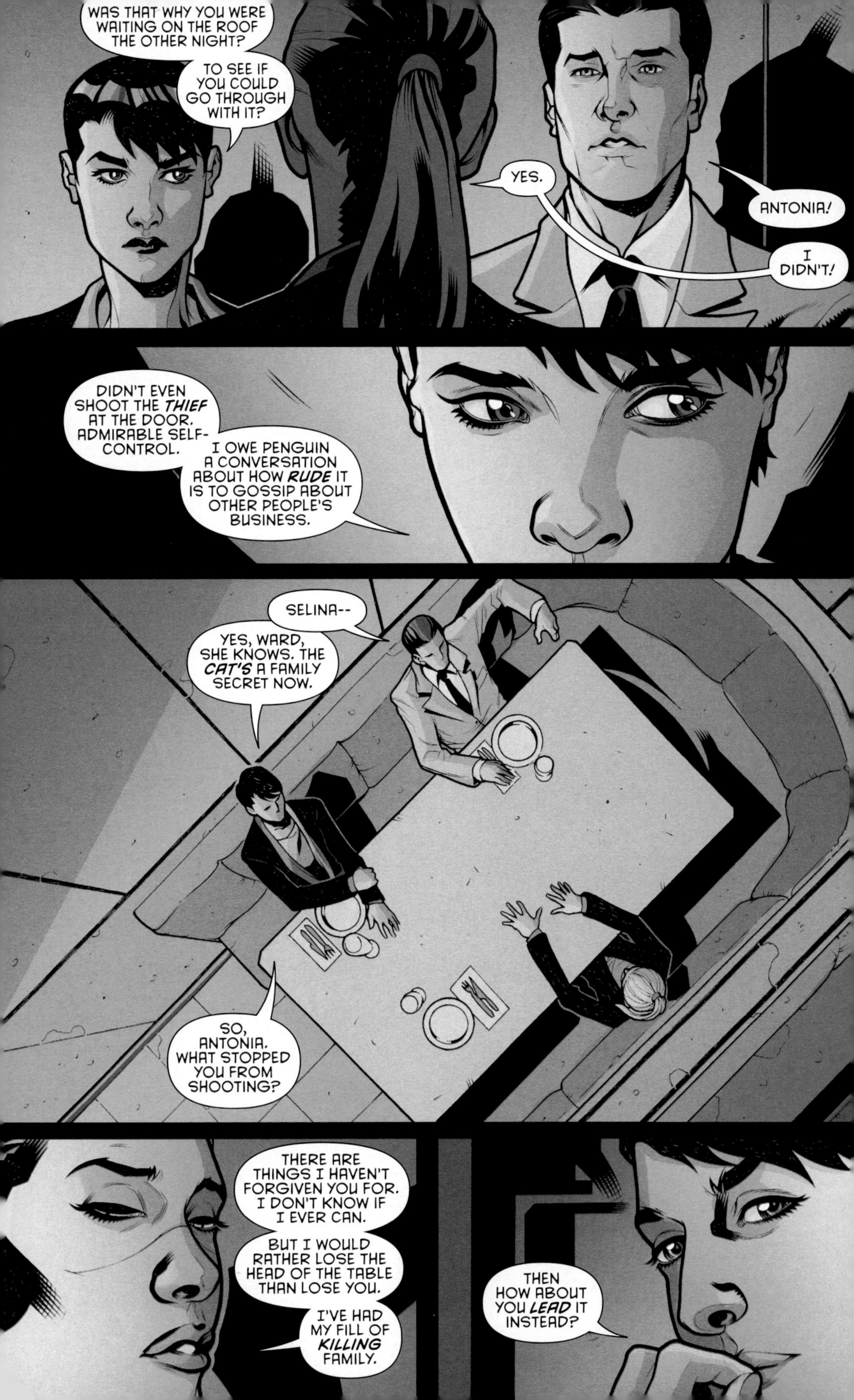
WAS THAT WHY YOU WERE WAITING ON THE ROOF THE OTHER NIGHT?
TO SEE IF YOU COULD GO THROUGH WITH IT?
YES.
ANTONIA!
I DIDN'T!
DIDN'T EVEN SHOOT THE *THIEF* AT THE DOOR. ADMIRABLE SELF-CONTROL.
I OWE PENGUIN A CONVERSATION ABOUT HOW *RUDE* IT IS TO GOSSIP ABOUT OTHER PEOPLE'S BUSINESS.
SELINA--
YES, WARD, SHE KNOWS. THE *CAT'S* A FAMILY SECRET NOW.
SO, ANTONIA. WHAT STOPPED YOU FROM SHOOTING?
THERE ARE THINGS I HAVEN'T FORGIVEN YOU FOR. I DON'T KNOW IF I EVER CAN.
BUT I WOULD RATHER LOSE THE HEAD OF THE TABLE THAN LOSE YOU.
I'VE HAD MY FILL OF *KILLING* FAMILY.
THEN HOW ABOUT YOU *LEAD* IT INSTEAD?

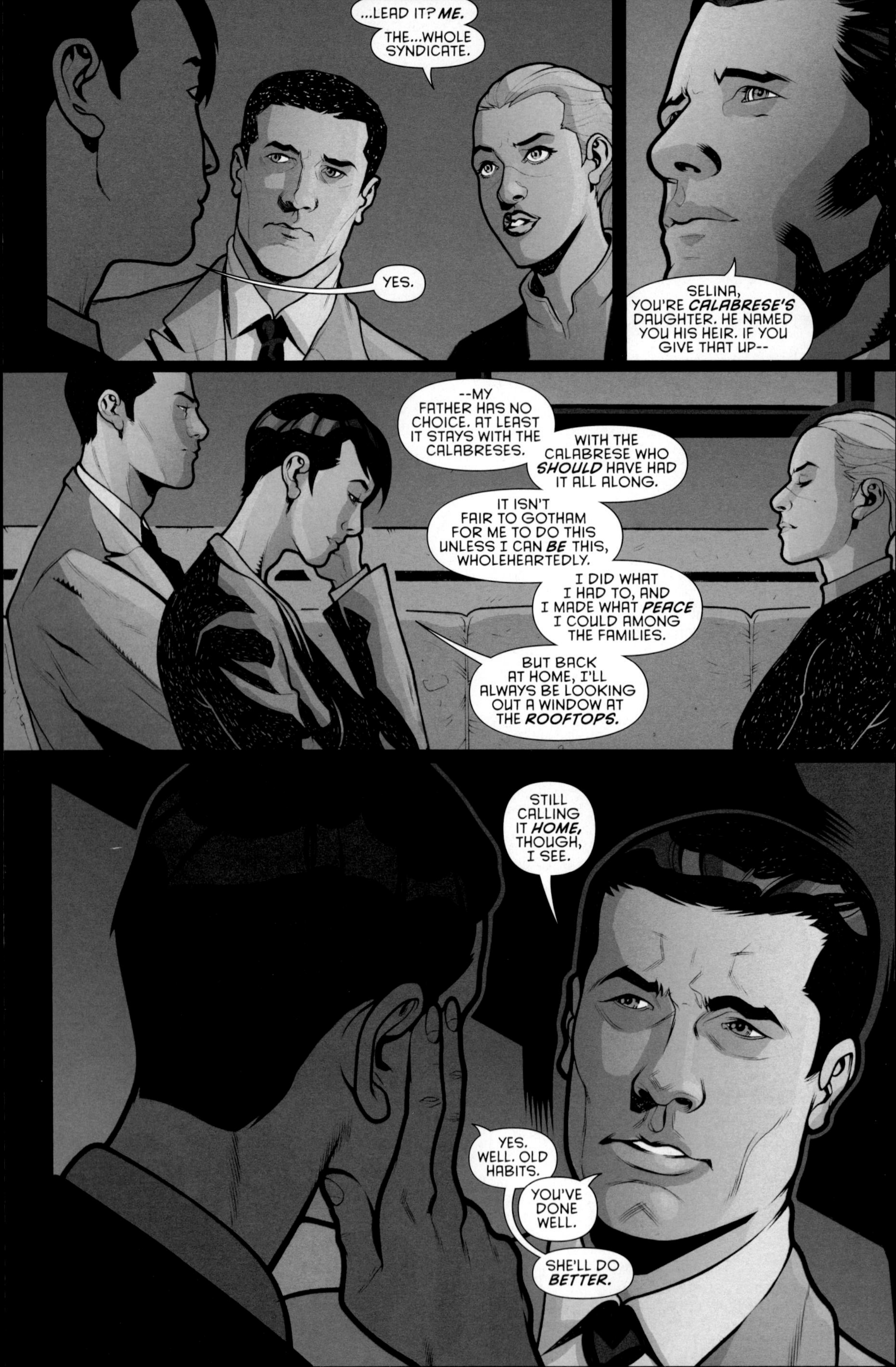
...LEAD IT? ME.
THE...WHOLE SYNDICATE.
YES.
SELINA, YOU'RE CALABRESE'S DAUGHTER. HE NAMED YOU HIS HEIR. IF YOU GIVE THAT UP--
--MY FATHER HAS NO CHOICE. AT LEAST IT STAYS WITH THE CALABRESES.
WITH THE CALABRESE WHO SHOULD HAVE HAD IT ALL ALONG.
IT ISN'T FAIR TO GOTHAM FOR ME TO DO THIS UNLESS I CAN BE THIS, WHOLEHEARTEDLY.
I DID WHAT I HAD TO, AND I MADE WHAT PEACE I COULD AMONG THE FAMILIES.
BUT BACK AT HOME, I'LL ALWAYS BE LOOKING OUT A WINDOW AT THE ROOFTOPS.
STILL CALLING IT HOME, THOUGH, I SEE.
YES. WELL. OLD HABITS.
YOU'VE DONE WELL.
SHE'LL DO BETTER.

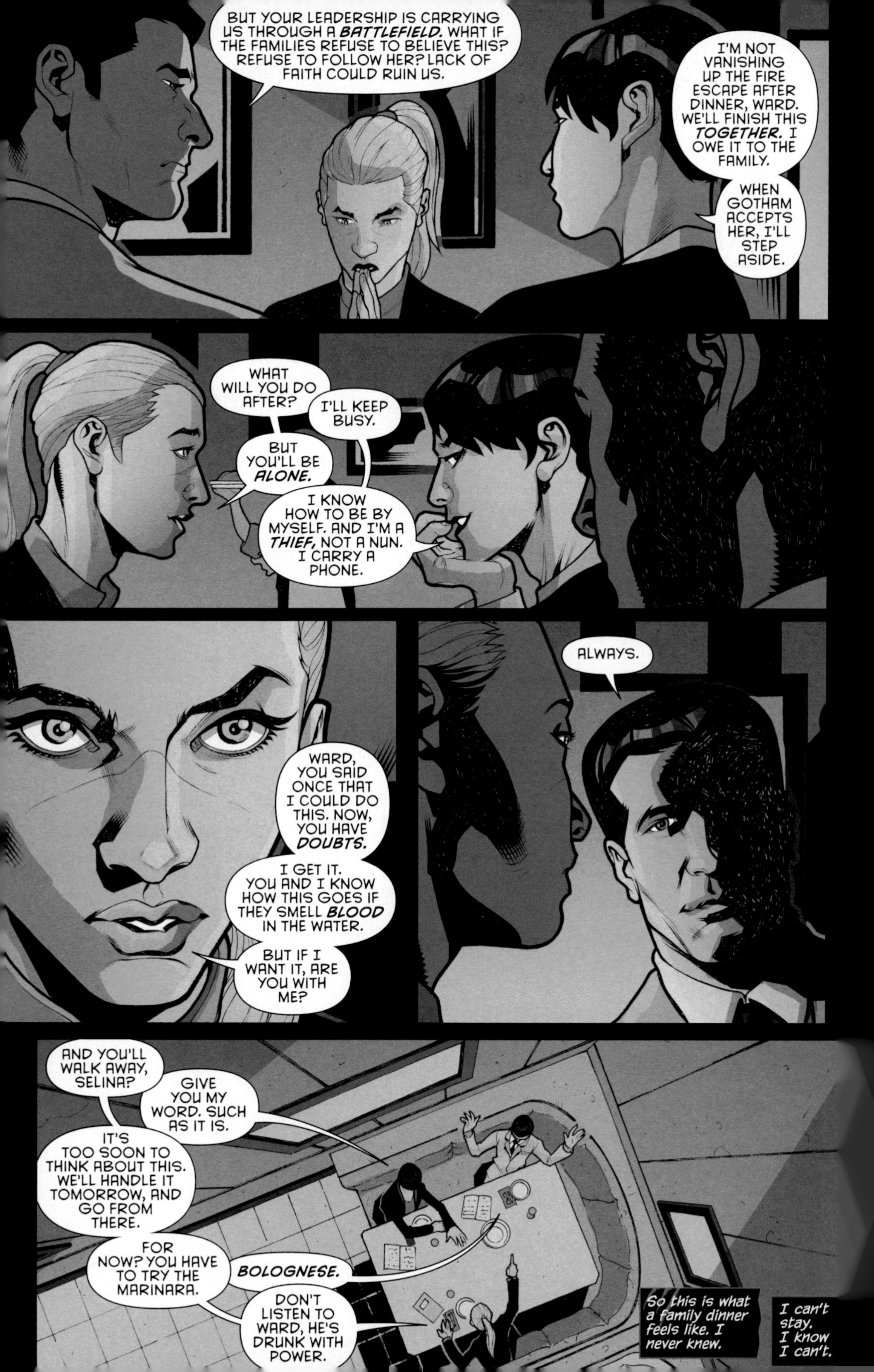
BUT YOUR LEADERSHIP IS CARRYING US THROUGH A BATTLEFIELD. WHAT IF THE FAMILIES REFUSE TO BELIEVE THIS? REFUSE TO FOLLOW HER? LACK OF FAITH COULD RUIN US.
I'M NOT VANISHING UP THE FIRE ESCAPE AFTER DINNER, WARD. WE'LL FINISH THIS TOGETHER. I OWE IT TO THE FAMILY.
WHEN GOTHAM ACCEPTS HER, I'LL STEP ASIDE.
WHAT WILL YOU DO AFTER?
I'LL KEEP BUSY.
BUT YOU'LL BE ALONE.
I KNOW HOW TO BE BY MYSELF. AND I'M A THIEF, NOT A NUN. I CARRY A PHONE.
WARD, YOU SAID ONCE THAT I COULD DO THIS. NOW, YOU HAVE DOUBTS.
I GET IT. YOU AND I KNOW HOW THIS GOES IF THEY SMELL BLOOD IN THE WATER.
BUT IF I WANT IT, ARE YOU WITH ME?
ALWAYS.
AND YOU'LL WALK AWAY, SELINA?
GIVE YOU MY WORD. SUCH AS IT IS.
IT'S TOO SOON TO THINK ABOUT THIS. WE'LL HANDLE IT TOMORROW, AND GO FROM THERE.
FOR NOW? YOU HAVE TO TRY THE MARINARA.
BOLOGNESE.
DON'T LISTEN TO WARD, HE'S DRUNK WITH POWER.
So this is what a family dinner feels like. I never knew.
I can't stay. I know I can't.

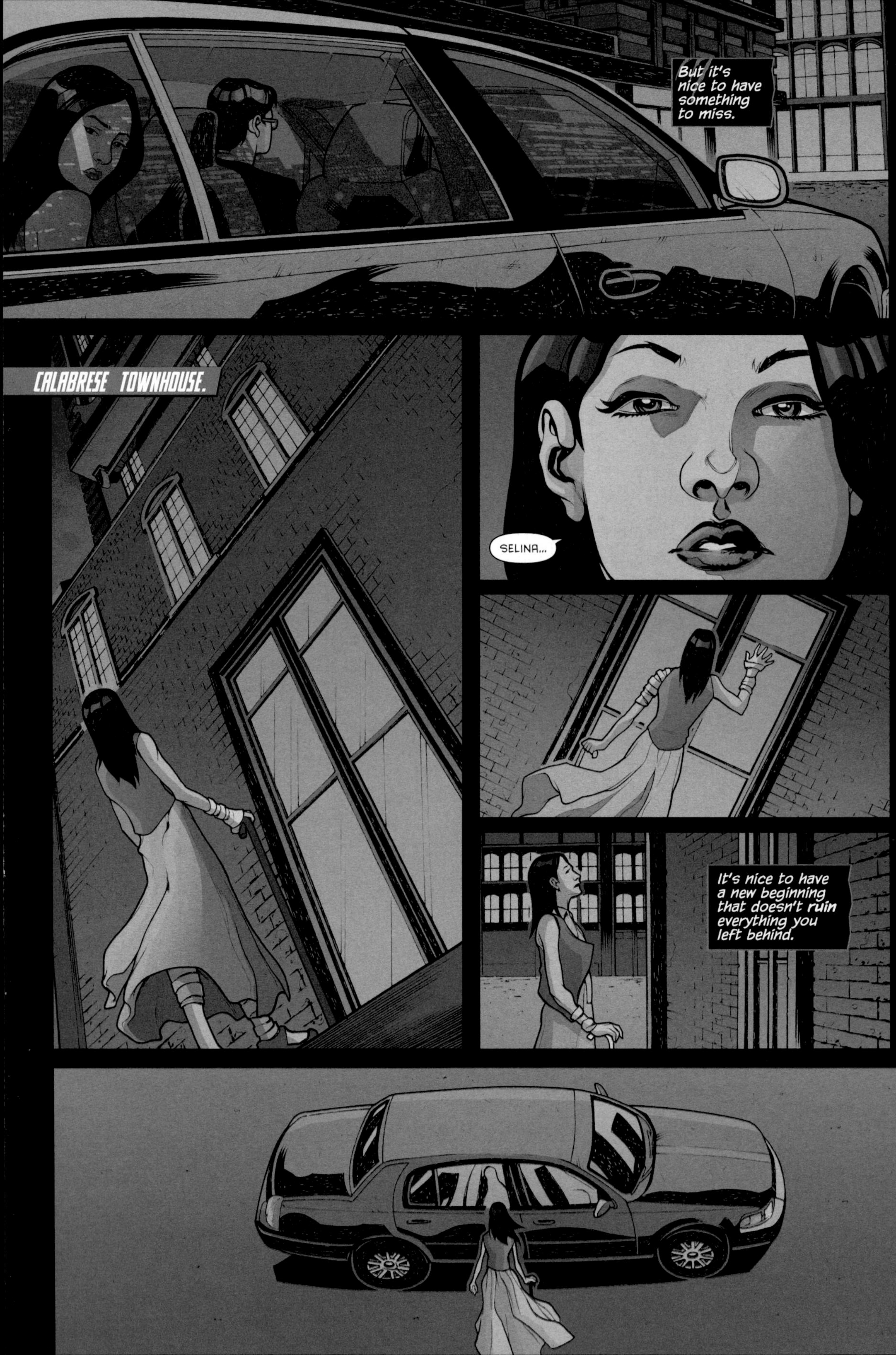

But it's nice to have something to miss.
CALABRESE TOWNHOUSE.
SELINA...
It's nice to have a new beginning that doesn't ruin everything you left behind.

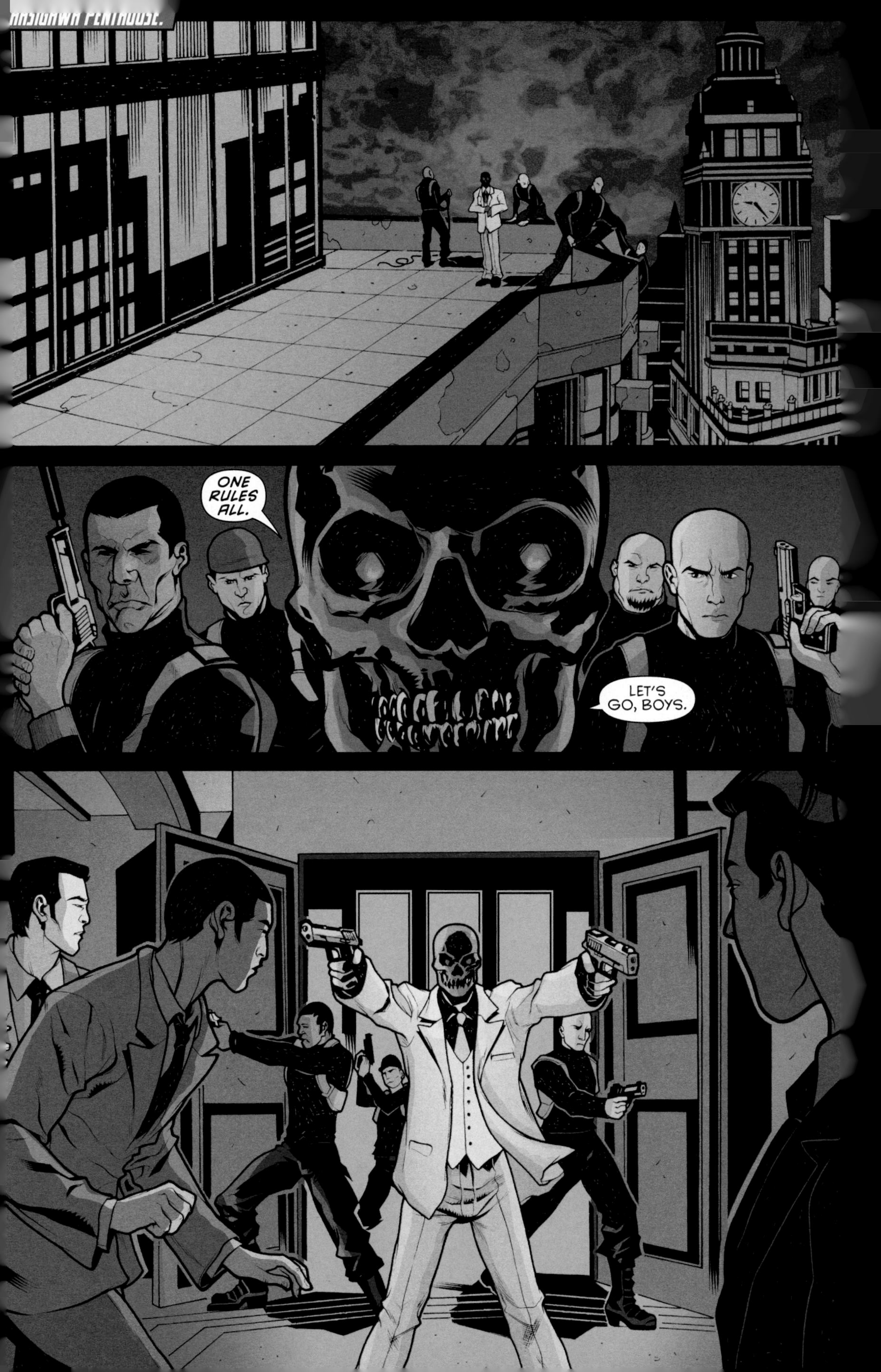
HASIGAWA PENTHOUSE.
ONE RULES ALL.
LET'S GO, BOYS.

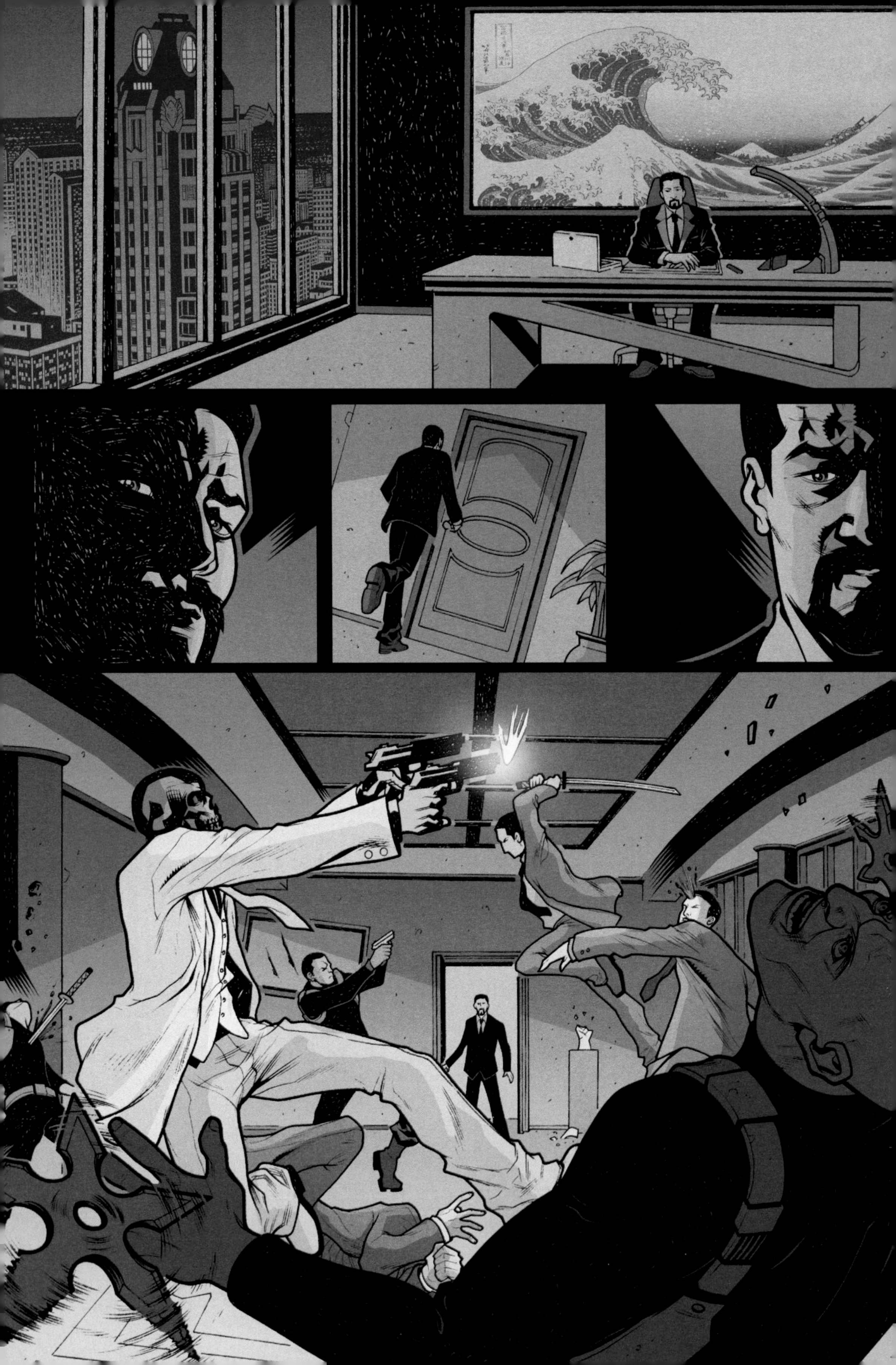

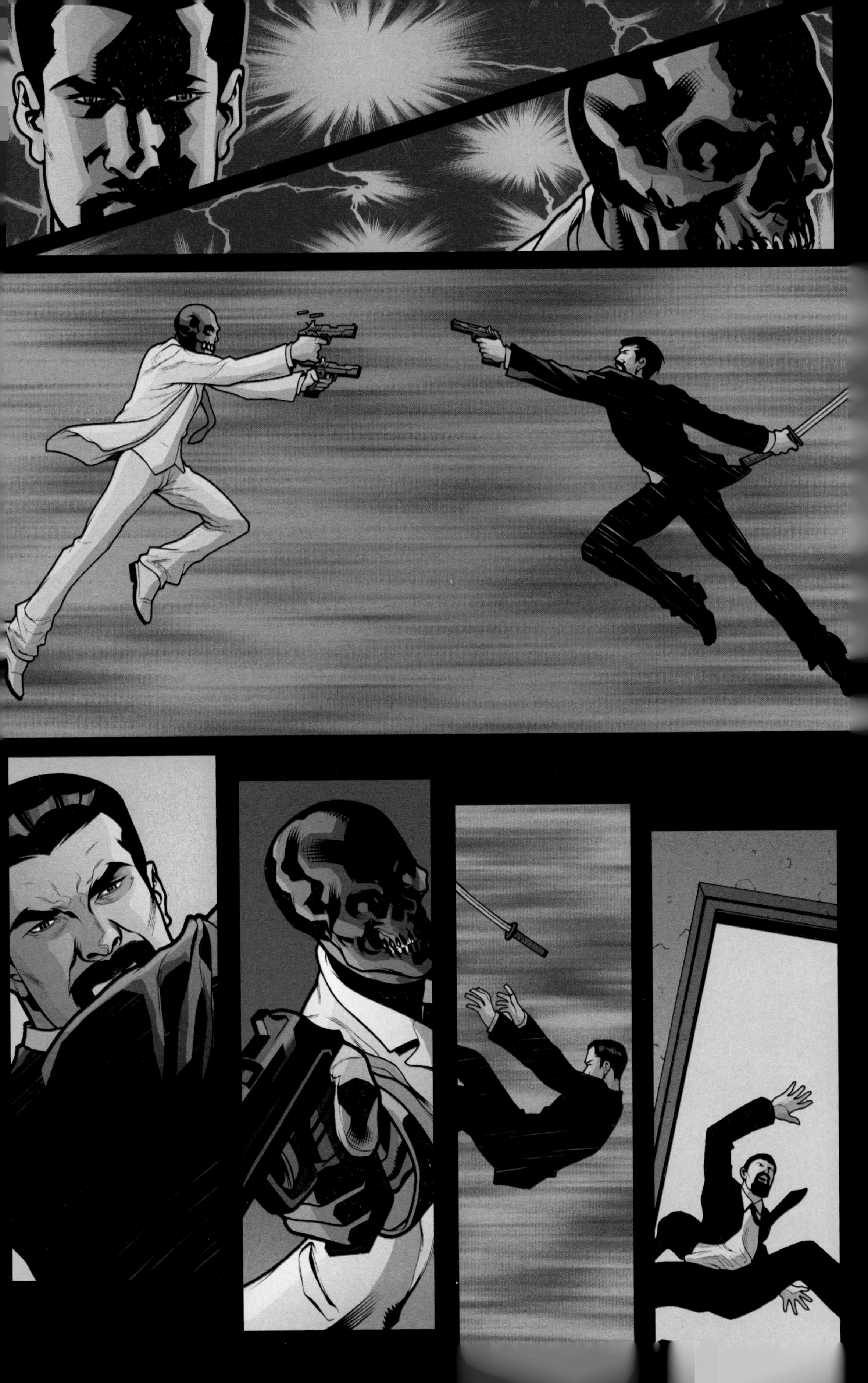

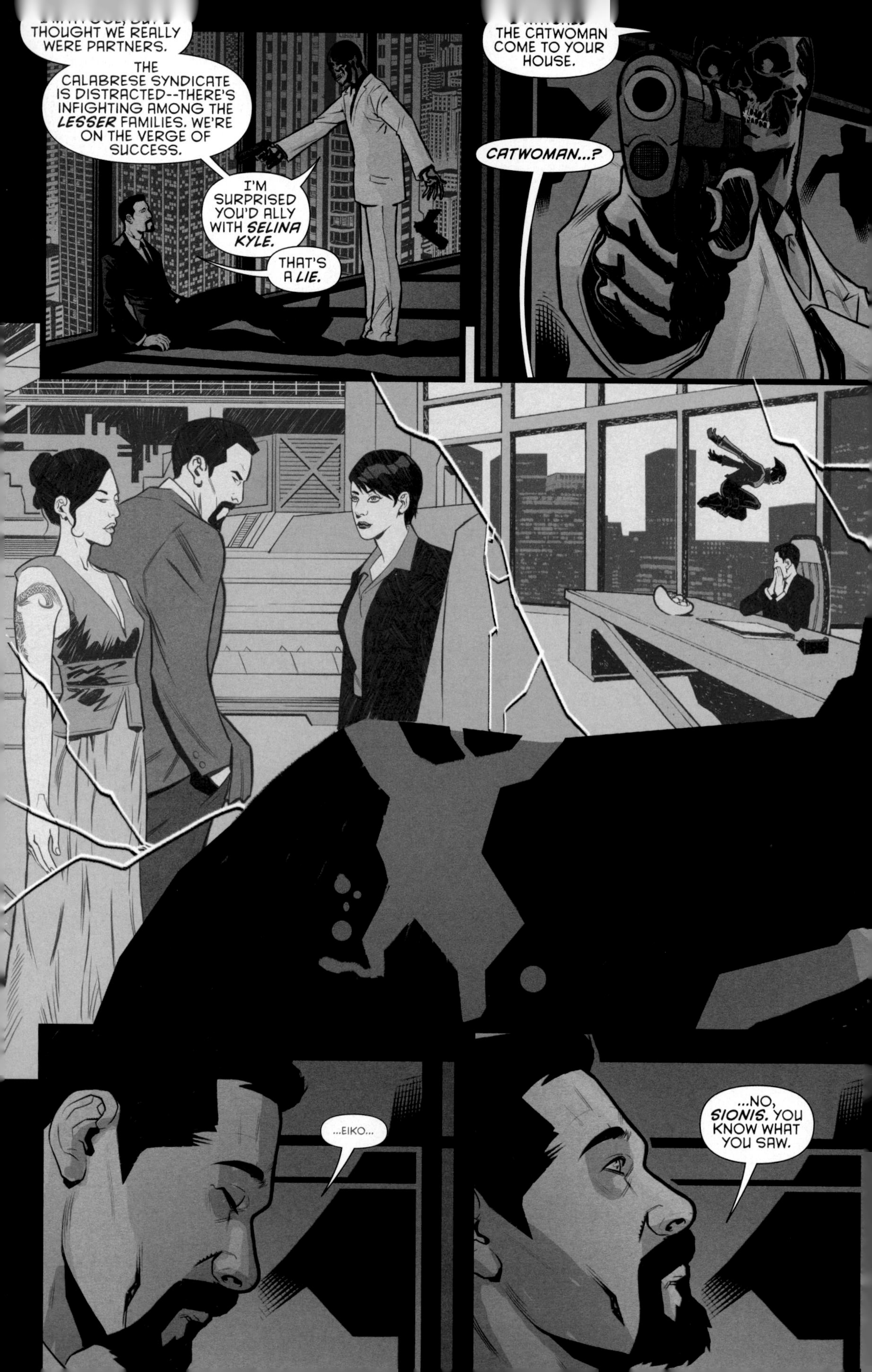
THOUGHT WE REALLY WERE PARTNERS.
THE CALABRESE SYNDICATE IS DISTRACTED--THERE'S INFIGHTING AMONG THE *LESSER* FAMILIES. WE'RE ON THE VERGE OF SUCCESS.
I'M SURPRISED YOU'D ALLY WITH *SELINA KYLE.*
THAT'S A *LIE.*
THE CATWOMAN COME TO YOUR HOUSE.
CATWOMAN...?
...EIKO...
...NO, *SIONIS.* YOU KNOW WHAT YOU SAW.

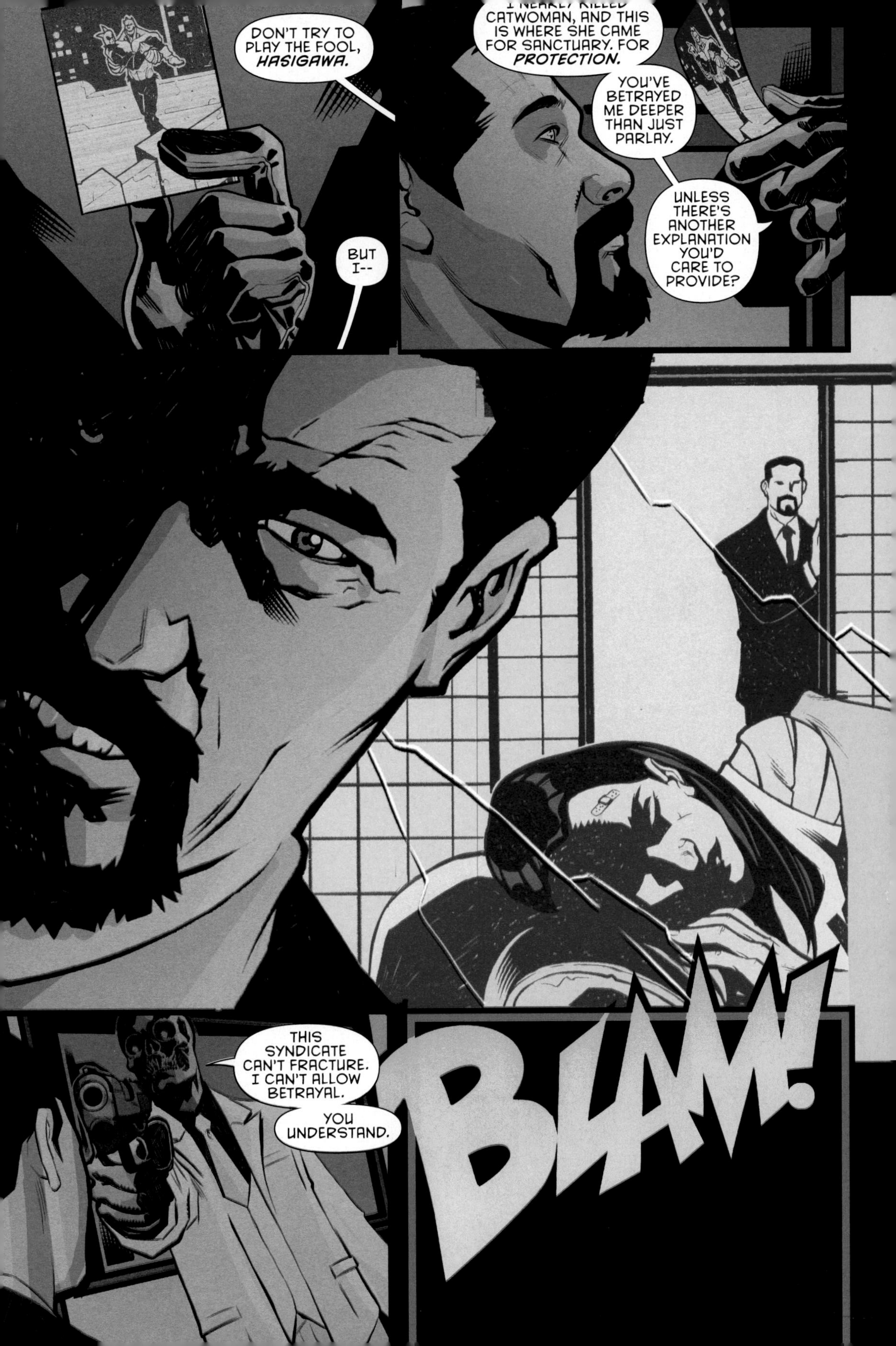
DON'T TRY TO PLAY THE FOOL, HASIGAWA.
BUT I--
CATWOMAN, AND THIS IS WHERE SHE CAME FOR SANCTUARY. FOR PROTECTION.
YOU'VE BETRAYED ME DEEPER THAN JUST PARLAY.
UNLESS THERE'S ANOTHER EXPLANATION YOU'D CARE TO PROVIDE?
THIS SYNDICATE CAN'T FRACTURE. I CAN'T ALLOW BETRAYAL.
YOU UNDERSTAND.
BLAM!

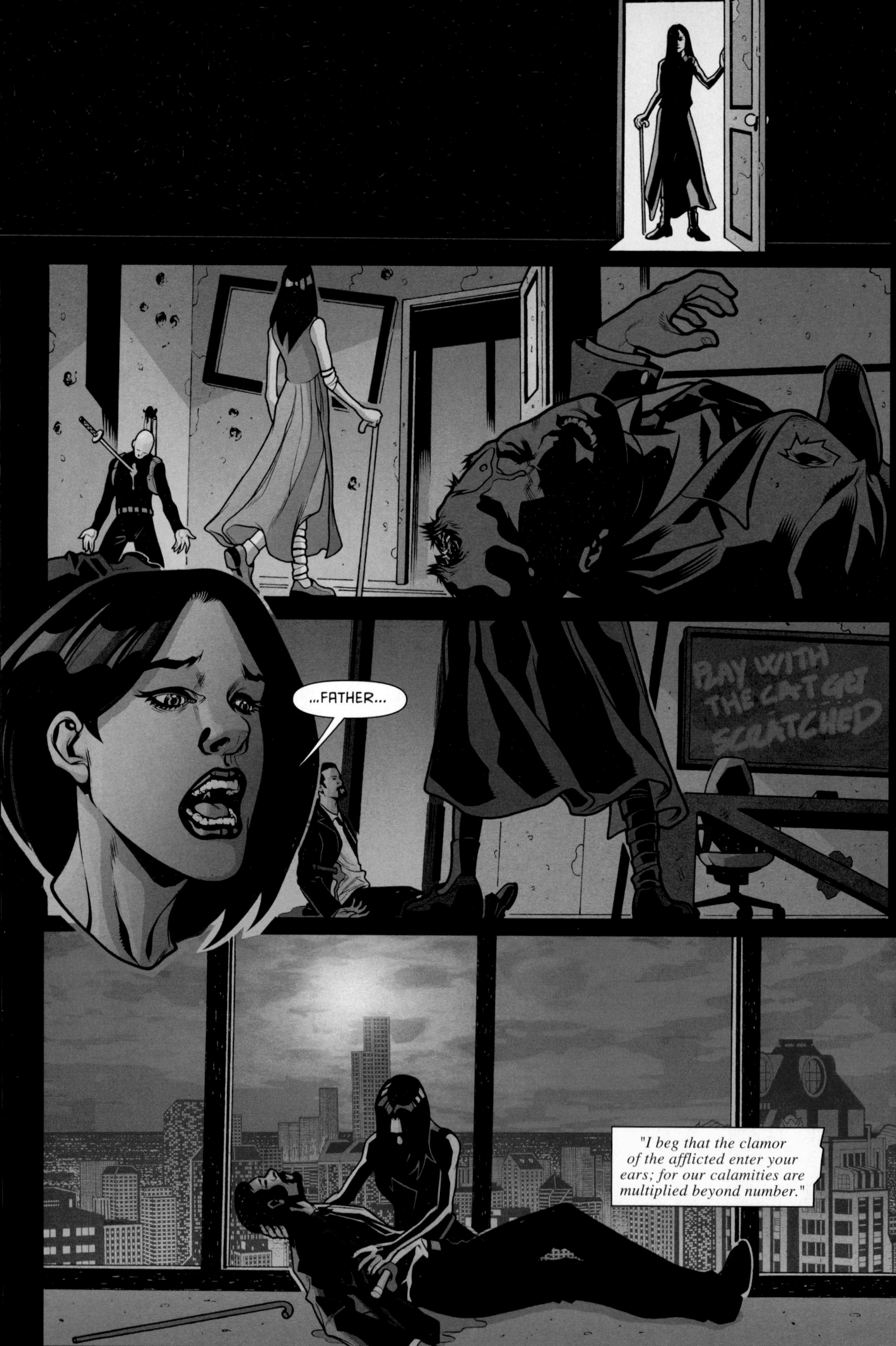
...FATHER...
PLAY WITH THE CAT GET SCRATCHED
"I beg that the clamor of the afflicted enter your ears; for our calamities are multiplied beyond number."

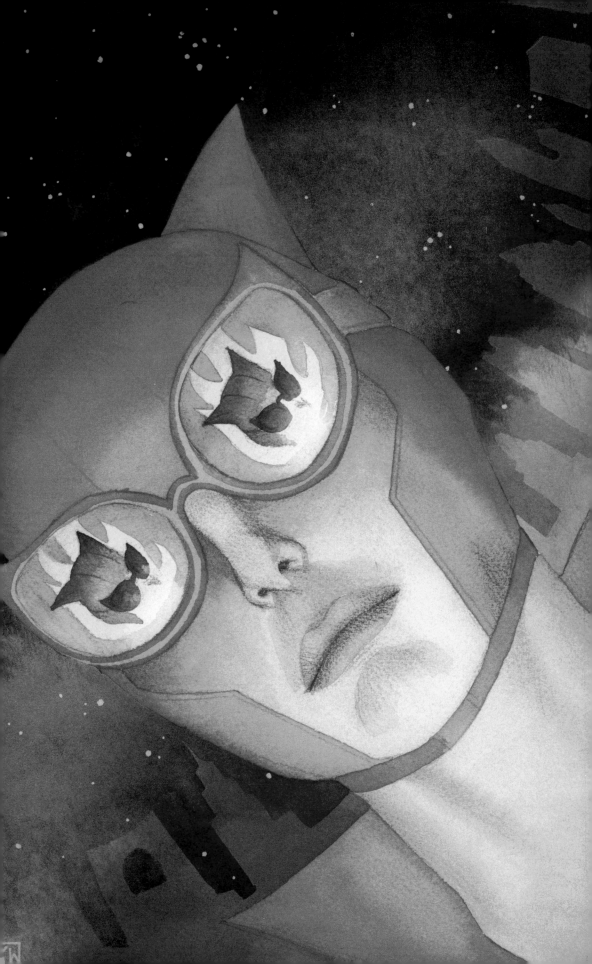

THE DAUGHTER OF ONE WHO HAD NO FEAR

GENEVIEVE VALENTINE writer DAVID MESSINA penciller GAETANO CARLUCCI inker LEE LOUGHRIDGE colorist TRAVIS LANHAM letterer cover art by KEVIN WADA

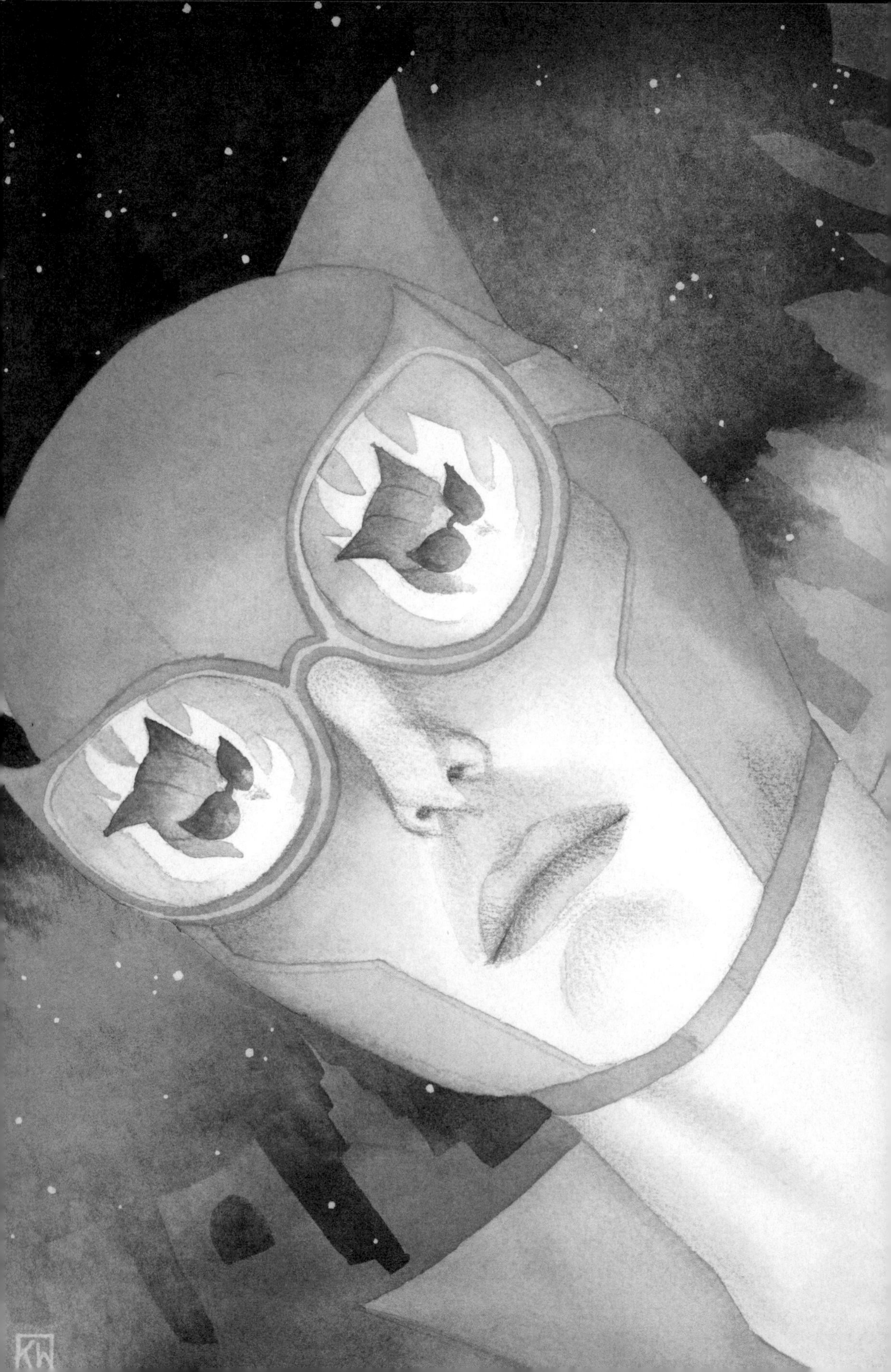
KW

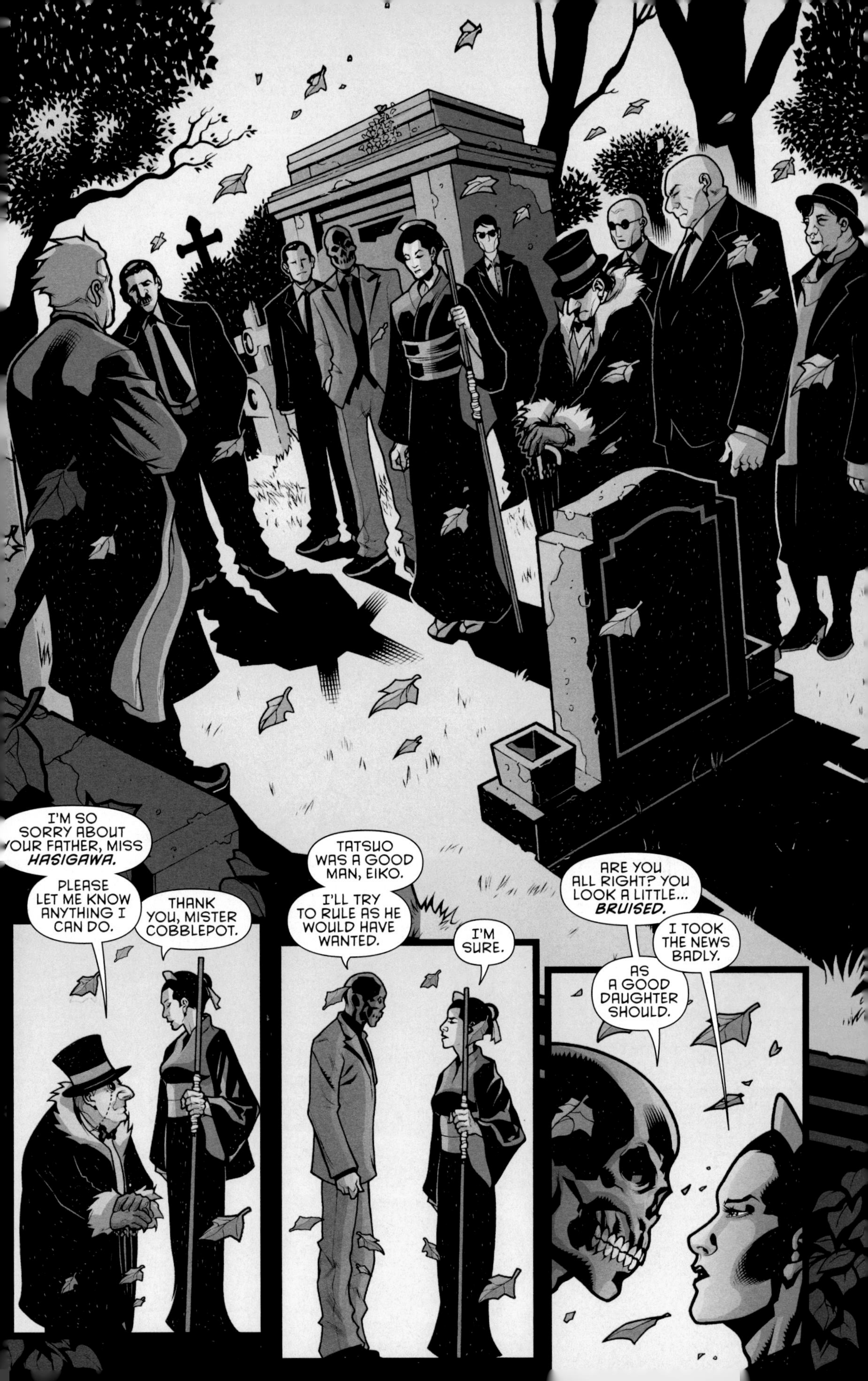
I'M SO SORRY ABOUT YOUR FATHER, MISS HASIGAWA.
PLEASE LET ME KNOW ANYTHING I CAN DO.
THANK YOU, MISTER COBBLEPOT.
TATSUO WAS A GOOD MAN, EIKO.
I'LL TRY TO RULE AS HE WOULD HAVE WANTED.
I'M SURE.
ARE YOU ALL RIGHT? YOU LOOK A LITTLE... BRUISED.
I TOOK THE NEWS BADLY.
AS A GOOD DAUGHTER SHOULD.

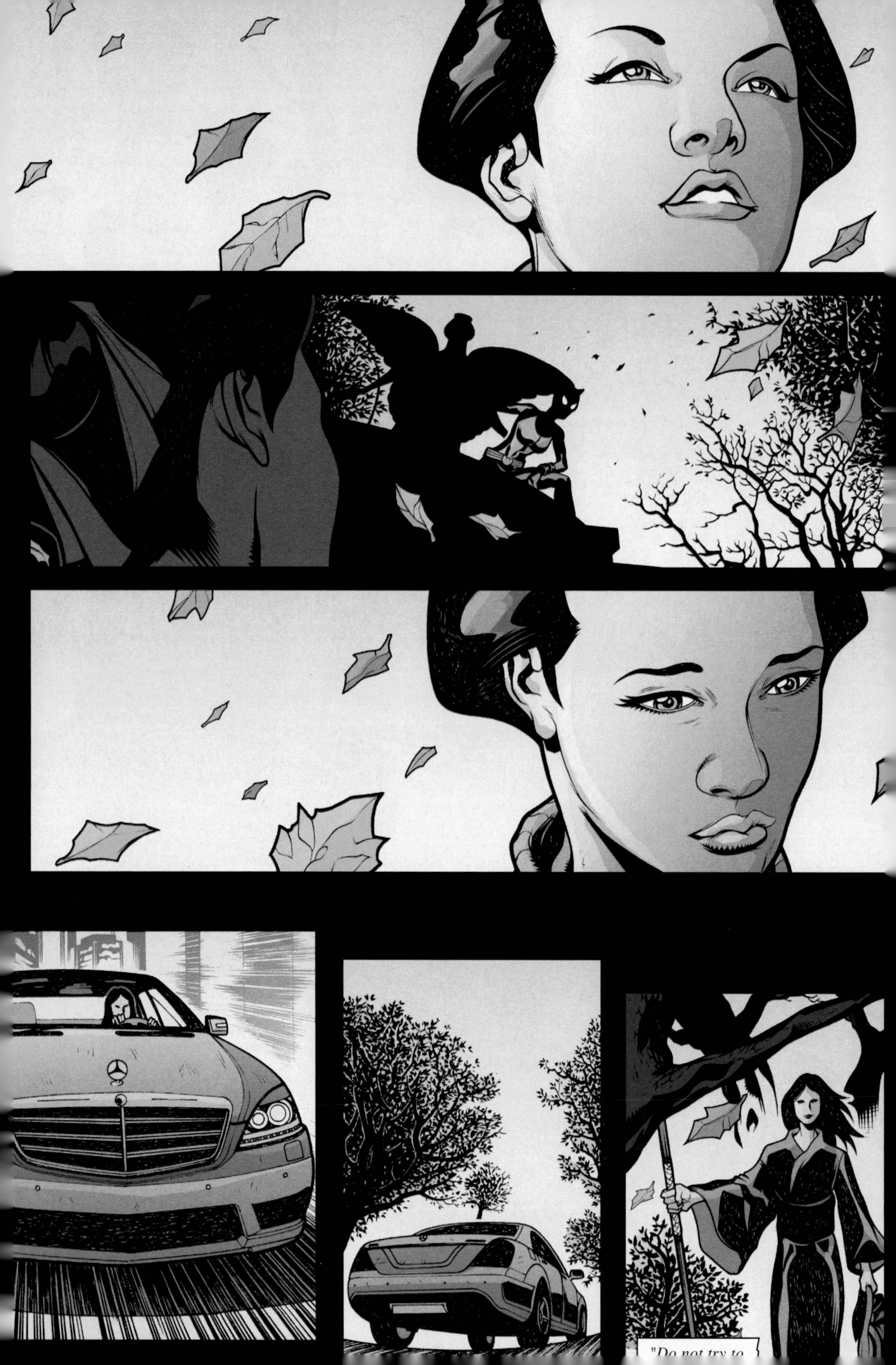
"Do not try to

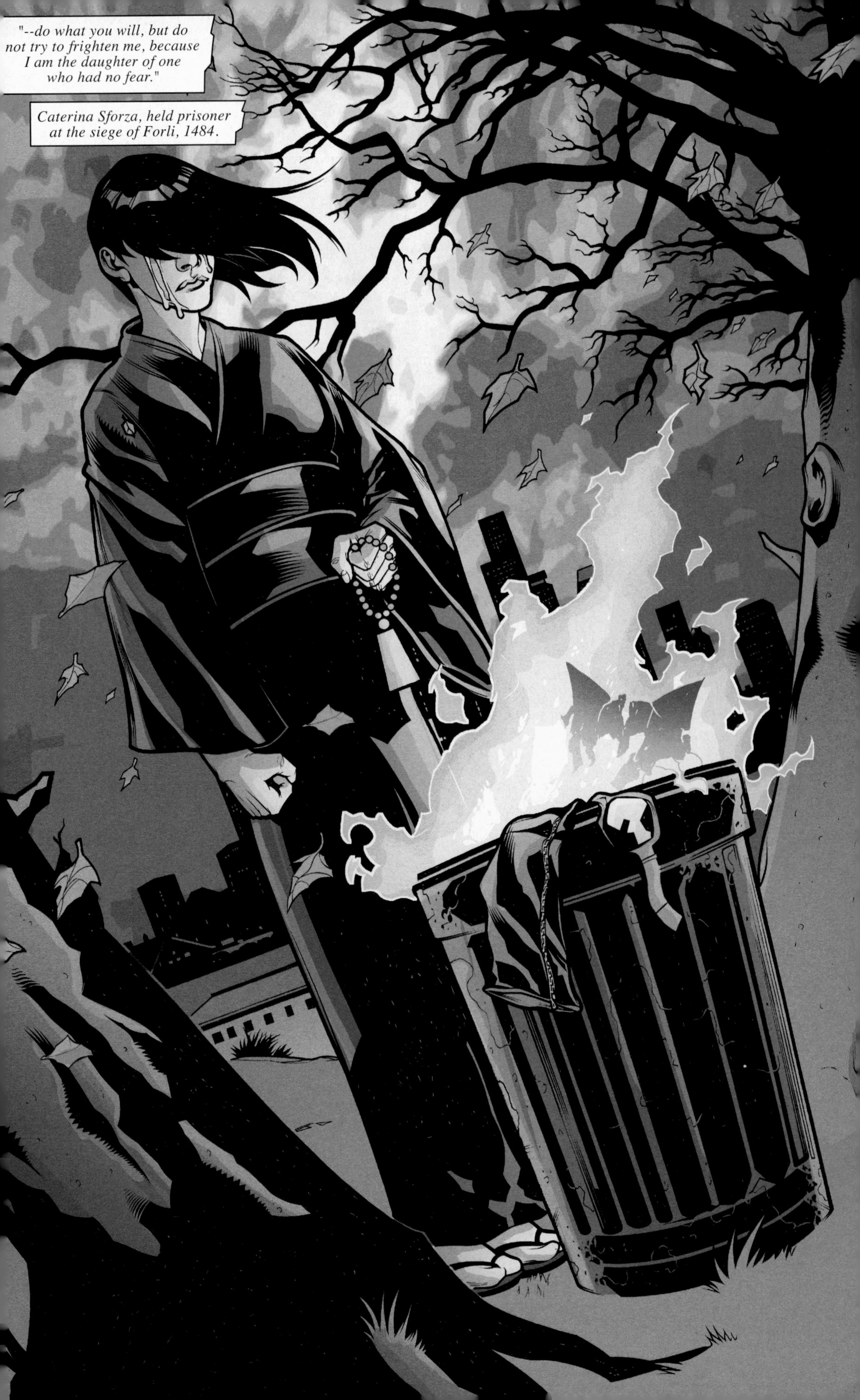
"--do what you will, but do not try to frighten me, because I am the daughter of one who had no fear."
Caterina Sforza, held prisoner at the siege of Forli, 1484.

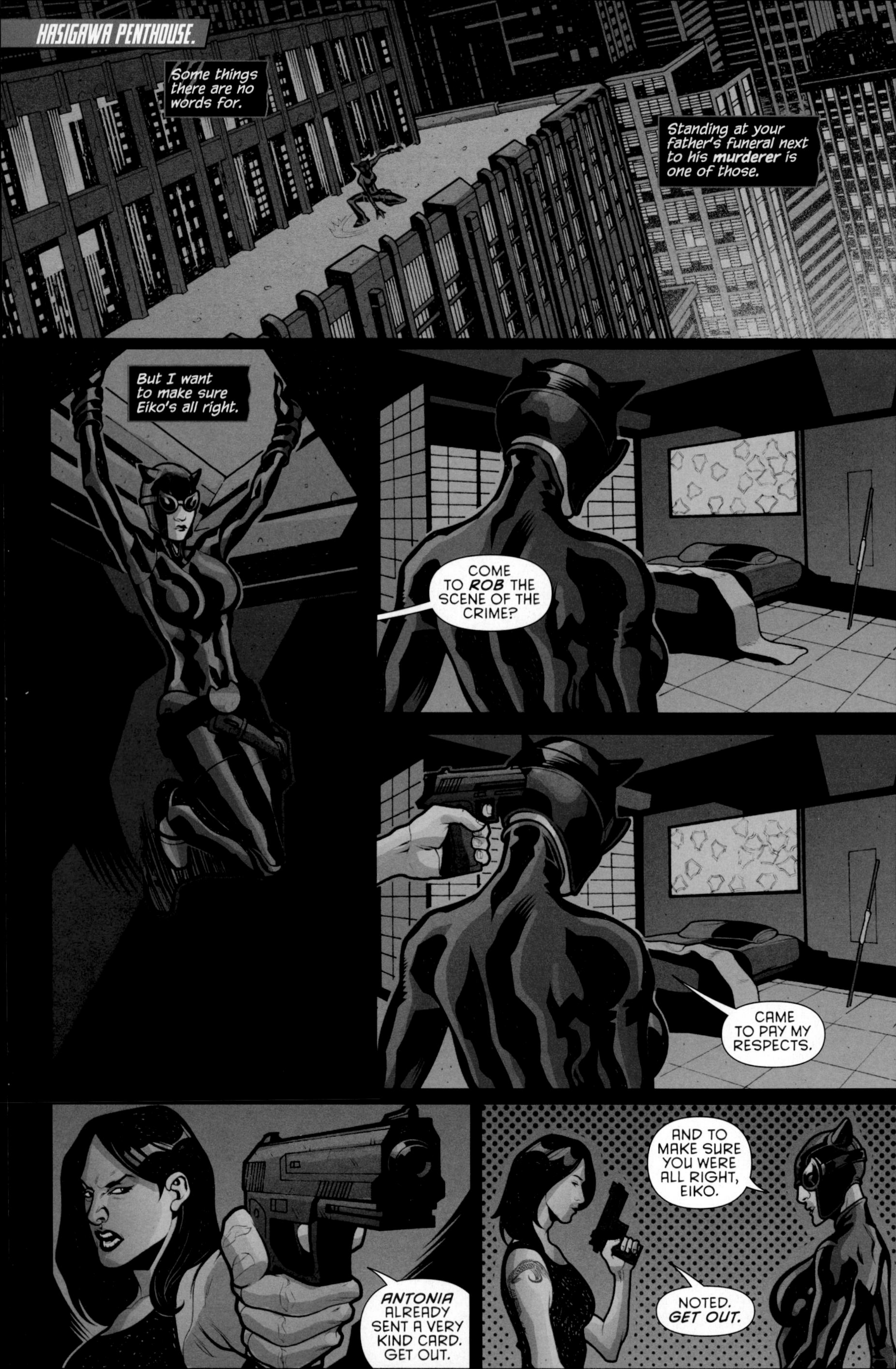
HASIGAWA PENTHOUSE.
Some things there are no words for.
Standing at your father's funeral next to his murderer is one of those.
But I want to make sure Eiko's all right.
COME TO ROB THE SCENE OF THE CRIME?
CAME TO PAY MY RESPECTS.
ANTONIA ALREADY SENT A VERY KIND CARD. GET OUT.
AND TO MAKE SURE YOU WERE ALL RIGHT, EIKO.
NOTED. GET OUT.

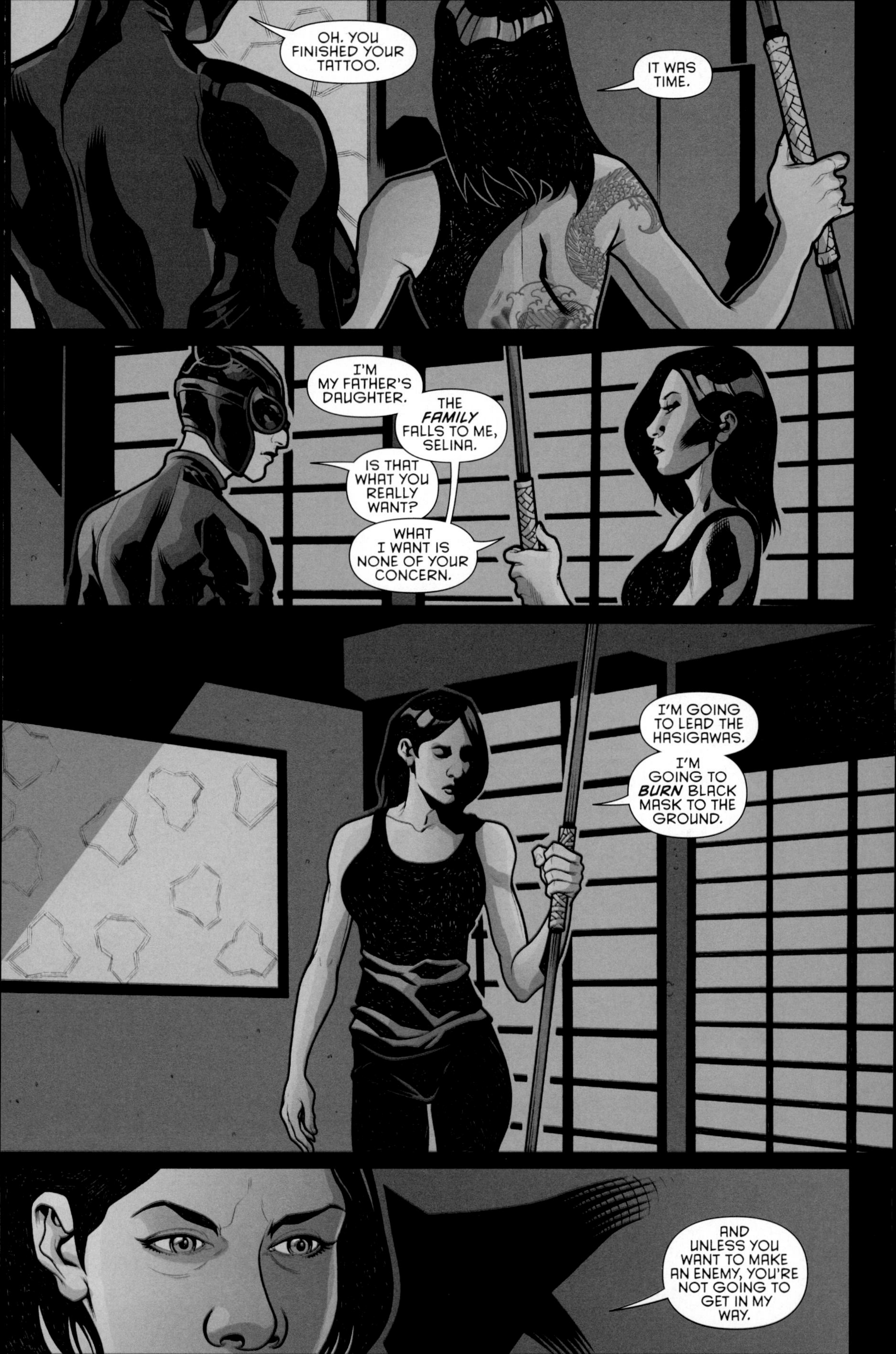
OH. YOU FINISHED YOUR TATTOO.
IT WAS TIME.
I'M MY FATHER'S DAUGHTER.
THE *FAMILY* FALLS TO ME, SELINA.
IS THAT WHAT YOU REALLY WANT?
WHAT I WANT IS NONE OF YOUR CONCERN.
I'M GOING TO LEAD THE HASIGAWAS.
I'M GOING TO ***BURN*** BLACK MASK TO THE GROUND.
AND UNLESS YOU WANT TO MAKE AN ENEMY, YOU'RE NOT GOING TO GET IN MY WAY.

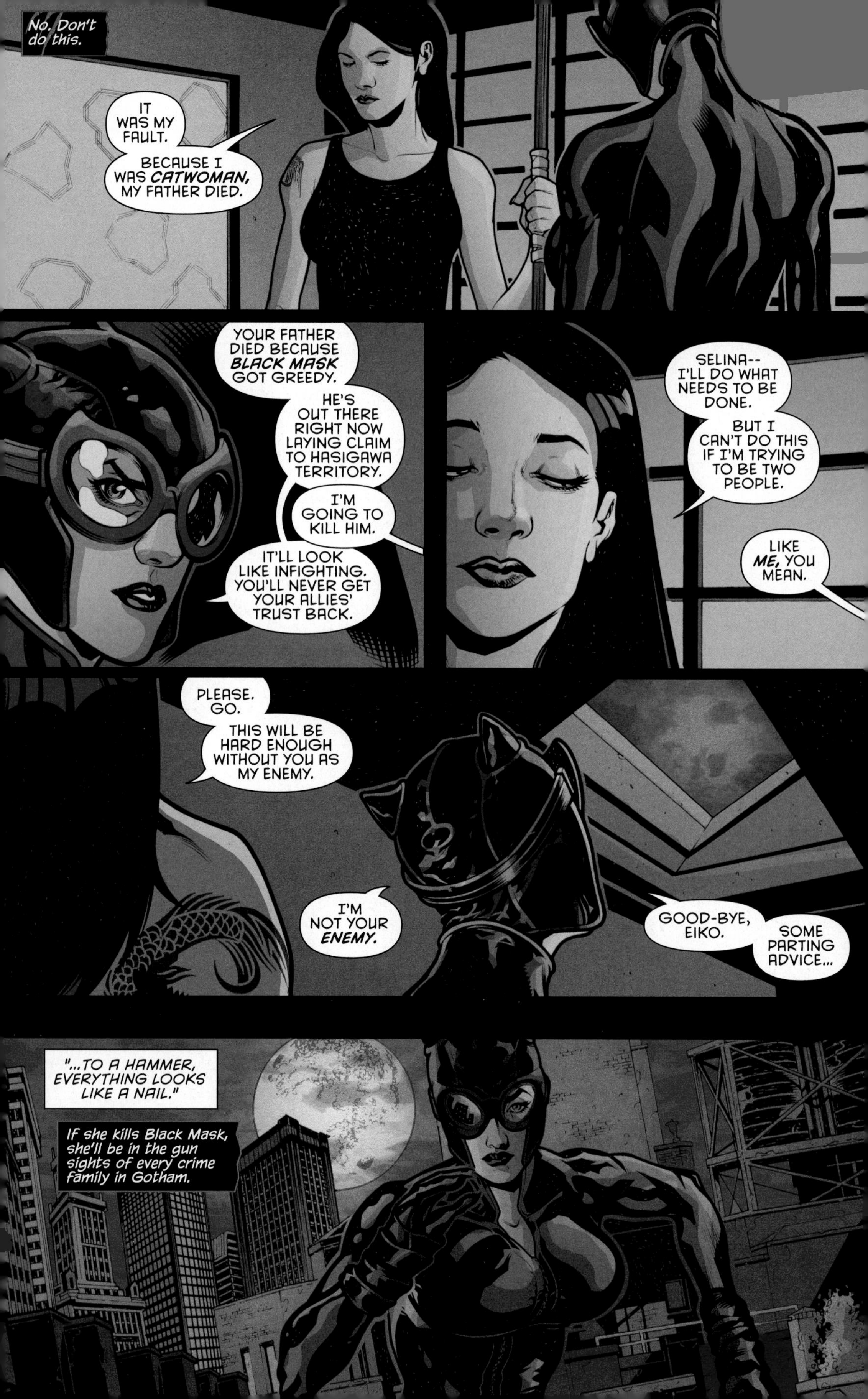
No. Don't do this.
IT WAS MY FAULT.
BECAUSE I WAS CATWOMAN, MY FATHER DIED.
YOUR FATHER DIED BECAUSE BLACK MASK GOT GREEDY.
HE'S OUT THERE RIGHT NOW LAYING CLAIM TO HASIGAWA TERRITORY.
I'M GOING TO KILL HIM.
IT'LL LOOK LIKE INFIGHTING. YOU'LL NEVER GET YOUR ALLIES' TRUST BACK.
SELINA-- I'LL DO WHAT NEEDS TO BE DONE.
BUT I CAN'T DO THIS IF I'M TRYING TO BE TWO PEOPLE.
LIKE ME, YOU MEAN.
PLEASE. GO.
THIS WILL BE HARD ENOUGH WITHOUT YOU AS MY ENEMY.
I'M NOT YOUR ENEMY.
GOOD-BYE, EIKO.
SOME PARTING ADVICE...
"...TO A HAMMER, EVERYTHING LOOKS LIKE A NAIL."
If she kills Black Mask, she'll be in the gun sights of every crime family in Gotham.

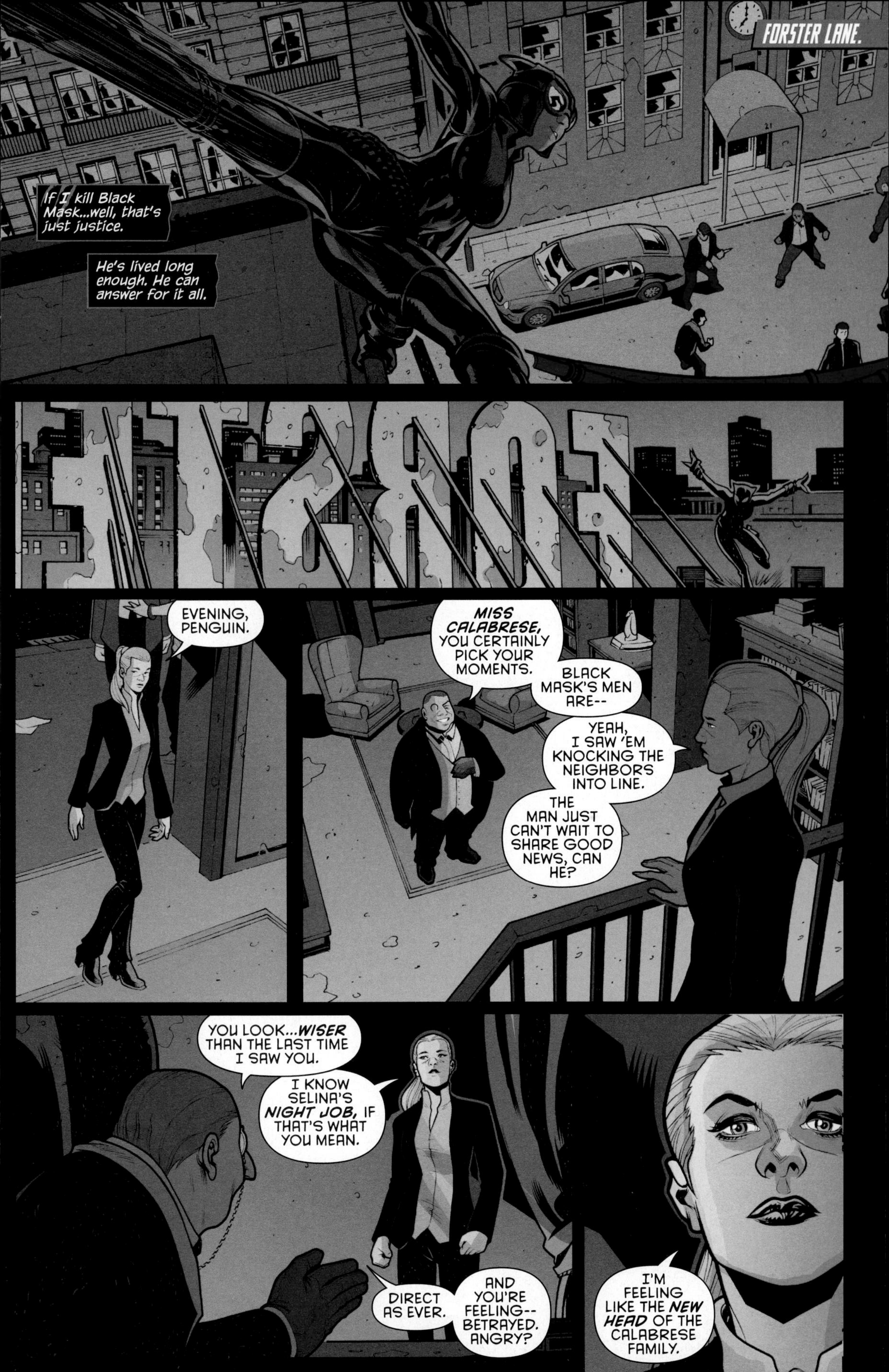
FORSTER LANE.
If I kill Black Mask...well, that's just justice.
He's lived long enough. He can answer for it all.
EVENING, PENGUIN.
MISS CALABRESE, YOU CERTAINLY PICK YOUR MOMENTS.
BLACK MASK'S MEN ARE--
YEAH, I SAW 'EM KNOCKING THE NEIGHBORS INTO LINE.
THE MAN JUST CAN'T WAIT TO SHARE GOOD NEWS, CAN HE?
YOU LOOK...WISER THAN THE LAST TIME I SAW YOU.
I KNOW SELINA'S NIGHT JOB, IF THAT'S WHAT YOU MEAN.
DIRECT AS EVER.
AND YOU'RE FEELING--BETRAYED. ANGRY?
I'M FEELING LIKE THE NEW HEAD OF THE CALABRESE FAMILY.

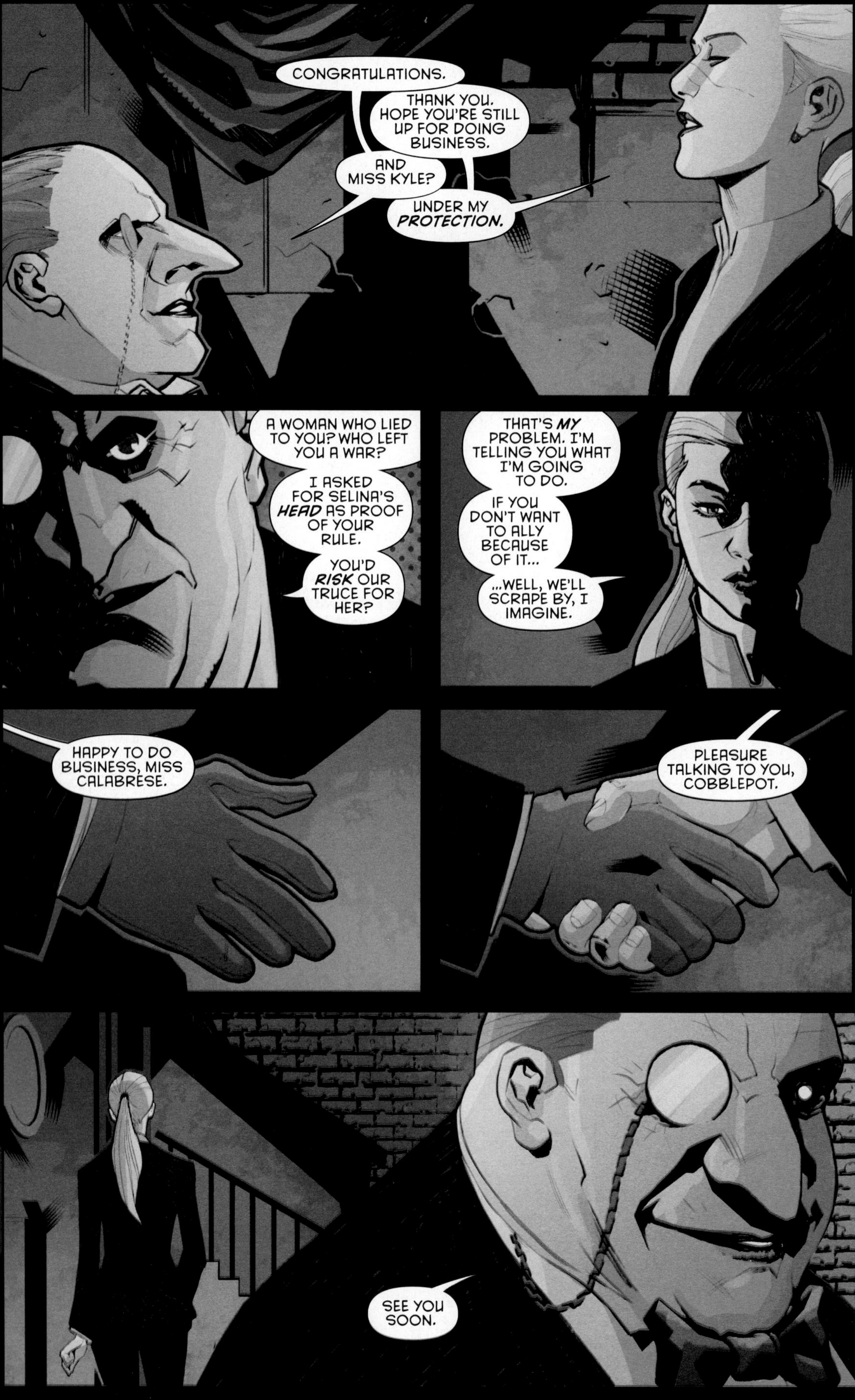
CONGRATULATIONS.
THANK YOU. HOPE YOU'RE STILL UP FOR DOING BUSINESS.
AND MISS KYLE?
UNDER MY *PROTECTION.*
A WOMAN WHO LIED TO YOU? WHO LEFT YOU A WAR?
I ASKED FOR SELINA'S *HEAD* AS PROOF OF YOUR RULE.
YOU'D *RISK* OUR TRUCE FOR HER?
THAT'S *MY* PROBLEM. I'M TELLING YOU WHAT I'M GOING TO DO.
IF YOU DON'T WANT TO ALLY BECAUSE OF IT...
...WELL, WE'LL SCRAPE BY, I IMAGINE.
HAPPY TO DO BUSINESS, MISS CALABRESE.
PLEASURE TALKING TO YOU, COBBLEPOT.
SEE YOU SOON.

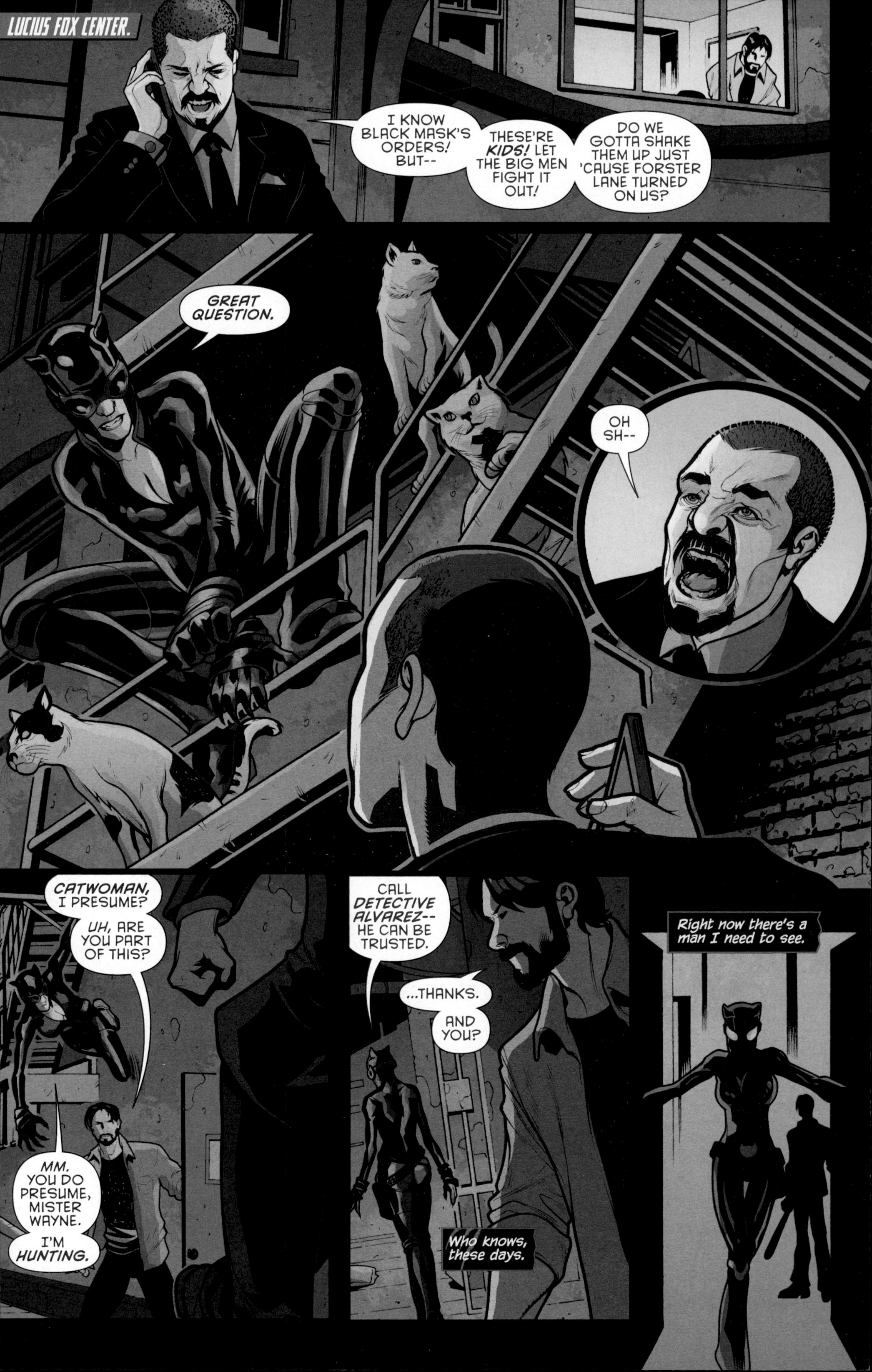
LUCIUS FOX CENTER.
I KNOW BLACK MASK'S ORDERS! BUT--
THESE'RE KIDS! LET THE BIG MEN FIGHT IT OUT!
DO WE GOTTA SHAKE THEM UP JUST 'CAUSE FORSTER LANE TURNED ON US?
GREAT QUESTION.
OH SH--
CATWOMAN, I PRESUME?
UH, ARE YOU PART OF THIS?
MM. YOU DO PRESUME, MISTER WAYNE.
I'M HUNTING.
CALL DETECTIVE ALVAREZ-- HE CAN BE TRUSTED.
...THANKS.
AND YOU?
Who knows, these days.
Right now there's a man I need to see.

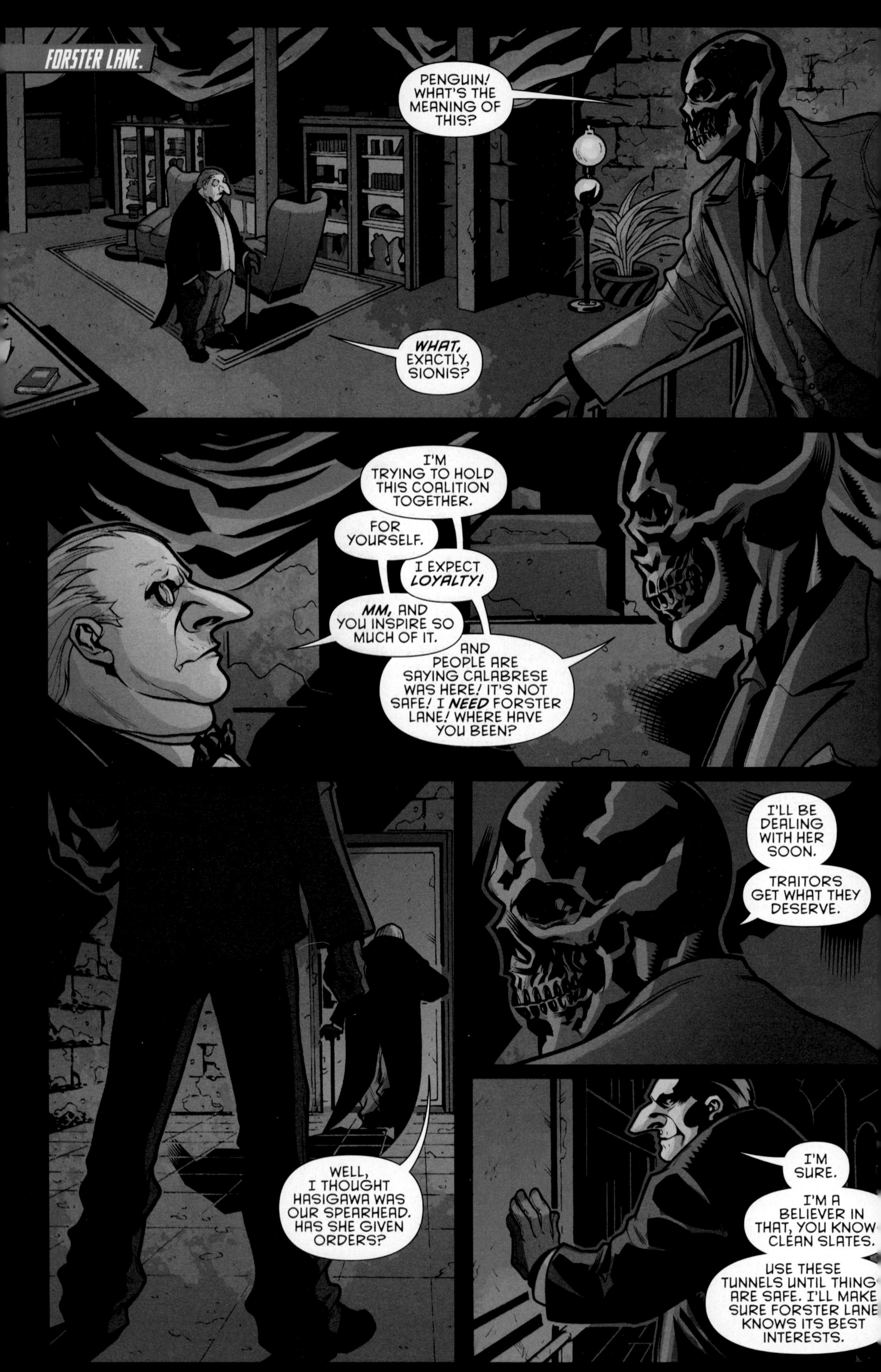
FORSTER LANE.
PENGUIN! WHAT'S THE MEANING OF THIS?
WHAT, EXACTLY, SIONIS?
I'M TRYING TO HOLD THIS COALITION TOGETHER.
FOR YOURSELF.
I EXPECT LOYALTY!
MM, AND YOU INSPIRE SO MUCH OF IT.
AND PEOPLE ARE SAYING CALABRESE WAS HERE! IT'S NOT SAFE! I NEED FORSTER LANE! WHERE HAVE YOU BEEN?
WELL, I THOUGHT HASIGAWA WAS OUR SPEARHEAD. HAS SHE GIVEN ORDERS?
I'LL BE DEALING WITH HER SOON.
TRAITORS GET WHAT THEY DESERVE.
I'M SURE.
I'M A BELIEVER IN THAT, YOU KNOW CLEAN SLATES.
USE THESE TUNNELS UNTIL THING ARE SAFE. I'LL MAKE SURE FORSTER LANE KNOWS ITS BEST INTERESTS.

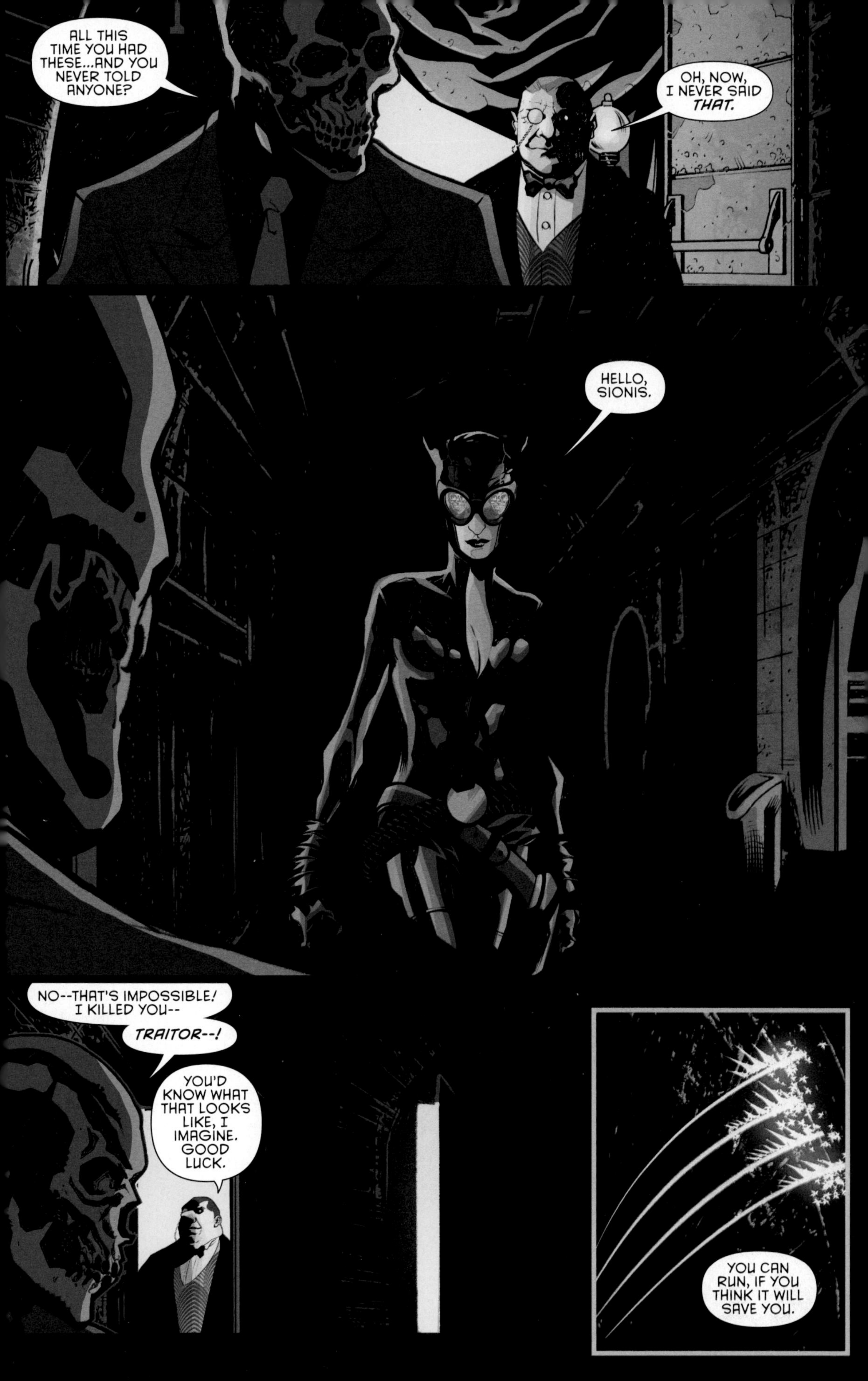
ALL THIS TIME YOU HAD THESE...AND YOU NEVER TOLD ANYONE?
OH, NOW, I NEVER SAID *THAT.*
HELLO, SIONIS.
NO--THAT'S IMPOSSIBLE! I KILLED YOU--
TRAITOR--!
YOU'D KNOW WHAT THAT LOOKS LIKE, I IMAGINE. GOOD LUCK.
YOU CAN RUN, IF YOU THINK IT WILL SAVE YOU.

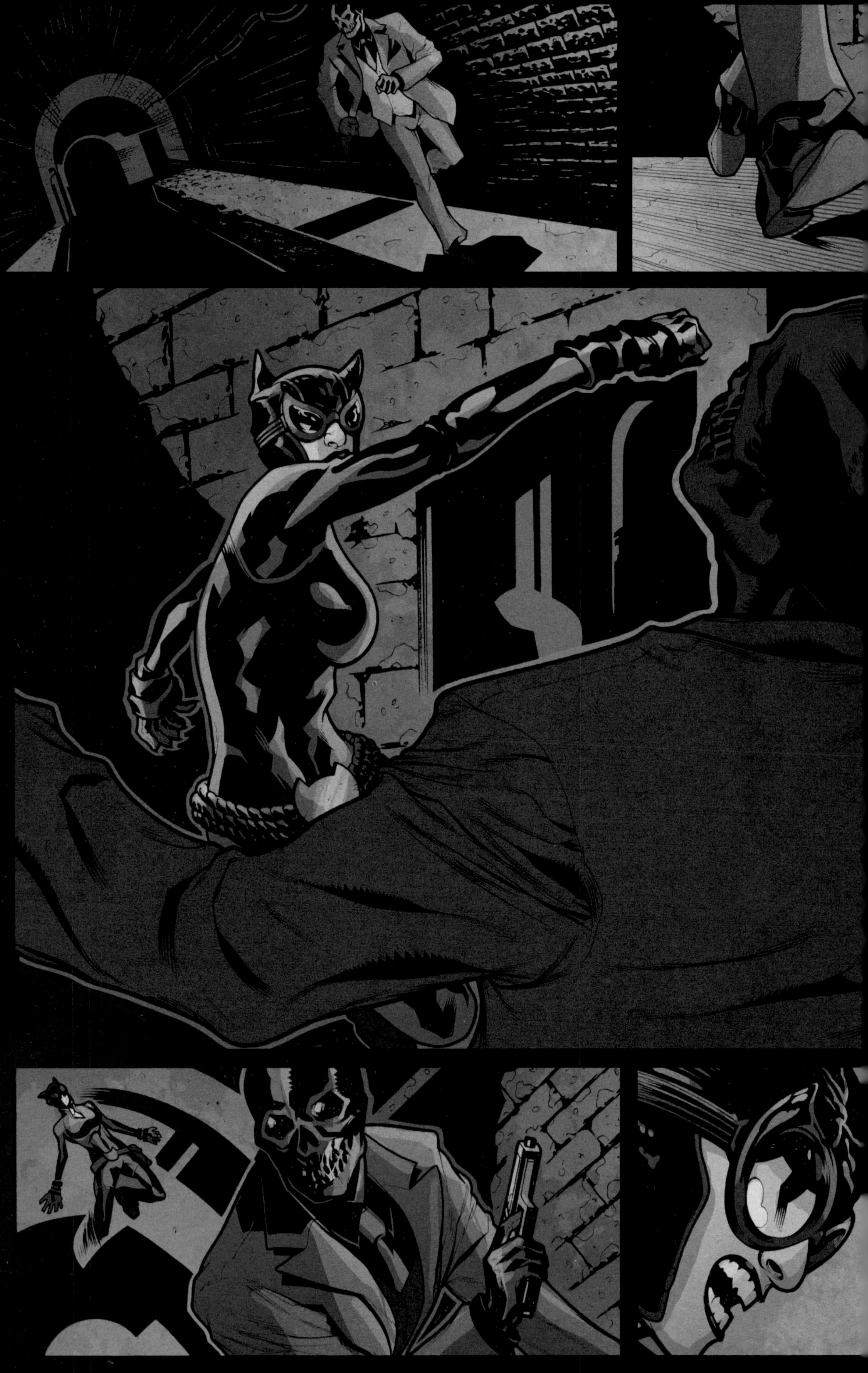

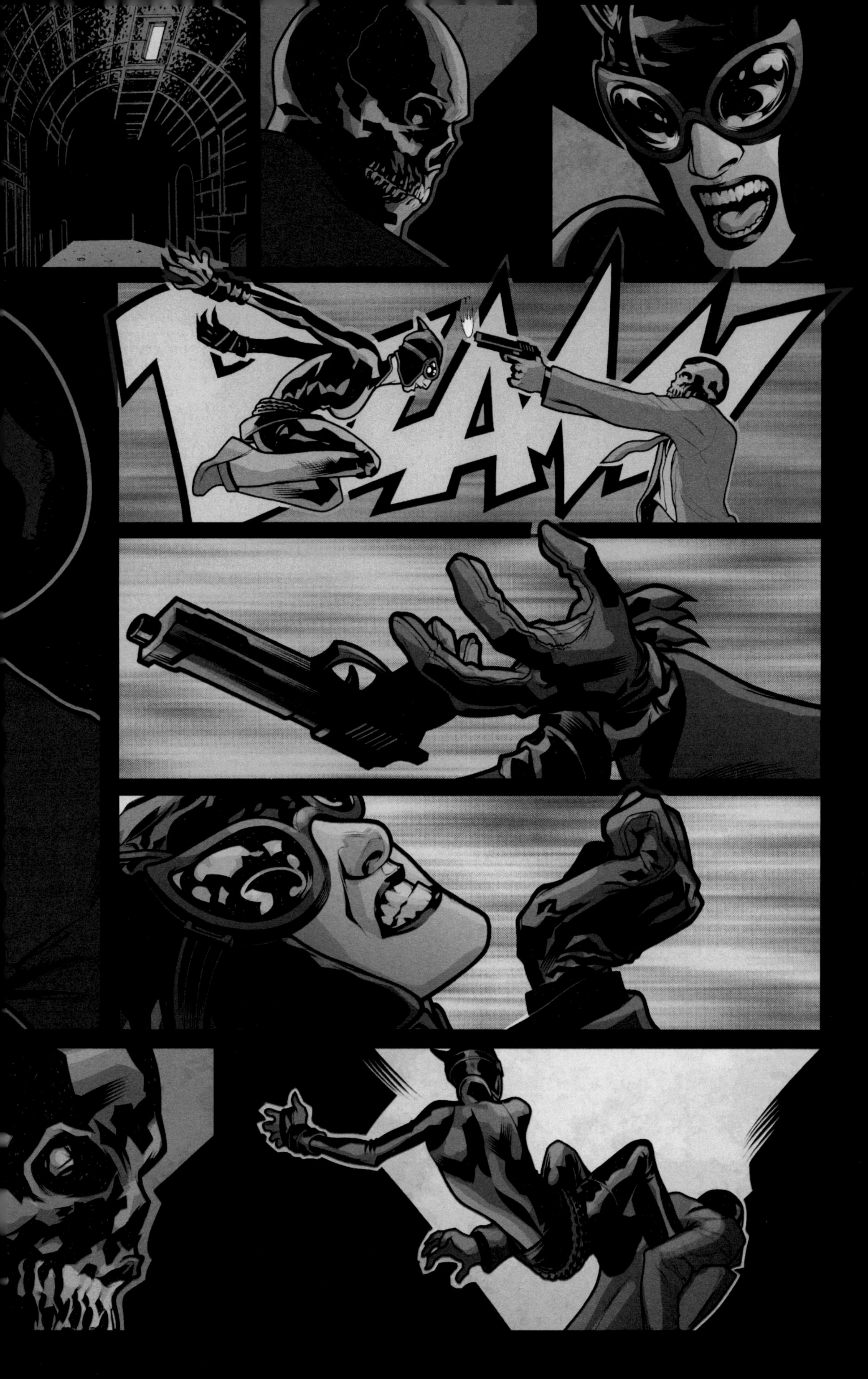

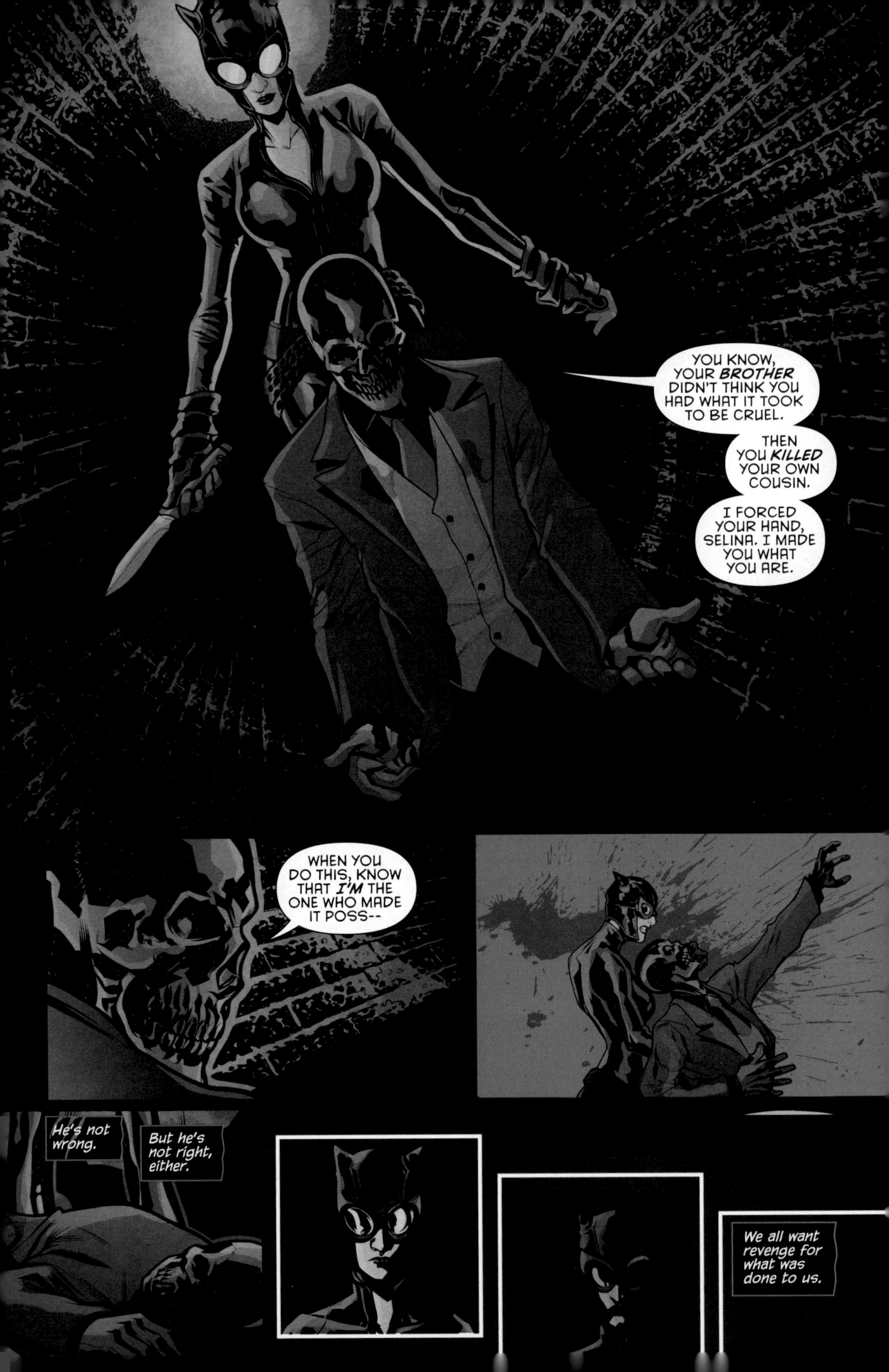
YOU KNOW, YOUR **BROTHER** DIDN'T THINK YOU HAD WHAT IT TOOK TO BE CRUEL.
THEN YOU **KILLED** YOUR OWN COUSIN.
I FORCED YOUR HAND, SELINA. I MADE YOU WHAT YOU ARE.
WHEN YOU DO THIS, KNOW THAT ***I'M*** THE ONE WHO MADE IT POSS--
He's not wrong.
But he's not right, either.
We all want revenge for what was done to us.

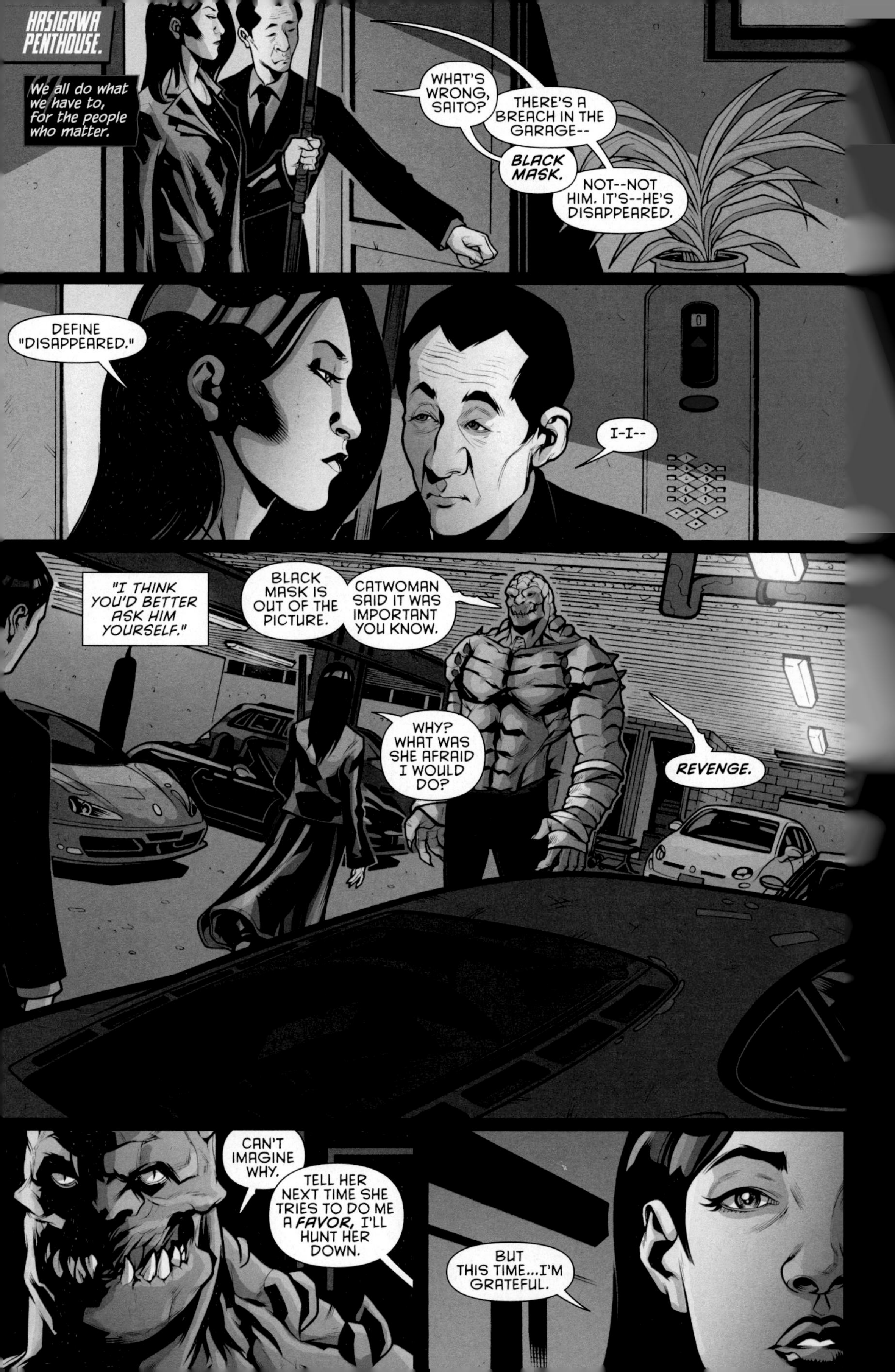
HASIGAWA PENTHOUSE.
We all do what we have to, for the people who matter.
WHAT'S WRONG, SAITO?
THERE'S A BREACH IN THE GARAGE--
BLACK MASK.
NOT--NOT HIM. IT'S--HE'S DISAPPEARED.
DEFINE "DISAPPEARED."
I-I--
"I THINK YOU'D BETTER ASK HIM YOURSELF."
BLACK MASK IS OUT OF THE PICTURE.
CATWOMAN SAID IT WAS IMPORTANT YOU KNOW.
WHY? WHAT WAS SHE AFRAID I WOULD DO?
REVENGE.
CAN'T IMAGINE WHY.
TELL HER NEXT TIME SHE TRIES TO DO ME A FAVOR, I'LL HUNT HER DOWN.
BUT THIS TIME...I'M GRATEFUL.

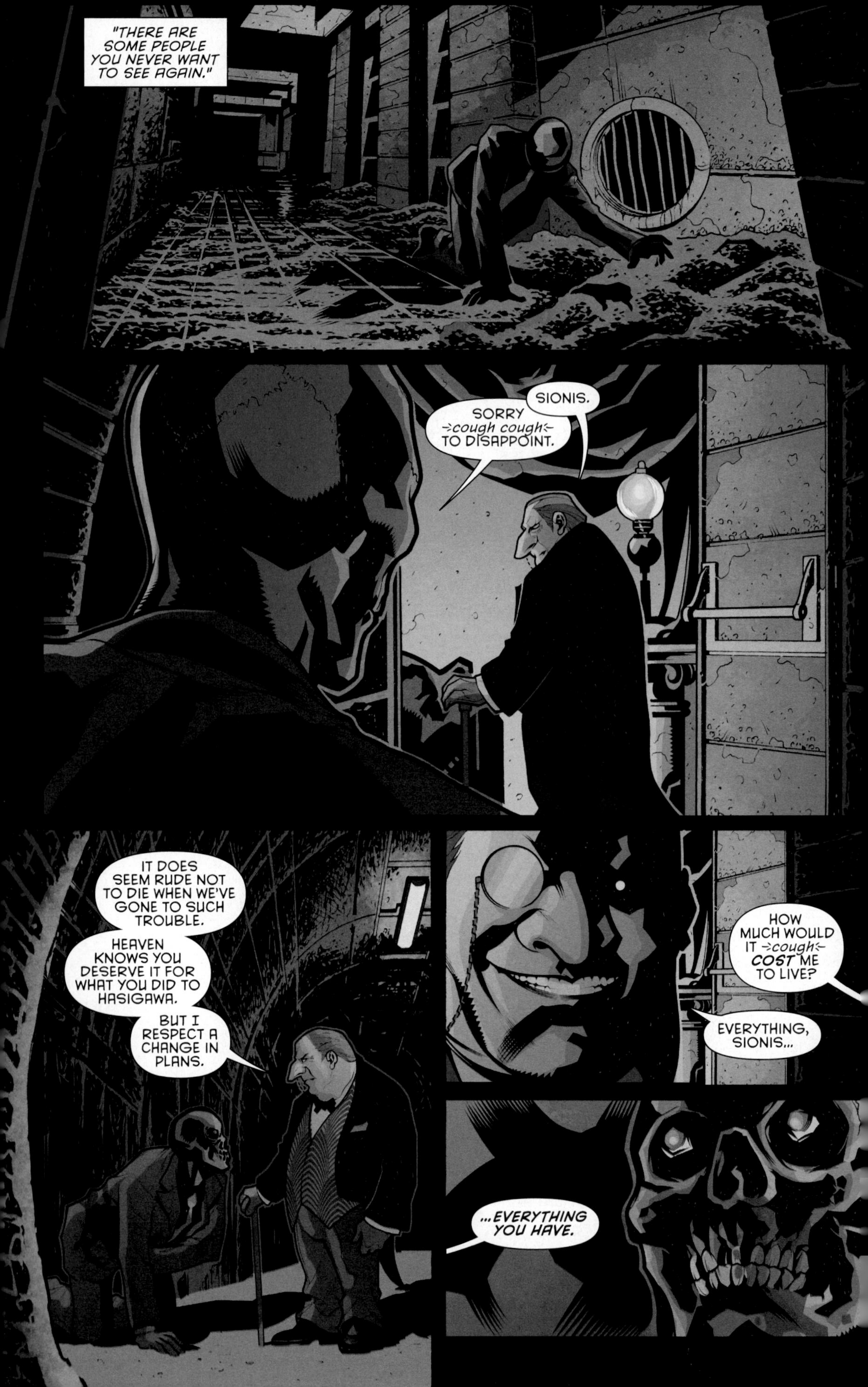
"THERE ARE SOME PEOPLE YOU NEVER WANT TO SEE AGAIN."
SIONIS.
SORRY ⇥cough cough⇤ TO DISAPPOINT.
IT DOES SEEM RUDE NOT TO DIE WHEN WE'VE GONE TO SUCH TROUBLE.
HEAVEN KNOWS YOU DESERVE IT FOR WHAT YOU DID TO HASIGAWA.
BUT I RESPECT A CHANGE IN PLANS.
HOW MUCH WOULD IT ⇥cough⇤ COST ME TO LIVE?
EVERYTHING, SIONIS...
...EVERYTHING YOU HAVE.

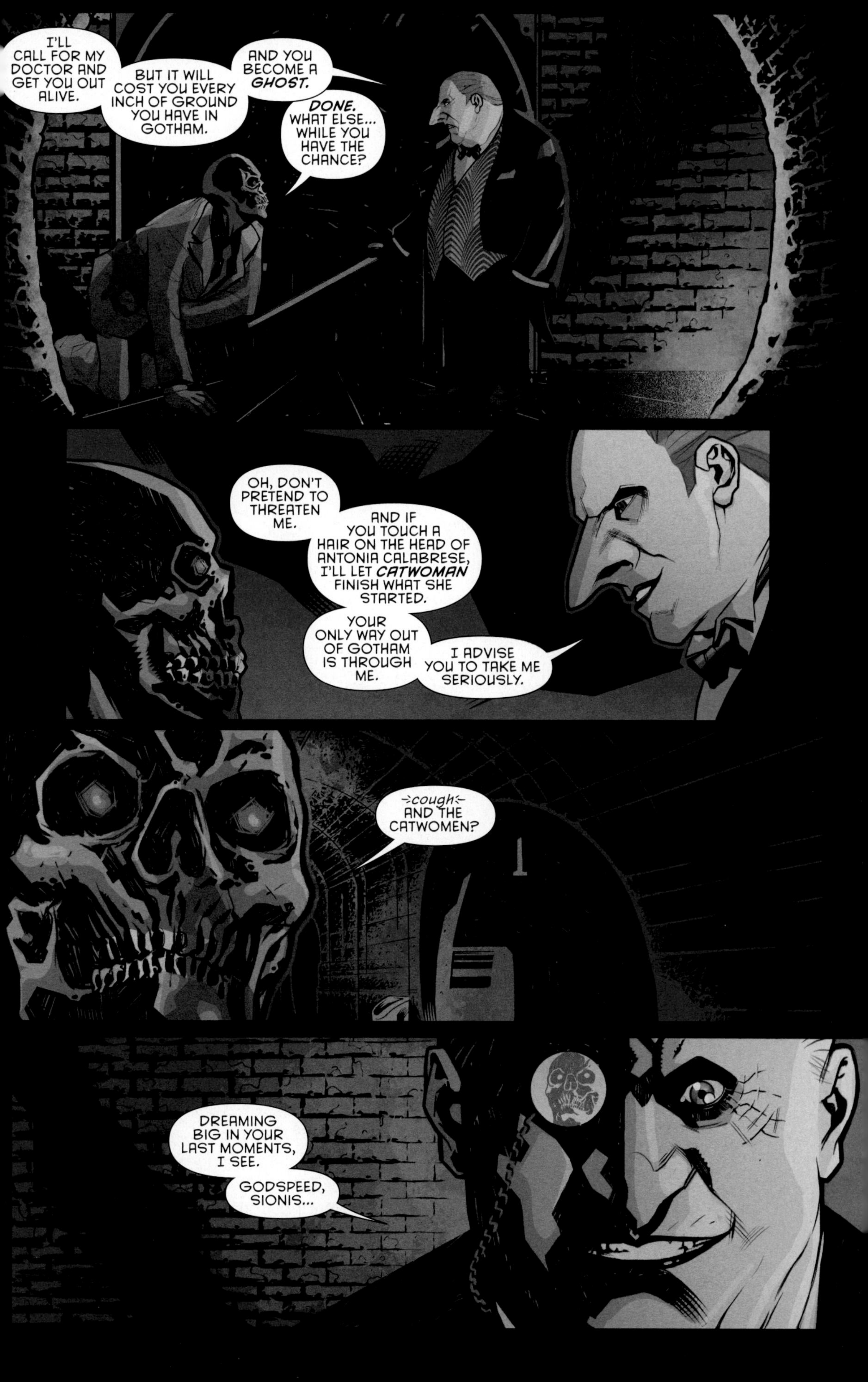
I'LL CALL FOR MY DOCTOR AND GET YOU OUT ALIVE.
BUT IT WILL COST YOU EVERY INCH OF GROUND YOU HAVE IN GOTHAM.
AND YOU BECOME A *GHOST.*
DONE. WHAT ELSE... WHILE YOU HAVE THE CHANCE?
OH, DON'T PRETEND TO THREATEN ME.
AND IF YOU TOUCH A HAIR ON THE HEAD OF ANTONIA CALABRESE, I'LL LET *CATWOMAN* FINISH WHAT SHE STARTED.
YOUR ONLY WAY OUT OF GOTHAM IS THROUGH ME.
I ADVISE YOU TO TAKE ME SERIOUSLY.
cough AND THE CATWOMEN?
DREAMING BIG IN YOUR LAST MOMENTS, I SEE.
GODSPEED, SIONIS...

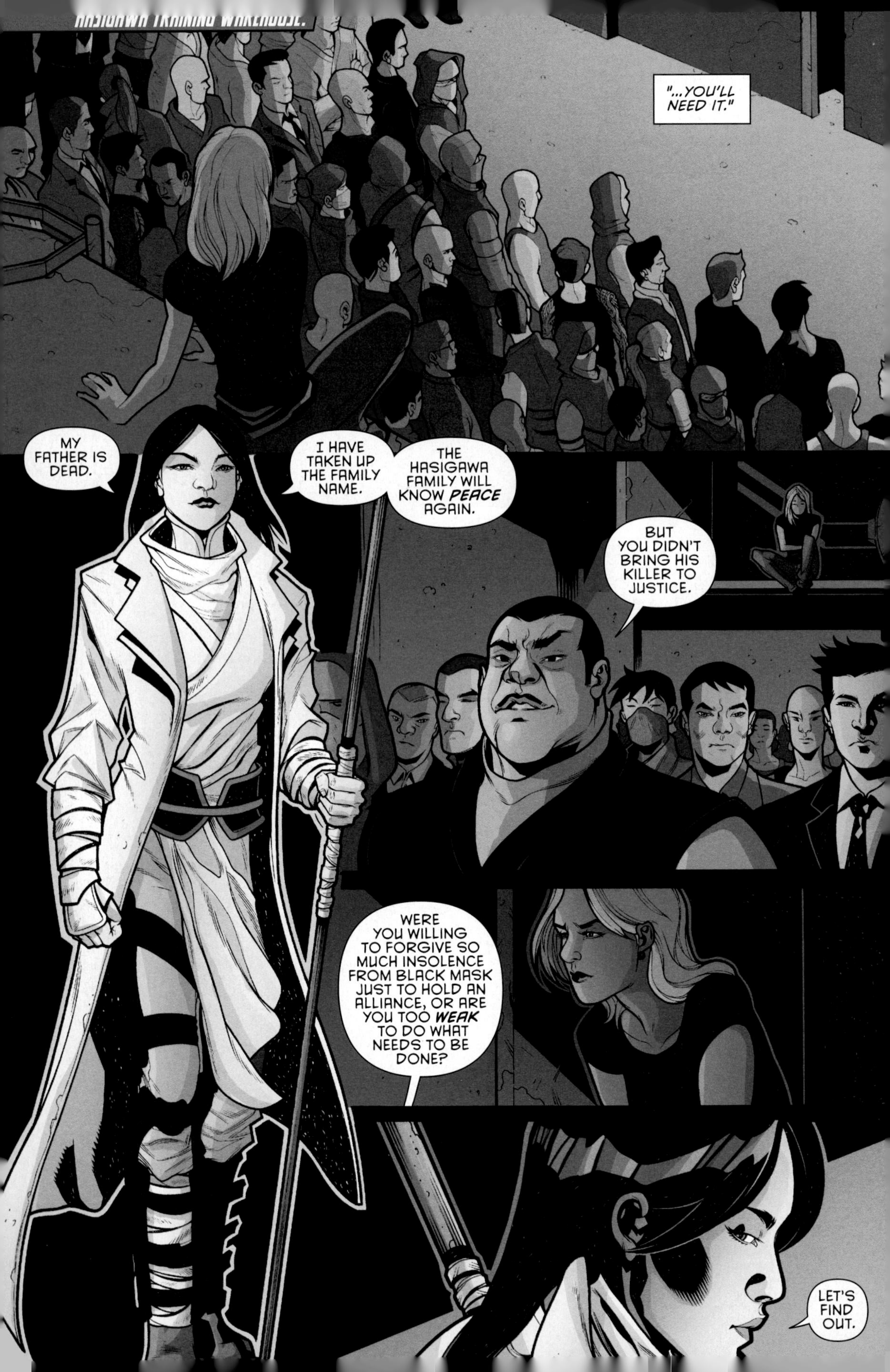
"...YOU'LL NEED IT."
MY FATHER IS DEAD.
I HAVE TAKEN UP THE FAMILY NAME.
THE HASIGAWA FAMILY WILL KNOW *PEACE* AGAIN.
BUT YOU DIDN'T BRING HIS KILLER TO JUSTICE.
WERE YOU WILLING TO FORGIVE SO MUCH INSOLENCE FROM BLACK MASK JUST TO HOLD AN ALLIANCE, OR ARE YOU TOO *WEAK* TO DO WHAT NEEDS TO BE DONE?
LET'S FIND OUT.

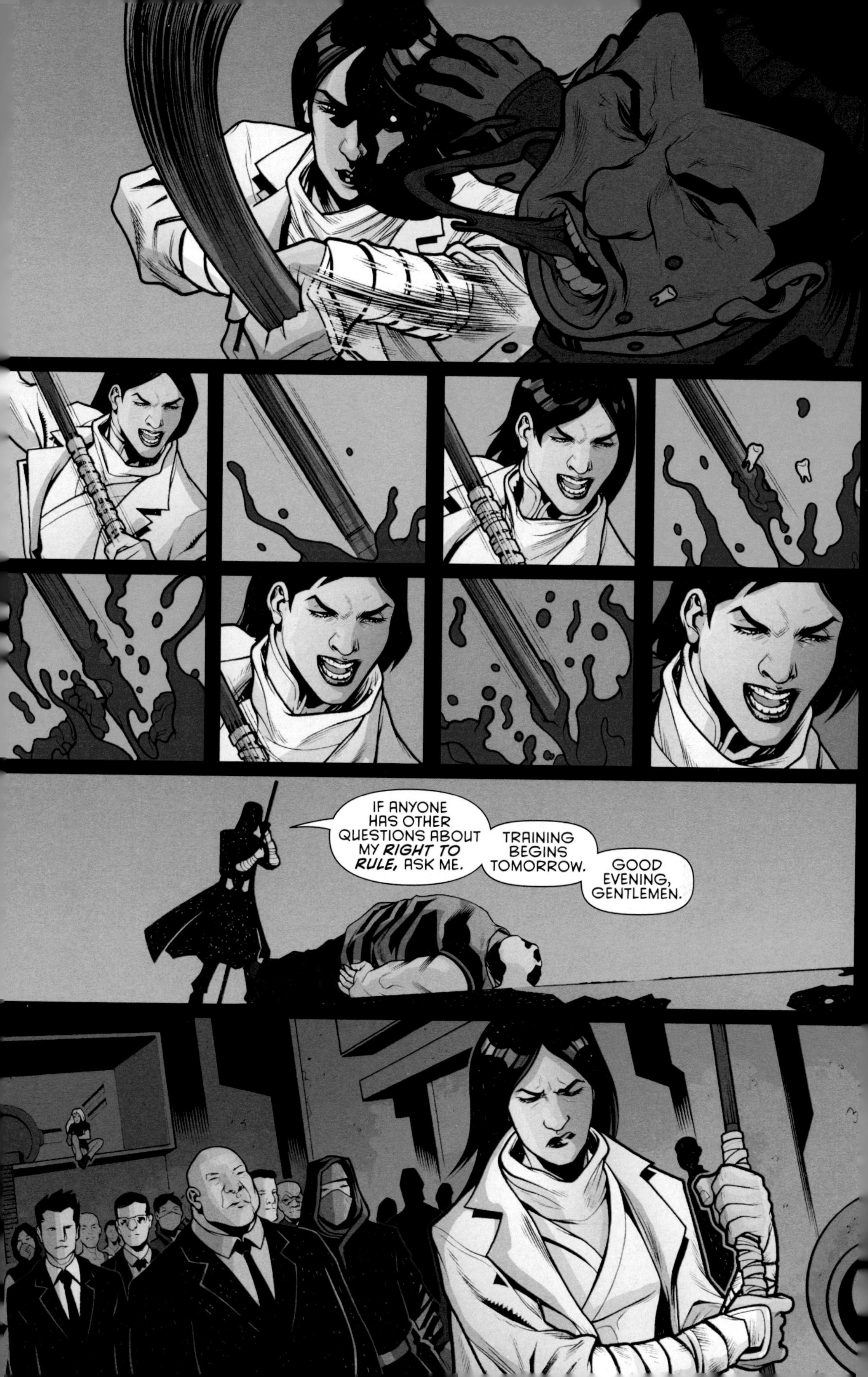
IF ANYONE HAS OTHER QUESTIONS ABOUT MY *RIGHT TO RULE,* ASK ME.
TRAINING BEGINS TOMORROW.
GOOD EVENING, GENTLEMEN.

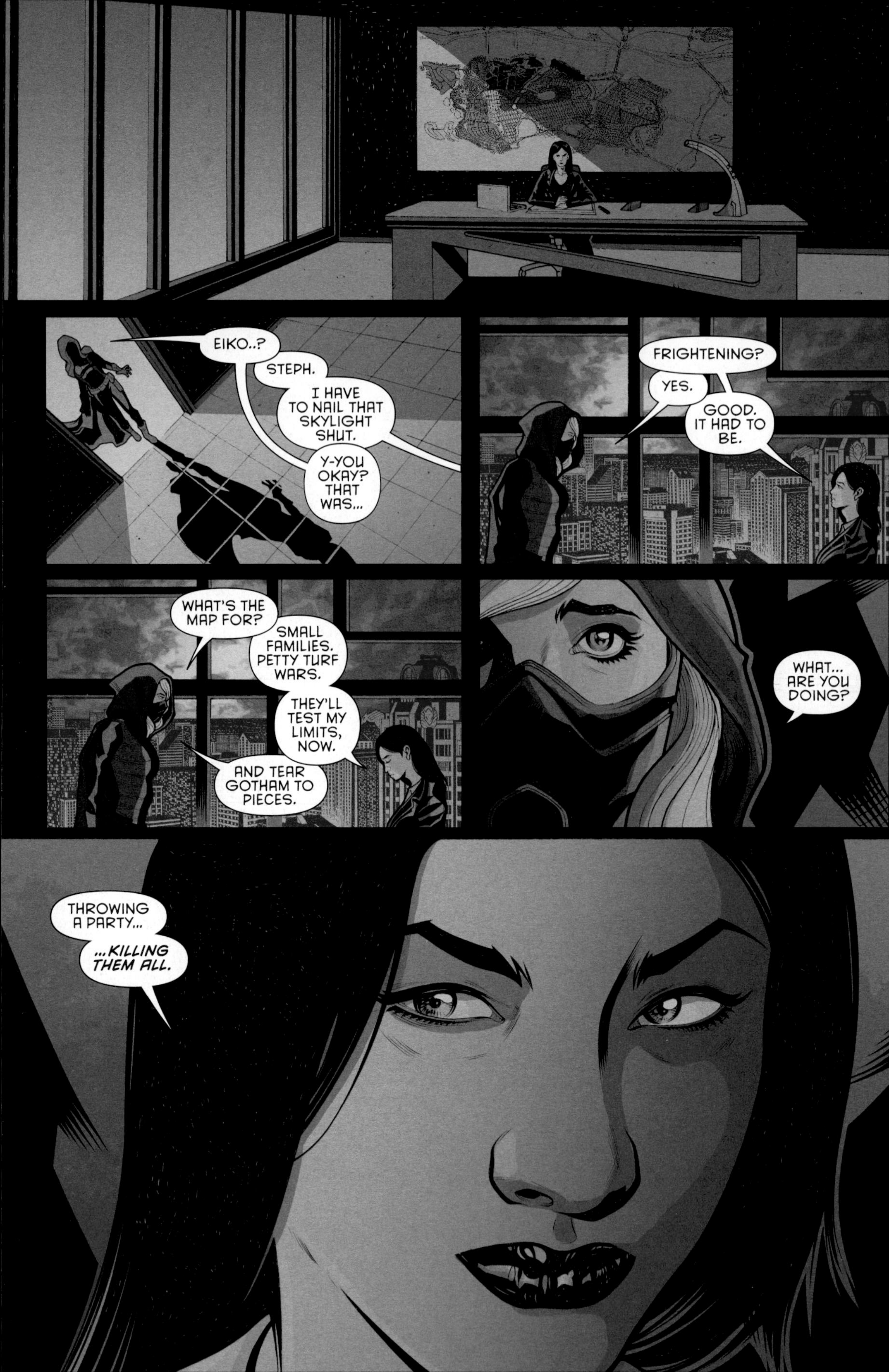
EIKO..?
STEPH.
I HAVE TO NAIL THAT SKYLIGHT SHUT.
Y-YOU OKAY? THAT WAS...
FRIGHTENING?
YES.
GOOD. IT HAD TO BE.
WHAT'S THE MAP FOR?
SMALL FAMILIES. PETTY TURF WARS.
THEY'LL TEST MY LIMITS, NOW.
AND TEAR GOTHAM TO PIECES.
WHAT... ARE YOU DOING?
THROWING A PARTY...
...KILLING THEM ALL.

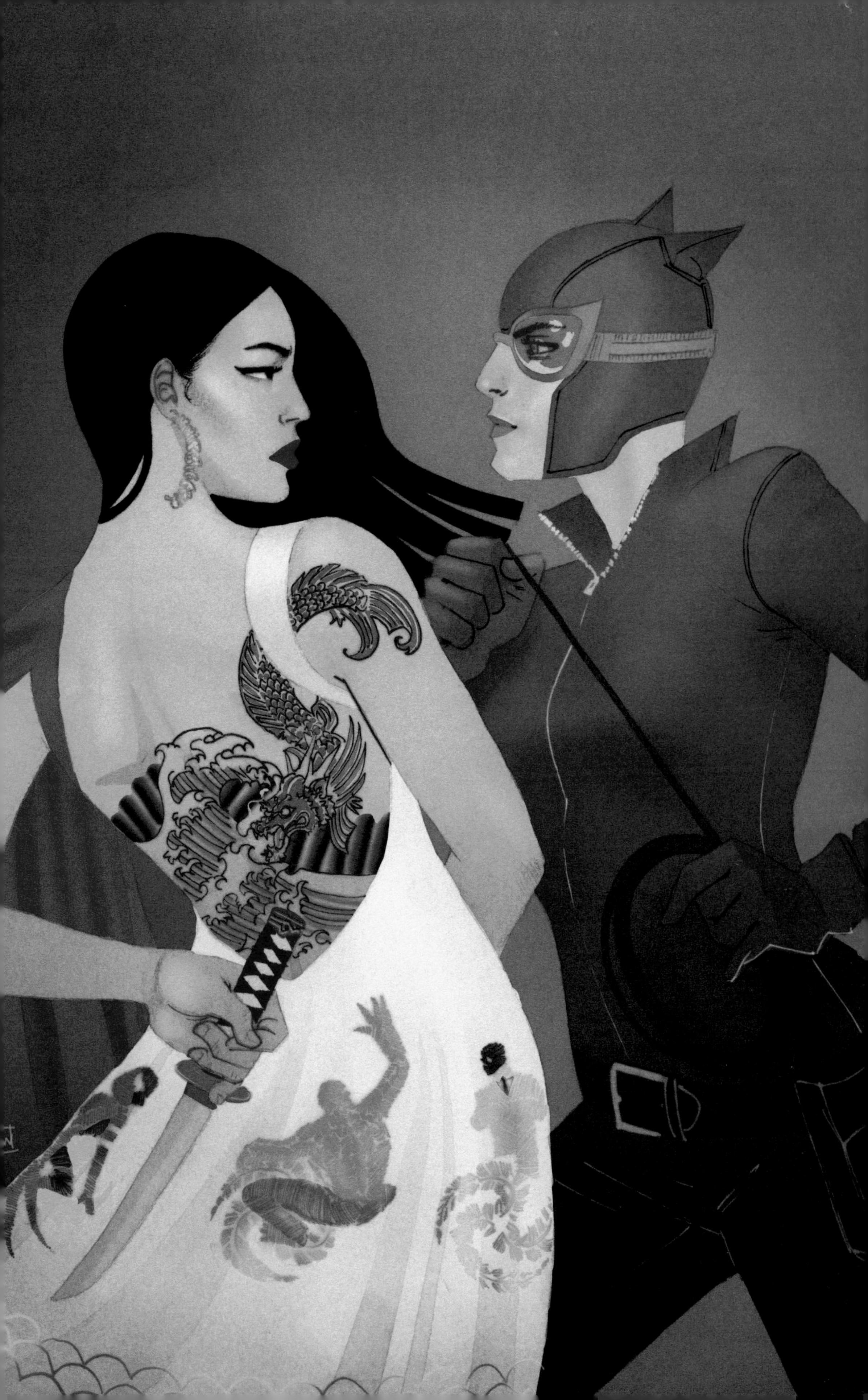

NOT FORGOTTEN

GENEVIEVE VALENTINE writer **DAVID MESSINA** penciller **GAETANO CARLUCCI** inker **LEE LOUGHRIDGE** colorist **TRAVIS LANHAM** letterer cover art by **KEVIN WADA**

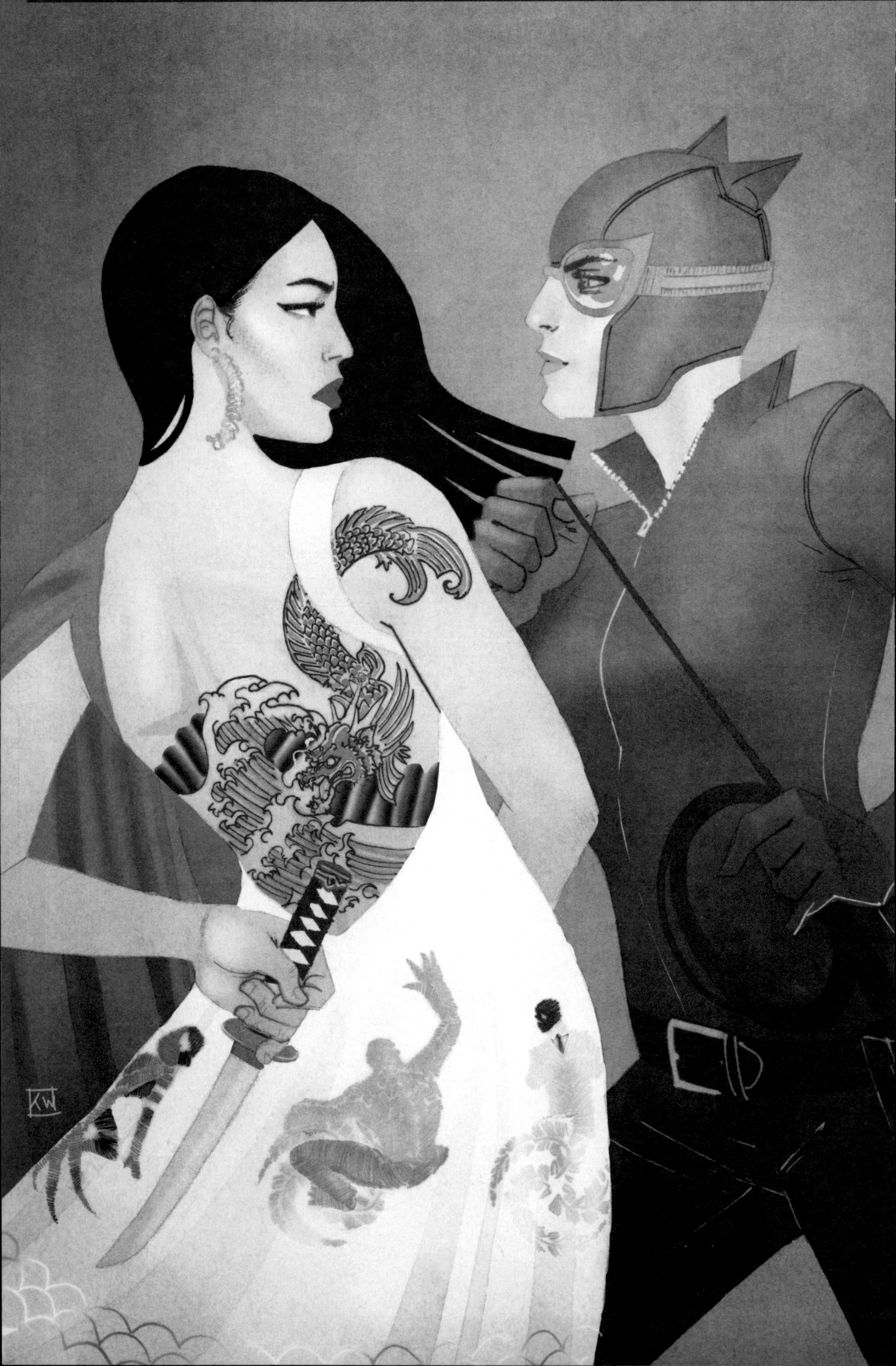
KW

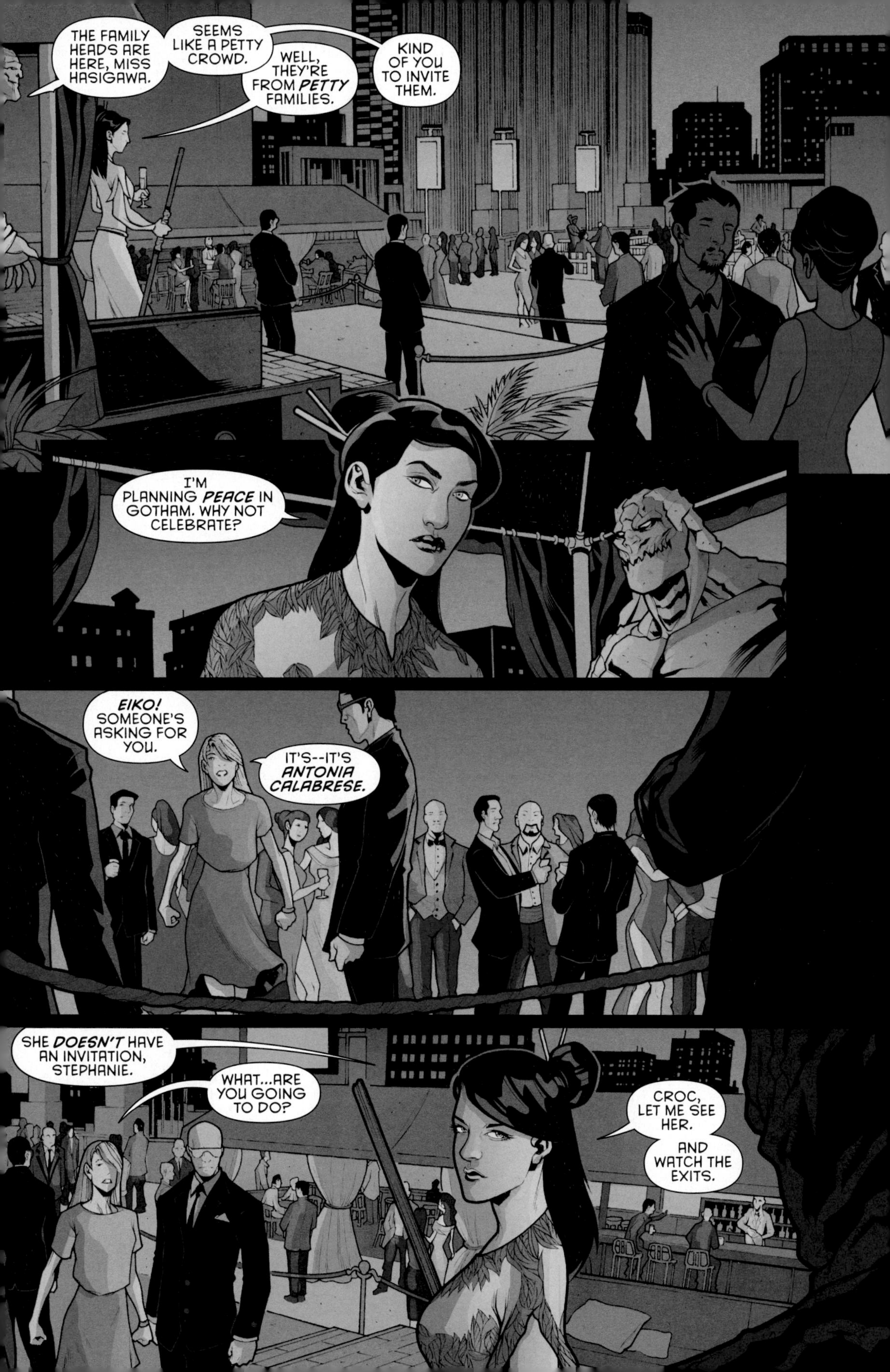
THE FAMILY HEADS ARE HERE, MISS HASIGAWA.
SEEMS LIKE A PETTY CROWD.
WELL, THEY'RE FROM PETTY FAMILIES.
KIND OF YOU TO INVITE THEM.
I'M PLANNING PEACE IN GOTHAM. WHY NOT CELEBRATE?
EIKO! SOMEONE'S ASKING FOR YOU.
IT'S--IT'S ANTONIA CALABRESE.
SHE DOESN'T HAVE AN INVITATION, STEPHANIE.
WHAT...ARE YOU GOING TO DO?
CROC, LET ME SEE HER.
AND WATCH THE EXITS.

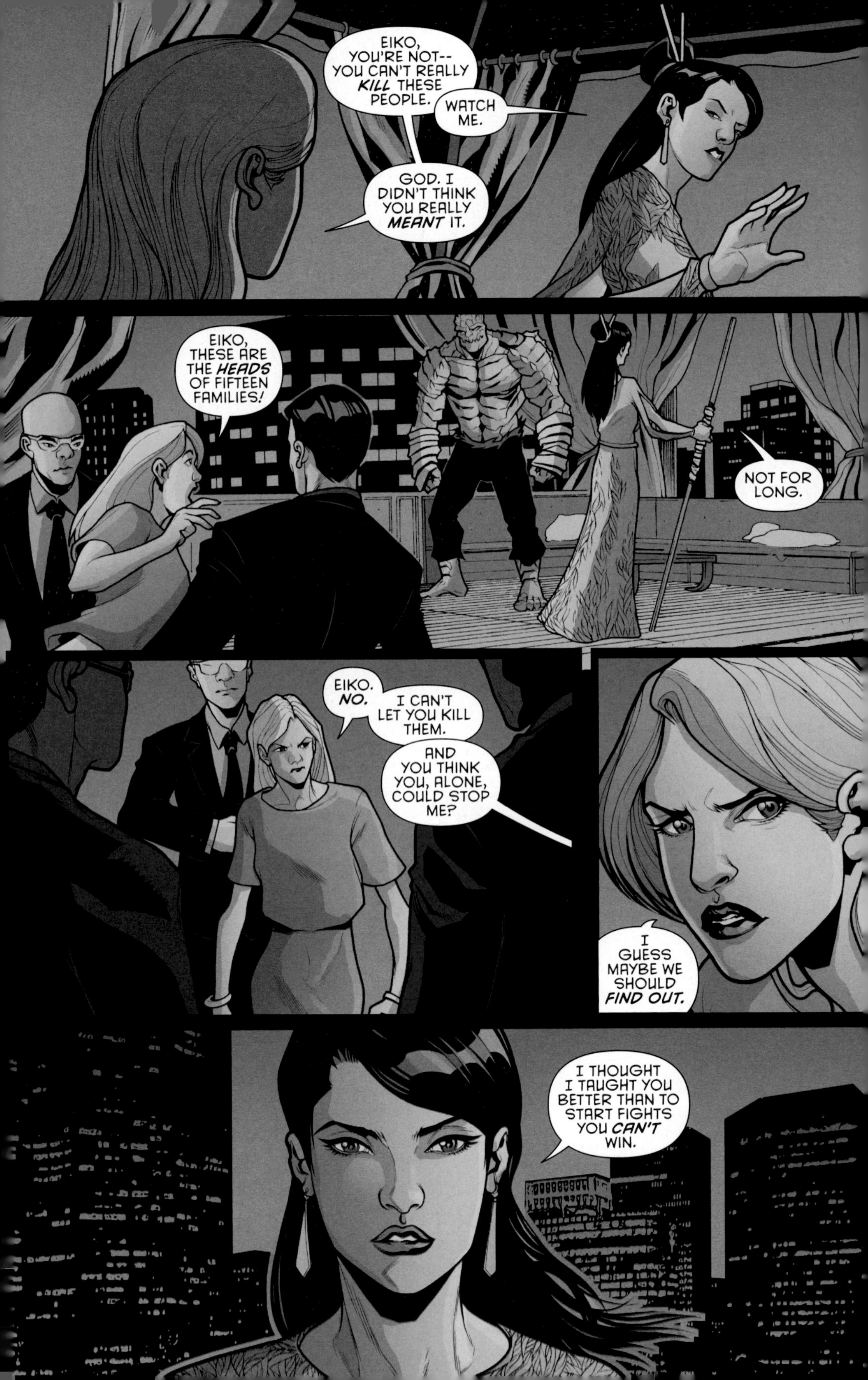
EIKO, YOU'RE NOT-- YOU CAN'T REALLY KILL THESE PEOPLE.
WATCH ME.
GOD. I DIDN'T THINK YOU REALLY MEANT IT.
EIKO, THESE ARE THE HEADS OF FIFTEEN FAMILIES!
NOT FOR LONG.
EIKO. NO.
I CAN'T LET YOU KILL THEM.
AND YOU THINK YOU, ALONE, COULD STOP ME?
I GUESS MAYBE WE SHOULD FIND OUT.
I THOUGHT I TAUGHT YOU BETTER THAN TO START FIGHTS YOU CAN'T WIN.

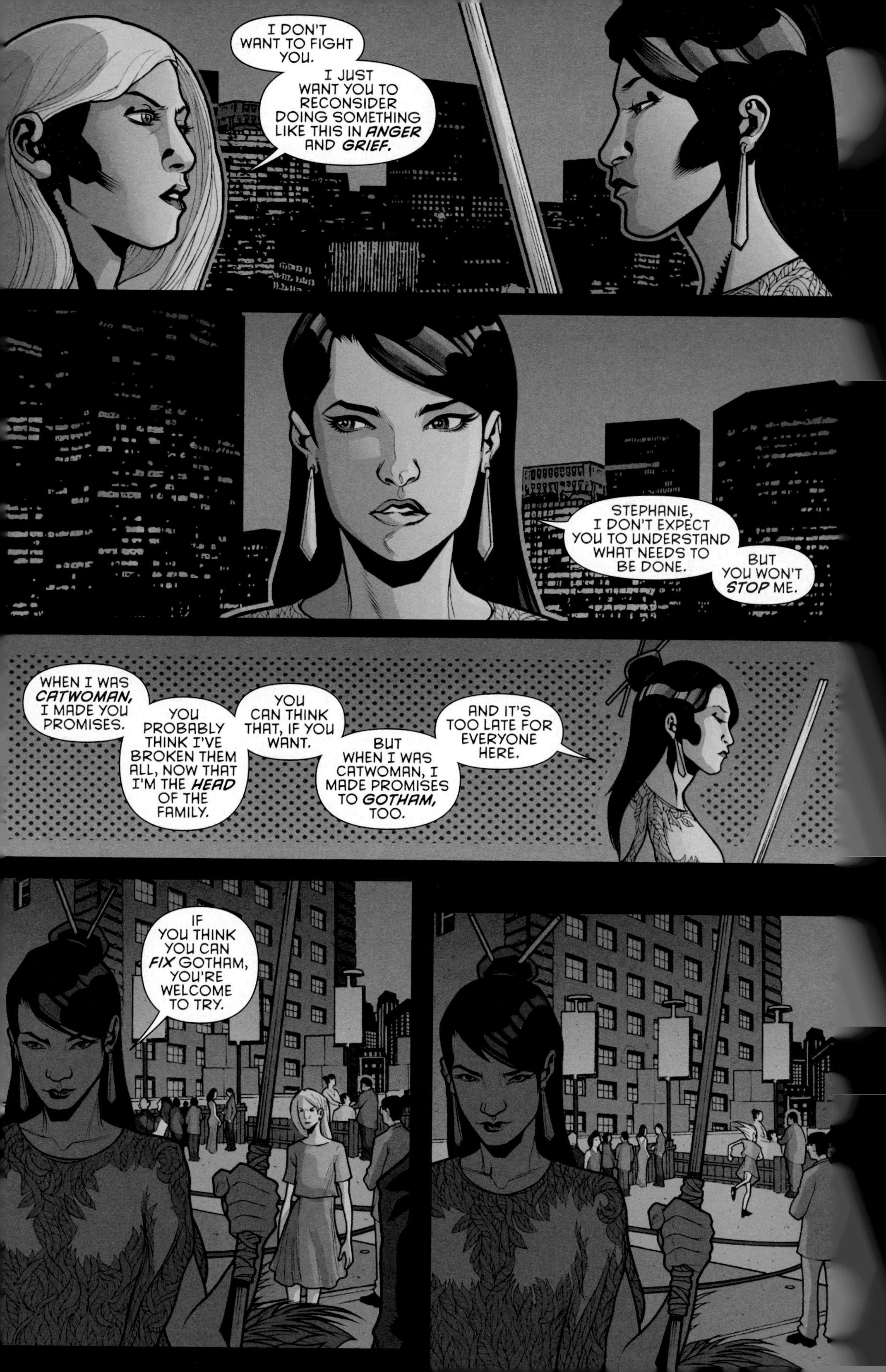
I DON'T WANT TO FIGHT YOU.
I JUST WANT YOU TO RECONSIDER DOING SOMETHING LIKE THIS IN *ANGER* AND *GRIEF.*
STEPHANIE, I DON'T EXPECT YOU TO UNDERSTAND WHAT NEEDS TO BE DONE.
BUT YOU WON'T *STOP* ME.
WHEN I WAS *CATWOMAN,* I MADE YOU PROMISES.
YOU PROBABLY THINK I'VE BROKEN THEM ALL, NOW THAT I'M THE *HEAD* OF THE FAMILY.
YOU CAN THINK THAT, IF YOU WANT.
BUT WHEN I WAS CATWOMAN, I MADE PROMISES TO *GOTHAM,* TOO.
AND IT'S TOO LATE FOR EVERYONE HERE.
IF YOU THINK YOU CAN *FIX* GOTHAM, YOU'RE WELCOME TO TRY.

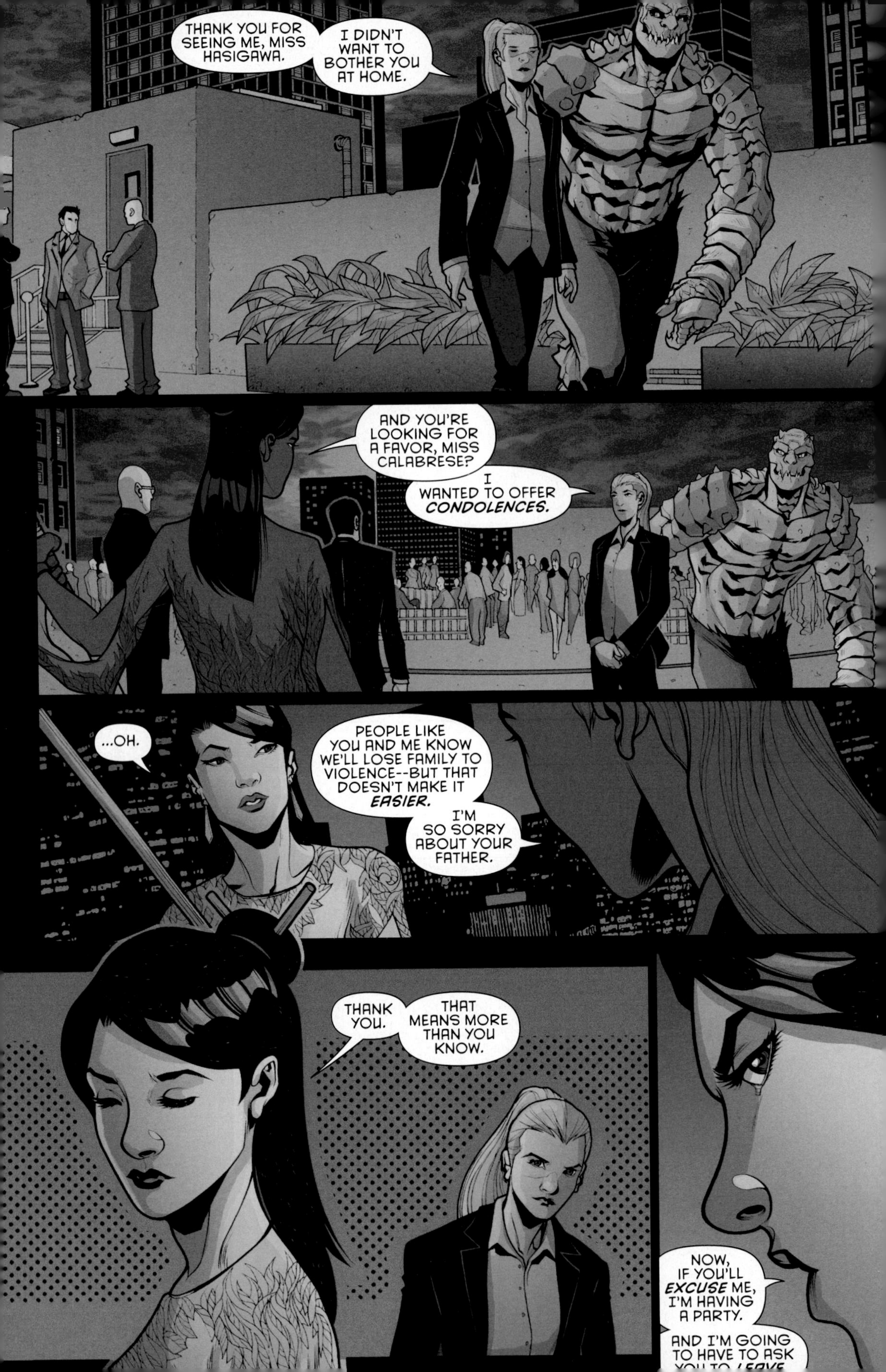
THANK YOU FOR SEEING ME, MISS HASIGAWA.
I DIDN'T WANT TO BOTHER YOU AT HOME.
AND YOU'RE LOOKING FOR A FAVOR, MISS CALABRESE?
I WANTED TO OFFER CONDOLENCES.
...OH.
PEOPLE LIKE YOU AND ME KNOW WE'LL LOSE FAMILY TO VIOLENCE--BUT THAT DOESN'T MAKE IT EASIER.
I'M SO SORRY ABOUT YOUR FATHER.
THANK YOU.
THAT MEANS MORE THAN YOU KNOW.
NOW, IF YOU'LL EXCUSE ME, I'M HAVING A PARTY.
AND I'M GOING TO HAVE TO ASK

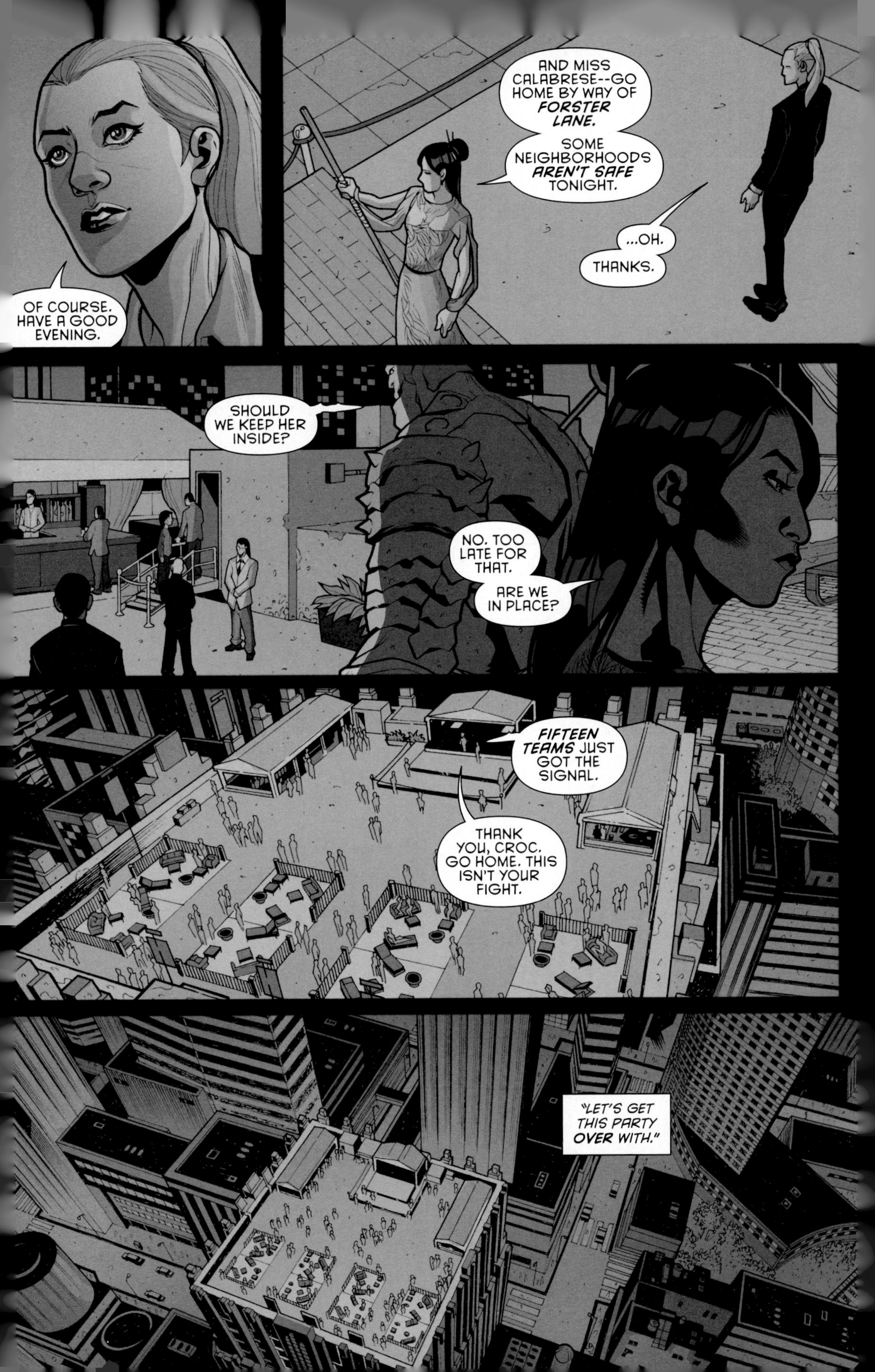
OF COURSE. HAVE A GOOD EVENING.
AND MISS CALABRESE--GO HOME BY WAY OF *FORSTER LANE.*
SOME NEIGHBORHOODS *AREN'T SAFE* TONIGHT.
...OH.
THANKS.
SHOULD WE KEEP HER INSIDE?
NO. TOO LATE FOR THAT.
ARE WE IN PLACE?
FIFTEEN TEAMS JUST GOT THE SIGNAL.
THANK YOU, CROC. GO HOME. THIS ISN'T YOUR FIGHT.
"LET'S GET THIS PARTY *OVER* WITH."

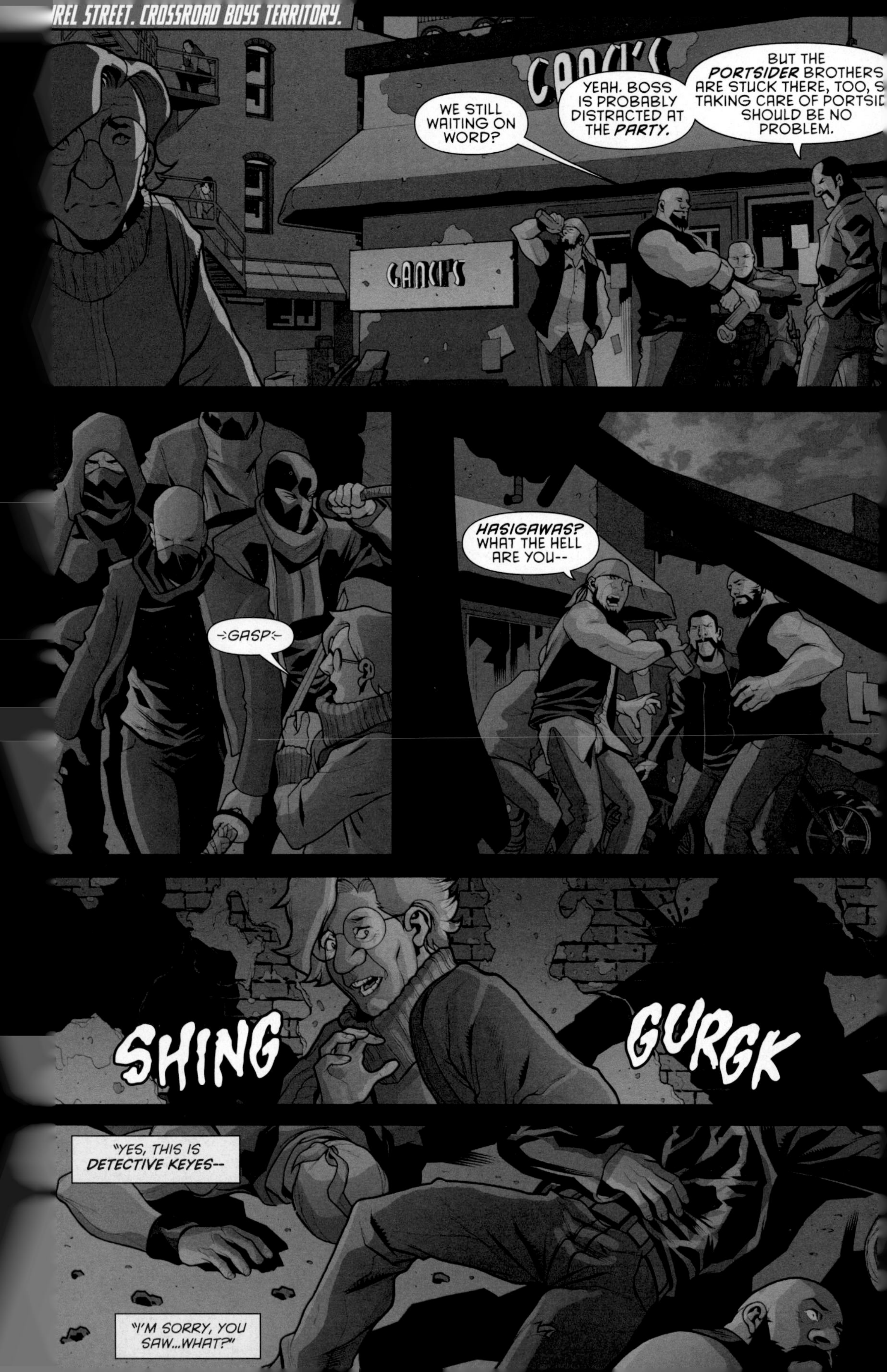

IREL STREET. CROSSROAD BOYS TERRITORY.
GANCI'S
WE STILL WAITING ON WORD?
YEAH. BOSS IS PROBABLY DISTRACTED AT THE PARTY.
BUT THE PORTSIDER BROTHERS ARE STUCK THERE, TOO, S TAKING CARE OF PORTSID SHOULD BE NO PROBLEM.
GANCI'S
GASP
HASIGAWAS? WHAT THE HELL ARE YOU--
SHING
GURGK
"YES, THIS IS DETECTIVE KEYES--
"I'M SORRY, YOU SAW...WHAT?"

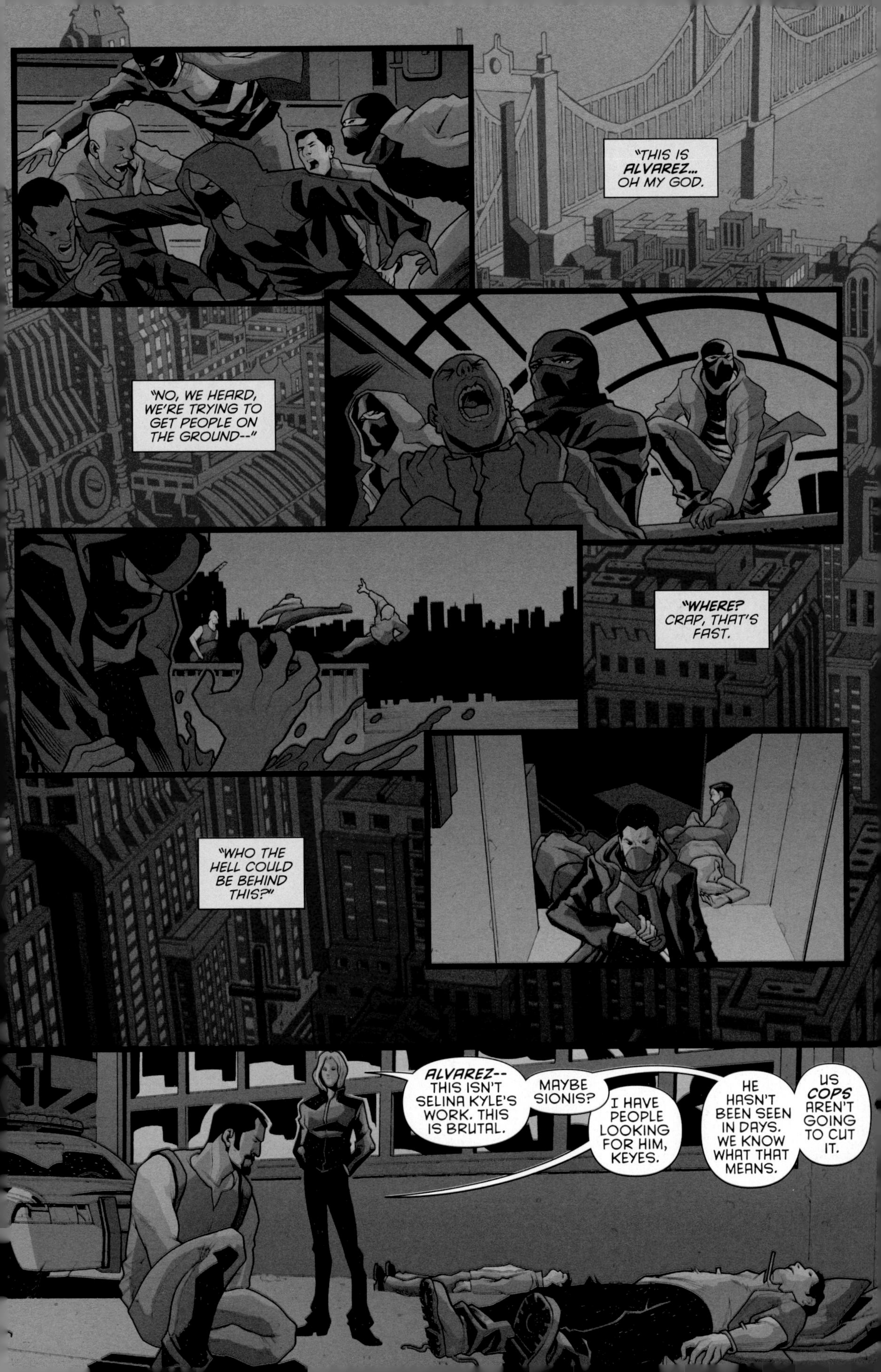
"THIS IS ALVAREZ... OH MY GOD.
"NO, WE HEARD, WE'RE TRYING TO GET PEOPLE ON THE GROUND--"
"WHERE? CRAP, THAT'S FAST.
"WHO THE HELL COULD BE BEHIND THIS?"
ALVAREZ-- THIS ISN'T SELINA KYLE'S WORK. THIS IS BRUTAL.
MAYBE SIONIS?
I HAVE PEOPLE LOOKING FOR HIM, KEYES.
HE HASN'T BEEN SEEN IN DAYS. WE KNOW WHAT THAT MEANS.
US COPS AREN'T GOING TO CUT IT.

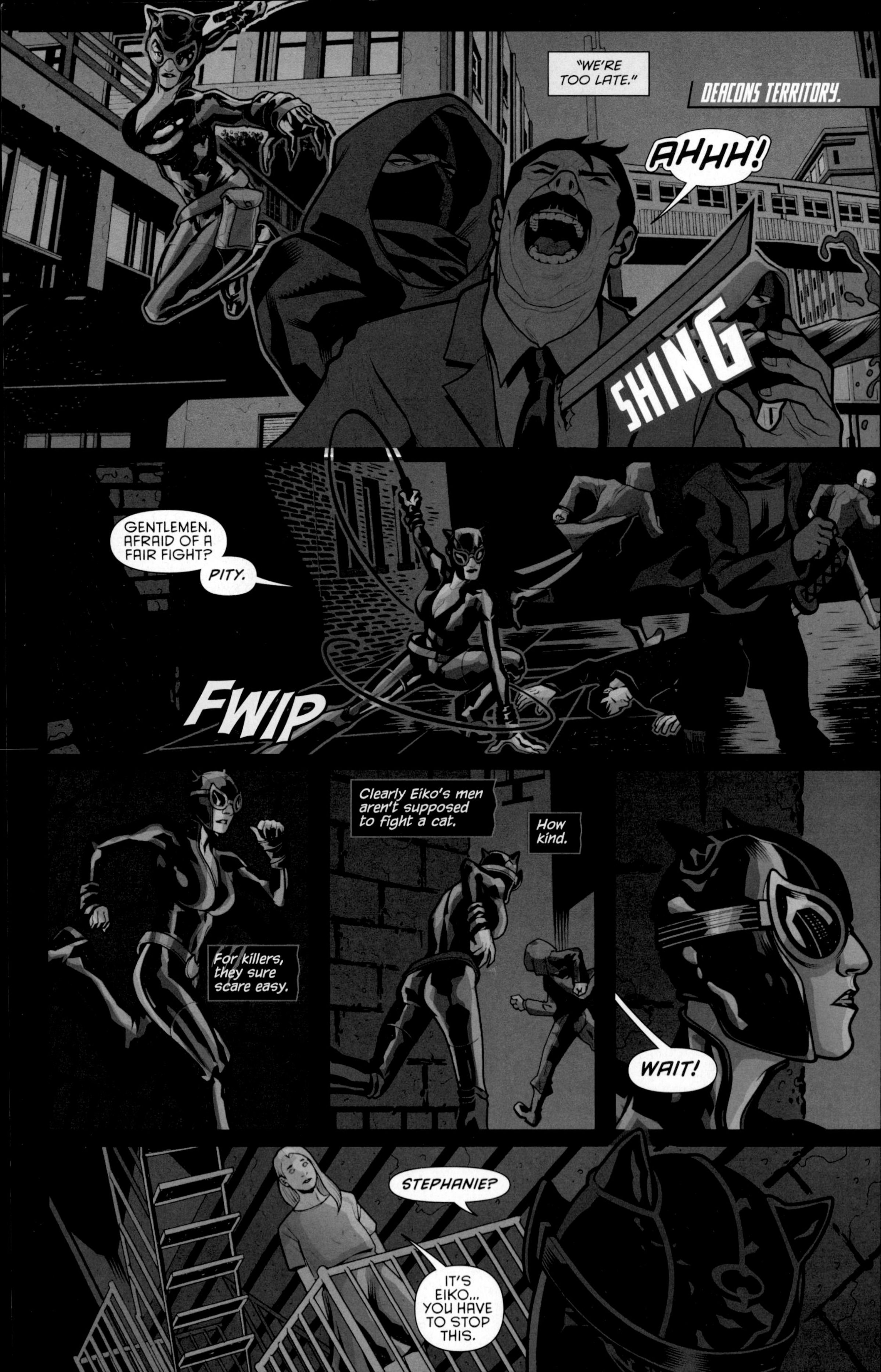
"WE'RE TOO LATE."
DEACONS TERRITORY.
AHHH!
SHING
GENTLEMEN. AFRAID OF A FAIR FIGHT?
PITY.
FWIP
For killers, they sure scare easy.
Clearly Eiko's men aren't supposed to fight a cat.
How kind.
WAIT!
STEPHANIE?
IT'S EIKO... YOU HAVE TO STOP THIS.

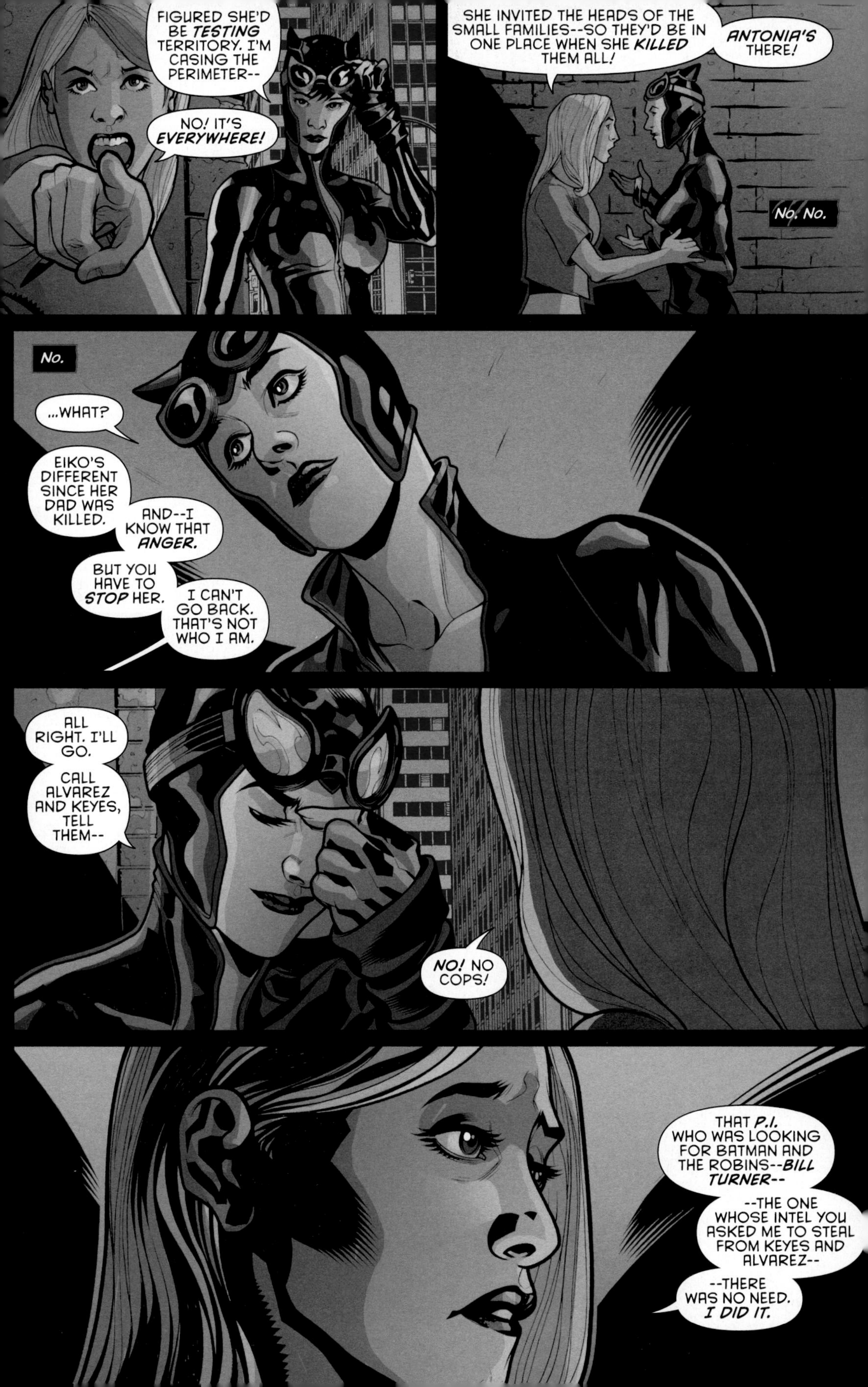

FIGURED SHE'D BE TESTING TERRITORY. I'M CASING THE PERIMETER--
NO! IT'S EVERYWHERE!
SHE INVITED THE HEADS OF THE SMALL FAMILIES--SO THEY'D BE IN ONE PLACE WHEN SHE KILLED THEM ALL!
ANTONIA'S THERE!
No. No.
No.
...WHAT?
EIKO'S DIFFERENT SINCE HER DAD WAS KILLED.
AND--I KNOW THAT ANGER.
BUT YOU HAVE TO STOP HER.
I CAN'T GO BACK. THAT'S NOT WHO I AM.
ALL RIGHT. I'LL GO.
CALL ALVAREZ AND KEYES, TELL THEM--
NO! NO COPS!
THAT P.I. WHO WAS LOOKING FOR BATMAN AND THE ROBINS--BILL TURNER--
--THE ONE WHOSE INTEL YOU ASKED ME TO STEAL FROM KEYES AND ALVAREZ--
--THERE WAS NO NEED. I DID IT.

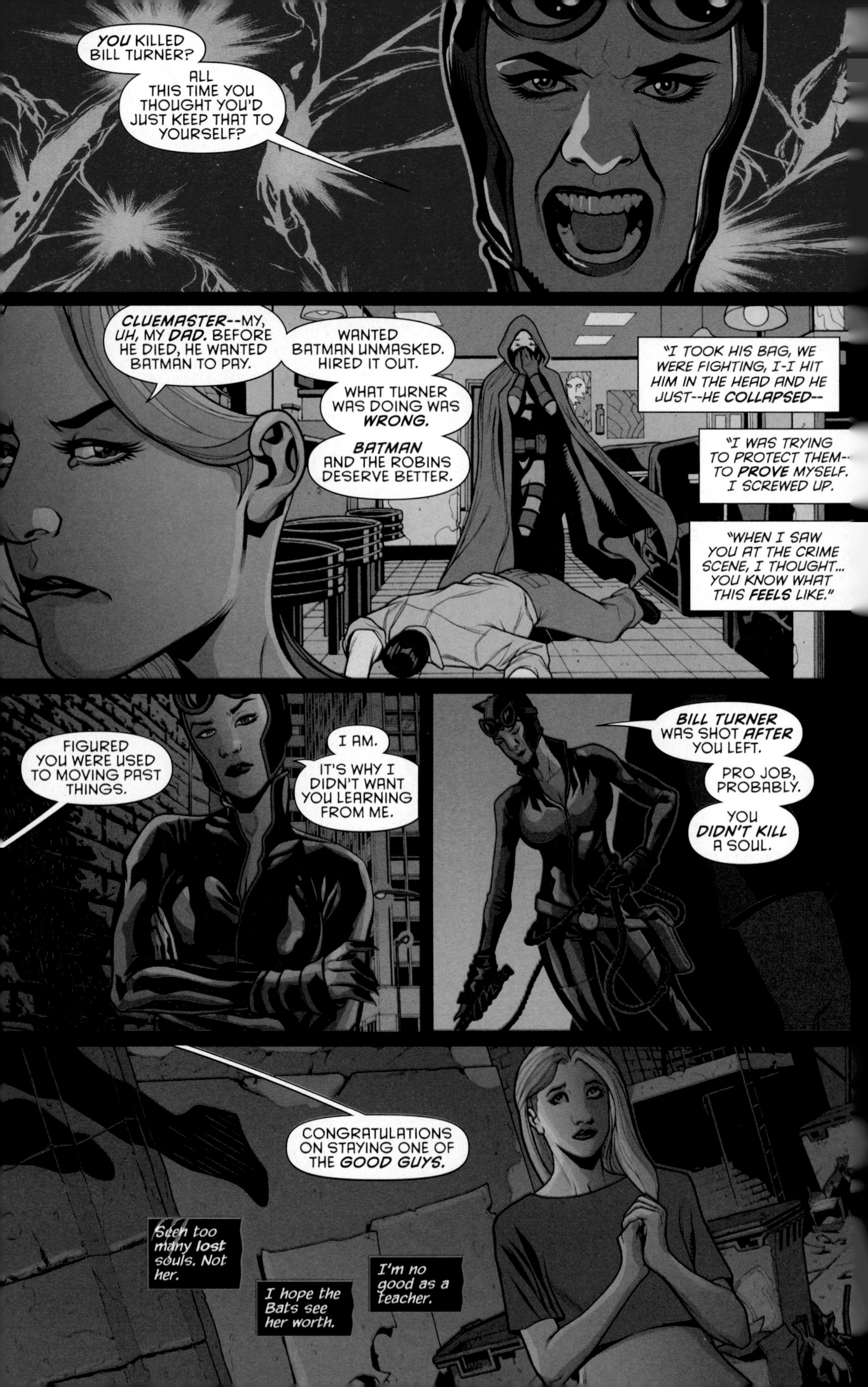

YOU KILLED BILL TURNER?
ALL THIS TIME YOU THOUGHT YOU'D JUST KEEP THAT TO YOURSELF?
CLUEMASTER--MY, UH, MY DAD. BEFORE HE DIED, HE WANTED BATMAN TO PAY.
WANTED BATMAN UNMASKED. HIRED IT OUT.
WHAT TURNER WAS DOING WAS WRONG.
BATMAN AND THE ROBINS DESERVE BETTER.
"I TOOK HIS BAG, WE WERE FIGHTING, I-I HIT HIM IN THE HEAD AND HE JUST--HE COLLAPSED--
"I WAS TRYING TO PROTECT THEM--TO PROVE MYSELF. I SCREWED UP.
"WHEN I SAW YOU AT THE CRIME SCENE, I THOUGHT... YOU KNOW WHAT THIS FEELS LIKE."
FIGURED YOU WERE USED TO MOVING PAST THINGS.
I AM.
IT'S WHY I DIDN'T WANT YOU LEARNING FROM ME.
BILL TURNER WAS SHOT AFTER YOU LEFT.
PRO JOB, PROBABLY.
YOU DIDN'T KILL A SOUL.
CONGRATULATIONS ON STAYING ONE OF THE GOOD GUYS.
Seen too many lost souls. Not her.
I hope the Bats see her worth.
I'm no good as a teacher.

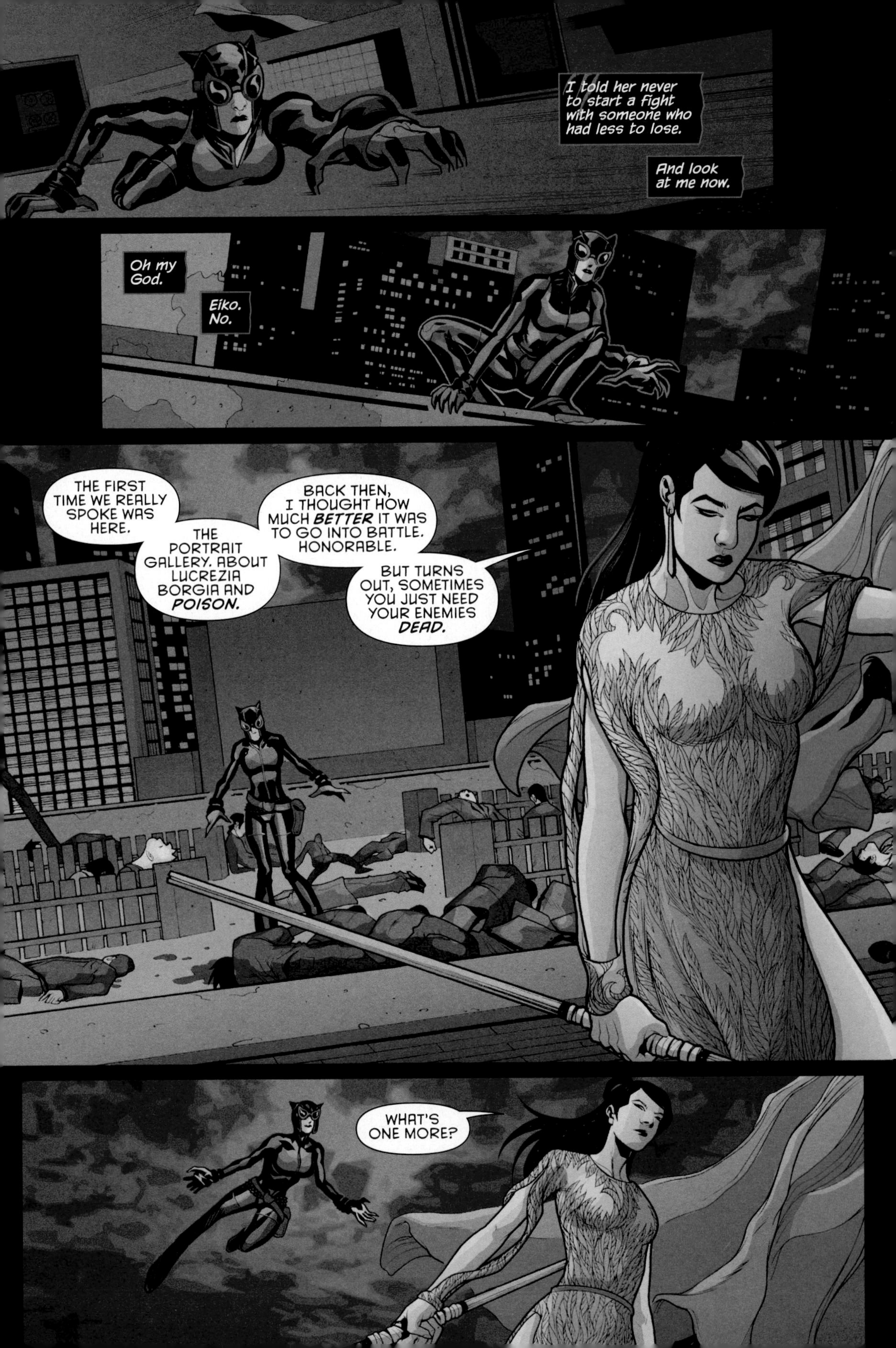
I told her never to start a fight with someone who had less to lose.
And look at me now.
Oh my God.
Eiko. No.
THE FIRST TIME WE REALLY SPOKE WAS HERE.
THE PORTRAIT GALLERY. ABOUT LUCREZIA BORGIA AND POISON.
BACK THEN, I THOUGHT HOW MUCH BETTER IT WAS TO GO INTO BATTLE. HONORABLE.
BUT TURNS OUT, SOMETIMES YOU JUST NEED YOUR ENEMIES DEAD.
WHAT'S ONE MORE?

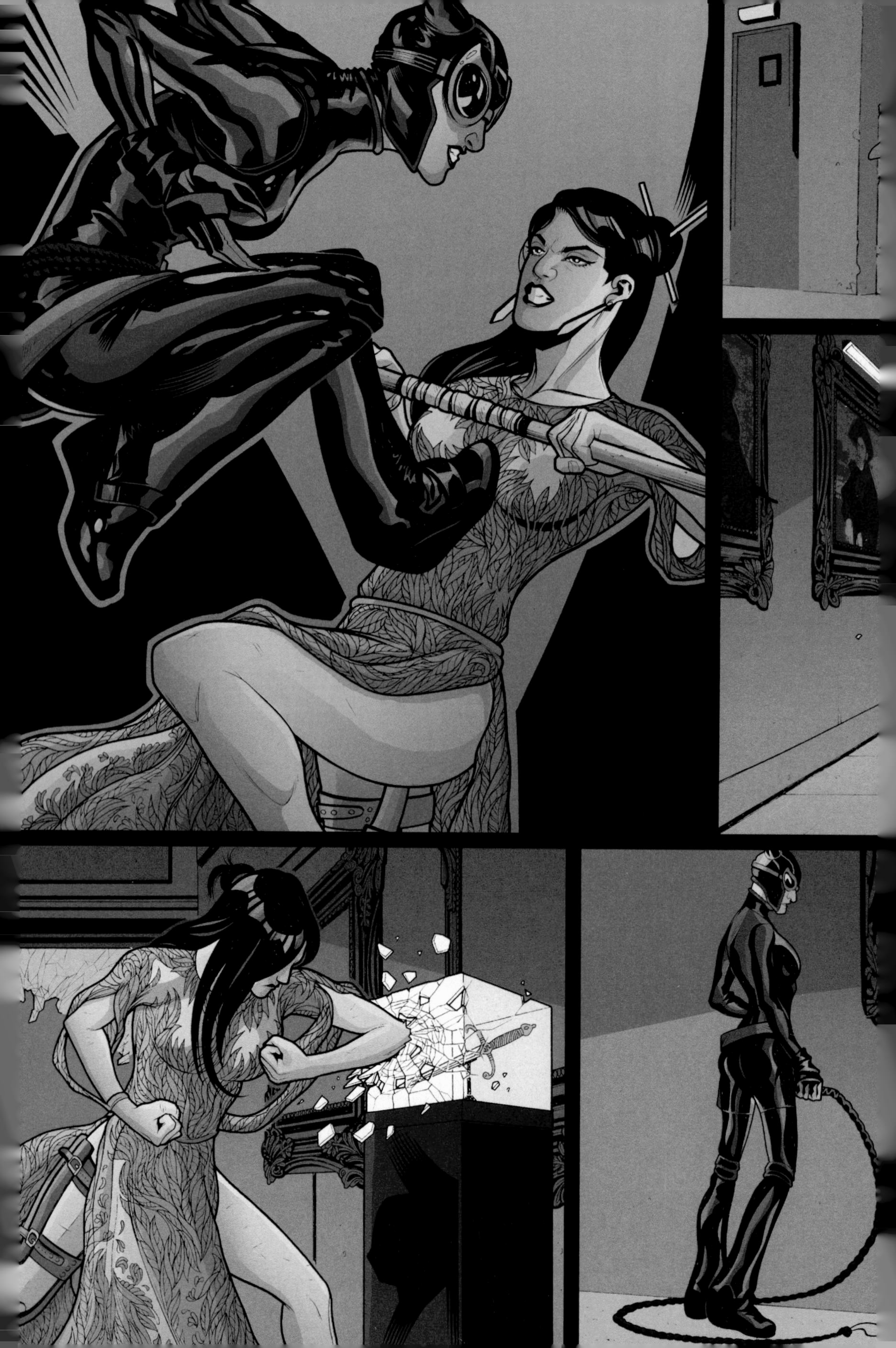

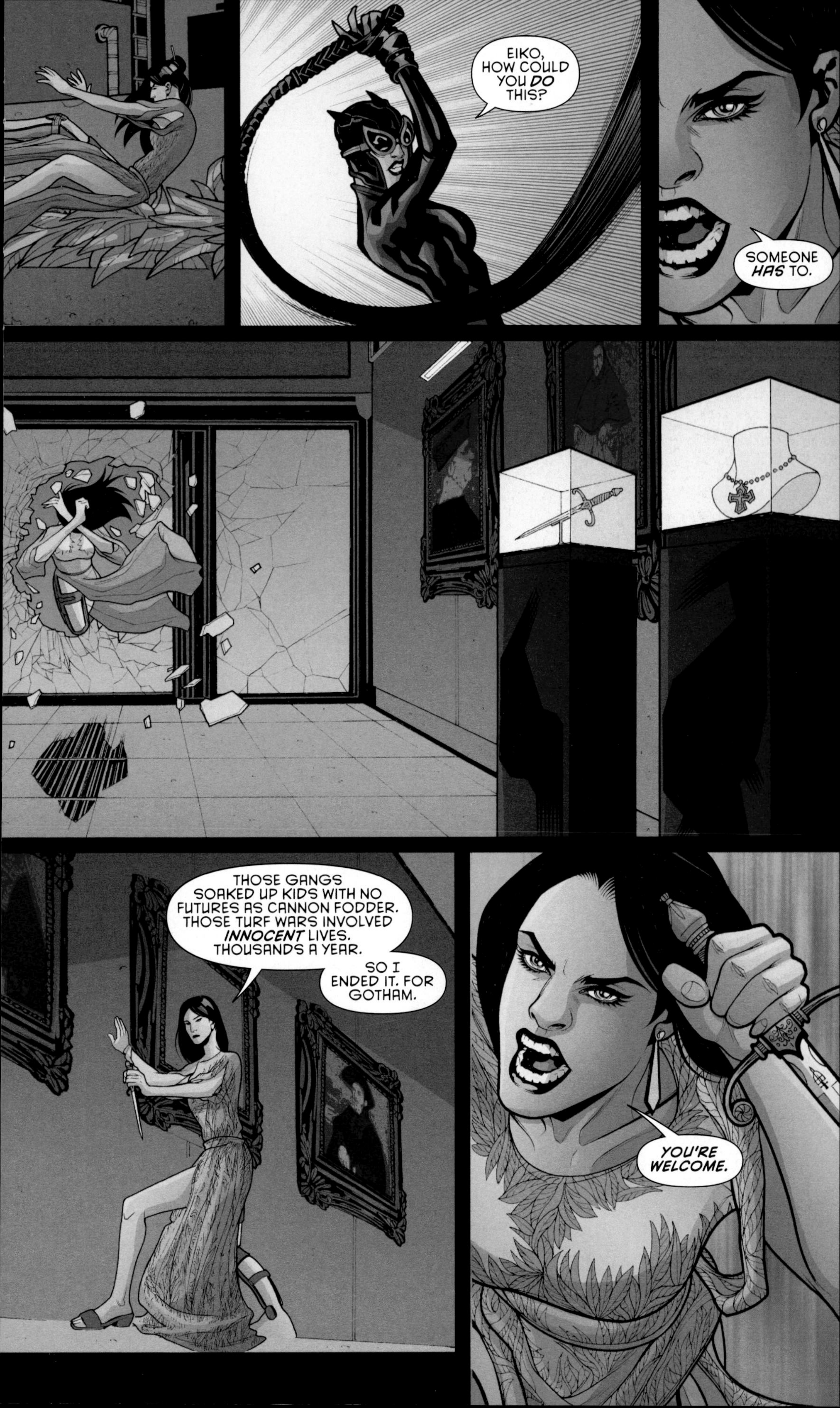
EIKO, HOW COULD YOU DO THIS?
SOMEONE HAS TO.
THOSE GANGS SOAKED UP KIDS WITH NO FUTURES AS CANNON FODDER. THOSE TURF WARS INVOLVED INNOCENT LIVES. THOUSANDS A YEAR.
SO I ENDED IT. FOR GOTHAM.
YOU'RE WELCOME.

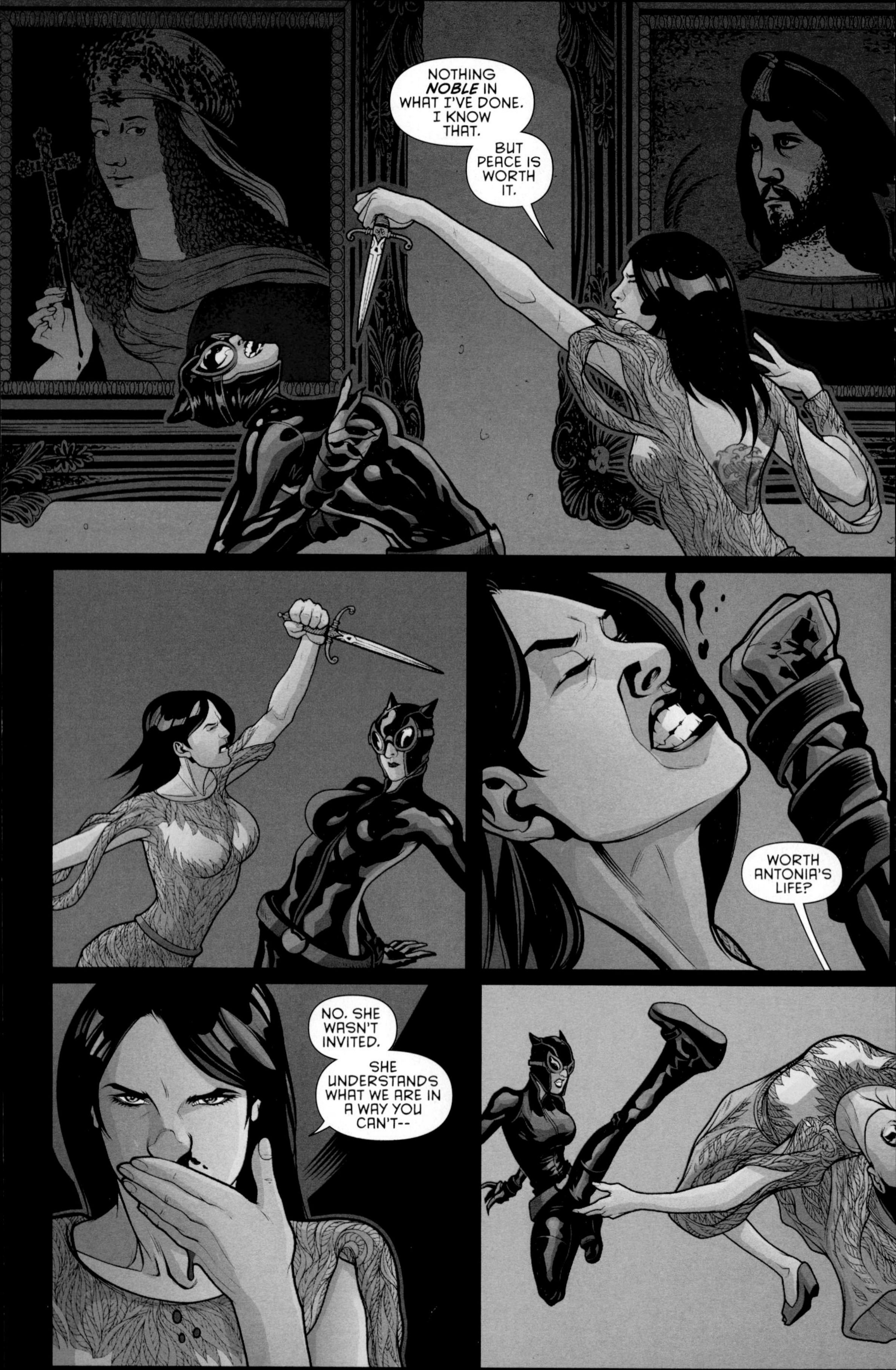
NOTHING *NOBLE* IN WHAT I'VE DONE. I KNOW THAT.
BUT PEACE IS WORTH IT.
WORTH ANTONIA'S LIFE?
NO. SHE WASN'T INVITED.
SHE UNDERSTANDS WHAT WE ARE IN A WAY YOU CAN'T--

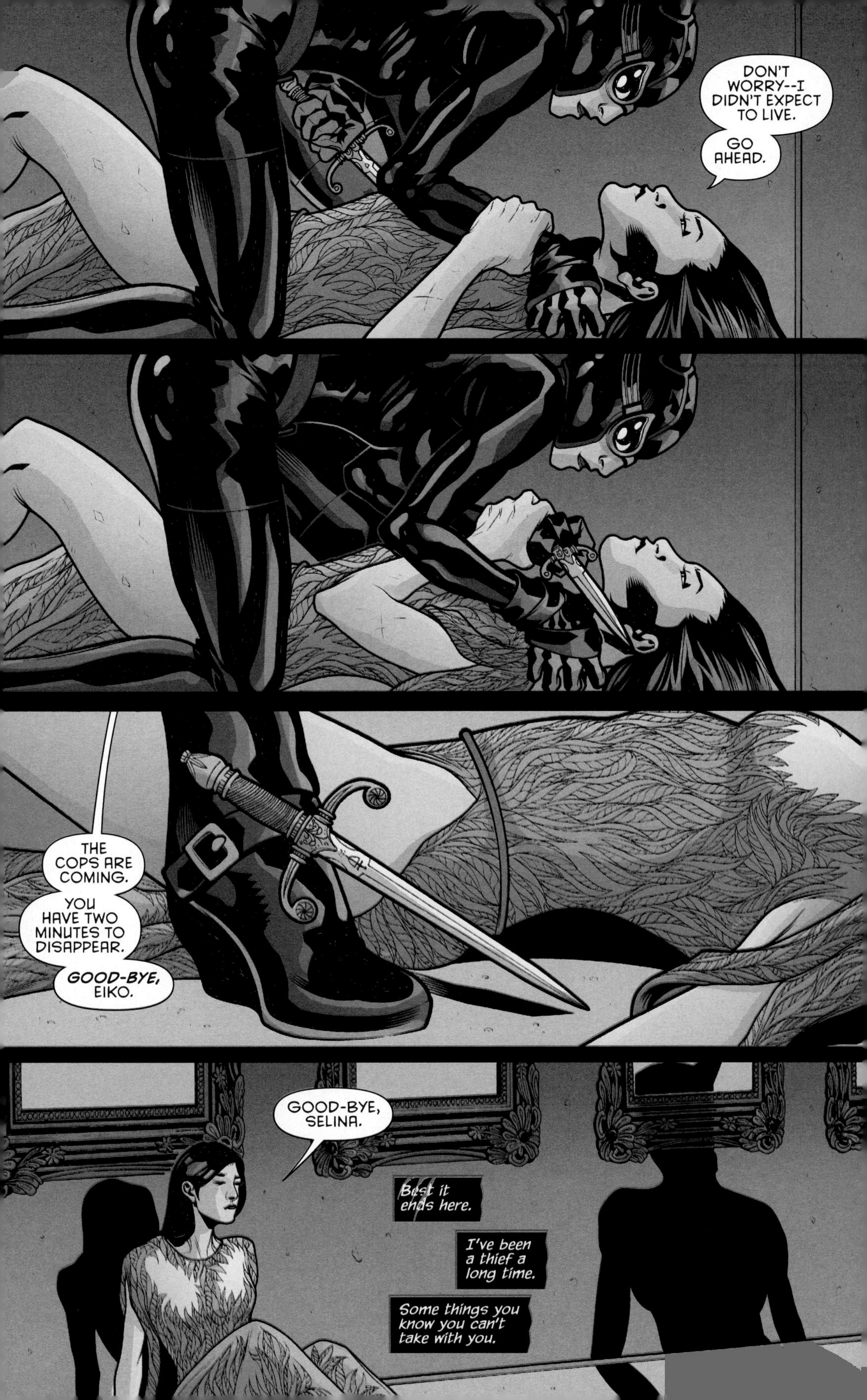
DON'T WORRY--I DIDN'T EXPECT TO LIVE.
GO AHEAD.
THE COPS ARE COMING.
YOU HAVE TWO MINUTES TO DISAPPEAR.
GOOD-BYE, EIKO.
GOOD-BYE, SELINA.
Best it ends here.
I've been a thief a long time.
Some things you know you can't take with you.

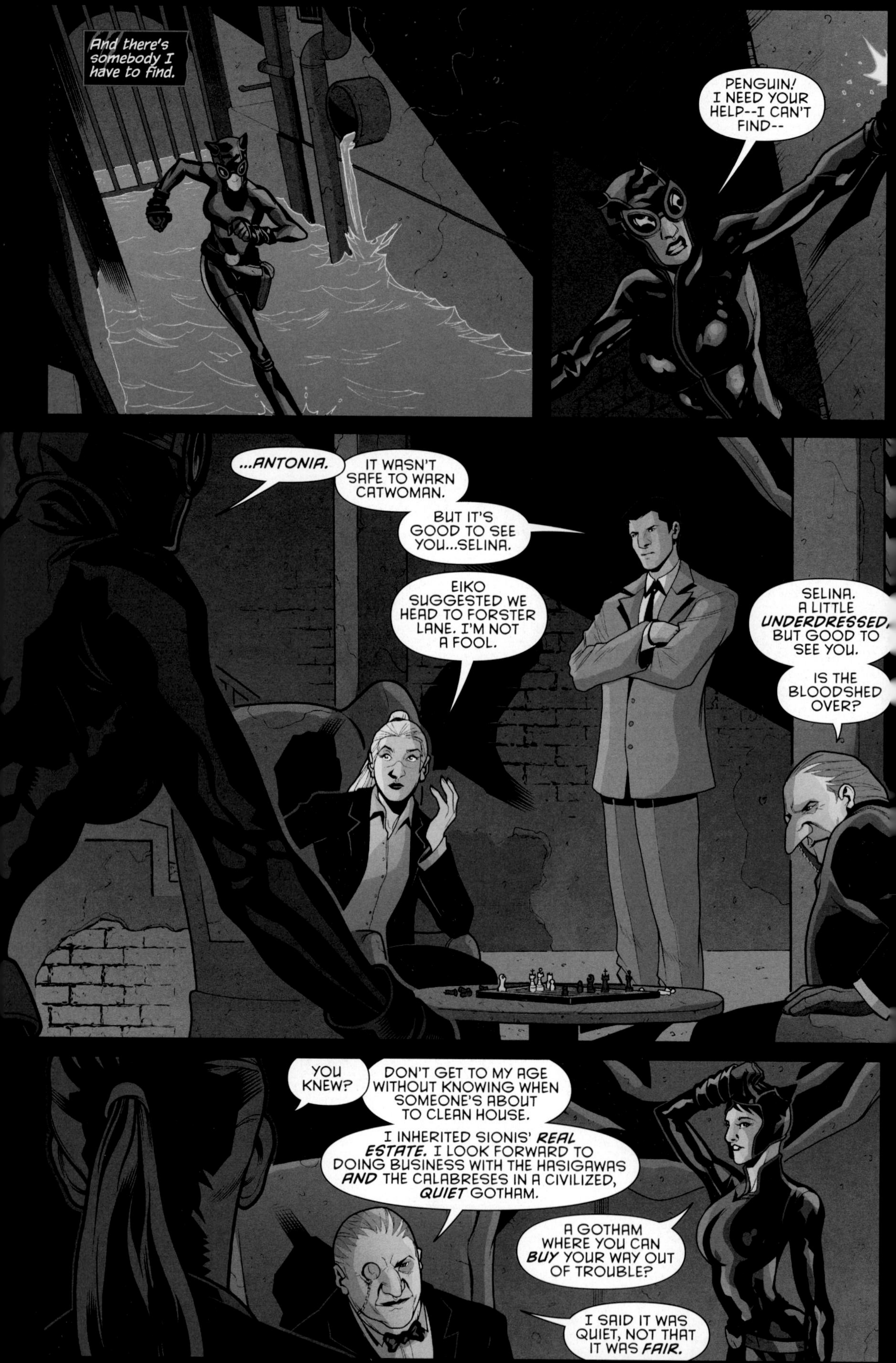
And there's somebody I have to find.
PENGUIN! I NEED YOUR HELP--I CAN'T FIND--
...ANTONIA.
IT WASN'T SAFE TO WARN CATWOMAN.
BUT IT'S GOOD TO SEE YOU...SELINA.
EIKO SUGGESTED WE HEAD TO FORSTER LANE. I'M NOT A FOOL.
SELINA. A LITTLE UNDERDRESSED, BUT GOOD TO SEE YOU.
IS THE BLOODSHED OVER?
YOU KNEW?
DON'T GET TO MY AGE WITHOUT KNOWING WHEN SOMEONE'S ABOUT TO CLEAN HOUSE.
I INHERITED SIONIS' REAL ESTATE. I LOOK FORWARD TO DOING BUSINESS WITH THE HASIGAWAS AND THE CALABRESES IN A CIVILIZED, QUIET GOTHAM.
A GOTHAM WHERE YOU CAN BUY YOUR WAY OUT OF TROUBLE?
I SAID IT WAS QUIET, NOT THAT IT WAS FAIR.

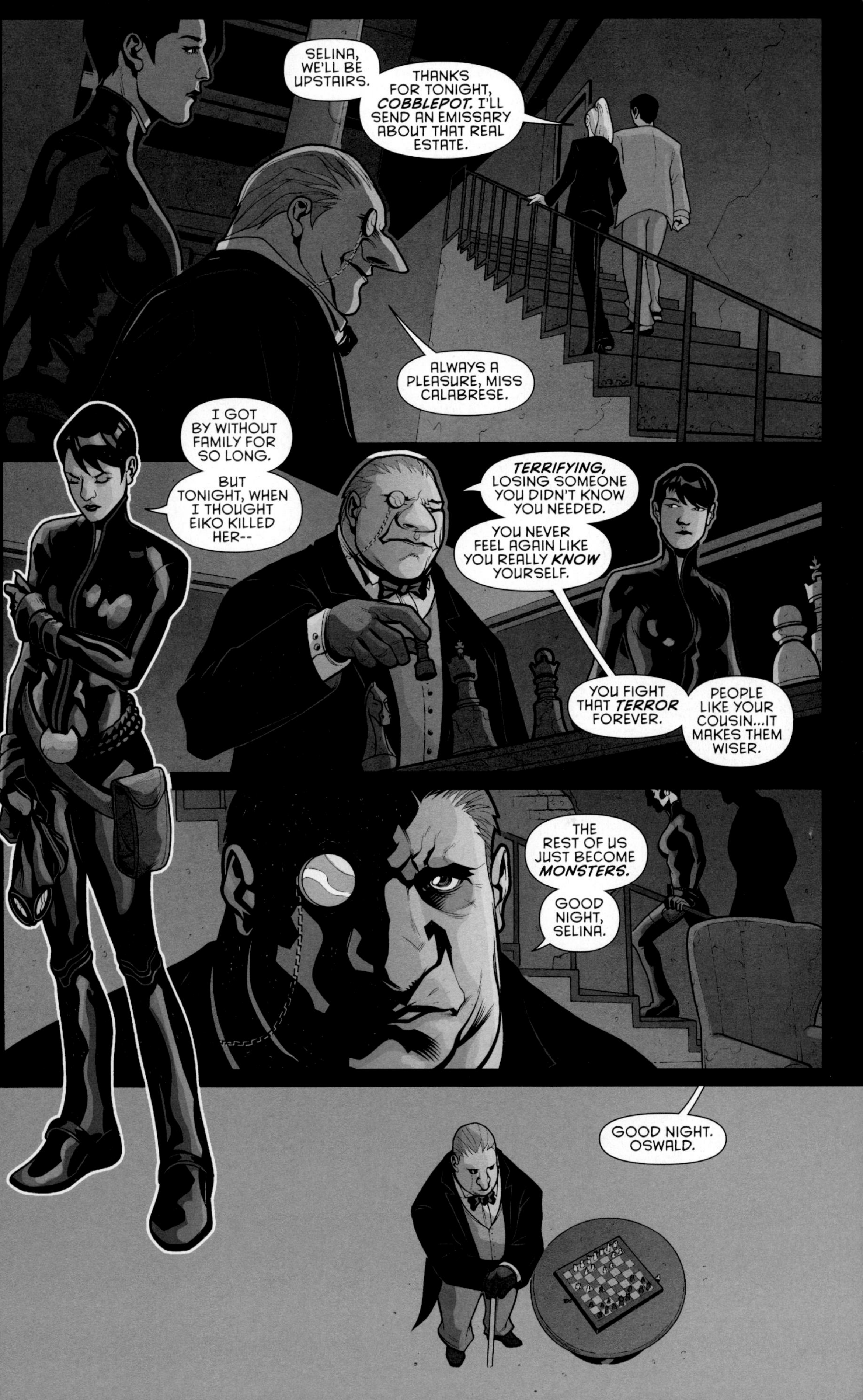
SELINA, WE'LL BE UPSTAIRS.
THANKS FOR TONIGHT, COBBLEPOT. I'LL SEND AN EMISSARY ABOUT THAT REAL ESTATE.
ALWAYS A PLEASURE, MISS CALABRESE.
I GOT BY WITHOUT FAMILY FOR SO LONG.
BUT TONIGHT, WHEN I THOUGHT EIKO KILLED HER--
TERRIFYING, LOSING SOMEONE YOU DIDN'T KNOW YOU NEEDED.
YOU NEVER FEEL AGAIN LIKE YOU REALLY KNOW YOURSELF.
YOU FIGHT THAT TERROR FOREVER.
PEOPLE LIKE YOUR COUSIN...IT MAKES THEM WISER.
THE REST OF US JUST BECOME MONSTERS.
GOOD NIGHT, SELINA.
GOOD NIGHT. OSWALD.

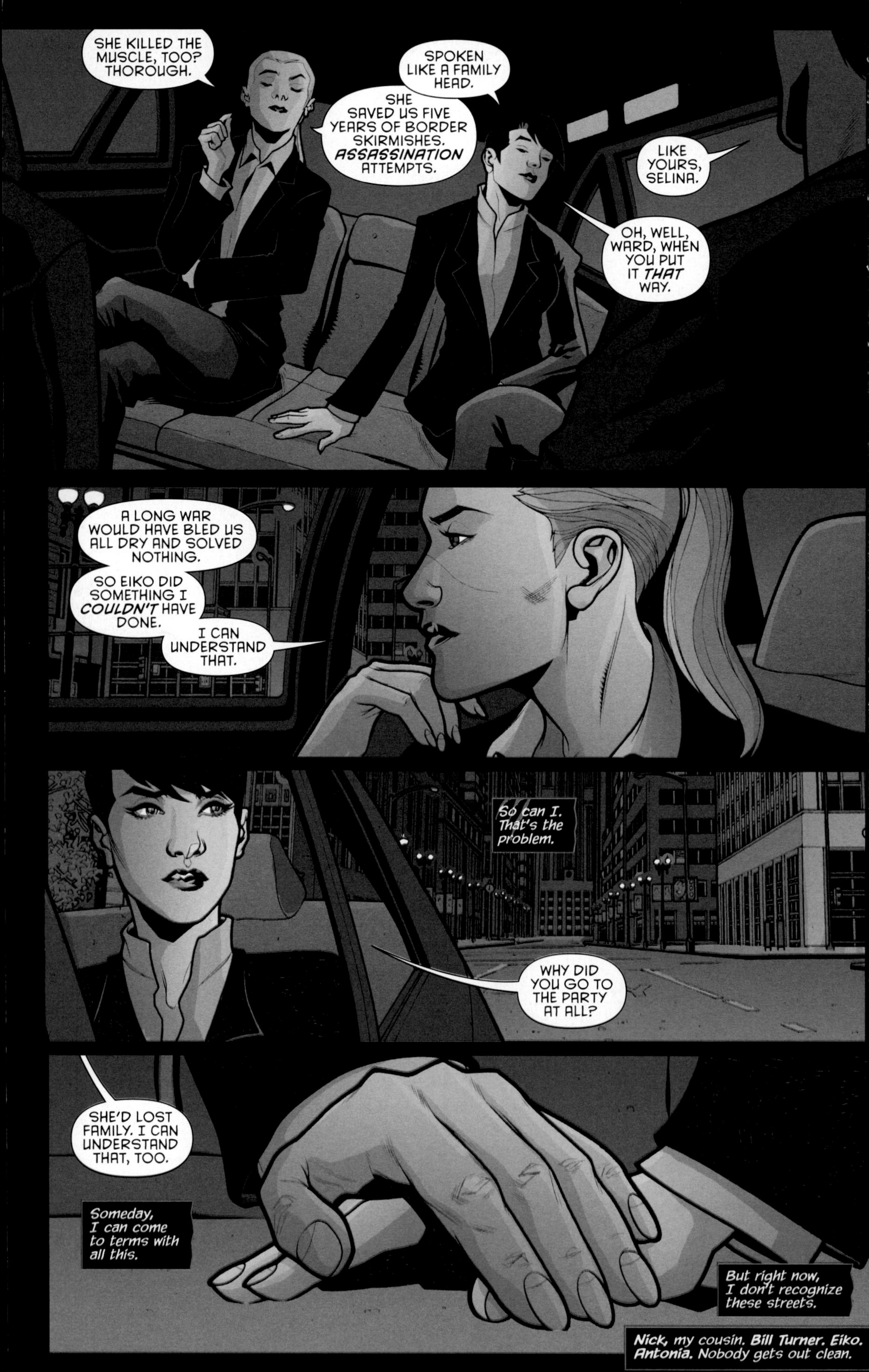
SHE KILLED THE MUSCLE, TOO? THOROUGH.
SPOKEN LIKE A FAMILY HEAD.
SHE SAVED US FIVE YEARS OF BORDER SKIRMISHES. ASSASSINATION ATTEMPTS.
LIKE YOURS, SELINA.
OH, WELL, WARD, WHEN YOU PUT IT THAT WAY.
A LONG WAR WOULD HAVE BLED US ALL DRY AND SOLVED NOTHING.
SO EIKO DID SOMETHING I COULDN'T HAVE DONE.
I CAN UNDERSTAND THAT.
So can I. That's the problem.
WHY DID YOU GO TO THE PARTY AT ALL?
SHE'D LOST FAMILY. I CAN UNDERSTAND THAT, TOO.
Someday, I can come to terms with all this.
But right now, I don't recognize these streets.
Nick, my cousin. Bill Turner. Eiko. Antonia. Nobody gets out clean.

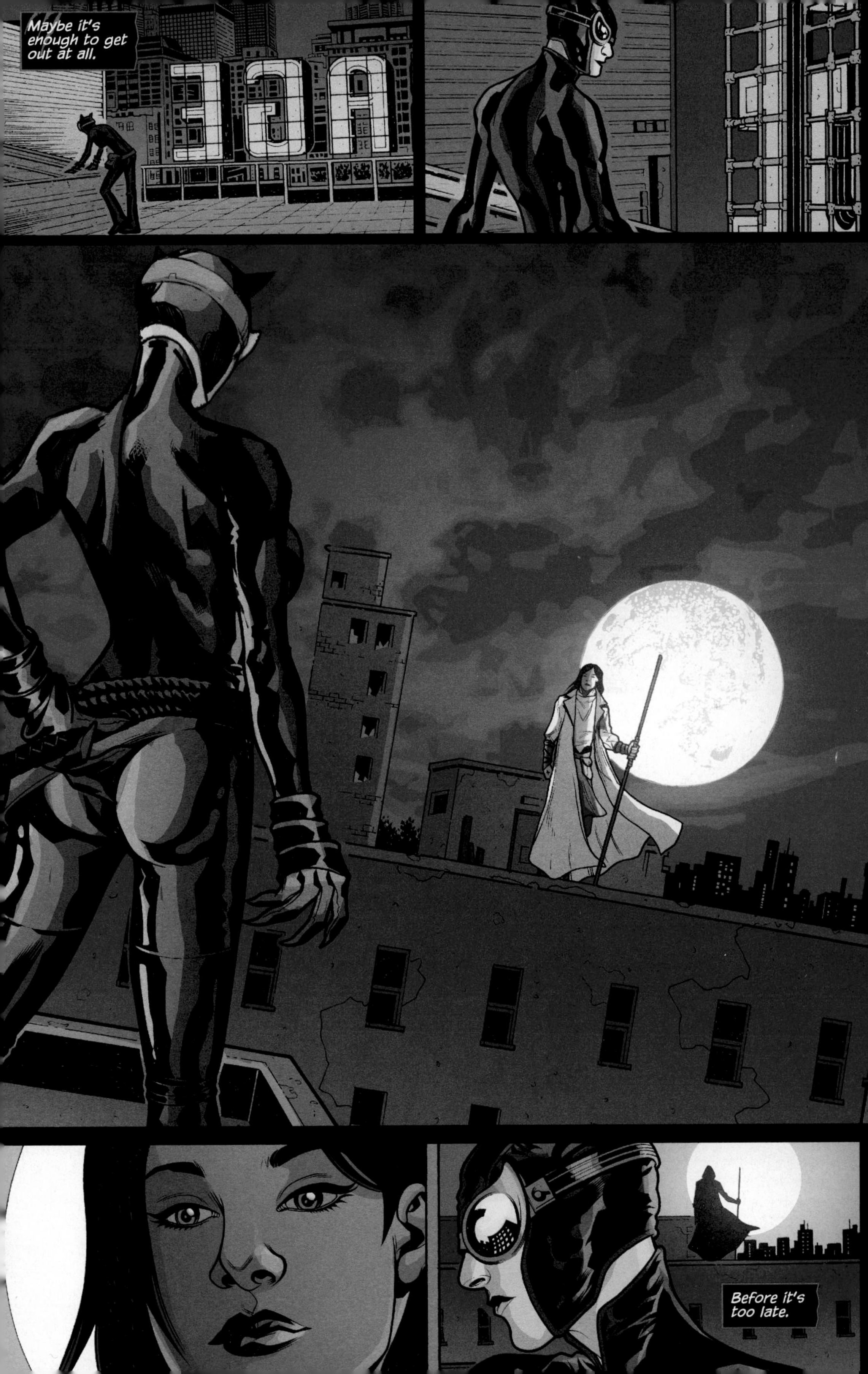
Maybe it's enough to get out at all.
Before it's too late.

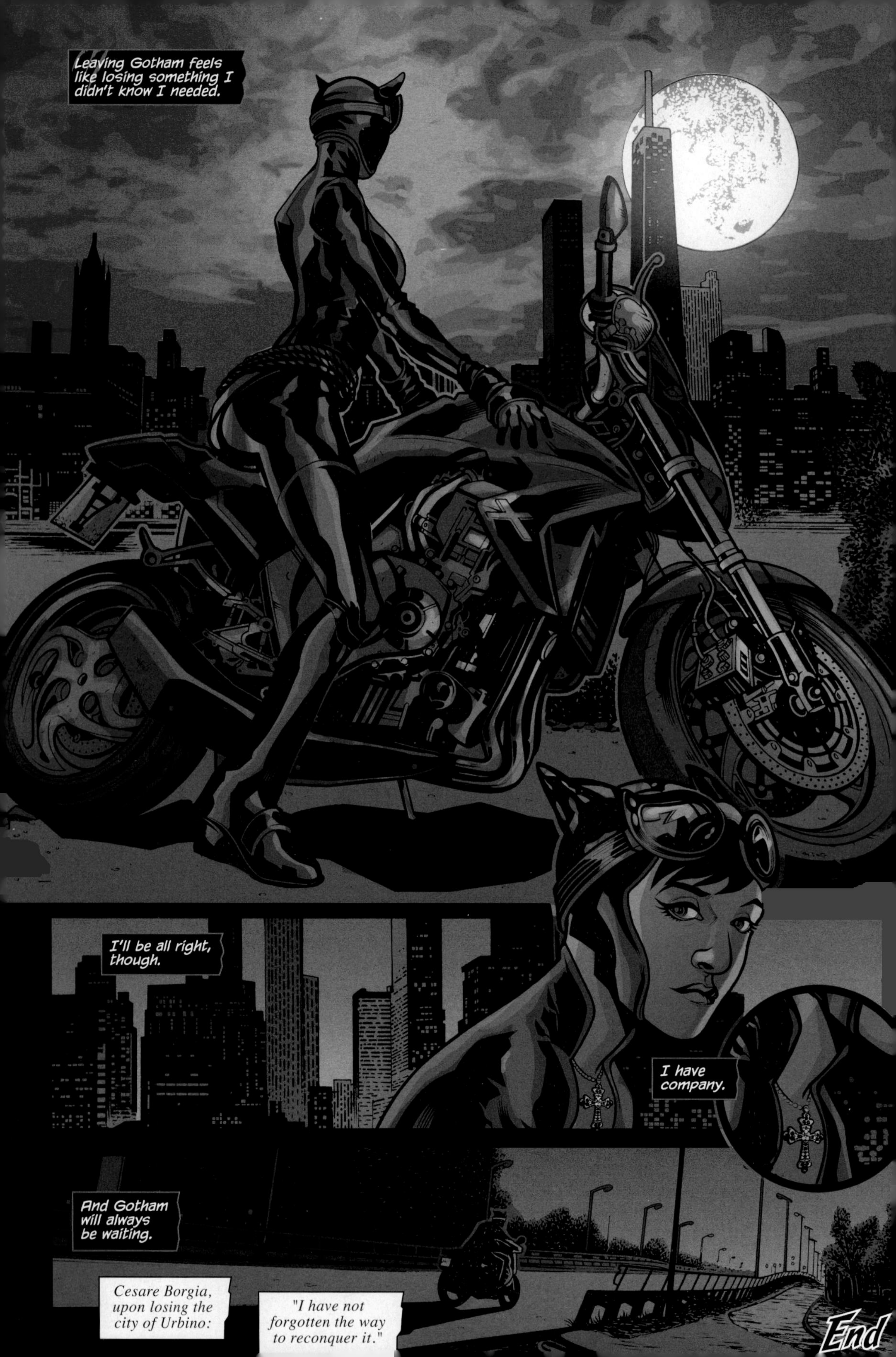
Leaving Gotham feels like losing something I didn't know I needed.
I'll be all right, though.
I have company.
And Gotham will always be waiting.
Cesare Borgia, upon losing the city of Urbino:
"I have not forgotten the way to reconquer it."
End

CATWOMAN COVER GALLERY

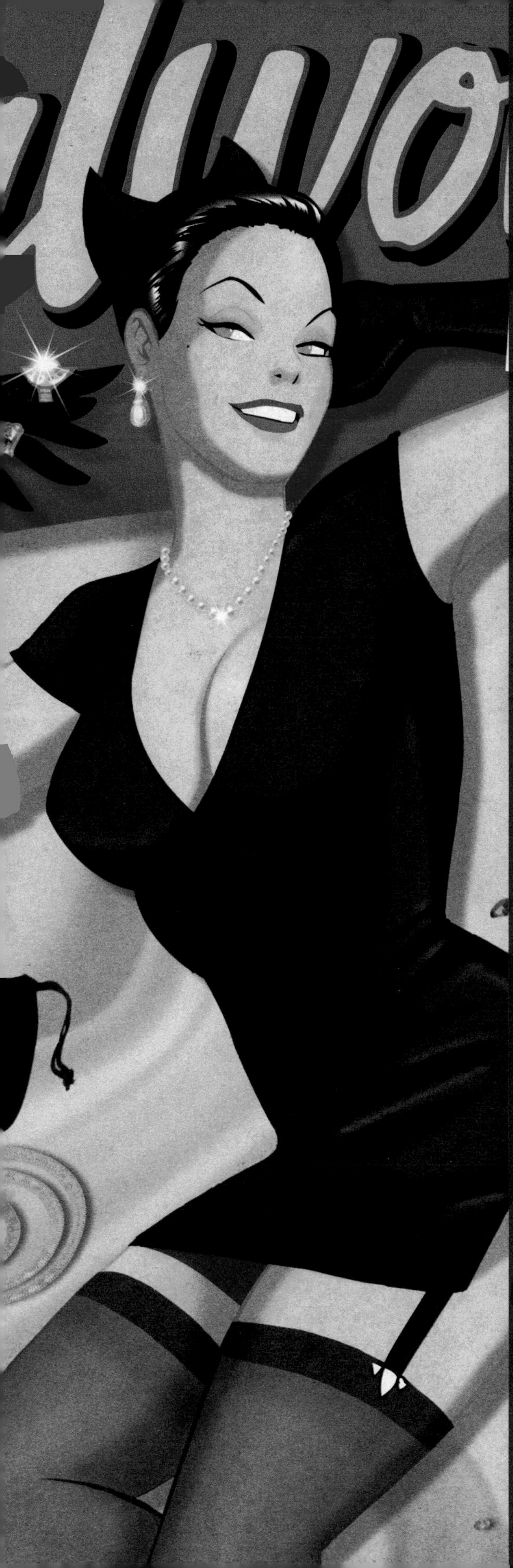

CATWOMAN #41
JOKER 75TH ANNIVERSARY
VARIANT BY JAVIER PULIDO

CATWOMAN #42
TEEN TITANS GO! VARIANT BY
BEN CALDWELL

CATWOMAN #43
BOMBSHELLS VARIANT BY
DES TAYLOR

CATWOMAN #44
GREEN LANTERN
75TH ANNIVERSARY VARIANT BY
EMANUELA LUPACCHINO
WITH LAURA MARTIN

CATWOMAN #45
MONSTER VARIANT BY
ROBBI RODRIGUEZ

CATWOMAN #46
LOONEY TUNES
VARIANT BY
DARWYN COOKE
AND SPIKE BRANDT

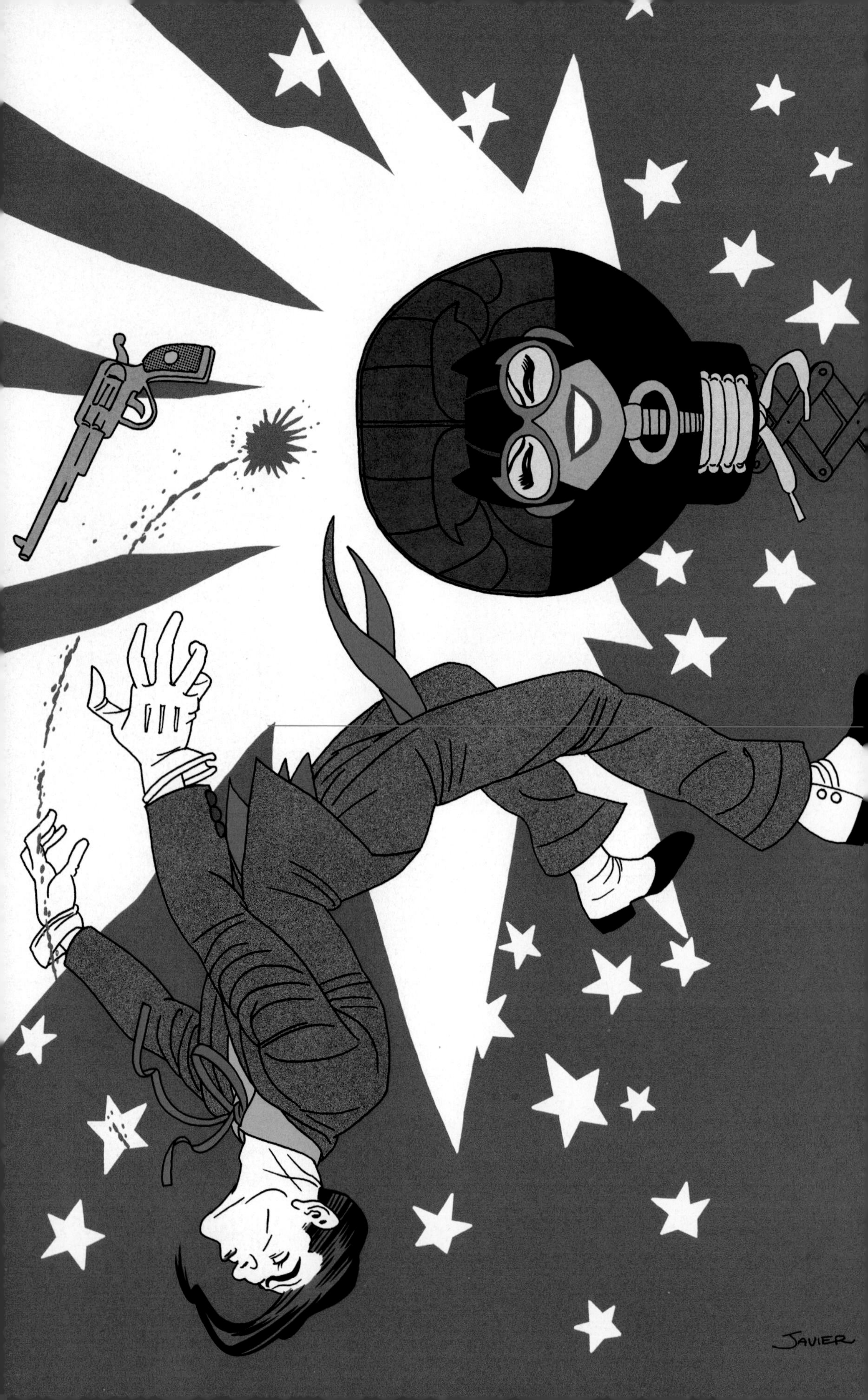
JAVIER

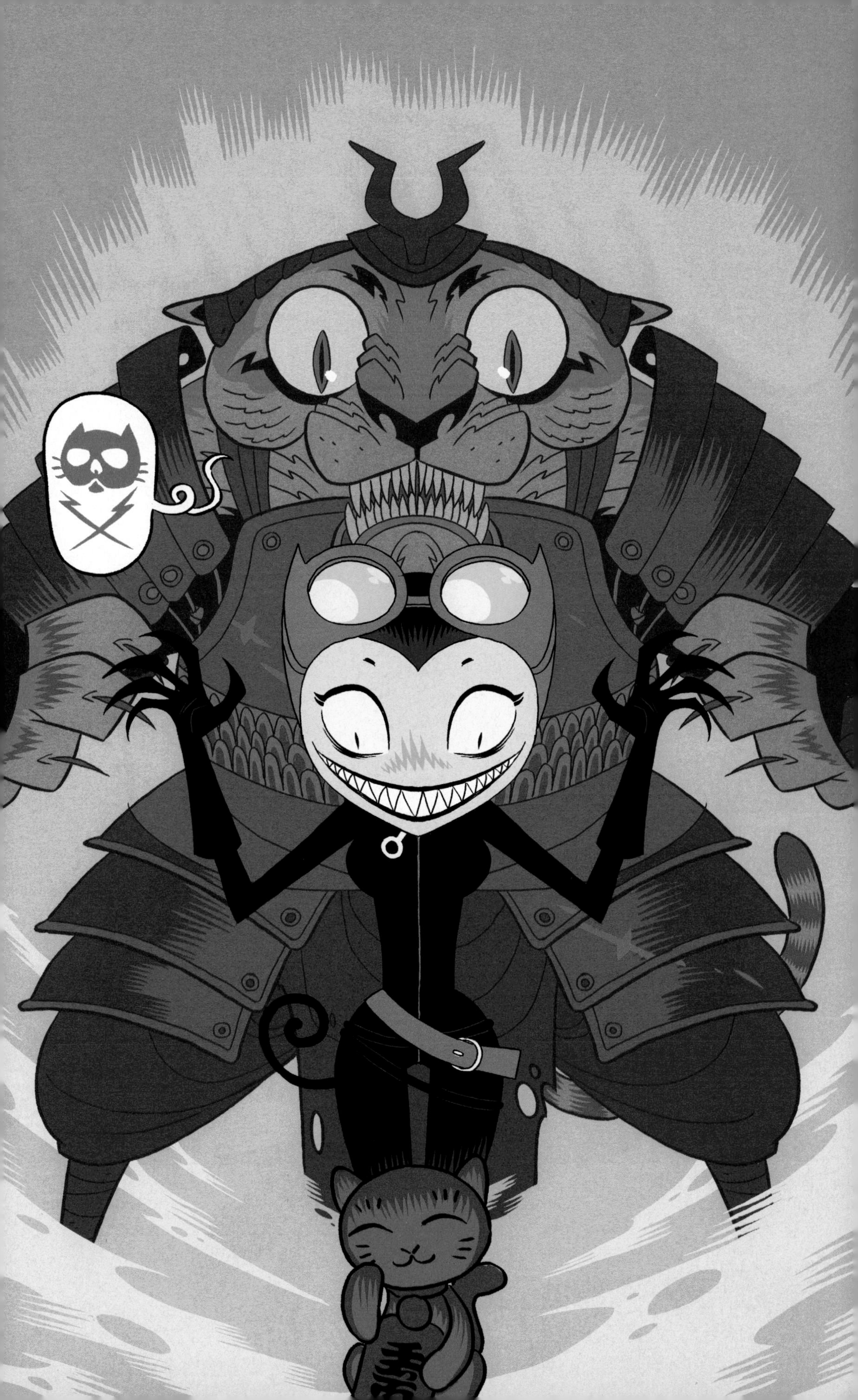

SU
Catwoman
MAGAZINE
ALL-NEW STORYL
STARTS TODAY
"Cat
Scratch
Feve
THE CAT IS BACK...SCRATCH ONE MORE HEIST!

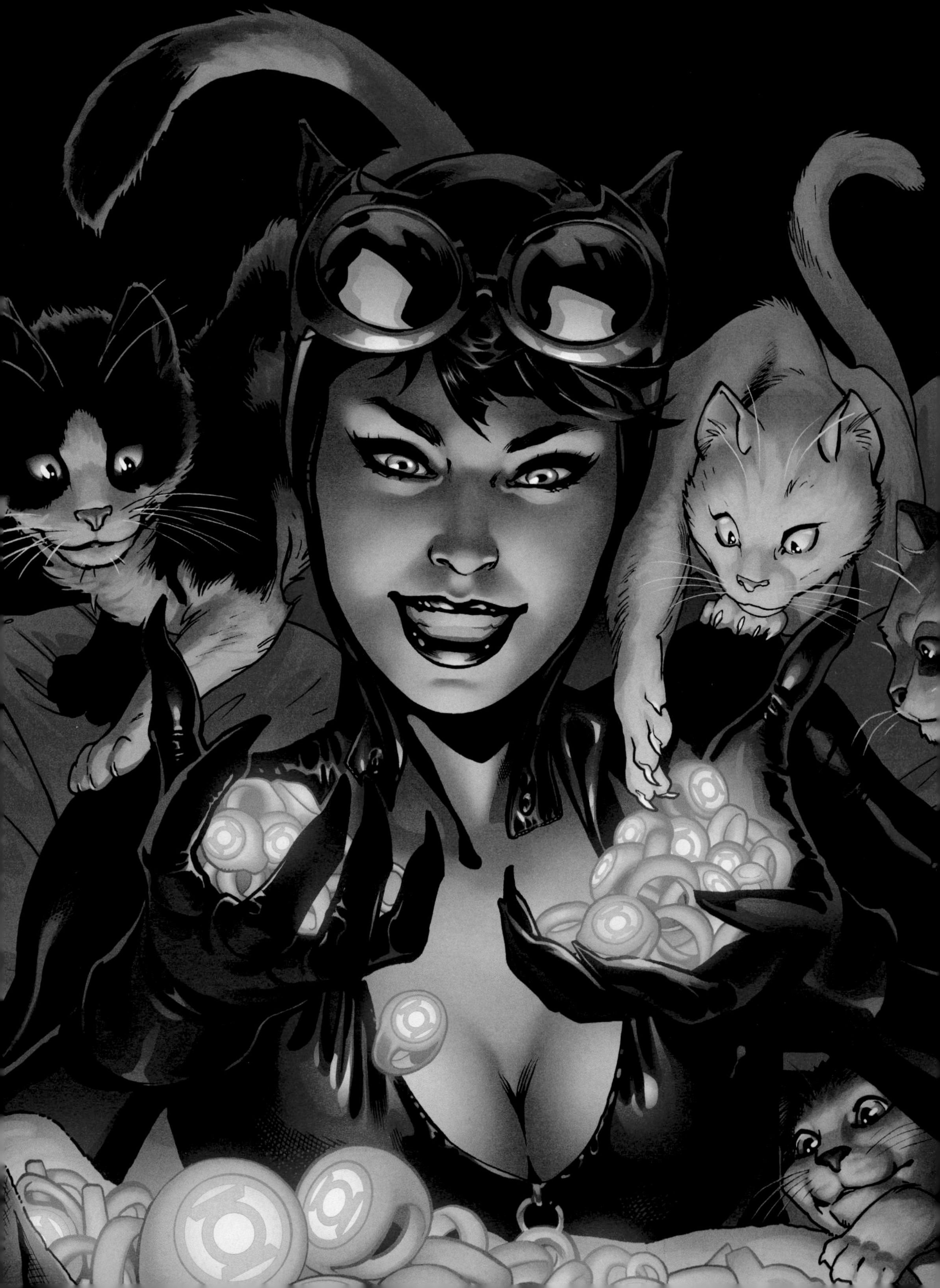

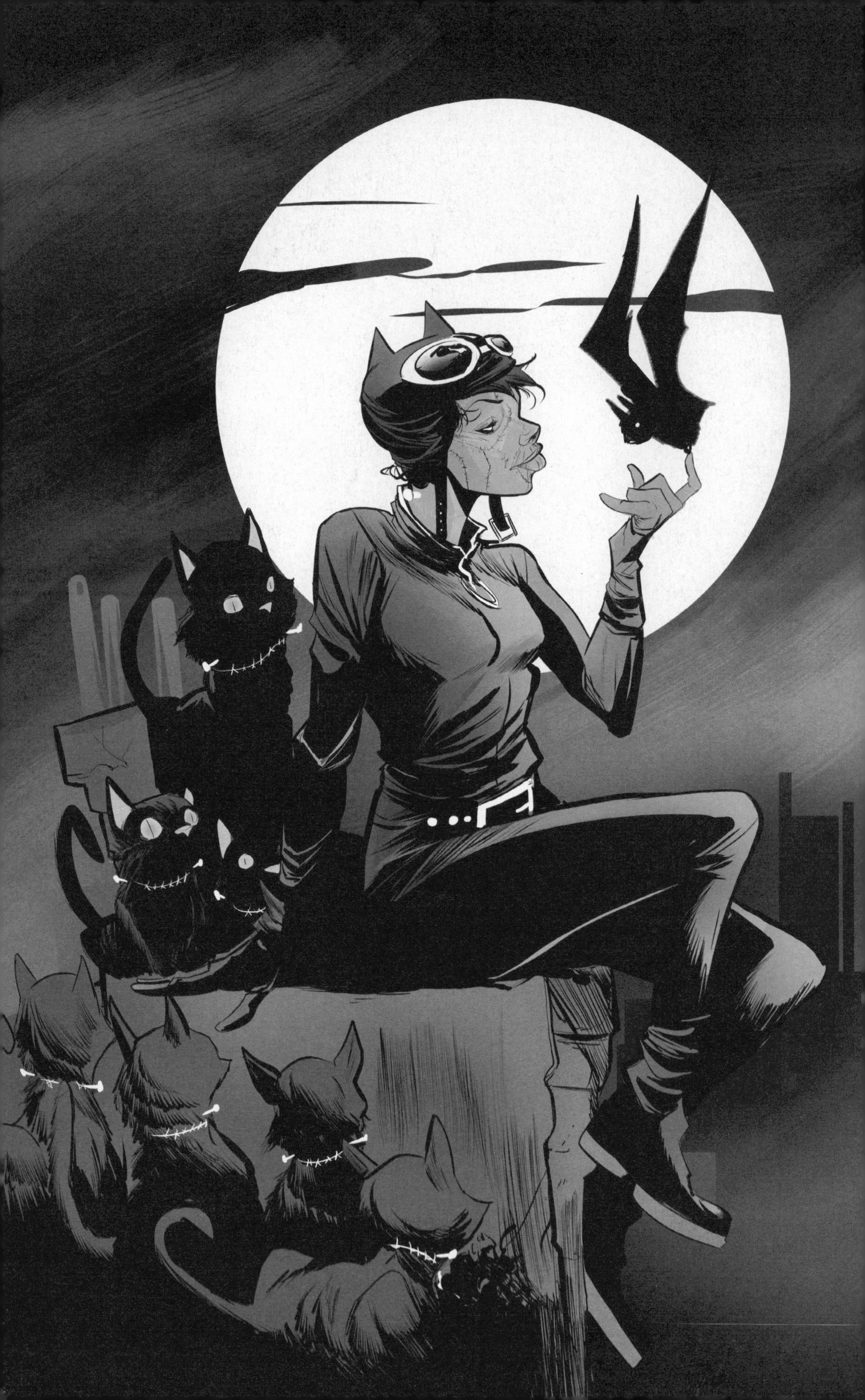

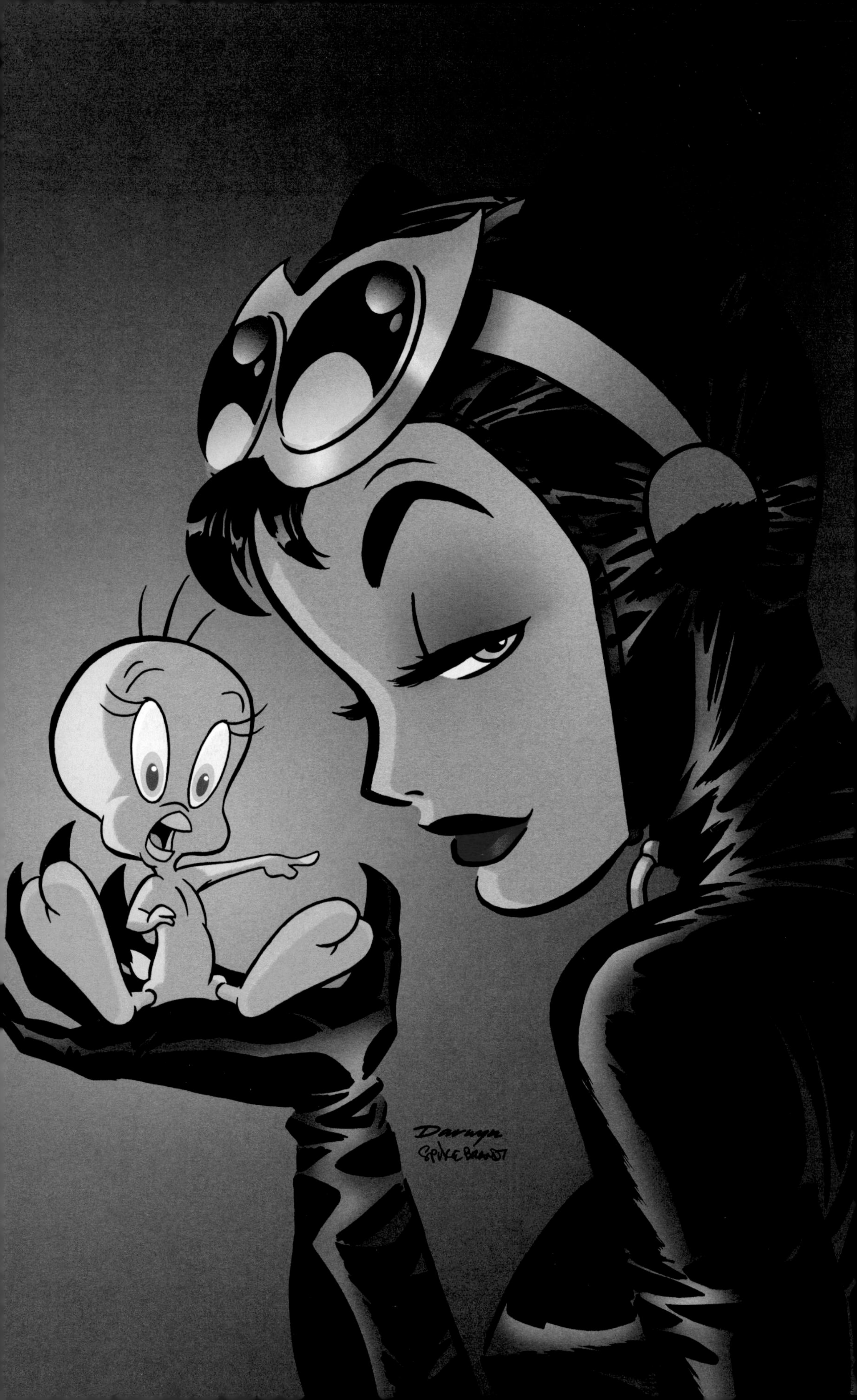
Darwyn
SPIKE BRANDT

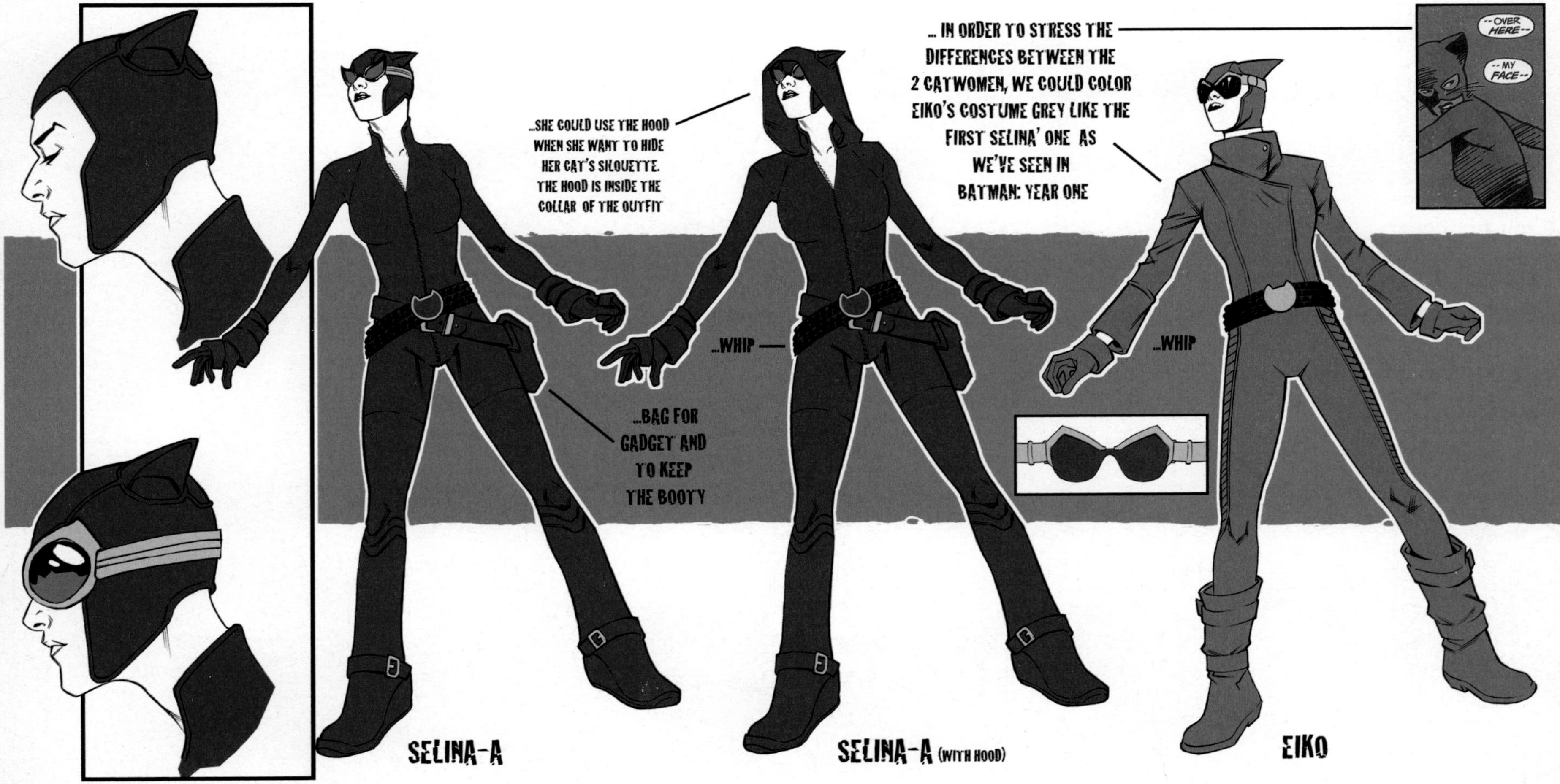
...SHE COULD USE THE HOOD WHEN SHE WANT TO HIDE HER CAT'S SILOUETTE. THE HOOD IS INSIDE THE COLLAR OF THE OUTFIT
... IN ORDER TO STRESS THE DIFFERENCES BETWEEN THE 2 CATWOMEN, WE COULD COLOR EIKO'S COSTUME GREY LIKE THE FIRST SELINA' ONE AS WE'VE SEEN IN BATMAN: YEAR ONE
--OVER HERE--
--MY FACE--
...WHIP
...WHIP
...BAG FOR GADGET AND TO KEEP THE BOOTY
SELINA-A
SELINA-A (WITH HOOD)
EIKO

Sketches by David Messina